BRITISH GOVERNMENT PUBLICATIONS

An index to
chairmen and authors

VOLUME III: 1941-1978

BRITISH GOVERNMENT PUBLICATIONS

An index to
chairmen and authors

VOLUME III: 1941-1978

Compiled by
Stephen Richard
for the
Reference, Special and Information Section
of the
Library Association

THE LIBRARY ASSOCIATION · LONDON

First published 1982

British Cataloguing in Publication Data

Richard, Stephen
    British government publications: an index to
    chairmen and authors.
    Vol. 3: 1941-1978
    1. Governmental investigations—Great Britain—
    Bibliography
    2. Great Britain—Government publications—
    Bibliography
    I. Title   II. Library Association
    Reference, Special and Information Section
    016.3209'041   Z2009

ISBN 0 85365 753 X

Designed by Ron Jones.
Typeset in Times Roman by Walker and Company Limited.

Contents

Introduction

This index of chairmen is a cumulation of the indexes by A. M. Morgan, British Government Publications; an Index to Chairmen and Authors, 1941 - 1966, 2nd ed., 1973 and A. M. Morgan and L. R. Stephen, British Government Publications, an Index to Chairmen, 1967 - 1971, 1976. The index also covers the period up to the end of 1978.

Annual reports, boiler explosion and railway accident inquiry reports etc. have been excluded in most cases. In addition to the published indexes cumulated here, the resources of the Bodleian Library, British Library and Edinburgh University Library have also been used, and any additional reports for the period 1941 - 71 which have been discovered have been added.

The arrangement of the index is alphabetical by latest form of the chairman's name used in the reports. Titles of persons are entered before surnames of the same spelling. Cross references are given from earlier forms of names. The reports are arranged chronologically under each chairman's name. The only exception to this arrangement is where it would break up a numbered sequence of reports or the reports of a single committee which reported over a number of years.

A few abbreviations are used in the entries, namely:

Cmd. Cmnd. }	Command papers
D.	Department
HC.	House of Commons papers
HL.	House of Lords papers
M.	Ministry
NEDO	National Economic Development Office

I wish to thank the compilers of the indexes which are cumulated here for permission to use their work, and the staff of the Bodliean, Edinburgh University, and British Library Official Publications libraries for their assistance.

Stephen Richard
Horton-cum-Studley
29 August, 1980

AARON, R. I.

1949 The future of secondary education in Wales. Central Advisory Council for Education (Wales). Report
M. of Education

1951 County Colleges in Wales. Report of the Central Advisory Council for Education (Wales)
M. of Education

1953 Place of Welsh and English in the schools of Wales. Report of the Central Advisory Council for Education (Wales)
M. of Education

1962 Rural transport problem in Wales. Report by the Council for Wales and Monmouthshire
Session 1961-62 Cmnd. 1821 xxiv.

1963 The Welsh holiday industry. Report by the Council for Wales and Monmouthshire
Session 1962-63 Cmnd. 1950 xxv.

Welsh language today. Report by the Council for Wales and Monmouthshire
Session 1963-64 Cmnd. 2198 xx.

AARVOLD, Carl D., Sir

1961 Magistrates' courts in London. Report of the interdepartmental committee
Session 1961-62 Cmnd. 1606 xviii.

1973 Procedures for the discharge and supervision of psychiatric patients subject to special restrictions. Report on the review
Session 1972-73 Cmnd. 5191 xiii.

ABEL, W. K. J.

1973 Signposts to success. A wholesaler's guide to the use of management information techniques. Distributive Trades E.D.C.
N.E.D.O.

ABERCROMBIE, Patrick, Sir

1944 Greater London plan, 1944. A report prepared on behalf of the standing conference on London regional planning
M. of Town and Country Planning

1949 Clyde Valley regional plan, 1946, by Sir P. Abercrombie and R. Matthew
D. of Health for Scotland

ADAM, R.

1944 Planning our new homes. Report of the Scottish Housing Advisory Committee on the design, planning and furnishing of new houses in Scotland
D. of Health for Scotland

ADAMS, John Roland

1967 Sea Gem. Report of the inquiry into the causes of the accident to the drilling rig Sea Gem
Session 1966-67 Cmnd. 3409 xxi.

ADAMS, Paul

1968 Civil judicial statistics. Report of the committee
Session 1967-68 Cmnd. 3684 xviii.

ADEANE, Michael Edward, Lord

1974 Ancient monuments of York, IV. 30th interim report of the Royal Commission on the Ancient and Historical Monuments and Constructions of England
Session 1974 Cmnd. 5577 vi.

Ancient monuments of east Dorset. 31st interim report of the Royal Commission on the Ancient and Historical Monuments and Constructions of England
Session 1974 Cmnd. 5578 vi.

1975 Archaeological sites in north-east Northampton-shire. 32nd interim report of the Royal Commission on the Ancient and Historical Monuments and Constructions of England
Session 1974-75 Cmnd. 6005 xi.

Iron age and Romano-British monuments in the Gloucestershire Cotswolds. 33rd interim report of the Royal Commission on the Ancient and Historical Monuments and Constructions of England
Session 1974-75 Cmnd. 6178 xi.

1976 Monuments threatened or destroyed, 1963-74. Interim report of the Royal Commission on the Ancient and Historical Monuments and Constructions of England
Session 1975-76 Cmnd. 6383 xli.

1977 Ancient and historical monuments in the City of Salisbury (excluding the Cathedral Close). 35th interim report of the Royal Commission on the Ancient and Historical Monuments and Constructions of England
Session 1976-77 Cmnd. 6679 xxxiii.

Archaeological sites in central Northampton-shire. Royal Commission on the Ancient and Historical Monuments and Constructions of England. 36th interim report
Session 1977-78 Cmnd. 6997 xvi.

ADRIAN, E. D., Lord

1959 Radiological hazards to patients. Interim report of the committee
M. of Health

1960 Radiological hazards to patients. 2nd report of the committee
M. of Health

1966 Radiological hazards to patients. Final report of the committee
M. of Health

AGLEN, A. J.

1955 Valuation for rating of waterworks in Scotland. Report of the working party
Scottish Home D.

Valuation for rating of gasworks in Scotland. Report of the working party
Scottish Home D.

AITKEN, J. K.

1954 General Nursing Councils for England and Wales and Scotland. Report of the committee set up to consider the function, status and training of nurse tutors
M. of Health

1956 Control of dangerous drugs and poisons in hospitals. Report of the standing medical, nursing and pharmaceutical advisory committees joint sub-committee
M. of Health, 1958

AITKEN, R. S., Sir

1957 University College of the West Indies teaching hospital. Hospital advisory committee report
Colonial Office

ALBEMARLE, D. C., Countess of

1960 Youth service in England and Wales. Report of the committee
Session 1959-60. Cmnd. 929 xix.

1965 Central Youth Employment Executive. The future development of the Youth Employment Service. Report of a working party of the National Youth Employment Council
M. of Labour

ALBEMARLE, D. C., Countess of *(continued)*

1968   The work of the Youth Employment Service, 1965-68. Report by the National Youth Employment Council
D. of Employment and Productivity

ALDEN, Jeremy

1977   Upper Afan Community Development Project. Final report
Univ. Wales Institute for Science and Technology for the Home Office

ALDINGTON, Austin Richard William Low, Lord

1974   Choice of thermal reactor systems. Report of the Nuclear Power Advisory Board
Session 1974 Cmnd. 5731 iii.

ALDWYN, M. J., Earl St.

See **ST. ALDWYN, M. J., Earl**

ALEXANDER, K. J. W.

1975   Adult education; the challenge of change. Report by a committee of inquiry
Scottish Education D.

ALLAN, T. M.

1961   Mental health services of local health authorities. Report by the Scottish Health Services Council Standing Advisory Committee on Local Authority Services
D. of Health for Scotland

ALLEN OF ABBEYDALE, Philip, Lord

1974   Occupational Pension Schemes (Preservation of Benefit) Amendment Regulations, 1974. Report of the Occupational Pensions Board
Session 1974-75 Cmnd. 5706 xvi.

1975   Occupational Pension Schemes (Perpetuities) Amendment Regulations, 1975. Report of the Occupational Pensions Board
Session 1974-75 HC. 410 xxxiv.

Solvency, disclosure of information and member participation in occupational pension schemes. Report of the Occupational Pensions Board
Vol. 1: Report. Session 1974-75 Cmnd. 5904 xxxiv.
Vol. 2: Written evidence submitted to the Board. Session 1974-75 Cmnd. 5904-I xxxiv.
Vol 3: Overseas practice. Session 1974-75 Cmnd. 5904-II xxxiv.

1976   Equal status for men and women in occupational pension schemes. Report of the Occupational Pensions Board
Session 1975-76 Cmnd. 6599 xlv.

Occupational Pension Schemes (Friendly Societies) Regulations, 1976. Report of the Occupational Pensions Board
Session 1975-76 HC. 347 xlv.

Occupational Pension Schemes (Preservation of Benefit) Amendment Regulations, 1976. Report of the Occupational Pensions Board
Session 1975-76 HC. 156 xlv.

1977   Contracted-Out Employment (Fire Services) (Amendment) Regulations, 1977; Contracted-Out Employment (Police) (Amendment) Regulations, 1977. Report of the Occupational Pensions Board
Session 1976-77 HC. 574 xlv.

Contracted-Out Employment (Miscellaneous Provisions) Regulations, 1977. Report of the Occupational Pensions Board
Session 1976-77 HC. 513.

Contracted-Out Employment (Transitional Arrangements) Regulations, 1977. Report of the Occupational Pensions Board
Session 1976-77 Cmnd. 6961 xlv.

Occupational pension scheme cover for disabled people. Report of the Occupational Pensions Board
Session 1976-77 Cmnd. 6849 xlv.

Occupational Pension Schemes (Certification of Employments—National Health Service) Regulations, 1977. Report cf the Occupational Pensions Board
Session 1977-78 HC. 55 lii.

Occupational Pension Schemes (Certification of Employments—Local Government, *etc.* Staffs) Regulations, 1977. Report of the Occupational Pensions Board
Session 1976-77 HC. 573 xlv.

Occupational Pensions Schemes (Preservation of Benefit) Amendment Regulations, 1977. Report of the Occupational Pensions Board
Session 1976-77 HC. 454 xlv.

Social Security (Earnings Factor) Amendment Regulations, 1977. Report of the Occupational Pensions Board
Session 1976-77 Cmnd. 6975 xlv.

Social Security Pensions Act, 1975 (Commencement, No. 11) Order, 1977. Report of the Occupational Pensions Board
Session 1977-78 Cmnd. 7053 lii.

1978   Contracted-Out Employment (Miscellaneous Provisions) Regulations, 1978. Report on the draft by the Occupational Pensions Board
Session 1977-78 HC. 260 lii.

Contracted-Out and Preservation (Further Provisions) Regulations, 1978. Report of the Occupational Pensions Board
Session 1977-78 Cmnd. 7309 lii.

Occupational Pensions Schemes (Public Service Pension Schemes) Regulations, 1978. Report of the Occupational Pensions Board
Session 1977-78 HC. 277 lii.

ALLEN OF HURTWOOD, Marjory, Lady

1943   Breast feeding of infants. Report of the advisory committee on mothers and young children. (Reports on public health and medical subjects No. 91)
M. of Health

ALLEN, G. C.

1944 &   Survey of international cartels and internal car-
1946   tels. 2 vols.
D. of Trade, published 1976

ALLEN, P., Sir

1948   Police Council. Report of a committee on special pensions
Home Office

ALLEN, P.

1973   Sedimentology. Report of the working party. *In* Research in the geological sciences (publications, series 'B' No. 7)
Natural Environment Research Council

ALLEN, R. G. D., Sir

1965   The impact of rates on households. Report of the committee of inquiry
Session 1964-65 Cmnd. 2582 xxii.

ALLISON, Charles W., Sir

1969   Teesside survey and plan. Final report to the steering committee.
Vol. 1 Policies and proposals
M. of Housing and Local Government
Vol. 2. See **WILSON, Hugh**

ALMENT, E. J. A.
1976   Competence to practice. Report of the committee
D. of Health and Social Security

ALNESS, R., Lord
1945   Agricultural education in Scotland. Report of the committee
Session 1945-46 Cmnd. 6704 x.

ALSOP, K.
See BISHOP, D.

ALSTON, R. C.
1978   Bibliography, machine readable cataloguing and the ESTC, by R. Alston and M. J. Jannetta
British Library

AMERY, J.
1957   Army cadet force. Report of the committee
Session 1956-57 Cmnd. 268 viii.

AMMON, G. C., Lord
1945   London dock dispute, March 1945. Report of the committee of enquiry
M. of Labour and National Service

ANDERSON, Colin, Sir
1960   Grants to students. Report of the committee
Session 1959-60. Cmnd. 1051 xxi.
Traffic signs for motorways. Final report of the advisory committee
M. of Transport

ANDERSON, David
1944   Steel structures. Report by a committee. (Post-war building studies No. 7)
M. of Works

ANDERSON, David Colville
1968   Report of inquiry in respect of the objection to the proposed compulsory amalgamation of the police areas of the counties of Caithness, Orkney and Zetland
Session 1967-68 Cmnd. 3695 xxx.
Report of inquiry in respect of the objection to the proposed compulsory amalgamation of the police areas of the County of Inverness and the Burgh of Inverness
Session 1967-68 Cmnd. 3634 xxx.

ANDERSON, David Steel
1970   Commercial rating. Report of the committee of inquiry
Session 1970-71 Cmnd. 4366 xxxii.

ANDERSON, J.
1945   Postal voting for the forces, seamen and war workers abroad. Report of the conference
Session 1944-45 Cmd. 6581 v.

ANDERSON, W. C.
1972   National Insurance (Assessment of Graduated Contributions) Amendment Regulations, 1972. Report of the National Insurance Advisory Committee
Session 1971-72 HC. 158 xxxviii.
National Insurance (General Benefit and Miscellaneous Amendment) Regulations, 1972. Report of the National Insurance Advisory Committee
Session 1970-71 HC. 185 xxxviii.

ANGWIN, Stanley, Sir
1948   Telecommunications. The fundamental research problems of telecommunications. Reports of the working parties of the telecommunications research committee
D. of Scientific and Industrial Research

ANNAN, Nöel Gilroy, Lord
1962   Teaching of Russian. Report of the committee
M. of Education
1977   Future of broadcasting. Report of the committee. 2 vols
Session 1976-77 Cmnd. 6753, 6753-I vi.

ANSELL, Michael Picton
1971   Riding for recreation. A digest of the report and the recommendations of the steering committee of the British Horse Society and the Sports Council
D. of the Environment

ANSON, Wilfred, Sir
1961   Work for prisoners. Report of the Advisory Council on the Employment of Prisoners
Home Office
1963   Work and vocational training in borstals (England and Wales). Report of the Advisory Council on the Employment of Prisoners
Home Office
1964   Organisation of work for prisoners. Report of the Advisory Council on the Employment of Prisoners
Home Office

APPLEBY, Robert
1969   Attainable production targets. A report by the Economic Development Committee for the Clothing Industry
N.E.D.O.
1970   Your future in clothing, an economic development study of the future market for the clothing industry. Clothing E.D.C.
N.E.D.O.

APPLETON, Edward V., Sir
1946   British Commonwealth scientific official conference, London, 1946. Report of proceedings
Session 1946-47 Cmnd. 6970 x.
1953   Scottish Peat Committee report
Scottish Home D.
1955   Supply of teachers of mathematics and science in Scotland. Report of the committee
Session 1954-55 Cmnd. 9419 iv.
1962   Scottish peat. 2nd report of the Scottish Peat Committee
D. of Agriculture and Fisheries for Scotland

APPLETON, J. H.
1970   Disused railways in the countryside of England and Wales. A report to the Countryside Commission, by J. H. and R. J. Appleton
Countryside Commission

APPLETON, R. J.
See APPLETON, J. H.

ARBUCKLE, R. H.
See WRIGHT, A. C. S.

ARCHER, H.
1974   Noise in public places. Report of a working group
Noise Advisory Council

ARCHER, J. N.
1978   Employment of non-domiciled seafarers. Report of the working party
D. of Trade

ARCHIBALD, E. S., Sir
1946   Imperial Agriculture Bureaux conference, London, 1946. Report of proceedings
Session 1946-47 Cmd. 6971 x.

ARDEN-CLARKE, Charles, Sir
1958   Chaguaramas joint commission report, 25 March, 1958. (Colonial No. 338)
Colonial Office

ARMER, F., Sir
1955   Training of district nurses. Report of the working party
M. of Health
1957   Trade effluents sub-committee of the Central Advisory Water Committee. 1st report
M. of Housing and Local Government
1960   Trade effluents sub-committee of the Central Advisory Water Committee. Final report
M. of Housing and Local Government

ARMITAGE, Arthur L., Sir
1964   Committee on the pay of postmen. Minutes of Evidence
Treasury
Committee on the pay of postmen. Report
Treasury
1978   Political activities of civil servants. Report of the committee
Session 1977-78 Cmnd. 7057 viii.

ARMSTRONG, A. G.
1974   The demand for new cars; an econometric model for short term forecasting. Motor Manufacturing E.D.C.
N.E.D.O.

ARONSON, V. R.
1949   Rubber proofed garment making industry. Report on an application for the establishment of a wages council by a commission of inquiry
M. of Labour and National Service

1949   Draft Blasting (Casting and Other Articles) Special Regulations, 1949. Report
M. of Labour and National Service

ARTHURSON, N. L., Miss
1971   Training for selling. A four step guide to the training of retail staff, based on a report by the staff training working group. Distributive Trades E.D.C.
N.E.D.O.

ASHBY, Eric, Lord
1954   Organisation and finance of adult education in England and Wales. Report of the committee
M. of Education
1971   Royal Commission on Environmental Pollution. First report
Session 1970-71 Cmnd. 4585 xvi.
1972   Royal Commission on Environmental Pollution. Second report
Session 1971-72 Cmnd. 4898 xii.
Royal Commission on Environmental Pollution. Third report: pollution in some British estuaries and coastal waters
Session 1971-72 Cmnd. 5054 xii.

Pollution: nuisance or nemesis? A report of the working party on the control of pollution
D. of the Environment
1975   Experimental manipulation of the genetic composition of micro-organisms. Report of the working party
Session 1974-75 Cmnd. 5880 xxix.
New postgraduate patterns; blending the natural and social sciences. Second report of the joint SRC/SSRC committee
Science Research Council

ASHCROFT, S. H.
1977   Structural model of British retail trade. Preliminary report—methodology and historical analysis. Distributive Trades E.D.C.
N.E.D.O.

ASSOCIATED INDUSTRIAL CONSULTANTS, LTD.
Hosiery and knitwear in the 1970s. **See RIGBY, N. L.**
Your future in clothing. **See APPLEBY, R.**

ASQUITH, C., Sir
1945   Commission on Higher Education in the Colonies. Report
Session 1944-45 Cmd. 6647 iv.
Royal Commission on Equal Pay. Minutes of evidence and appendices
Royal Commission on Equal Pay
1946   Royal Commission on Equal Pay. Report
Session 1945-46 Cmd. 6937 xi.

ASSHETON, Ralph
See CLITHEROE, R., Lord

ASTLEY, I. D.
1968   The Certificate of Secondary Education: the place of the personal topic—history. Report of the steering committee (Examinations bulletin No. 18)
Schools Council

ATCHERLEY, Harold W., Sir
1972   Review body on armed forces pay. First report
Session 1971-72 Cmnd. 4954 xxx.
1973   Review body on armed forces pay. Second report
Session 1972-73 Cmnd. 5336 xxx.
Review body on armed forces pay. Supplement to second report
Session 1972-73 Cmnd. 5450 xxx.
1974   Review body on armed forces pay. Third report
Session 1974. Cmnd. 5631 xiv.
Review body on armed forces pay. Pay of service medical and dental officers, supplement to the third report
Session 1974 Cmnd. 5729 xiv.
1975   Review body on armed forces pay. London weighting and separation allowance, second supplement to third report
Session 1974-75 Cmnd. 5853 xxxii.
Review body on armed forces pay. Fourth report
Session 1974-75 Cmnd. 6063 xxxii.
Review body on armed forces pay. Supplement to the fourth report
Session 1974-75 Cmnd. 6146 xxxii.
1976   Review body on armed forces pay. Second supplement to fourth report: London weighting
Session 1975-76 Cmnd. 6420 xli.
Review body on armed forces pay. Fifth report
Session 1975-76 Cmnd. 6470 xli.

ATCHERLEY, Harold W., Sir *(continued)*

Review body on armed forces pay. Supplement to the fifth report
Session 1975-76 Cmnd. 6515 xli.

1977   Review body on armed forces pay. Sixth report
Session 1976-77 Cmnd. 6801 xlii.

1978   Review body on armed forces pay. Seventh report
Session 1977-78 Cmnd. 7177 xlviii.

Review body on armed forces pay. Service medical and dental officers, supplement to the seventh report
Session 1978-79 Cmnd. 7288

ATKINS, H. J. B., Sir

1962   Emergency treatment in hospital of cases of acute poisoning. Report of the sub-committee of the standing medical advisory committee, Central Health Services Council
M. of Health

ATKINS, W. S.

See **BULMER, W. P.**
See **SUSSMAN, N. F.**
See **WOOD, J. I.**

ATKINSON, E. H. Tindal

1946   Prices of radio valves. Report of the central price regulation committee
Board of Trade

ATKINSON, Richard

1976   Capital provision for university libraries. Report of a working party
University Grants Committee

AUCKLAND, John George

See **KENNEDY, P. J. M.**

AULD, A. T.

1970   Handicapped children in care of local authorities and voluntary organisations. Report of the committee. Scottish Advisory Council on Child Care
Scottish Education D.

AVONSIDE, I. H., Lord

1958   Tenancy of Shops (Scotland) Act, 1949. Report of the committee
Session 1957-58 Cmnd. 472 xviii.

AWBERRY, S. S.

1948   Labour and trade union organisation in the Federation of Malaya and Singapore. Report by S. S. Awberry and F. W. Dalley (Colonial No. 234)
Colonial Office

AYERST, D. G. O.

1967   The Certificate of Secondary Education trial examinations: Religious knowledge. Report of the steering committee. (Examinations bulletin No. 17)
Schools Council

AYRE, Amos L., Sir

1945   Committee on hydrocarbon oil duties. Report
Session 1944-45 Cmd. 6615 v.

BACON, Edmund C., Sir

1968   Agriculture's import saving role, a report. Agriculture E.D.C.
N.E.D.O.

1973   Farm productivity, a report on factors affecting productivity at the farm level by the productivity steering group. Agriculture E.D.C.
N.E.D.O.

BACON, R. W.

1974   Age of U.S. and U.K. machinery. (Monograph No. 3)
N.E.D.O.

BADER, Douglas

1973   Flight time limitations. Report of the committee
Civil Aviation Authority

BADHAM, D. G.

1975   National health service staff commission for Wales. Report 1972-1975
Welsh Office

BAILEY, D. C., Sir

1952   Quicker completion of house interiors. Report of a committee
M. of Housing and Local Government

BAILLIEU, Clive, Sir

1946   Central institute of management. Report of a committee appointed to formulate detailed proposals for setting up a central institute for all questions connected with management
Board of Trade

BAILLIE, E. O.

1968   Protective clothing for workers on construction sites, report on a competition. The method of assessment, the techniques employed in serviceability testing and the results
M. of Public Building and Works, Directorate of Building Development

BAIN, A. D.

1978   Financing of North Sea oil. Report of the working party. (Committee to review the functioning of financial institutions, research report No. 2)
Treasury

BAINS, M. A.

1972   The new local authorities: management and structure. Report of a study group on local authority management structure
D. of the Environment.

BAKER, A. S.

1976   Rank structure of the police, part 2: ranks above chief superintendent. Report of the joint working party of the Police Advisory Boards of England and Wales, and of Scotland
Home Office

Special constabulary. Report of the working party of the Police Advisory Board for England and Wales
Home Office

BAKER, D. W.

1972   Not so much a warehouse. . . . The CWS automated grocery distribution centre, Birtley
D. of Trade and Industry

BAKER, E. B. H.

1962   Inter-library co-operation in England and Wales. Report of the working party
M. of Education

BAKER, G., Sir

1965   Mechanical recording of court proceedings. Interim report of the committee
Session 1964-65 Cmnd. 2733 xiii.

1966   Mechanical recording of court proceedings. Final report of the committee
Session 1966-67 Cmnd. 3096 xxvi.

1973   Collapse of false work for the viaduct over the River London on 24 October, 1972. Report by H.M. Factory Inspectorate
Session 1972-73 HC. 425 viii.

BAKER, G. G.

1956   Proposed British egg marketing scheme. Report on the public inquiry into objections
Session 1955-56 Cmd. 9805 x.

BAKER, Harold T.

1947   New Forest committee report
Session 1947-48 Cmd. 7245 xiv.

BAKER, M. G. J.

1972   Data base management systems, their use in hospital data processing. Report of the data base sub-groups on software and programming
D. Health and Social Security

BAKER, S. J., Sir

1944   Income tax on rent allowances. Report of the sub-committee of the Police Council
Home Office

1947   Local conditions of service for the police. Report of the committee of the Police Council
Home Office

1951   Standardisation of promotion examinations. Report of the committee of the Police Council
Home Office

1952   Police representative organisations and negotiating machinery. Report of the committee of the Police Council
Home Office

1955   Sale of old metals and the control of dealers in old metals. Report of the working party
Home Office

BALFOUR OF BURLEIGH, G. J. G., Lord

1944   Committee on hill sheep farming in Scotland. Report
Session 1943-44 Cmd. 6494 iii.

1949   Housing management. Management of municipal housing estates. Second report of the housing management sub-committee of the Central Housing Advisory Committee
M. of Health

1955   Hill lands (north of Scotland) commission. Report
Session 1955-56 Cmd. 9759 x.

1957   Export of live cattle. Report of the committee of enquiry into the export of live cattle to the continent for slaughter
Session 1956-57 Cmnd. 154 xii.

BALFOUR, G.

1941   Committee on cement production. Report
Session 1940-41 Cmd. 6282 iv.

BALFOUR, R. A. L., Earl

1954   Royal Commission on Scottish affairs. Report
Session 1953-54 Cmd. 9212 xix.

BALL, J. G.

    See ADAMS, J. R.

BALL, R. J.

1978   Policy optimisation. Report of the committee
Session 1977-78 Cmnd. 7148 xiv.

BALLANTYNE, J. C.

1976   Services for hearing-impaired children. Interim report of a sub-committee of the Advisory Committee on Services for Hearing Impaired People
D. of Health and Social Security

BAMFORD, Eric St. J., Sir

1949   Taxation and overseas minerals. Report of the departmental committee
Session 1948-49 Cmd. 7728 xviii.

BANFIELD, J.

1977   Training for health and safety, a guide for the industry. Report of the working party
Air Transport and Travel Industry Training Board

BANKS, Maurice Alfred Lister

1970   British patent system. Report of the committee to examine the patent system and patent law
Session 1970-71 Cmnd. 4407 xliii.

BANNERMAN, J. W. M.

1977   Late medieval monumental sculpture in the West Highlands. Royal Commission on the Ancient and Historical Monuments of Scotland

BANTOCK, G. H.

1969   Education through the use of materials, the possible role of school workshops in the education of secondary-school pupils. Report of the advisory committee. (Working paper, 26)
Schools Council

BANWELL, Harold, Sir

1964   The placing and management of contracts for building and civil engineering work. Report of the committee
M. of Public Building and Works.

1967   Action on the Banwell report.
See POTTS, P. G.

1968   Contracting in civil engineering since Banwell.
See HARRIS, W. G., Sir

BARBER, A.

1973   Industrial review to 1977
N.E.D.O.

BARKER, H.

1972   Data transmission: the future, the next ten years
N.E.D.O.

BARKER, James

1972   Contract farming. Report of the committee of inquiry
Session 1971-72 Cmnd. 5099 vi.

BARLOW, Alan, Sir

1946   Scientific manpower. Report of a committee
Session 1945-46 Cmd. 6824 xiv.

BARLOW, J. A.

1944   Civil Service. Recruitment to established posts in the Civil Service during the reconstruction period. Statement of government policy and report of the committee of the Civil Service National Whitley Council
Session 1943-44 Cmd. 6567 viii.

BARLOW, J. A. *(continued)*
1946   Marriage bar in the Civil Service. Report of the Civil Service National Whitley Council Committee Session 1945-46 Cmd. 6886 x.

BARNES, D. C., Sir
1962   Selection and training of supervisors. Report of the committee
M. of Labour

BARNES, G. G.
    See WRIGHT, N. C.

BARNES, H. Jefferson
1971   Art in secondary schools. Report of the working party. (Consultative committee on the curriculum, curriculum papers No. 9)
Scottish Education D.

BARNES, J.
1975   Educational priority, vol. 3: curriculum innovation in London's EPAs
D. of Education and Science

BARNES, Michael
1977   Note on the objectives of energy policy as described in chapter two of the Energy Commission Paper No. 1 (ENCOM (77) 5)
Energy Commission
1978   Energy pricing, an alternative approach. (Energy Commission Paper No. 11)
Energy Commission

BARNES, W. C.
1953   Police pensions. Report of the working party of The Scottish Police Council
Scottish Home D.

    Extraneous duties. Report of the committee of the Scottish Police Council
Scottish Home D.

BARNES, W. L. Gorell, Sir
    See GORELL-BARNES, W. L., Sir

BARNETT, G. B.
1945   Mule spinners' cancer and automatic wiping-down motions. Interim report of the joint advisory committee on the cotton industry
M. of Labour
1946   The cotton industry. Interim reports of the joint advisory committee
M. of Labour and National Service
1947   Cotton industry. Spacing of machinery and cotton weaving. Report of the joint advisory committee on conditions of work in the cotton trade. 1st. report
M. of Labour and National Service

    Cotton industry. Ventilation, temperature, use of steam in humidification and lighting. Interim report
M. of Labour and National Service

    Milling machines. Interim report of the committee on the safeguarding of milling machines
M. of Labour and National Service

BARRATT, John
1974   Remainder waterways of the British Waterways Board
Inland Waterways Amenity Advisory Council

    Scottish waterways: Forth and Clyde Canal, Union Canal Report to the Secretary of State for the Environment
Inland Waterways Amenity Advisory Council

1974   Upgrading of remainder waterways
Inland Waterways Amenity Advisory Council

    Water shortage of British Waterways Board system
Inland Waterways Amenity Advisory Council
1975   Angling on the British Waterways Board system
Inland Waterways Amenity Advisory Council

    Priorities for action on the waterways of the British Waterways Board
Inland Waterways Amenity Advisory Council
1976   Observations on the review of the water industry in England and Wales; the government consultative document
Inland Waterways Amenity Advisory Council

    Scotland's remainder waterways. Progress report on the Forth and Clyde, and Union Canals
Inland Waterways Amenity Advisory Council

BARRINGTON-WARD, V. M., Sir
1949   London plan working party report. Report by the working party appointed by the British Transport Commission
M. of Transport

BARRY, P. R., Sir
1959   Treatment of young offenders. Report of the Advisory Council on the Treatment of Offenders
Home Office
1960   Corporal punishment. Report of the Advisory Council on the Treatment of Offenders Session 1960-61 Cmnd. 1213 xiii.
1962   Non-residential treatment of offenders under 21. Report of the Advisory Council on the Treatment of Offenders
Home Office

BARTLETT, F., Sir
1958   Human relations in industry, 1954-57. Final report of the joint committee
D. of Scientific and Industrial Research *and* the Medical Research Council

BASDEN, B. E.
1975   Bernard Russell Ltd. Report of investigations under the Companies Act
D. of Trade
1975   Blande Ltd. (now named Black Arrow Group Ltd). Report of investigations under the Companies Act
D. of Trade

BASKETT, R., Sir
    See CUTHBERTSON, D., Sir

BASNETT, D.
1973   Chemical manpower in Europe. Report of a comparative study of industrial relations and manpower productivity in the U.K., France, Germany and Holland. Chemicals E.D.C.
N.E.D.O.

BATCHELOR, I. R. C.
1970   The staffing of mental deficiency hospitals. Report of a sub-committee constituted jointly by the Standing Medical Advisory Committee and the Standing Nursing and Midwifery Advisory Committee of the Scottish Health Services Council
Scottish Home and Health D.

BATEMAN, James A.

1975   Biological recording working group for Wales. Reports and records of field meetings, 1974-75
National Museum of Wales

BATESON, Dingwall L.

1950   Employment of children. Report of the departmental committee on the employment of children as film actors, in theatrical work and in ballet
Session 1950 Cmd. 8005 vii.

BATHO, W. J. S.

1976   Dogs. Report of the working party
D. of the Environment

BATSON, E.

1976   Industrial democracy; European experience, two reports for the industrial democracy committee
D. of Trade

BAVIN, A. R. W.

1973   Reorganisation of the N.H.S. and local government in England and Wales. Report from the working party on collaboration between the N.H.S. and local government on its activities to the end of 1972
D. of Health and Social Security

1973   Reorganisation of the N.H.S. and local government in England and Wales. Report from the working party on collaboration on its activities from January to July 1973
D. of Health and Social Security

1974   Reorganisation of the N.H.S. and local government in England and Wales. Report from the working party on collaboration on its activities from July 1973 to April 1974
D. of Health and Social Security

BAWDEN, F. C., Sir

1964   Technical assistance from Britain in agriculture, animal health, forestry and fisheries overseas. Report of the advisory committee
Session 1963-64 Cmnd. 2286 xix.

BAXTER, G. H.

1951   Central African territories. Report of conference on closer association
Session 1950-51 Cmd. 8233 x.

BAXTER, J. W.

1971   Price adjustment formulae for civil engineering contracts. Report. Civil Engineering E.D.C.
N.E.D.O.

1974   Price adjustment formulae for civil engineering contracts, 2: structural steelwork. Civil Engineering E.D.C.
N.E.D.O.

BAYLISS, B. T.

1969   Transport for industry (summary report). A study of the determinants of demand for transport in manufacturing industry, by B. T. Bayliss and and S. L. Edwards
M. of Transport

1970   Industrial Demand for transport, by B. T. Bayliss and S. L. Edwards
M. of Transport

1973   Road haulage industry since 1968
D. of the Environment

BEACH, S. T.

1975   Manpower policy in the hotels and restaurant

industry. Manpower policy working group.
Hotels and Catering E.D.C. 2 vols
Summary and recommendations
Research findings
N.E.D.O.

1977   Employment policy and industrial relations in hotels and catering industry. Report of the manpower working group of the Hotels and Catering E.D.C.
N.E.D.O.

BEACHAM, A.

See OGDEN, W. M.

BEALE, Samuel, Sir

1942   Small retailers of clothing. Scheme for ensuring fair shares of supplies
Board of Trade

BEAMENT, J. W. L.

1973   Research in the soil sciences. Report of the working party (Publications series B, No. 6)
Natural Environment Research Council

BEARD, James R.

1944   Electrical installations. Report of a committee convened by the Institution of Electrical Engineers (Post-war building studies 2)
M. of Works

BEATON, Neil S.

1947   Ferries in Great Britain. Report of the committee
M. of Transport

BEAUMONT, P. B.

1978   Labour shortages in manpower policy. (Manpower studies No. 1978-2)
D. of Employment

BEAVER, Hugh, Sir

1953   Power stations. Report of the committee of inquiry into the construction of power stations
M. of Power

1954   Air pollution committee. Interim report
Session 1953-54 Cmnd. 9011 viii.
Air pollution committee. Report
Session 1953-54 Cmnd. 9322 viii.

BEEBY, George Harry

1967   Manpower in the chemical industry. A comparison of British and American practices. Working party report. Chemicals E.D.C.
N.E.D.O.

BEECHING, Richard, Lord

1963   British Railways Board: Reshaping of British Railways. Report and maps
M. of Transport

1969   Royal Commission on assizes and quarter sessions. Report
Session 1968-69 Cmnd. 4153 xxiii.

1971   Royal Commission on assizes and quarter sessions. Written evidence submitted to the Royal Commission

See also ROSE, G. N. G.

BEESTON, G. R.

1966   The arts in Wales. Report of a study of the organisation, finance, accommodation and other

BEESTON, G. R. *(continued)*
provisions for the arts in Wales. Council for Wales and Monmouthshire
Session 1966-67 Cmnd. 2983 li.

BEHREND, H.
1974   Attitudes to price increases and pay claims (Monograph No. 4)
N.E.D.O.

BELCHAMBERS, Anthony Murray
1978   The Birmingham and Midland Canal Carrying Co. Ltd. Report of investigations under the Companies Act
D. of Trade

BELL, Kathleen
1975   Research study on supplementary benefit appeal tribunals. Review of main findings: conclusions, recommendations
D. of Health and Social Security

BELLAMY, R. G.
1966   Training of training officers, introductory courses. A report by the committee on training of training officers of the Central Training Council
M. of Labour

1967   Training of training officers, a pattern for the future. A report by the Central Training Council's committee on the training of training officers
M. of Labour

BELLIS, B. T.
1969   Computers and the schools. An interim report prepared by the consultative committee on the curriculum. (Curriculum papers No. 6)
Scottish Education D.

1972   Computers and the schools. Final report by the consultative committee on the curriculum (Curriculum paper No. 11)
Scottish Education D.

BELOE, R.
1960   Secondary schools examinations other than the G.C.E. Report of a committee of the Secondary School Examinations Council
M. of Education

BENEY, F. W.
1955   Diseases provisions of the National Insurance (Industrial Injuries) Act. Report of the departmental committee
Session 1955-56 Cmd. 9548 xxii.

BENINGTON, John
1976   Local government becomes big business, 2nd ed.
Home Office, Community Development Project

BENJAMIN, B.
1973   Government actuary's department; actuary's role in financial management
D. of Health and Social Security

BENNETT, C. J. M.
1971   Reaching world markets. A report on international marketing in the pharmaceuticals industry. Chemicals E.D.C. Repr. in 1973
N.E.D.O.

1972   Focus on pharmaceuticals. A report by the pharmaceuticals working party. Chemicals E.D.C.
N.E.D.O.
Organising R. & D. Chemicals E.D.C.
N.E.D.O.

1973   Innovative activity in the pharmaceuticals industry. A report by the pharmaceuticals working party. Chemicals E.D.C.
N.E.D.O.

BENNETT, P. H. P.
1978   The future of agrément in the U.K. Report of the agrément study group
D. of the Environment

BENNETT, S. J.
1971   Lorry parking. Report of the working party on the parking of lorries
D. of the Environment

BENSON, H., Sir
1958   Disposal of scrap cable. Report of an inquiry into the methods adopted by the London Electricity Board for the disposal of scrap cable
Session 1958-59 Cmnd. 605 xvi.

1977   Royal Commission on legal services. Report on progress
Session 1976-77 Cmnd. 6770 xviii.

BENTHALL, E., Sir
1954   Markets in the Middle East. Report of the United Kingdom trade mission to Iraq, Kuwait, the Lebanon, Syria and Saudi Arabia, November to December. 1953
Board of Trade

BERRIE, A. D.
1976   Freshwater biological surveillance. Working party report (Publications series B, No. 18)
Natural Environment Reseach Council

BERRILL, Kenneth E., Sir
1970   Teaching computing in universities. Report of a joint working party
University Grants Committee *and* Computer Board for Universities anad Research Councils

1977   Review of overseas representation. Report by the Central Policy Review Staff
Cabinet Office

BESSELL, J. E.
1973   Younger worker in agriculture; projections to 1980. (Discussion paper No. 2)
N.E.D.O.

BESSEY, G. S.
1962   Training of part-time youth leaders and assistants. Report of the working party
M. of Education

1966   Service by youth. Report of a committee of the Youth Service Development Council
D. of Education and Science

BEST, Roy
1972 to   Out of sight, out of mind. Report by a working
1976   party on sludge disposal in Liverpool Bay
Vol. 1: Report. 1972
Vol. 2: Appendices. 1972
Vol. 3: Report for 1972-73. 1973
Vol. 4: Report for 1973-75. 1976
D. of the Environment

1977   Disposal of sewage to sludge to land. Report of the working party. (Standing technical committee reports No. 5)
National Water Council

1978   Sewage sludge disposal data and reviews of disposal to sea. Standing technical committee on the disposal of sewage sludge. (Standing tech-

9

BEST, Roy *(continued)*

nical committee reports No. 8)
National Water Council

BEST, R. D.

1944   Design and designer in the light metal trades.
Report of a committee of the council for art
and industry set up to consider how to give
practical effect to the recommendations in
"Design and the Designer in Industry"
Board of Trade

BETTENSON, A. S.

1957   Dust in card rooms. 3rd interim report of the
Joint Advisory Committee of the Cotton Industry
M. of Labour and National Service

1960   Dust in card rooms. 4th interim report of the
Joint Advisory Committee of the Cotton Industry
M. of Labour

1961   Dust in card rooms. Final report of the Joint
Advisory Committee of the Cotton Industry
M. of Labour

BEVERIDGE, William H., Lord

1941   Skilled men in the Services. Interim report of
committee
Session 1940-41 Cmd. 6307 viii.

Fuel rationing. Report
Session 1941-42 Cmd. 6352 iv.
Treasury

1942   Social insurance and allied services. Report
Session 1942-43 Cmd. 6404 vi.
Social insurance and allied services. Appendix
G: memoranda from organisations
Session 1942-43 Cmd. 6405 vi.
Social insurance and allied services; the Beve-
ridge report in brief
Treasury

1950   Broadcasting. Report of the broadcasting committee
Session 1950-51 Cmd. 8116 ix.

BEVIN, Ernest

1947   European economic co-operation, July to Sep-
tember 1947. Report of the committee. Vol. 1:
General report (report of the Marshall Plan)
Foreign Office

BIEBUYCH, Tony

1978   Policy and provision for the single homeless; a
position paper by M. Drake and T. Biebuych
Personal Social Services Council

BIELBY, G. H.

1978   Salmon propagation in England and Wales.
Report by the Association of River Authorities/
National Water Council working party, ed. by
G. S. Harris
National Water Council

BINGHAM, T. H.

1978   The supply of petroleum and petroleum products
to Rhodesia
Foreign and Commonwealth Office

BIGNELL, S. G. L.

1977   Provision on nursing care in special schools
D. of Health and Social Security

BINNEY, G., Sir

1959   United Kingdom trade and industrial mission
to Ghana
Board of Trade

BINNEY, Marcus

1977   Chapels and churches; who cares, an independent report
British Tourist Authority

BINNIE AND PARTNERS
See CHANTLER, P.

BINNS, E. U. E. ELLIOTT-
See ELLIOTT-BINNS, E. U. E.

BINNS, P. D.

1970   Basic face end layouts. Report of a working
group
National Coal Board

BIRCH, J. G.

1971   Indoor sports centres. Report of an enquiry
undertaken for the sports council (Sports Council studies No. 1)
D. of the Environment

BIRD, Barbara

1977   Mobile homes in England and Wales, 1975.
Report of surveys by B. Bird and A. O'Dell
D. of the Environment

BIRD, T.

1975   Rehabilitation of the adult hearing-impaired.
Report of a sub-committee of the advisory
committee on services for hearing-impaired
people
D. of Health and Social Security

BIRKETT, Norman., Lord

1957   Interception of communications. Report of the
committee of privy councillors
Session 1956-57 Cmnd. 283 xv.

BIRKS, J.

1976   Marine technology. Report of a task force of
the Engineering Board
Science Research Council

BIRSAY, H. R., Lord

1957   Nuclear generating station. Report on the public
local inquiries into the applications by the South
of Scotland Electricity Board for consent to the
construction of a nuclear generating station at
Hunterston, Ayrshire, and into the South of
Scotland Electricity Board (Hunterston) Compulsory Purchase Order, 1956
Scottish Home D.

1960   Custodial sentences for young offenders. Report
of the Scottish Advisory Council on the Treatment of Offenders
Scottish Home D.

Extension of compulsory after-care to addi-
tional categories of inmates and prisoners.
Report of the Scottish Advisory Council on the
Treatment of Offenders
Scottish Home D.

1963   Organisation of after-care in Scotland. Report
of a committee of the Scottish Advisory Council
on the Treatment of Offenders
Scottish Home and Health D.

BIRSAY, H. R., Lord *(continued)*

1967   General medical services in the highlands and islands. Report of a committee
Session 1966-67 Cmnd. 3257 xxxv.

BISHOP, D.

1969   A study of coding and data co-ordination for the construction industry. Report prepared for the sub-committee on coding and data co-ordination of the committee on the application of computers in the construction industry, by D. Bishop and K. Alsop
M. of Public Building and Works

BLACK, D.

1974   Decentralised clinical research scheme in England and Wales. Report of the joint working party
D. of Health and Social Security

BLACK, Douglas Andrew Kilgour

1970   Biochemical research in psychiatry, survey and proposals. Report by a Council committee
Medical Research Council

BLACK, H. B.

1973   Social subjects for young school leavers. Central committee on social subjects. (Consultative committee on the curriculum bulletin No. 1)
Scottish Education D.

1976   The social subjects in secondary schools. Scottish Central Committee on Social Subjects. (Curriculum paper No. 15)
Scottish Education D.

BLACK, Harold, Sir

1976   The handling of complaints against the police. Report of a working party for Northern Ireland
Session 1975-76 Cmnd. 6475 xxxiv.

BLACK, Harold K.

1968   Report on a fatal accident and fire at the West London Terminal of Esso Petroleum Company Ltd. on 1 April, 1967.
Home Office

BLACKLEY, J. L.

1974   U.K. farming and the common market: hills and uplands. Agriculture E.D.C.
N.E.D.O.

BLAGDEN, J. B.

1957   Bankruptcy law and deeds of arrangement law amendment. Report of the bankruptcy law amendment committee
Session 1956-57 Cmnd. 221 viii.

1958   Bankruptcy law and deeds of arrangement law amendment committee. Minutes of Evidence
Board of Trade

BLAIR HARDIE, J.

1969   Dental services in health centres. Report of a sub-committee of the Standing Dental Advisory Committee of the Scottish Health Services Council
Scottish Home and Health D.

BLAKE, G. D.

1967   Report of the inquiry into local objections to the proposed development of land at Stansted as the third airport for London, 6 December, 1965-11 February, 1966
M. of Housing and Local Government

1971   New homes in the cities; the role of the private developer in urban renewal in England and Wales. Report by a working party. Building E.D.C.
N.E.D.O.

BLAND, C. E.
See WINN, C. R. N., Sir, 1969

BLEDISLOE, B. L., Viscount

1961   Salmon and freshwater fisheries. Report of the committee
Session 1960-61 Cmnd. 1350 xv.

BLENKHARN, Allan

1970   Birmingham canal navigations. Report on the 'remainder' waterways
British Waterways Board

BLENKINSOP, A.

1977   Advisory council on the misuse of drugs. Treatment and rehabilitation working group. First interim report
D. of Health and Social Security

BLENKINSOP, Arthur

1950   Publicity for local government. Final report of the consultative committee
M. of Health

BLENNERHASSETT, Francis Alfred

1967   Report of inquiry in respect of the objections to the proposed compulsory amalgamation of the police areas of the County of Yorkshire, East Riding, and the cities of Kingston upon Hull and York
Session 1966-67 Cmnd. 3406 xlvi.

1976   Drinking and driving. Report of the departmental committee
D. of the Environment

BLOOD, Hilary, Sir

1955   Plan for a British Caribbean Federation. Report of the Civil Service Commission
Session 1955-56 Cmd. 9619 xii.

1960   Malta constitutional commission. Report
Session 1960-61 Cmnd. 1261 x.

BLOOM, M. J.

1972   Regional forecasting for construction, a pilot study in Yorkshire and Humberside, 1970-75. Building and Civil Engineering E.D.C.s
N.E.D.O.

1974   Regional construction forecasts to 1977. Building and Civil Engineering E.D.C.s. 4 vols.
N.E.D.O.

BODMER, W. F.

1978   Review of clinical genetics. Report by the sub-committee
Medical Research Council

BOGLE, D. B.
See TENBY, G., Viscount

BOLTON, John Everleigh

1971   Small firms. Report of the committee of inquiry
Session 1971-72 Cmnd. 4811 ix.

11

BOMFORD, R. R.

1973   Report of the professional investigation into medical and nursing practice on certain wards at Napsbury Hospital near St. Albans
D. of Health and Social Security

BONDI, Hermann

1974   Interchange of scientists. Report of the task force
Civil Service Department

BONHAM-CARTER, A. Desmond, Sir

1969   The functions of the district general hospital. Report of the committee. Central Health Services Council
D. of Health and Social Security

BONHAM-CARTER, G. E. D.

1971   Construction industry prospects to 1979. Report by the joint working party on demand and output forecasts. Building and Civil Engineering E.D.C.'s.
N.E.D.O.

1972   Construction industry prospects to 1979. Report by the joint working party on demand and output forecasts. Building and Civil Engineering E.D.C.s
N.E.D.O.

BONN, Max J., Sir

1942   Memorandum on the problems of post-war entry of juveniles into employment, by the London Regional Advisory Council for Juvenile Employment
M. of Labour

BOORMAN, L. A.

1977   Ecology of Maplin Sands and the coastal zones of Suffolk, Essex and North Kent
Institute of Terrestrial Ecology

BOR, W. G.

    See LLEWELYN-DAVIES, R., Lord

BOREHAM, Leslie Kenneth Edward

1969   Report of inquiry in respect of the objections to the proposed amalgamation of the Police areas of the County of Warwick, the City of Coventry and the County Borough of Solihull
Session 1968-69 Cmnd. 3947 xliii.

BORNER, R. S.

1973   Valuers in the public service. Report of the committee
Session 1973-74 Cmnd. 5518 iv.

BOSANQUET, C. I. C.

1956   Pigs and bacon. Reorganisation committee report
Session 1955-56 Cmd. 9795 xxvi.

1964   Demand for agricultural graduates. Report of an interdepartmental committee
Session 1963-64 Cmnd. 2419 viii.

BOSTOCK, G.

1971   Approach to the training of staff with training officer roles. Discussion document by the training of trainers committee
Manpower Services Commission, Training Services Division

1978   Training of trainers. First report of the committee
Manpower Services Commission, Training Services Division

BOSTON CONSULTING GROUP LTD.

1975   Strategy alternatives for the British motorcycle industry. Report and appendices. 2 vols.
Session 1974-75 HC. 532, 532-I. xiv.

BOSWORTH, George S.

1966   Education and training requirements for the electrical and mechanical manufacturing industries. Report of the committee on manpower resources for science and technology
D. of Education and Science

1970   Graduate training in manufacturing technology. Working group on engineering training and the requirements of industry
M. of Technology

BOTT, M. H. P.

1973   Marine geology and geophysics. Report of the working party In: Research in the geological sciences. (publications series 'B', No. 7)
Natural Environment Research Council

BOTTINI, R. N.

1972   Agricultural manpower in England and Wales. Report by the manpower working group. Agriculture E.D.C.
N.E.D.O.

1977   Agriculture into the 1980s: manpower. Agriculture E.D.C.
N.E.D.O.

BOTTOMLEY, Arthur

1975   House of Commons administration. Report to Mr. Speaker
Session 1974-75 HC. 624 xii.

BOTTOMLEY, J. K.

1967   Manpower in the chemical industry. A comparison of British and American practices. Report by a working party. Chemicals E.D.C.
N.E.D.O.

BOURDILLON, H. T.

1962   Standards of public library service in England and Wales. Report of the working party
M. of Education

BOWDEN, K.

1973   Ocean circulation. Report of the working party. In: Research in the physical marine sciences. (publications series B, No. 8)
Natural Environment Research Council

BOWE, Colette

1977   Industrial efficiency and the role of government
D. of Industry

BOWEN, G.

1973   Value for money; report of the Consumer Safeguards Group
Metrication Board

BOWEN, Gordon

1977   Survey of fringe bodies
Civil Service Dept.

BOWEN, Martin

1977   Grass fleece experiment; a report of monitoring at Crystal Palace National Sports Centre and Finsbury Park. (Sports Council study No. 12)
Sports Council

BOWEN, Roderick

1966   Aden. Report on procedures for the arrest, interrogation and detention of suspected terrorists in Aden. (Miscellaneous No. 15, 1966)
Session 1966-67 Cmnd. 3165 xxv.

1972   Bilingual traffic signs. Report of a committee of inquiry
Session 1971-72 Cmnd. 5110 xxxix.

BOWES, H. L.

1958   Inland waterways. Report of the committee of inquiry
Session 1957-58 Cmnd. 486 xviii.

BOYD OF MERTON, A. T., Viscount

1957   Singapore constitutional conference held in London in March and April, 1957. Report
Session 1956-57 Cmnd. 147 x.
Nigeria constitutional conference. Report by the Nigeria Constitutional Conference held in London in May and June 1957
Session 1956-57 Cmnd. 207 x.

1958   Nigeria. Report by the resumed Nigeria constitutional conference held in London in September and October 1958
Session 1958-59 Cmnd. 569 x.

BOYD-BARRETT, Oliver

1977   Studies on the press. (Working paper No. 3)
Royal Commission on the Press

BOYD-ORR, J., Lord

1943   Infant mortality in Scotland. Report of a sub-committee of the Scientific Advisory Committee
D. of Health for Scotland

1974   Limitation of actions in personal injury claims. Interim report (Law Reform Committee 20th report)
Session 1974-75 Cmnd. 5630 vii.

For previous reports See PEARSON, C. H., Lord

BOYLE OF HANDSWORTH, Edward Charles Gurney, Lord

Review body on top salaries

1971   1st report: Ministers of the Crown and Members of Parliament
Session 1971-72 Cmnd. 4836 xxxiv.

1972   2nd report: Interim report on top salaries
Session 1971-72 Cmnd. 5001 xxxiv.

1973   3rd report: 2nd interim report on top salaries
Session 1972-73 Cmnd. 5372 xxx.

1974   4th report: 3rd interim report on top salaries
Session 1974 Cmnd. 5595 xv.

5th report: Members of Parliament allowances
Session 1974 Cmnd. 5701 xv.

6th report: Report on top salaries
Session 1974-75 Cmnd. 5846 xxxii.

1975   7th report: Ministers of the Crown and Members of Parliament and the Peers' expenses allowance, part 1
Session 1974-75 Cmnd. 6136 xxxii.

1976   8th report: Ministers of the Crown and Members of Parliament and the Peers' expenses allowance, part II
Session 1975-76 Cmnd. 6574 xli.

1977   9th report: Ministers of the Crown and Members of Parliament and the Peers' expenses allowance, part III
Session 1976-77 Cmnd. 6749 xlii.

1978   10th report: Top salaries, second report
Session 1977-78 Cmnd. 7253 xlviii.

BRABAZON OF TARA, J. T. C., Lord

1945   Severn barrage committee report, 1933, incorporating general plan No. 3, reprinted 1945. Economic Advisory Council
Treasury

1951   Landing and taking-off of aircraft in bad weather. Report of the inquiry into the relative responsibilities of the captain of an aircraft, the operator and aerodrome authority in deciding whether an aircraft can safely land at or take off from an aerodrome in bad weather conditions
Session 1950-51 Cmd. 8147 viii.

BRABIN, D. J., Sir

1966   Case of Timothy John Evans. Report of an inquiry
Session 1966-67 Cmnd. 3101 xxvi.

BRADBEER, A. F.

1954   Internal administration of hospitals. Report of the committee. Central Health Services Council
M. of Health

BRADLAW, R. V., Sir

1950   New Zealand school dental nurses. Report of United Kingdom mission February to March 1950
M. of Health

BRADSHAW, A. D.

1977   Amenity grasslands, the needs for research. Report by the amenity grass committee. (Publications series C No. 19)
Natural Environment Research Council

See also CLARK, R. B.

BRADY, G. A.
See LEWES, F. M. M.

BRAGG, S. L.

1974   Falsework. Interim report of the advisory committee
D. of Employment *and* D. of the Environment

1976   Falsework. Final report of the advisory committee
Health and Safety Executive

BRAIN, Russell, Lord

1960   Drug addiction. Interim report of the interdepartmental committee
M. of Health

1961   Drug addiction. Report of the interdepartmental committee
M. of Health

1965   Drug addiction. Second report of the interdepartmental committee
M. of Health

BRAITHWAITE, J. Gurney

1952   Bus accident on 4 December, 1951 at Gillingham. Road Safety Committee
M. of Transport

Highway code. Report of the Road Safety Committee
M. of Transport

Motor Cycle accidents. Report of the Road Safety Committee
M. of Transport

BRAMBELL, F. W. R.

1965 Welfare of animals kept under intensive live-stock husbandry systems. Report of the technical committee
Session 1965-66 Cmnd. 2836 iv.

BRAMLEY-HARKER, R.

1952 Fencing of hydraulic presses. Report of the joint standing committee on safety in the use of power presses
M. of Labour and National Service

Fencing of press brakes. Joint standing committee in the use of power presses
M. of Labour and National Service

1953 Drop forging industry. Report of the committee on conditions
M. of Labour and National Service

Safety in the use of power presses. 2nd report of proceedings of the joint standing committee
M. of Labour and National Service

1957 Non-ferrous foundries. First report on safety, health and welfare conditions by the joint standing committee
M. of Labour and National Service

Safety in the use of power presses. 4th report of proceedings of the joint standing committee
M. of Labour and National Service

1959 Safety in the use of power presses. 4th report of the proceedings of the joint standing committee
M. of Labour and National Service

BRAND, M.

1963 Dust control in potteries. First report of the joint standing committee
M. of Labour

BRAY, F.

1948 Art examinations. Report of the committee
M. of Education

BRECKENRIDGE, A. M.

1976 Addition of drugs to intravenous fluids. Report of the working party
D. of Health and Social Security

BREESE, P. L. LEIGH-

See LEIGH-BREESE, P. L.

BRENNAN, A. J. E.

1974 Vagrancy and street offences. Working paper of the working party
Home Office

1976 Vagrancy and street offences. Report of the working party
Home Office

BRESLIN, J. J.

1954 Matchwood working party. Report
Board of Trade

BRETT, M. J.

1977 Ownership of land by agricultural landlords in England and Wales Agriculture E.D.C.
N.E.D.O.

BRIAULT, E. W. H.

1972 Sixteen to nineteen; growth and response, 1: curricular bases; some suggestions for consideration from the second sixth form working party with a discussion of the certificate of extended education
Schools Council, published by Evans/Methuen Educational

1973 Sixteen to nineteen: growth and response, 2: examination structure. Proposals by the second sixth form working party
Schools Council

BRIDGE, C. G.

1973 Chemical manpower in Europe. Report of a comparative study of industrial relations and manpower productivity in the U.K., France, Germany and Holland. Chemicals E.D.C.
N.E.D.O.

BRIDGE, Nigel, Lord

1971 Remedies in administrative law. Report of a consultative panel (working paper No. 43)
Law Commission

1978 Judicial studies and information. Report of the working party
Home Office

BRIDGEMAN, W. C., Viscount

1959 Financial provisions of the Legal Aid and Advice Act 1949 and the Legal Aid (assessment and resources) Regulations 1950. Report of the Advisory Committee
Session 1959-60 Cmnd. 918 xvii.

1960 Report of the advisory committee upon the proviso to Sect. 2(1) of the Legal Aid and Advice Act 1949
Session 1959-60 Cmnd. 962 xvii.

BRIDGES, E., Lord

1962 Security at the National Gallery
Session 1961-62 Cmnd. 1750 xviii.

1963 Training in public administration for overseas countries. Report of the committee
D. of Technical Co-operation

BRIERLY, J. L.

1947 Double day shift working
Session 1947-47 Cmd. 7147 xiii.

1950 London Master Printers' Association and the London Society of Compositors. Report of a court of inquiry into the causes and circumstances of a dispute between them
Session 1950 Cmd. 8074 xiii.

BRIGGS, Asa

1972 Nursing. Report of the committee
Session 1971-72 Cmnd. 5115 xvi.

BRIGGS, B. S.

See HARGREAVES, W. S.

BRIMELOW, Thomas, Lord

1978 Contracted-out Employment (Miscellaneous Provisions) (No. 2) Regulations 1978. Report of the Occupational Pensions Board
Session 1978-79 Cmnd. 7424

BRITTON, D. K.

1977 Agriculture in the 1980s: animal feeding stuffs Agriculture E.D.C.
N.E.D.O.

BRITTON, D. R.

See WINN, C. R. N., Sir

BROADLEY, L.

1972 Training for purchasing and supply. Report by the sub-committee of the committee for com-

BROADLEY, L. *(continued)*
mercial and administrative training
D. of Employment

BRODRICK, Norman John Lee
1971   Death certification and coroners. Report of the
committee
Session 1971-72 Cmnd. 4810 xxi.

BROOK, Frank, Sir
Police uniform. Report of the committee of the
Police Council
Home Office

BROOKE, H.
1952   Living in flats. Report of the flats sub-committee
of the Central Housing Advisory Committee
M. of Housing

1953   Transfers, exchanges and rents. Housing manage-
ment sub-committee of the Central Housing
Advisory Committee. 4th report
M. of Housing and Local Government

BROOK, Norman, Sir
1958   Misuse of official facilities. Report of an inquiry
into an allegation of misuse of official facilities
for the circulation of documents
Session 1958-59 Cmnd. 583 ix.

BROTHERSTON, John H. F.
1963   Experimental nurses training at Glasgow Royal
Infirmary. Final report of the assessment committee
Scottish Home and Health D.

1967   Organisation of medical work in the hospital
service in Scotland. 1st report of the joint working party
Scottish Home and Health D.

1970   Vitamin D. Interim report by the panel on child
nutrition. (Reports on public health and medical
subjects No. 123)
D. of Health and Social Security

1971   Doctors in an integrated health service. Report
of a joint working party
Scottish Home and Health D.

1973   Towards an integrated child health service.
Report of the joint working party on the inte-
gration of medical work
Scottish Home and Health D.

1978   Morbidity and its relationship to resource allo-
cation. Papers and proceedings of a workshop,
Abergavenny, January 1978
Welsh Office

BROWN, Arthur, J.
1968   Advisory panel on student maintenance grants, a
report
D. of Education and Science

BROWN, D. CLIFTON-
See CLIFTON-BROWN, D.

BROWN, E. H. Phelps
1963   Pay and conditions of employment of drivers and
conductors of the London Transport Board's
road services. Interim report of the committee of
inquiry
M. of Labour

1964   Pay and conditions of employment of the drivers
and conductors of the London Transport Board's
road services. Report of the committee of inquiry
M. of Labour

1968   Labour in building and Civil Engineering. Report
of the committee of inquiry
Session 1967-68 Cmnd. 3714 xvii.
Research supplement
Session 1967-68 Cmnd. 3714-I xvii.

BROWN, G. A.
1949   Allotments advisory committee. Report respect-
ing amendment of existing allotments legislation
M. of Agriculture and Fisheries

Smallholdings. 1st report of the Smallholdings
Advisory Council
M. of Agriculture and Fisheries

1950   Domestic food production. Report of the committee on the organisation of domestic food
producers
M. of Agriculture, Fisheries and Food

Survey staffs. Report of the inter-departmental
committee
Ordnance Survey

BROWN, G. M.
1975   Growth areas in the geological sciences. Report
of the ad hoc working party for 1974. (Publications series B, No. 12)
Natural Environment Research Council

BROWN, J.
1974   Telecommunications. Report of a panel
Science Research Council

BROWN, L. FARRER-
See FARRER-BROWN, L.

BROWN, Stephen
1968   Report of inquiry in respect of the objections
to the proposed compulsory amalgamation of the
police areas of the County of Glamorgan, the
City of Cardiff and the County Boroughs of
Merthyr Tydfil and Swansea
Session 1967-68 Cmnd. 3790 xxx.

Report of the inquiry in respect of the objections
to the proposed compulsory amalgamation of the
police areas of the County of Glamorgan, the
City of Cardiff and the County Boroughs of
Merthyr Tydfil and Swansea
Session 1968-69 Cmnd. 3843 xliv.

BROWNE, E. H.
1955   Roadway conveyors. Report of the committee
National Coal Board

BROWNE, G. St. J., Sir, ORDE-
See ORDE-BROWNE, G. St. J., Sir

BROWNE, H. H.
1967   Refuse storage and collection. Report of the
working party
M. of Housing and Local Government

BROWNE, J. N.
See CRAIGTON, J. N., Lord

BROWNING, Robert
1969   Hospital endowments. Report of a working party
set up to review the allocation of hospital endowments
Scottish Home and Health D.

BROWNLIE, Charles C.

1970   Rent rebates for council tenants. Report of the Scottish Housing Advisory Committee's sub-committee on local authority rent rebate schemes
Scottish Development D.

BRUCE, Robert Hunter Wingate

1967   Highland transport services. Report of the Highland Transport Board
D. of Agriculture and Fisheries for Scotland

BRUNDRETT, Frederick, Sir

1964   Technical assistance for overseas geology and mining. Report of the committee
Session 1963-64 Cmnd. 2351 xix.

BRUNT, David, Sir

1956   Basic design temperatures for space-heating, by a study committee convened by the councils of the Institution of Mechanical Engineers, the Institute of Electrical Engineers, the Institution of Gas Engineers and the Institution of Heating and Ventilating Engineers (Post-war building studies No. 33)
M. of Works

BRUNT, H.

1974   Organised recreation in the East Midlands, an initial appraisal by the countryside pursuits panel
East Midlands Sports Council

BRUNTON, J. S.

1959   Curriculum of the senior secondary school. Report of the working party. Introduction of the ordinary grade of the Scottish leaving certificate
Scottish Education D.

1963   From school to further education. Report of a working party on the linkage of secondary and further education
Scottish Education D.

1972   Training of graduates for secondary education. Report by the working party
Scottish Education D.

BRYAN, Andrew M, Sir

1950   Safety in the use of explosives in coal mines. Report of the committee of enquiry into the precautions necessary to secure safety in the use of explosives in coal mines
Ministry of Fuel and Power

1953   The coal miner
National Coal Board

1959   Mining explosions. Report of the sub-committee
National Coal Board

BRYCE, I. G.

1969   National staff committee. Progress report for the period 1964-1968. Recruitment, training and development of administrative and clerical staff in the hospital service
D. of Health and Social Security

BRYDEN, W. J.

1962   Custodial training for young offenders. Report of a committee of the Scottish Advisory Council on the treatment of offenders
Scottish Home and Health D.

1977   Identification procedure under Scottish Criminal Law. Report of the working group
Session 1977-78 Cmnd. 7096 xx.

BUCHANAN, Colin D.

1963   Traffic in towns. A study of the long-term problems of traffic in urban areas. Reports of the steering group and working group
M. of Transport

1967   Ashford study, consultants proposals for designation. A report by Colin Buchanan and Partners in association with Economic Consultants Ltd., John Taylor and Sons, Cyril Sweett and Partners and Peter Youngman
M. of Housing and Local Government

1969   Bath, a study in conservation. Report for the preservation policy group
M. of Housing and Local Government

1972   Urban research and the private developer, report of a conference on new homes in the cities. Building E.D.C.
N.E.D.O.

See also GRIMMITT, H. W.

BUCHANAN, George

1952   Reception centres for persons without a settled way of living. Report of the National Assistance Board
M. of National Insurance

BUCHANAN, W. D.

1978   Audiometry in industry; discussion document. Report of the working group
Health and Safety Executive

BUCK, A. C.

1971   Out of stock; report of a study in wholesale grocer's warehouse. Report of the working party
N.E.D.O.

BULLARD, Edward, Sir

1973   Geophysics (pure and applied). Report of the working party. In: Research in the geological sciences. (Publications series B No. 7)
Natural Environment Research Council

BULLARD, Reader, Sir

1948   Notes on awards made to post-graduate students by the Treasury committee for studentships in foreign languages and cultures
Treasury

BULLEN, F. R.

1969   Advisory committee on tip safety. Guidance notes for the initial inspection of disused tips
M. of Power

BULLOCK, Alan, L. C., Lord

1965   Demand and for supply of teachers, 1963-1986. 9th report of the national advisory council on the training and supply of teachers
D. of Education and Science

1968   Curriculum innovation in practice — Canada, England and Wales, United States. A report of the third international curriculum conference, Oxford, September 17-22, 1967
Schools Council

1975   Language for life. Report of the committee
D. of Education and Science

1977   Industrial democracy. Report of the committee of inquiry
Session 1976-77 Cmnd. 6706 xvi.

See also BATSON, E. and DAVIES, P. L.

BULLOCK, R. H. W.

1966   Problems arising from the cyclical pattern of machine tool orders. Report of the working party
M. of Technology

BULMER, W. P.

1969 The strategic future of the wool textile industry. A report by W. S. Atkins and Partners for the marketing study steering group of the Wool Textile E.D.C.
N.E.D.O.

1976 Trends in textile technology. Joint Textile Committee
N.E.D.O.

Textile trends, 1966-75. An economic profile of the U.K. textile and clothing industries. Joint Textile Committee
N.E.D.O.

BURGHARD, Geoffrey F.

1967 Common standards for electronic parts. 2nd report of the committee
M. of Technology

BURGHLEY, D. G. B., Lord

See EXETER, D. G. B., Marquis of

BURMAN, Peter

1977 Chapels and churches; who cares? An independent report
British Tourist Authority

BURNETT, P. V.

1952 Lighting of office buildings. Report by the lighting committee of the building research board. (Post-war building studies No. 30)
M. of Works

BURNHAM, H. L. W., Viscount

Burnham committee

See

CREED, T. P., Sir
JACK, D. T., Sir
MACNAIR, A. D., Lord
PELHAM, H., Sir
PERCY OF NEWCASTLE, E., Lord
SILSOE, A. M. T., Lord
SOULBURY, H., Lord

BURNS, Tom

1963 Child care service at work. Report prepared for the Scottish Advisory Council on Child Care
Scottish Education D.

BURNS, W.

1970 Hearing and noise in industry
D. of Health and Social Security

1972 New roads in towns. Report of the Urban motorways committee
D. of the Environment

BURR, E. C.

1977 Appropriate technology. Report of the working party. (Overseas development paper No. 8)
M. of Overseas Development

BURRELL, J. H.

1948 Police rent and supplementary allowances. Report of the committee of the Police Council

1953 Police extraneous duties. Report of the committee
Home Office

BURROWS, F. J., Sir

1949 Romney Marsh investigation. Agricultural Land Commission report
M. of Agriculture and Fisheries

1952 Lakenheath Fen investigation. Report of the Agricultural Land Commission
M. of Agriculture and Fisheries

Over and Bare fens investigation. Report of the Agricultural Land Commission
M. of Agriculture and Fisheries

Swaffham Prior and Burwell fens investigation. Report of the Agricultural Land Commission
M. of Agriculture and Fisheries

Yetminster farm boundary report. Adjustment of farm boundaries and amalgamation of farms in the Yetminster area of Dorset
M. of Agriculture and Fisheries

1956 Land in the Brue Valley and Northmoor, Somerset. Report of the Agricultural Land Commission
M. of Agriculture, Fisheries and Food

BURROWS, G. S.

1969 Chichester, a study in conservation. Report to the preservation policy group
M. of Housing and Local Government

BURROWS, Roland, Sir

1944 Newcastle upon Tyne inquiry. Report of the tribunal appointed under the Tribunal of Inquiry (Evidence) Acts, 1921, to inquire into the administration by the Council of the City and County of Newcastle upon Tyne and its committees and officers of their function in relation to the fire, police and civil defence services
Session 1943-44 Cmd. 6522 iv.

1950 Boundary Commission for England. Report with respect to the areas comprised in the constituencies in the City of Leeds, and the constituencies of Torrington, Bootle, Liverpool, Walton, Ormskirk, Carlisle, Penrith and the Border, Doncaster, Don Valley, Gloucester, Stroud and Thornbury, West Gloucestershire, Norwich North, Central Norfolk, South Shields and Jarrow
Session 1950-51 Cmd. 8100 viii.

1951 Boundary Commission for England. Report with respect to the areas comprised in the constituencies of Oldham East, Oldham West and Ashton under Lyne
Session 1950-51 HC.203 viii.

BURT, C. S. S.

1957 Carlisle and District State Management. Inquiry into certain allegations made by the Civil Service Union. Report
Session 1956-57 Cmnd. 168 xv.

BURT, George M., Sir

1943 House construction. Report by an interdepartmental committee. (Post-war building studies No. 1)
M. of Works

1945 House construction. 2nd report by an interdepartmental committee. (Post-war building studies No 23)
M. of Works

1947 House construction. 3rd report by an interdepartmental committee. (Post-war building studies No. 25)
M. of Works

BURTON OF COVENTRY, E. F., Baroness

1968 Special report to the Lord Chancellor by the Council on Tribunals under the Tribunal and Inquiries Acts, 1958 and 1966. Stansted Airport
Session 1967-68 Cmnd. 3559 xxxiii.

BURTON, A. L.

1969 Local authority purchasing. Report of the joint review body
M. of Housing and Local Government

BURTON, N. E. D.

1971 Marketing in a small business. Hotel and Catering E.D.C.
N.E.D.O.

BUTE, John Crichton-Stuart, 6th Marquess

1974 North Sea oil and the environment. Report to the Oil Development Council for Scotland
Scottish Development D.

BUTLER OF SAFFRON WALDEN, Richard Austen, Lord

1974 Mentally abnormal offenders. Interim report of the committee
Session 1974 Cmnd. 5698 vii.

1975 Mentally abnormal offenders. Report of the committee
Session 1974-75 Cmnd. 6244 xvi.

BUTLER, R. A., Lord

1962 Nyasaland constitutional conference. Report of the conference held in London in November 1962
Session 1962-63 Cmnd. 1887 x.

1963 Central Africa conference. Report
Session 1962-63 Cmnd. 2093 x.

BUTTERWICK, M. W.

1969 Vertical integration in agriculture and the role of the co-operatives
Central Council for Agricultural and Horticultural Co-operation

BUTTERWORTH, H. S.

1945 The cotton spinning industry. Report of a commission set up to review the wages arrangements and methods of organisation of work and to make recommendations
M. of Labour

BUTTERWORTH, J. B.

1972 Work and pay of probation officers and social workers. Report of the Butterworth inquiry
Session 1971-72 Cmnd. 5076 xxxiv.

BUXTON, M. J.

1978 Allocating health resources: a commentary on the report of the resource allocation working party. (Research paper No. 3)
Royal Commission on the National Health Service

BYNG, E. S.

1948 Youth employment, 1948. London regional advisory council report
M. of Labour and National Service

BYRNE, L. A.

1948 Depositions. Report of the departmental committee
Session 1948-49 Cmd. 7639 xiv.

CADBURY, Egbert

1952 Increase in passenger fares. Report of the central transport consultative committee for G.B. on the British Transport Commission (Passenger) Charges Scheme, 1952
Session 1951-52 Cmd. 8513 xviii.

CADBURY, George Adrian

1971 West Midlands, an economic appraisal. Report of the working party appointed by the West Midlands Economic Planning Council
D. of the Environment

CAINE, Sydney, Sir

1955 Plan for a British Caribbean federation. Report of the fiscal commission
Session 1955-56 Cmd. 9618 xii.

1958 Grassland utilisation. Report of the committee
Session 1958-59 Cmnd. 547 viii.

CAIRNCROSS, Alec, Sir

1975 Channel tunnel and alternative cross channel services. Report by the Channel Tunnel Advisory Group
D. of the Environment

CAIRNS, David A. S., Sir

1953 Calico printing. Report on the process by the Monopolies and Restrictive Practices Commission
Session 1953-54 HC. 140 xvi.

1954 Supply of buildings in the Greater London area. Report of the Monopolies and Restrictive Practices Commission
Session 1953-54 HC. 264 xvi.

1955 Supply and export of certain semi-manufactures of copper and copper-based alloys. Report of the Monopolies and Restrictive Practices Commission
Session 1955-56 HC. 56 xxiv.

Collective discrimination: report on exclusive dealing, collective boycotts, aggregated rebates and other discriminatory trade practices by the Monopolies and Restrictive Practices Commission
Session 1955-56 Cmnd. 9504 xxiv.

Supply and export of pneumatic tyres. Report of the Monopolies and Restrictive Practices Commission
Session 1955-56 HC. 133 xxiv.

Supply of sand and gravel in central Scotland. Report of the Monopolies and Restrictive Practices Commission
Session 1955-56 HC. 222 xxiv.

Supply of hard fibre cordage. Report of the Monopolies and Restrictive Practices Commission
Session 1955-56 HC. 294 xxiv.

1956 Supply of linoleum. Report of the Monopolies and Restrictive Practices Commission
Session 1955-56 HC. 366 xxiv.

Supply of certain rubber footwear. Report of the Monopolies and Restrictive Practices Commission
Session 1955-56 HC. 328 xxiv.

Supply of certain industrial and medical gases. Report of the Monopolies and Restrictive Practices Commission
Session 1956-57 HC. 13 xvii.

Supply and exports of electrical and allied machinery and plant. Report of the Monopolies and Restrictive Practices Commission
Session 1956-57 HC. 42 xvi.

Supply of electronic valves and cathode ray tubes. Report by the Monopolies and Restrictive Practices Commission
Session 1956-57 HC. 16 xvi.

Supply of Tea. Report of the Monopolies and Restrictive Practices Commission
Session 1956-57 HC. 15 xvii.

Supply of standard metal windows and doors. Report by the Monopolies and Restrictive Practices Commission
Session 1956-57 HC. 14 xvii.

1960 Civil aircraft accident investigation and licence control. Report of the committee
M. of Aviation

CALDECOTE, R. A., Viscount

1966   Through transport to Europe. Movement of Exports E.D.C.
N.E.D.O.

1967   Exports by air, a report by a working party. Movement of Exports E.D.C.
N.E.D.O.

1971   Interim review: Supplementary report on the treatment of marketing and selling expenses
Review Board for Government Contracts

CALLAGHAN, James

1949   Committee on road safety. Report on the desirability and practicability of amending the pedestrian crossing places (Traffic) Regulations, 1941
M. of Transport

   See also NOEL-BAKER, Philip
   STRAUSS, G. R.

CALLICK, E. B.

1974   Education and training. 2nd report by the committee for terotechnology
D. of Industry

CALVERT, J. T.
   See KEY, A.

CAMERON, A. B.

1976   Gifted young musicians and dancers. Report of a working group
Scottish Education D.

1978   Music in Scottish schools. Report of the working party. (Curriculum paper 15)
Scottish Education D.

CAMERON, John, Lord

1946   Legal aid and legal advice in Scotland. Report of the committee
Session 1945-46 Cmd. 6925 xiii.

1947   Port Transport industry. Report of an inquiry
M. of Labour and National Service

1953   Dispute between the National Federated Electrical Association and the Electrical Trades Union. Report of a court of inquiry
Session 1952-53 Cmd. 8968 xiii.

1955   Dispute between the British Transport Commission and the National Union of Railwaymen. Court of inquiry
Interim report. Session 1954-55 Cmd. 9352 v.
Final report. Session 1954-55 Cmd. 9372 v.

1957   Dispute at Briggs Motor Bodies Limited, Dagenham, existing between the Ford Motor Company Limited and members of the Trade unions represented on the trade union side of the Ford National Joint Negotiating Committee. Report of the court of inquiry
Session 1956-57 Cmnd. 131 xiv.

1958   Dispute between employers who are members on the employers' side and work people who are represented on the work people's side of the National Joint Council for the Port Transport Industry. Report of a court of inquiry
Session 1957-58 Cmnd. 510 xv.

1961   Highland transport enquiry. 'Bus services in the highlands and islands
M. of Transport

1962   Report of the inquiry into the complaint made by the National Union of Bank Employees on March 12, 1962 to the committee on freedom of association of the International Labour Organisation
M. of Labour

1963   Transport services in the highlands and islands
See KILBRANDON, C. J. D., Lord

1964   Land use in the highlands and islands. Report of the advisory panel on the highlands and islands
D. of Agriculture and Fisheries for Scotland

1967   Report of a court of inquiry into the problems caused by the introduction of web-offset machines in the printing industry, and the problems arising from the introduction of other modern printing techniques and the arrangements which should be adopted within the industry for dealing with them
Session 1966-67 Cmnd. 3184 xxxvi.

   Report of a court of inquiry into trade disputes at the Barbican and Horseferry Road Construction sites in London
Session 1966-67 Cmnd. 3396 xxxvii.

1970   Regulations of Scottish inshore fisheries. Report of the committee
Session 1970-71 Cmnd. 4453 xvii.

CAMERON, John A.

1949   Knoydart Estate. Report
D. of Agriculture for Scotland

CAMERON, K. J.

1973   Local inquiry in relation to the implementation by Kilmarnock Town Council of parts II and IV of the Housing (Financial Provisions) (Scotland) Act, 1972. Report
Scottish Development D.

CAMMOCK, R. M.

1973   Health centres, reception, waiting and patient call. Report of the study
D. of Health and Social Security

CAMPBELL, Archibald Duncan

1965   Hydro-electric schemes. Report of the public inquiry into the North of Scotland Hydro-Electric Board's constructional scheme No. 39 (Fada/Fionn project) and constructional scheme No. 38 (Laidon project)
Scottish Development D.

1967   Hair, Bass and Fibre Wages Council (G.B.) and the Brush and Broom Wages Council (G.B.). Report of a commission of inquiry
M. of Labour

1969   The organisation of demand. A study of the organisation of demand on the construction industries with special reference to hospital building and civil engineering for water and sewerage. A report by a joint working party of the Building and Civil Engineering E.D.C.s
N.E.D.O.

1970   Report of a court of inquiry into a dispute between the parties represented on the National Joint Board for the Electricity Supply Industry
Session 1970-71 Cmnd. 4410 xxv.

   Salaries of teachers employed whole-time in further education centres, Scotland. Report of the arbitration body
Scottish Education D.

   Tayside: potential for development, by A. D. Campbell and W. D. C. Lyddon
Scottish Development D.

1971   Report of a committee of inquiry into the causes of dispute between the Amalgamated Union of Engineering Workers and Transport and General Workers Union and Fine Tubes Ltd.
D. of Employment

CAMBELL, Archibald Duncan (*continued*)

1973 Construction forecasts, 1973-74-75. Joint forecasting committee. Building and Civil Engineering E.D.C.s
N.E.D.O.

1974 Construction forecasts, 1974-75. Joint forecasting committee. Building and Civil Engineering E.D.C.s
N.E.D.O.

CAMPBELL, Colin, Sir

1954 Gatwick Airport. Report of an inquiry into proposed development
Session 1953-54 Cmd. 9215 viii.

CAMPBELL, H.

1975 Housing co-operatives. Final report of the working party
D. of the Environment

CAMPBELL, Lennox H.

1978 Forth ornithological working party report
Nature Conservancy Council

CANTAUR (Archbishop of Canterbury)

See LANG, Cosmos Gordon, 1928-42

TEMPLE, William, 1942-45 (formerly Archbishop of York, 1929-42)

FISHER, Geoffrey Francis, 1945-61

RAMSEY, Arthur Michael, 1961-74 (formerly Archbishop of York, 1956-61)

COGGAN, Frederick Donald, 1974-80 (formerly Archbishop of York, 1961-74)

CARESS, Alfred

1972 The plastics industry and its prospects. A report of the working party. Chemicals E.D.C.
N.E.D.O.

CARMICHAEL, A. D.

1942 Small retailers of hollow-ware. Scheme for ensuring fair shares of supplies
Board of Trade

CARNEGY, Elizabeth

1977 Professional education and training for community education. Report of the working party
Scottish Education D.

CARR, C. F.

1972 Safety at the reel-up on paper making machines. 2nd report of the Joint Standing Committee for Paper Mills
D. of Employment

CARR, Cecil, Sir

1945 Electoral law reform. Interim report of the committee
Session 1944-45 Cmd. 6606 v.

1948 Electoral law reform. Final report of the committee
Session 1947-48 Cmd. 7286 xvi.

CARR, Robert

1957 Training for skill, recruitment and training of young workers in industry. Report by a sub-committee on the National Joint Advisory Council
M. of Labour

CARR-SAUNDERS, Alexander M., Sir

1947 Commission on university education in Malaya. Report
Colonial Office

1949 Education for commerce. Report of the special committee
M. of Education

1950 Papers of the royal commission on population. Vol. 2: Reports and selected papers of the Statistics committee
Royal Commission on Population

1955 Higher education overseas. Inter-University Council report and review
Session 1955-56 Cmd. 9515 xiv.

CARRINGTON, P. A. R., Lord

1953 Agricultural education. Report of the working party
M. of Agriculture and Fisheries

1954 Myxomatosis. Report of the advisory committee
M. of Agriculture and Fisheries
See also ST. ALDWYN, M. J., Earl of

CARRINGTON, William S., Sir
See SKELHORN, N. J., Sir

CARTER, Archibald, Sir

1950 Supply of dental goods. Report of the Monopolies and Restrictive Practices Commission
Session 1950-51 HC. 18 xvii.

1951 Supply of electric lamps. Report of the Monopolies and Restrictive Practices Commission
Session 1950-51 HC. 287 xvii.

1952 Supply of insulated electric wires and cables. Report of the Monopolies and Restrictive Practices Commission
Session 1951-52 HC. 209 xvii.

Supply of insulin. Report of the Monopolies and Restrictive Practices Commission
Session 1951-52 HC. 296 xvii.

Supply and export of matches and the supply of match-making machinery. Report of the Monopolies and Restrictive Practices Commission
Session 1952-53 HC. 161 xv.

1953 Supply of imported timber. Report of the Monopolies and Restrictive Practices Commission
Session 1952-53 HC. 281 xv.

CARTER, A. D. BONHAM-, Sir
See BONHAM-CARTER, A. D., Sir

CARTER, C. F.

1960 Industrial research and development expenditure, 1958. Report by the economics committee of the council for scientific and industrial research
D. of Scientific and Industrial Research

1977 Post Office review committee
Report. Session 1976-77 Cmnd. 6850 xxxix.
Appendix. Session 1976-77 Cmnd. 6954 xxxix.

CARTER, Charles F.

1976 Social responsibilities of business. Report of an advisory panel
Social Science Research Council

CARTER, David

1977 Industrial design education in the U.K. Report of the sub-committee
Design Council

CARTER, W. B.

1973 Great Ouse and its tributaries; capacity and density survey
Sports Council, Eastern Region

CARTWRIGHT, Ann
1974   Survey of abortion patients (for the committee on the working of the Abortion Act)
D. of Health and Social Security

CARY, Michael, Sir
1970   Construction research. A report on the work of the construction research advisory council and the Construction Industry Research and Information Association. Research and Development. R. & D. bulletins
M. of Public Building and Works

CASSELS, J. M.
1978   Heat load density study: Leeds. Combined heat and power group, heat load density working party
D. of Energy

CASTREN, Erik
1978   Arbitration between the United Kingdom and France on delimitation of the Continental shelf. Decisions of the court of arbitration, dated 30 June, 1977 and 14 March, 1978. (Miscellaneous, No. 15, 1978)
Session 1978-79 Cmnd. 7438

CATHCART, E. P.
1940   Industrial health in war. Report of the industrial health research board
Medical Research Council

1946   Rehabilitation. Report of the sub-committee of the medical advisory committee
Scottish Health D.

CATTERELL, J.
1974   Training of key personnel in the application of computer controlled systems to industrial processes. Report by the joint committee of industrial training boards
D. of Employment

CATTO, T. S., Lord
1952   Scottish financial and trade statistics. Report of the committee
Session 1951-52 Cmd. 8609 xiii.

CHADWICK, W. Owen
1970   Church and state. Report of the Archbishops' commission
Church Information Office

CHALLONER, H. G.
See JAMES, A. E., Sir

CHALMERS, Robert
1943   Mechanical installations. Report by a committee convened by the institution of Mechanical Engineers
M. of Works

CHAMBERS, S. P., Sir
1955   London Transport. Report of the committee of inquiry
M. of Transport

CAMPION, A. J., Lord
1952   Veterinary Surgeons Act, 1948. Report of the committee on licenses under Sect. 7
M. of Agriculture and Fisheries

CHANCE, Hugh, Sir
1958   Technical education. Report of the advisory panel on the provision of advanced technical education at the technical colleges at Wrexham, Denbighshire and Kelsterton, Flintshire
M. of Education (Welsh Dept.)

CHANCELLOR, John R., Sir
1945   Veterinary practice by unregistered persons. Report of the committee
Session 1944-45 Cmd. 6611 v.

CHANDOS, O., Viscount
1953   West Indian Federation. Report by the conference held in London in April 1953
Session 1952-53 Cmd. 8837 viii.

West Indian constitution. Report by the conference on the Nigerian constitution held in London in July and August 1953
Session 1952-53 Cmd. 8934 viii.

1954   Nigeria. Report by the resumed conference on the Nigerian constitution held in January and February 1954 in Lagos
Session 1953-54 Cmd. 9059 xi.

CHANNON, P.
1972   Building maintenance. Report of the committee. (R. & D. bulletin)
D. of the Environment

CHANTLER, P.
1967   Dee crossing study phase 1. A report to the technical working party
M. of Housing and Local Government

CHAPLIN, F. L.
1947   Rubber proofed clothing. Working party report
Board of Trade

CHAPLIN, M. F.
1970   Condensation in dwellings, part 1: a design guide prepared by the interdepartmental working party on condensation and mould in buildings
M. of Public Building and Works

CHAPPELL, E. P.
1978   Investment and employment, an approach to improving performance. A joint paper by representatives of management and trade unions
N.E.D.O.

CHARNOCK, H.
1973   Marine sedimentation. Report of the working party. In: Research in the physical marine sciences (publications series B, No. 8)
Natural Environment Research Council

CHASTENEY, H. E.
1944   Dust in steel foundries. 1st report of a committee appointed to consider methods of preventing the production or the inhalation of dust and the possibility of reducing the use of materials containing free silica in steel foundries
M. of Labour and National Service

1947   Conditions in iron foundries. Joint advisory committee report
M. of Labour and National Service

CHATFIELD, June E.
1975   Biological recording working group for Wales. Reports and records of field meetings, 1973/75
National Museum of Wales

CHATTERTON, W. O.

1955　Hospital costing. Report of the working party set up to devise a system of costing the departments and services of a hospital
M. of Health

CHESHAM, J. C. C., Lord

1964　Control of motor rallies. Report of the motor rallies advisory committee
M. of Transport

CHESTER, Daniel Norman

1968　Football. Report of the committee
D. of Education and Science

CHILVER, A. H.

1977　Computers in higher education and research: the next decade. A statement by the computer board for universities and research councils
D. of Education and Science

CHORLEY, R. S. T., Lord

1948　Higher Civil Service remuneration. Report of the committee
Session 1948-49 Cmd. 7635 xii.

CHUTER-EDE, James, Lord

1949　Island of Alderney. Report of the committee of the Privy Council
Session 1948-49 Cmd. 7805 xi.

CITRINE, Walter McL., Lord

1942　Committee on regional boards. Report
Session 1941-42 Cmd. 6360 iv.

CLAPHAM, John, Sir

1946　Committee on social and economic research. Report
Session 1945-46 Cmd. 6868 xiv.

CLARK, A. J. O.

1970　Community service and Scottish secondary schools. The report of the committee on community service and the schools. (Consultative committee on the curriculum, curriculum papers No. 8)
Scottish Education D.

CLARK, A. W.

1975　Metrication and elderly people
Metrication Board

CLARK, K., Sir

1959　Housing the arts in Great Britain
Arts Council

CLARK, D. H.

1968　Psychiatric nursing, today and tomorrow. Report of the joint sub-committee of the standing mental health and the standing nursing advisory committees of the Central Health Services Council
D. of Health and Social Security

CLARK, E.

1967　Housing management in Scotland. Report of the sub-committee on housing management
Scottish Development D.

CLARK, R. B.

1973　Marine wildlife conservation. Report of the working party (Publications series B, No. 5)
Natural Environment Research Council

1976　Research on pollution of the natural environment. Report of the ad hoc preparatory group 'F'. Publications series B, No. 15)
Natural Environment Research Council

Role of taxonomy in ecological research. Report of the working party. (Publications series B, No. 14)
Natural Environment Research Council

CLARK, Richard
See JAUNCEY, C. E.

CLARKE, A. W.

1968　Carriage of dangerous goods in ships. Report of the standing advisory committee, 1966 (The Blue Book)
Board of Trade

CLARKE, C. ARDEN-, Sir
See ARDEN-CLARKE, C., Sir

CLARKE, E.

1967　Housing management in Scotland. Report of the sub-committee of the Scottish housing advisory committee
Scottish Development D.

CLARKE, Frederick, Sir

1946　School and life. Enquiry into the transition from school to independent life. Central Advisory Council for Education (England). 1st report
M. of Education

1948　Out of school. Central Advisory Council for Education (England). 2nd report
M. of Education

CLARKSON, D. J.

1977　Edward Wood and Co. Ltd., Skibben Winton Construction, Ltd. Report of investigations under the Companies Act
D. of Trade

CLARKSON, F.

1976　Offences against discipline at H.M. Borstal Feltham
Home Office

CLATWORTHY, A. A.
See EASTHAM, T.

CLAYE, Andrew, Sir

1961　Prevention of prematurity and the care of premature infants. Report of the sub-committee of joint standing maternity and midwifery advisory committee and standing medical advisory committee of the Central Health Services Council
M. of Health

CLAYSON, Christopher

1973　Scottish licensing law. Report of the departmental committee
Session 1972-73 Cmnd. 5354 xv.

CLEARY, William Cleary, Sir

1946　School sites and building procedure. Report of the committee
M. of Education

CLEARY, William Cleary, Sir *(continued)*

1948   School construction. Report of the technical working party
M. of Education

CLEGG, H. A.

1966   Dispute concerning the operation of fork lift trucks at the Albert Edward Dock, North Shields. Report of a court of inquiry
Session 1966-67 Cmnd. 3061 xxxvi.

1978   Leeds district bus dispute. Committee of inquiry into a dispute between the West Yorkshire Passenger Transport Executive and the General and Municipal Workers Union concerning platform crews (report No. 15)
Advisory, Conciliation and Arbitration Service

CLIFTON-BROWN, D.

1944   Conference on electoral reform and redistribution of seats. Letter, dated May 24, 1944, from Mr. Speaker to the Prime Minister
Session 1943-44 Cmd. 6534 iii.

1945   Boundary Commission for England, 1944. Report of the commission in regard to certain abnormally large constituencies
Session 1944-45 Cmd. 6634 iv.

1947   Boundary Commission for England. Initial report
Session 1947-48 Cmd. 7260 xv.

         Boundary Commission for Northern Ireland. Initial report
Session 1946-47 Cmd. 7231 x.

         Boundary Commission for Scotland. Initial report
Session 1947-48 Cmd. 7270 xv.

         Boundary Commission for Wales. Initial report
Session 1947-48 Cmd. 7274 xv.

CLITHEROE, Ralph, Lord

1944   Committee on the training of civil servants. Report
Session 1943-44 Cmd. 6525 iii.

CLOTHIER, C. M.

1972   Report of the committee appointed to inquire into the circumstances including the production which led to the use of contaminated infusion fluids in the Devonport section of Plymouth General Hospital
Session 1971-72 Cmnd. 5035 xv.

1977   The dispensing of N.H.S. prescriptions in rural areas. Report of the national joint committee of the medical and pharmaceutical professions
D. of Health and Social Security

CLOW, Andrew, Sir

1948   Electricity peak load problem. Report of the committee to study the peak load problem in relation to non-industrial consumers
Session 1947-48 Cmd. 7464 xi.

CLYDE, J. L. McD., Lord

1942   Government contracts in Scotland; allocation to Messrs. George Wimpey and Co. Ltd. during the war. Report
Session 1941-42 Cmd. 6393 iv.

1946   Homeless children (Scotland). Report of the committee
Session 1945-46 Cmd. 6911 x.

COALES, H. W.

1952   Water pipes. Report of the working party on small diameter water pipes
M. of Housing and Local Government
See also ELLIOTT, R. A.

COATSWORTH, James M.

1977   Northumberland National Park plan. National park and countryside committee
Northumberland National Park

COBB, John F. S.

1968   Findings and recommendations following inquiries into allegations concerning the care of elderly patients in certain hospitals. IV: St. James's Hospital, Leeds. V: Storthes Hall Hospital, Kirkburton. National Health Service
Session 1967-68 Cmnd. 3687 xxvii.

COBBOLD, C. F., Lord

1962   North Borneo and Sarawak. Report of the commission of inquiry
Session 1961-62 Cmnd. 1794 xi.

COCKBURN, Cynthia

1968   Directory of construction statistics. A report prepared by C. Cockburn and M. Verstage (R. & D. Bulletin)
M. of Public Building and Works

COCKBURN, Robert

1972   Television advisory committee. Report
Post Office

1973   Television advisory committee. Papers of the technical sub-committee
Post Office

COCKCROFT, Janet R.

1977   Effect of the potato marketing scheme on consumers. Report of the Agricultural Marketing Act Consumers' Committee for Great Britain
M. of Agriculture, Fisheries and Food

COCKCROFT, John, Sir

1964   The exposure of the population to radiation from fallout. A report by a committee on protection against ionizing radiations
Medical Research Council

COCKERILL, G. F.

1975   Nutrition in schools. Report of the working party on the nutritional aspects of school meals
D. of Education and Science

COCKFIELD, Arthur, Sir

1974   Fresh food reference: prices, margins and channels of distribution for fruit and vegetables. An interim report
Price Commission

         Fresh food reference. Second report: marketing of eggs
Session 1974 HC. 329 xiv.

1977   Beer prices and margins. (Price Commission report No. 31)
Price Commission

COCKRAM, J.

1963   Water charges. Report of the sub-committee of the Central Advisory Water Committee
M. of Housing and Local Government

COGGAN, Donald, Archbishop of Canterbury (formerly of York)

1972   Deaconesses and Lay Ministry Measure. 166th report of the Ecclesiastical Committee
Session 1971-72 HC.455 vii; HL.180

         Clergy Pensions (Amendment) Measure. 167th report of the Ecclesiastical Committee
Session 1971-72 HC.457 vii; HL.182

COGGAN, Donald, Archbishop of Canterbury *(continued)*

1976   Endowments and Glebe Measure. 176th report of the Ecclesiastical Committee
Session 1975-76 HC.493 ix; HL.216

Church of England (Miscellaneous Provisions) Measure. 177th report of the Ecclesiastical Committee
Session 1975-76 HC.531 ix; HL.244

1977   Incumbents (Vacation of Benefices) Measure. 178th report of the Ecclesiastical Committee
Session 1976-77 HC.279 vi; HL.116

Dioceses Measure. 179th report of the Ecclesiastical Committee
Session 1976-77 HC.558 vi; HL.266

Parochial Registers and Records Measure. 180th report of Ecclesiastical Committee
Session 1976-77 HC.602 vi; HL.279

1978   Church of England (Miscellaneous Provisions) Measure. 181st report of the Ecclesiastical Committee
Session 1977-78 HC.340 vii; HL.123

COHEN, B.

1977   Review of dental research. Report of the physiological systems disorders board by the central committee
Medical Research Council

COHEN, L. L., Lord

1945   Committee on company law amendment
Report
Session 1944-45 Cmd. 6659 iv.
Minutes of Evidence, 26 days, 1943-45
Board of Trade

Royal Commission on Awards to Inventors
1948   1st report. Session 1948-49 Cmd. 7586 xvii.
1949   2nd report. Session 1948-49 Cmd. 7832 xvii.
1953   3rd report. Session 1952-53 Cmd. 8743 vi.
1956   4th and final report. Session 1955-56 Cmd. 9744 xi.

1951   Royal Commission on taxation of profits and income
Minutes of evidence taken before the Royal Commission. 1st to 17th days
Royal Commission on Taxation of Profits and Income
For the report **See RADCLIFFE, C. J., Lord**

1957   Use of invention and designs by government departments. Compendium of the principles and procedure adopted by the Royal Commission on Awards to Inventors
Royal Commission on Awards to Inventors

COHEN OF BIRKENHEAD, Henry, Lord

1950   Prescribing. 2nd interim report of the joint committee of the Central Health Services Council and the Scottish Health Services Council
M. of Health

1951   Definition of drugs. 3rd report of the joint subcommittee of the standing medical, pharmaceutical and general practitioner advisory committees
M. of Health

1953   Clinical research in relation to the National Health Service. Report of the council advisory committee on medical research in Scotland
Medical Research Council

1954   Prescribing. Report of the joint committee of the Central Health Services Council and the Scottish Health Services Council
M. of Health

General Practice within the National Health Service. Report of the Central Health Services Council committee
M. of Health

1956   Medical care of epileptics. Report of the subcommittee of the Central Health Services Council
M. of Health

Flour. Report of the panel on composition and nutritive value of flour
Session 1955-56 Cmd. 9757 xxii.

1957   Welfare foods. Report of the joint sub-committee of the Standing Medical Advisory Committees of the Central and Scottish health services councils
M. of Health

1959   Classification of proprietary preparations. Report of the Standing Joint Committee of the Central and Scottish health services council

Definition of Drugs. Report
M. of Health

Staphylococcal infections in hospitals. Report of the Standing Medical Advisory Committee
M. of Health

1961   Classification in category S. Report of the standing joint committee on classification of proprietary preparations. Central and Scottish health service councils
M. of Health

1963   Safety of drugs. Final report of the joint sub-committee of the standing medical advisory committees. Central and Scottish health services councils
M. of Health

Communications between doctors, nurses and patients. An aspect of human relations in the hospital service. Joint sub-committee of the standing medical and standing nursing advisory committees
M. of Health

1964   Health education. Report of a joint committee of the Central and Scottish health services council
M. of Health

COHEN, Brunel, Sir

1945   Artificial limbs. Report of the departmental committee
M. of Pensions

COHEN, John

1948   Recruitment and training of nurses. Minority report from the working party
M. of Health

COHEN, Karl C., Sir

1971   Housing associations. A working paper of the Central Housing Advisory Committee
D. of the Environment

COHEN, R. H. L.

1972   Publication of tar and nicotine yields of packeted cigarettes. Report of the Standing Scientific Liaison Committee on the Scientific Aspects of Smoking and Health
D. of Health and Social Security

COLDSTREAM, William M., Sir

1960   National Advisory Council on Art Education. 1st report
M. of Education

1962   Vocational Courses in colleges and schools of art. 2nd report of the National Advisory Council on Art Education.
M. of Education

1964   Post-diploma studies in art and design. 3rd report of the National Advisory Council on Art Education
D. of Education and Science

COLDSTREAM, William M., Sir *(continued)*

1970   Structure of art and design education in the further education sector. Report of a joint committee of the National Advisory Council on Art and Education and the National Council for Diplomas in Art and Design
D. of Education and Science

COLE, H. G.

1958   Corrosion of metals by vapours from organic materials, a survey (Inter-service metallurgical research council)
M. of Supply

COLERAINE, R. K., Lord

1956   Work of the youth employment service, 1953-56. Report by the National Youth Employment Council
M. of Labour and National Service

1958   Lewes-East Grinstead Branch Railway. Report on the proposed withdrawal of train services by the Central Transport Consultative Committee Session 1957-58 Cmnd. 360 xviii.

1959   Work of the youth employment service, 1956-59. Report by the National Youth Employment Council
M. of Labour

1961   Employment and training of young people, April 1959-October 1961. Interim report of the National Youth Employment Council
M. of Labour

COLLEDGE, Maureen

1978   Young people and work, research studies. (Manpower studies, 1978/81)
Manpower Services Commission

COLLINS, H. E.

1958   Coal mining in Poland. Report by the technical mission
National Coal Board

COLLINS, M. F.

1977   Indoor swimming pools in Britain; summary of results of a national survey of attendance and public use (Research working paper, No. 1)
Sports Council

COLLISON, H. F., Lord

1971   Cohabitation: the administration of the relevant provisions of the Ministry of Social Security Act, 1966. Report by the Supplementary Benefits Commission
D. of Health and Social Services

COLWELL, Maria
        See FIELD-FISHER, T. G.

COMPTON, Edmund, Sir

1971   Allegations against the security forces of physical brutality in Northern Ireland arising out of events on 9th August 1971. Report of the inquiry Session 1971-72 Cmnd. 4823 xxxii.

1972   Memorandum on the draft proposals for new districts in English non-metropolitan counties proposed in the Local Government Bill
Local Government Boundary Commission for England

1973   Defence services inquiry committee. Report
M. of Defence

COMYN, J. P.

1975   Court Line Ltd. Final report of investigation under the Companies Act
D. of Trade

CONFAIT, Maxwell
        Inquiry on trial arising from his death
        See FISHER, Henry, Sir

COOK, Edward R.

1949   Exports to Canada. Report of the United Kingdom clothing mission to Canada
Board of Trade

COOK, Frederick C., Sir

1944   Traffic signs. Report of the departmental committee
M. of Transport

1945   Roads design and layout of roads in built-up areas. Report of the departmental committee
M. of Transport

COOK, James W., Sir

1960   Milk composition in the United Kingdom. Report of an inter-departmental committee
Session 1959-60 Cmnd. 1147 xix.

1964   Review of the persistent organochlorine pesticides. Report by the advisory committee on poisonous substances used in agriculture and food storage
M. of Agriculture, Fisheries and Food

Review of persistent organochlorine pesticides. Supplementary report by the advisory committee on pesticides and other toxic chemicals
M. of Agriculture, Fisheries and Food

1967   Review of the present safety arrangements for the use of toxic chemicals in agriculture and food storage. Report by the advisory committee on pesticides and other toxic chemicals
D. of Education and Science

COOK, K. W.

1974   Manpower and pay in retail distribution. Report of the working party on pay and efficiency in retail distribution
N.E.D.O.

Manpower and pay in retail distribution. Summary of the report
N.E.D.O.

1975   Finance for investment; a study of mechanisms available for financing industrial investment *and* appendices. 2 vols.
N.E.D.O.

COOKE, Leonard, Sir

1970   Loans for hotel development. Report of the hotel loans advisory committee
Board of Trade

COOKE, Samuel

1973   Family law. First report on family property, a new approach (Law Com. No. 52)
Session 1972-73 H.C. 274 xiv.

Family law. Report on solemnisation of marriage in England and Wales. (Law Com. No. 53)
Session 1972-73 HC. 250 xiv.

Law reform, third programme. (Law Com. No. 54)
Session 1972-73 HC. 293 xiv.

Criminal law: report on forgery and counterfeit currency. (Law Com. No. 55)
Session 1972-73 HC. 320 xiv.

Personal injury litigation—assessment of damages. Report. (Law Com. No. 56)
Session 1972-73 HC. 373 xiv.

COOKE, Samuel *(continued)*

Statute law revision, fifth report. Draft Statute Law (Repeals) Bill. (Law Com. No. 57; Scot. Law Com. No. 32)
Session 1973-74 Cmnd. 5493 iv.

1974   8th annual report. (Law Com. No. 58)
Session 1973-74 HC. 34 iv.

Friendly Societies Bill. Report on the consolidation of the Friendly Societies Acts, 1896 to 1971 (Law Com. No. 59; Scot. Law Com. No. 35).
Session 1974 Cmnd. 5634 vii.

Injuries to unborn children. Report. (Law Com. No. 60)
Session 1974-75 Cmnd. 5709 vii.

Family law. Second report on family property: family provision on death. (Law Com. No. 61)
Session 1974 HC. 324 vii.

Transfer of land. Report on local land charges (Law Com. No. 62)
Session 1974-75 HC. 71 xvii.

Statute law revision, 6th report. Draft Statute Law (Repeals) Bill. (Law Com. No. 63; Scot. Law Com. No. 36)
Session 1974-75 Cmnd. 5792 xvii.

9th annual report, 1973-74 (Law Com. No. 64)
Session 1974-75 HC. 40 xvii.

1975   Transfer of land. Report on " subject to contract " agreements. (Law Com. No. 65)
Session 1974-75 HC. 119 xvii.

Supply Powers Bill. Report on the consolidation of certain enactments. (Law Com. No. 66; Scot. Law Com. No. 38)
Session 1974-75 Cmnd. 5850 xvii.

Codification of landlord and tenant. Report on obligations of landlords and tenants. (Law Com. No. 67)
Session 1974-75 HC. 377 xvii.

Transfer of land: report on " subject to contract " agreements. (Law Com. No. 68)
Session 1974-75 HC. 119 xvii.

Exemption clauses, 2nd report. (Law Com. No. 69; Scot. Law Com. No. 39)
Session 1974-75 HC. 605 xvii.

Statute law revision, 7th report. Draft Statute Law (Repeals) Bill. (Law Com. No. 70; Scot. Law Com. No. 40)
Session 1975-76 Cmnd. 6303 xx.

10th annual report, 1974-75. (Law Com. No. 71)
Session 1975-76 HC. 51 xx.

1976   Jurisdiction of certain ancient courts. (Law Com. No. 72)
Session 1975-76 Cmnd. 6385 xx.

Remedies in administrative law. Report (Law Com. No. 73)
Session 1975-76 Cmnd. 6407 xx.

Charging orders. (Law Com., No. 74)
Session 1975-76 Cmnd. 6412 xx.

Report on liability for damage or injury to trespassers and related questions of occupiers' liability. (Law Com. No. 75)
Session 1975-76 Cmnd. 6428 xx.

Criminal law. Report on conspiracy and criminal law reform. (Law Com. No. 76)
Session 1975-76 HC. 176 xx.

Family law. Report on matrimonial proceedings in magistrates' courts. (Law Com. No. 77)
Session 1975-76 HC. 637 xx.

1977   11th annual report, 1975-76. (Law Com. No. 78)
Session 1976-77 HC. 94 xviii.

Law of contract. Report on contribution. (Law Com. No. 79)
Session 1976-77 HC. 181 xviii.

Law Com. No. 80
See SCARMAN, Leslie, Lord

Rent Bill; report on the consolidation of the Rent Act 1968, parts III, IV, and VIII of the Housing Finance Act 1972, the Rent Act 1974, sections 7-10 of the Housing and Rents and Subsidies Act 1975, and certain related enactments. (Law Com. No. 81)
Session 1976-77 Cmnd. 6751 xviii.

Law Com. No. 82
See SCARMAN, Leslie, Lord

Criminal law. Report on defences of general application. (Law Com. No. 83)
Session 1976-77 HC. 556 xix.

Law of contract. Report on the proposed E.E.C. directive on the law relating to commercial agents. (Law Com. No. 84)
Session 1976-77 Cmnd. 6948 xix.

12th annual report. (Law Com. No. 85)
Session 1976-77 HC. 96 xxii.

1978   Family law, 3rd report on family property. The matrimonial home (co-ownership and occupation rights) and household goods. (Law Com. No. 86)
Session 1977-78 HC. 450 xxii.

Statute law revision, 9th report. Draft Statute Law (Repeals) Bill. (Law Com. No. 87; Scot. Law Com. No. 48)
Session 1977-78 HC. 7189 xxiii.

Law Com. No. 88
See KERR, M. R. E.

Criminal law. Report on the mental element in crime. (Law Com. No. 89)
Session 1977-78 HC. 499 xxiii.

Interpretation Bill. Report on the Interpretation Act, 1889 and certain other enactments relating to the construction and operation of Acts of Parliament and other instruments. (Law Com. No. 90; Scot. Law Com. No. 53)
Session 1977-78 Cmnd. 7235 xxiii.

See also KERR, M. R. E.

COOMBE, G. A.

1949   Present and future supply and demand for persons with professional qualifications in technical or scientific register. Valuation and estate management surveyors' panel (valuation-estate management) of the building and civil engineering sub-committee report
M. of Labour and National Service

COOMES, T. J.

1978   Survey of vinyl chloride content of polyvinyl chloride for food contact and of foods. 2nd report of the steering group on food surveillance, working party on vinyl chloride. (Food surveillance paper No. 2)
M. of Agriculture, Fisheries and Food

COOPER, A. J.

1972   International price comparison. A study of the prices of pharmaceuticals in the U.K. and eight other countries, 1970. Pharmaceutical working party
N.E.D.O.

COOPER, Cary L.

1976   Evaluation of two approaches to social skill training in the catering industry
Hotel and Catering Industry Training Board

COOPER, Cary L. *(continued)*

1977   Hurt or helped? A study of the personal impact on managers of experimental, small group training programmes. (Training information paper No. 10)
Training Services Agency

COOPER, M. H.

    See COOPER, A. J.

COOPER, T. M. Lord

1942   Hydroelectric development in Scotland. Report of the committee
Session 1942-43 Cmd. 6406 iv.

1945   Clyde estuary committee. Report
M. of Transport

1946   Universities of Scotland (increased grant). Report of the special committee
Session 1945-46 Cmd. 6853 xi.

1949   The organisation of university education in Dundee and its relationship with St. Andrews University. Report of the inquiry
Scottish Office

COPE, V. Zachary, Sir

1950   Medical auxiliaries. Report of the committees
Session 1950-51 Cmd. 8188 xv.

COPPOCK, R., Sir

1950   Care and maintenance of fittings and equipment in the modern house. Report of a sub-committee of the Central Housing Advisory Committee
M. of Health

CORBETT, A.

1978   The libraries' choice. Report of the working party on the public library service to the disadvantaged (Library information series No. 10)
D. of Education and Science

CORBETT, J.

1975   Ardmore International Film Studios Ltd. (formerly New Brighton Tower Co., Ltd.). Report of investigation under the Companies Act
D. of Trade

CORFIELD, K. G.

1977   Foundrymen's views. An attitude survey in the ferrous foundries industry
N.E.D.O.

CORK, Kenneth

1976   E.E.C. preliminary draft convention on bankruptcy, winding-up, arrangements, compositions, and similar proceedings. Report of the advisory committee
Session 1975-76 Cmnd. 6602 ix.

CORRIE, W. R.

1972   Morecambe Bay estuary storage. Report by the economic study group
Water Resources Board

COTTERELL, J.

1972   Training of computer operators. Report by the joint board computer training policy committee
D. of Employment

COTTESLOE, J. W. H., Lord

1964   Sale of works of art by public bodies. Report of the committee of inquiry
Treasury

COTTON, B. E.

1976   Yorkshire and Humberside regional strategy review, 1975. The next ten years, by the economic planning council
D. of the Environment

COURT, S. D. M.

1976   Fit for the future. Report of the committee on child health services. 2 vols
Session 1976-77 Cmnd. 6684 xi.

COURTNEY, Christopher, Sir

    Tudor aircraft committee of inquiry

1947   Interim report. Session 1947-48 Cmd. 7307 xvi.

1948   Final report. Session 1947-48 Cmd. 7478 xvi.

COUSINS, Frank

1970   Review of the central training council. Report of a committee
Session 1969-70 Cmnd. 4335 xvi.

1972   Training of computer programmers. Report by a joint committee of industrial training boards
D. of Employment

COUSSEY, J. H.

1949   Gold Coast. Constitutional reform. Report to His Excellency the Governor by the committee. (Colonial, No. 248)
Colonial Office

COWAN, J. R.

1975   Steep seam working in British coal mines. 1st report of the national committee
Health and Safety Executive

1978   Steep seam workings in British coal mines. Final report of the national committee
Health and Safety Executive

COX, C. W. M., Sir

1944   Mass education in African society. Report of the adult and mass education sub-committee of the advisory committee on education in the colonies
Colonial Office

COX, J. G.

1970   Survey of professional scientists, 1968. (Studies in technological manpower No. 2)
M. of Technology

COX, O.

    See SHANKLAND, G.

COX, P.

1973   Government Actuary's Department, the actuary's role in financial management
D. of Health and Social Security

COX, P. J.

1974   Smallpox outbreak in London in March and April 1973. Report of the committee of inquiry
D. of Health and Social Security

COYNE, Charles

1970   Make your market. A practical guide to marketing garage workshop services. Motor Vehicle Distribution and Repair E.D.C.
N.E.D.O.

CRAFTON, J. W.

1973 Future of the chest service in Scotland. Report by the Scottish standing medical advisory committee
Scottish Home and Health D.

CRAIGIE, James

1962 Consultation on educational matters. Report of the working party on consultation between the teachers' associations and the Scottish Education Department on educational matters
Scottish Education D.

CRAIGTON, J. Nixon, Lord

1955 Operation of the exchequer equalisation grants in Scotland. Report of the committee's second investigation
Scottish Home D.

CRAMP, Stanley

1977 Bird conservation in Europe
Nature Conservancy Council

CRANBROOK, J. D., Earl

1958 Maternity services committee. Report
M. of Health

CRANE, H. W. V., Sir

1969 Industrial noise and its effect on hearing. Appraisal by the Industrial Injuries Advisory Council of the final report of the research made into noise in industry and its effect on hearing
Session 1968-69 Cmnd. 4145 xxxiii.

1970 Vibration syndrome. Interim report by the Industrial Injuries Advisory Council on the question whether diseases of bones, joints, muscles, blood-vessels or nerves of the hand, arm or shoulder (including Raynaud's phenomenon) caused by vibrating machines should be prescribed under the Act.
Session 1970-71 Cmnd. 4430 xxii.

1972 Brucellosis. Report by the Industrial Injuries Advisory Council
Session 1971-72 Cmnd. 4971 xv.

1973 Occupational deafness. Report by the Industrial Injuries Advisory Council
Session 1973-74 Cmnd. 5461 iii.

Pneumoconiosis and byssinosis. Report by the Industrial Injuries Advisory Council
Session 1972-73 Cmnd. 5443 viii.

CRANE, T. D.

1978 The biological information review committee. Final report. (R. & D. report, No. 5438)
British Library

CRATHORNE, T. L., Lord

1964 Law on Sunday observance. Report of the departmental committee
Session 1964-65 Cmnd. 2528 xxiii.

CRAWFORD AND BALCARRES, R. A., Earl

1958 Preservation of Downing Street. Report of the committee
Session 1957-58 Cmnd. 457 x.

CRAWFORD, Stewart, Sir

1974 Broadcasting coverage. Report of the committee
Session 1974-75 Cmnd. 5774 vi.

CRAWSHAY, G.

1951 Co-operative farms and smallholdings with centralised services in Wales. Review for the years 1936-50 and accounts for 1949-50 submitted by the Welsh Land Settlement Society Ltd.
M. of Agriculture and Fisheries

CREED, Thomas P., Sir

1958 Report of the Forest of Dean committee
Session 1958-59 Cmnd. 868 xiii.

1959 Report of the Burnham committee on scales of salaries for teachers in primary and secondary schools maintained by local education authorities, England and Wales
M. of Education

Report of the Burnham committee on scales of salaries for teachers in establishments for further education maintained by local education authorities in England and Wales
M. of Education

Report of the committee on scales of salaries for the teaching staff of farm institutes and for the teachers of agricultural (including horticultural) subjects of the staff of local education authorities, England and Wales
M. of Education

Report of the committee on scales of salaries for the teaching staff of training colleges, England and Wales
M. of Education

1961 Report of the Burnham committee on scales of salaries for teachers in primary and secondary schools maintained by local education authorities, England and Wales
M. of Education

Report of the Burnham committee on scales of salaries for teachers in establishments for further education maintained by local education authorities, England and Wales
M. of Education

Report of the committee on scales of salaries for the teaching staff of training colleges, England and Wales
M. of Education

Report of the committee on scales of salaries for the teaching staff of farm institutes and for teachers of agricultural (including horticultural) subjects on the staff of local education authorities, England and Wales
M. of Education

1963 Report of the committee on scales of salaries for the teaching staff of training colleges, England and Wales
M. of Education

CREMER, H. W.

1950 Chemical engineering research. Report of the committee
D. of Scientific and Industrial Research

1965 Effect of polluting discharges on the Thames estuary. Reports of the Thames survey committee (Water research technical paper No. 11)
D. of Scientific and Industrial Research

CREW, F. A. E.

1946 Control of midges. An interim report of the sub-committee of the scientific advisory committee
D. of Health for Scotland
See also MACGREGOR, A. S. M., Sir

CRIBBETT, George, Sir

1950 Helicopter. Interdepartmental helicopter committee, 1st report
M. of Aviation

CRICK, W. F.

1950 Government accounts. Final report of the committee on the form of government accounts
Session 1950 Cmd. 7969 vi.

CRICK, W. F. *(continued)*

1964   A higher award in business studies. Report of the advisory sub-committee of the National Advisory Council on Education for Industry and Commerce
M. of Education

CRIPPS, John S.

1970   Coastal preservation and development. Planning of the coastline. Report on a study of coastline preservation and development in England and Wales
Countryside Commission

1977   Accommodation for gypsies. A report on the working of the Caravan Sites Act, 1968
D. of the Environment

CRICHLEY, C. E.

1952   Survey of the trade in agricultural machinery. 36th report of the Commonwealth Economic Committee
Commonwealth Economic Committee

CROFT, E. D.

1968   Investment in hotels and catering. Economic and finance working group
N.E.D.O.

CROFTON, J. W.

1973   The future of the chest services in Scotland. Report by a sub-committee of the Scottish standing medical advisory committee
Scottish Home and Health D.

CROMER, G. R. S., Earl

1968   Export business from capital projects overseas. Report of an enquiry
Session 1967-68 Cmnd. 3516 xxi.

CROOK, R. D., Lord

1952   Statutory registration of opticians. Interdepartmental committee report
Session 1951-52 Cmd. 8531 xv.

CROOKS, J.

1973   General practitioners in the hospital service. Report of the sub-group of the joint working party on the integration of medical work
Scottish Home and Health D.

CROOM, J. Halliday

1974   Careers in dentistry. Scottish Council for Post-Graduate Medical Education
Scottish Home and Health D.

CROOM-JOHNSON, D. P.

1968   Report of an inquiry in respect of the objection to the proposed compulsory amalgamation of the police areas of the County of Lancaster and thirteen county boroughs
Session 1967-68 Cmnd. 3538 xxx.

CROSLAND, Anthony

1975   Greater London development plan statement
D. of the Environment

CROSS, Crispin

1978   Ethnic minorities in the inner city
Commission for Racial Equality

CROSS, G., Sir

1963   Private international law committee, 7th report. Law of Domicile
Session 1962-63 Cmnd. 1955 xx.

CROSSLAND, Anthony

1975   Greater London development plan statement
D. of the Environment

CROSSLAND, R. A.

1975   Teaching classical studies. Report on curriculum content and resource materials from a working party. (Curriculum bulletin No. 6)
Schools Council

CROWTHER OF HEADINGLEY, Geoffrey, Lord

1958   Future demand for teachers. Correspondence between the chairman of the Central Advisory Council for Education (England) and the Minister of Education, February to March 1958
M. of Education

1959-60   15 to 18. Report of the Central Advisory Council for Education, England. Vol. 1: Report, Vol. 2: Surveys
M. of Education

1963   Traffic in towns. A study of the long-term problems of traffic in urban areas. Reports of the steering group and working group
M. of Transport

Commission on the Constitution
Written evidence

1969   1. The Welsh Office
2. Scottish Office, Lord Advocate's Department and the Crown Office
3. Home Office (Note on the status of Northern Ireland within the United Kingdom), Government departments of Northern Ireland

1970   4. Civil Service Department, Department of Economic Affairs, Ministry of Housing and Local Government, Post Office, Ministry of Power, Board of Trade, Ministry of Transport

1972   5. Scotland
6. Northern Ireland
7. Wales
8. England
9. United Kingdom

1973   10. Revenue departments

Minutes of Evidence

1970   1. Wales
2. Scotland

1971   3. Northern Ireland
4. Scotland
5. Wales

1972   6. Channel Islands and the Isle of Man

Commission on the Constitution

1973   Report
Vol. 1: Report
Session 1973-74 Cmnd. 5460 xi.
Vol. 2: Memorandum of dissent by Lord Crowther-Hunt and A. T. Peacock
Session 1973-74 Cmnd. 5460-I xi.

1971   Consumer credit. Report of the committee. 2 vols.
Session 1970-71 Cmnd. 4596 ix.

CRUICKSHANK, H. J.

1974   Dimensional co-ordination. Report of the national consultative council of the building and civil engineering industries working party
D. of the Environment

1974   Metrication in the construction industry. Report
Metrication Board

CRUICKSHANK, Robert

1954   Air disinfection with ultra-violet irradiation; its effect on illness among school children. Report by the air hygiene committee. (Special report series No. 283)
Medical Research Council

1967   Rheumatic fever in Scotland. Report of a sub-committee of the Standing Medical Advisory Committee of the Scottish Health Services Council
Scottish Home and Health D.

CUCKNEY, J.

1976   Professions in the construction industries. Building
        and Civil Engineering E.D.C.s
        N.E.D.O.

CULLINGWORTH, John Barry

1967   The needs of new communities. A report on
        social provision in new and expanding commun-
        ities by a sub-committee of the Central Housing
        Advisory Committee
        M. of Housing and Local Government
        Scottish housing in 1965
        Scottish Development D.

        Scotland's older houses. Report of the sub-
        committee on unfit housing of the Scottish
        Housing Advisory Committee
        Scottish Development D.

1968   The ownership and management of housing in the
        new towns. Report by J. B. Cullingworth and
        V. A. Karn
        M. of Housing and Local Government

1969   Council housing, purposes, procedures and
        priorities. 9th report of the Housing Management
        sub-committee of the Central Housing Advisory
        Committee
        M. of Housing and Local Government

1971   Housing in Clydeside, 1970. Reports on a house-
        hold survey and a house condition survey in the
        central Clydeside conurbation, by J. B. Culling-
        worth and C. J. Watson
        Scottish Development D.

        West Yorkshire conurbation housing survey, 1969
        (Housing survey reports No. 7)
        D. of the Environment

1972   Planning for housing needs: pointers towards a
        comprehensive approach. Report of the working
        party of the Scottish Housing Advisory Committee
        Scottish Development D.

CULYER, A. J.

        See LEWES, F. M. M.

CUNLIFFE, R., Lord

1960   Hospital laundry arrangements. Report of the
        committee of the Central Health Services Council
        M. of Health

CUNLIFFE, Geoffrey

1951   British Standards Institution. Report of the
        committee on organisation and constitution
        Board of Trade

CUNNINGHAM, A.

1952   Child health. Report of the committee of the
        Scottish Health Services Council
        D. of Health for Scotland

CUNNINGHAM, Charles C., Sir

1953   Exchequer equalisation grants. Report of the
        committee
        Scottish Home D.

1962   Vassall case. Interim report by the committee of
        enquiry
        Session 1962-63 Cmnd. 1871 xxiv.

1971   Work of the fire service. Report of the Cunning-
        ham enquiry
        Session 1971-72 Cmnd. 4807 xiii.

1973   Uganda Resettlement Board. Interim report
        Session 1972-73 Cmnd. 5296 xxxi.

1974   Uganda Resettlement Board. Final report
        Session 1974-75 Cmnd. 5594 xv.

CUNNINGHAM, I. W.

1974   Health education in schools. Report of the
        working party (Curriculum paper No. 14)
        Scottish Education D.

CUNNINGHAM, W.

1970   Modern languages and the less able pupil. 2nd
        report of the national steering committee for
        modern languages
        Scottish Education D.

        Modern languages in further education. Report
        of a working party
        Scottish Education D.

        Modern languages in S I and S II of the compre-
        hensive school. Report of the national steering
        committee for modern languages
        Scottish Education D.

1971   Alternatives to French as a first foreign language
        in secondary schools. 3rd report of the national
        steering committee for modern languages
        Scottish Education D.

1972   The place and aims of modern language teaching
        in secondary schools. 4th report of the Scottish
        central committee for modern languages
        Scottish Education D.

CURRIE, W. J.

1976   Safe manriding in mines. 1st report of the national
        committee for safety of manriding in shafts and
        unwalkable outlets
        Health and Safety Executive

CURTIS, Myra, Dame

1946   Training in child care. Interim report of the child
        care committee
        Session 1945-46 Cmd. 6760 x.
        Care of children committee report
        Session 1945-46 Cmd. 6922 x.

CUSHING, D. H.

1976   Marine biological surveillance working party.
        Report (Publications series, B, No. 18)
        Natural Environment Research Council

CUTHBERTSON, David, Sir

1967   Nutrient requirements of farm livestock, No. 3:
        Pigs. Summaries of estimated requirements, tech-
        nical reviews and summaries
        Agricultural Research Council

D'ABREU, Alphonso L.

1968   Surgery for the newborn. Report of the joint sub-
        committee of the standing medical advisory com-
        mittees. Central and Scottish health services
        council
        M. of Health

DAINTON, Frederick S., Sir

1966   Enquiry into the flow of candidates in science
        and technology into higher education. Interim
        report
        Session 1965-66 Cmnd. 2893 vii.

1968   Enquiry into the flow of candidates in science
        and technology into higher education. Report
        Session 1967-68 Cmnd. 3541 xxxi.

1969   National libraries. Report of the committee
        Session 1968-69 Cmnd. 4028 xxxvii.
        Session 1968-69 Cmnd. 4028-I microfiche edition

1971   The future of the research council system. A
        report of a working group of the Council for
        Scientific Policy. In a framework for govern-
        ment research and development
        Session 1971-72 Cmnd. 4814 xxxv.
        See also ROTHSCHILD, N. M. V., Lord

DAINTON, Frederick S., Sir *(continued)*

1972   Council for scientific policy. 3rd report
        Session 1971-72 Cmnd. 5117 xxxv.

DALE, Edgar T.

1948   Industrial disease. Report of the departmental
        committee
        Session 1948-49 Cmd. 7557 xxxv.

1950   Industrial health services. Report of the com-
        mittee of enquiry
        Session 1950-51 Cmd. 8170 xv.

DALLEY, F. W.

1947   Trade union organisations and industrial relations
        in Trinidad. Report. (Colonial, No. 215)
        Colonial Office

1948   Labour and trade union organisation in the
        Federation of Malaya and Singapore

        See also AWBERRY, S. S.

DANIEL, Charles D.

1953   Television advisory committee. 1st report
        Post Office

1954   Television advisory committee. 2nd report
        Post Office

1960   Television advisory committee. Report
        Post Office

DANIEL, Goronwy, Sir

1975   Water charges in the area of the Welsh National
        Water Development Authority. Report of the
        committee of enquiry
        Welsh Office

DARLING OF HILLSBOROUGH, G., Lord

1977   Computers. Report of the informal joint com-
        mittee on computers
        Session 1976-77 HC. 78 xiii; HL. 35

DARTMOUTH, R. L., Countess

1972   How do you want to live? A report on the
        human habitat
        D. of the Environment

DARWIN, Charles G., Sir

1947   Artificial limbs. 1st report of the standing
        advisory committee
        M. of Pensions

1948   Artificial limbs. 2nd report of the standing
        advisory committee
        M. of Pensions

1949   Artificial limbs. 3rd report of the standing
        advisory committee
        M. of Pensions

1951   Artificial limbs. 4th and 5th reports of the stand-
        ing advisory committee
        M. of Pensions

1957   Code of practice for the protection of persons
        exposed to ionizing radiations. Part A: Use of
        X-rays for diagnosis; use of X-rays and γ-ray
        beam units for therapy. Part B: Use of radio-
        active isotopes. Supplement; protection against
        ionizing radiations—fundamental data. Radio-
        active substances standing advisory committee
        M. of Health

DAVIDSON, A. H. B.

1970   Projects in practice. Central project group of the
        central committee on English
        Scottish Education D.

DAVIDSON, D. Du B.

1941   Expenditure in respect of evacuated school chil-
        dren. 2nd report of the committee
        Board of Education

DAVIDSON, Ian Hay

1977   London Capital Group Ltd. (formerly British
        Bangladesh Trust Ltd.). Report of investigation
        under the Companies Act
        Dept. of Trade

DAVIDSON, J. C. C., Viscount

1946   Iraq, Syria, the Lebanon and Cyprus. British
        goodwill trade mission. Report
        Board of Trade

DAVIES, A., Sir

1958   Matrimonial proceedings. Report of the depart-
        mental committee on matrimonial proceedings in
        magistrates' courts. December, 1958
        Session 1958-59 Cmnd. 638 xvi.

DAVIES, A. B., OLDFIELD-

        See OLDFIELD-DAVIES, A. B.

DAVIES, A. E. Miles

1955   Grants to training college students. Report of
        the working party
        Board of Education

DAVIES, A. W. Michael

1967   Report of enquiry in respect of objections to the
        proposed compulsory amalgamation of the police
        areas of the County of Yorkshire, North Riding,
        and the new County Borough of Teesside
        Session 1966-67 Cmnd. 3407 xlvi.

1970   Public enquiry into a fire at Dudgeons Wharf on
        17 July, 1969. Report
        Session 1970-71 Cmnd. 4470 xvii.

DAVIES, Clement

1946   London regional planning. Advisory committee.
        Report and technical sub-committee report
        M. of Town and Country Planning

1949   London planning administration committee.
        Report
        M. of Town and Country Planning

DAVIES, D. R. Seaborne

1957   Agriculture and dairy diploma courses in Wales.
        Report of the Committee
        M. of Agriculture, Fisheries and Food

DAVIES, Elwyn

1978   Library services in rural areas; library services
        to Welsh industry. Two reports by the Library
        Advisory Council, Wales. (Library information
        series No. 9)
        D. of Education and Science

DAVIES, Herbert Edmund, Lord

1962   Limitation of actions in cases of personal injury.
        Report of the committee
        Session 1961-62 Cmnd. 1892 xx

1967   Report of the tribunal appointed to inquire into
        the disaster at Aberfan on October 24, 1966
        Session 1966-67 HC. 553 xxi; HL. 316
        See also PENMAN, A. D. M.

1972   Evidence (general). 11th report of the Criminal
        Law Revision Committee.
        Session 1971-72 Cmnd. 4991 xxi.

DAVIES, Herbert Edmund, Lord *(continued)*

1973   Penalty for murder. 12th report of the Criminal Law Revision Committee
Session 1972-73 Cmnd. 5184 xiv.

1974   Section 16 of the Theft Act, 1968. (Criminal Law Revision Committee working paper)
Home Office

1976   Criminal Law Revision Committee. Working paper on offences against the person
Home Office

1977   Criminal Law Revision Committee. 13th report: Section 16 of the Theft Act, 1968
Session 1976-77 Cmnd. 6733 xviii.

1978   Committee of inquiry on the police. Reports on negotiating machinery and pay
Session 1977-78 Cmnd. 7283 xlvi.

DAVIES, J. R.

1972   Small firms in manufacturing sector. (Committee of inquiry on small firms research report No. 3)
D. Trade and Industry

DAVIES, Jack Gale Wilmot

1969   The method II system of selection (for the administrative class of the home civil service). Report of the committee of inquiry
Session 1968-69 Cmnd. 4156 xxvii.

DAVIES, Joseph M.

1968   Findings and recommendations following inquiries into allegations concerning the care of elderly patients in certain hospitals, VII: Springfield Hospital, Manchester. National Health Service
Session 1967-68 Cmnd. 3687 xxviii.

DAVIES, M.

1973   Hospital complaints procedure. Report of the committee
D. of Health and Social Security

DAVIES, P. L.

1976   Industrial democracy; European experience, two reports. Industrial democracy committee
D. of Trade

DAVIES, R. I.

1971   Residual value of applied nutrients. Proceedings of a conference organised by the soil scientists of the National Agricultural Advisory Service, February 27-28, 1968. (Technical bulletin No. 20)
M. of Agriculture, Fisheries and Food

DAVIES, R. Llewelyn-, Lord
    See LLEWELYN-DAVIES, R., Lord

DAVIES, T. A. Lloyd-
    See LLOYD-DAVIES, T. A.

DAVIES, W. Tudor

1946   Nigeria. Inquiry into the cost of living and the control of the cost of living in the colony and protectorate of Nigeria. Part 1: report by W. Tudor Davies, April 15, 1946; Part 2: Despatch from Secretary of State for the Colonies to Governor of Nigeria, July 9, 1946. (Colonial No. 204)
Colonial Office

DAVIS, Alan

1977   Management of deprivation. Final report of the Southwark Community Development Project

Home Office, published by the Polytechnic of the South Bank

DAVIS, I. T. M.

1963   Winter building. An interim review by the committee
M. of Public Building and Works

DAVIS, J. A.

1966   Conditions in the drop-forging industry, 1954-64. Report of the joint standing committee on health, safety and welfare in the drop-forging industry
M. of Labour

1971   Pattern for progress. 2nd report of the joint standing committee for the pottery industry
D. of Employment

DAVIS, R. Harvard
    See HARVARD DAVIS, R.

DAVISON, I. H.

1977   Housing for all, a document for discussion. Housing strategy committee
N.E.D.O.

DAVISON, W. A.

1973   Remuneration of electricians employed in the National Health Service. Report of an inquiry
D. of Employment

DAWSON OF PENN, B., Viscount

1942   Committee on tuberculosis in wartime. Report. (special report, series 246)
Medical Research Council

DAWSON, D.

1973   Revenue and equalisation in Australia, Canada, West Germany and the U.S.A. (Commission on the constitution research papers No. 9)
Commission on the Constitution

DAYMOND, D. G.

1977   Selection of specialists. Report of the working party
Civil Service Commission

DEAKIN, W.

1973   Urban motorways project team. Report to the urban motorways committee
D. of the Environment

DEARING, G. E.

1966   East Midlands study. East Midlands Economic Planning Council
D. of Economic Affairs

DEBENHAM, F.

1949   Study of African swamp. Report of the Cambridge University expedition to the Bangweulu swamps, Northern Rhodesia, 1949
Colonial Office

DE DENEY, G. I.
    See HAYZELDEN, J. E.

DEER, W. A.

1973   Mineralogy, petrology and crystallography. Report of the working party. In Research in the geological sciences (publication series B, No. 7)
National Environmental Research Council

DELAFONS, John

1969   Housing revenue accounts. Report of the working party on the housing revenue account
M. Housing and Local Government

DE LA WARR, H. E. D. B., Earl

1943   Hill sheep farming in England and Wales. Committee appointed by the Agricultural Improvement Council for England and Wales. Report
Session 1943-44 Cmd. 6498 iii.

1958   Education for Agriculture. Report of the committee on further education for agriculture provided by local education authorities
Session 1958-59 Cmd. 614 xi.

DELEVINGNE, Malcolm, Sir

1942   Coal dust explosions. Special report by the safety in mines research board
Session 1942-43 Cmd. 6450 vi.

DENINGTON, E. J.

1966   Our older homes, a call for action. Report of the sub-committee on standards of housing fitness
M. of Housing and Local Government

DENNING, A. T., Lord

Procedure in matrimonial causes

1946   1st interim report. Session 1945-46 Cmd. 6881 xiii.
2nd interim report. Session 1945-46 Cmd. 6945 xiii.

1947   Final report. Session 1946-47 Cmd. 7024 xiii.

1960   Report of the committee on legal education for students from Africa
Session 1960-61 Cmnd. 1255 xviii.

1963   Lord Denning's report [on the Profumo affair]
Session 1962-63 Cmnd. 2152 xxiv.

1966   Report of the committee on legal records
Session 1966-67 Cmnd. 3084 xxxix.

DENNY, M. B. A.

1970   Future of the artificial limb service in Scotland. Report of a working party
Scottish Home and Health D.

DESAI, M. J.

1955   Vietnam. International commission for supervision and control in Vietnam
1st and 2nd interim reports. (Vietnam No. 1, 1955)
Session 1954-55 Cmd. 9461 xix.
3rd interim report. (Vietnam No. 2, 1955)
Session 1955-56 Cmd. 9499 xlv.

DEVERELL, Colville, Sir

1967   Seychelles. Proposals for constitutional advance. (Commonwealth No. 1)
Commonwealth Office

DEVEREUX, W. A.

1978   Preparatory courses. Report of the Training Services Agency/Adult Literary Resources Agency working group
Training Services Agency

DEVLIN, P. A., Lord

1956   Port transport industry. Report of a committee to inquire into the operation of the dock workers (regulation of employment) scheme, 1947
Session 1955-56 Cmd. 9813 xxiv.

1959   Report of the Nyasaland commission of inquiry
Session 1958-59 Cmnd. 814 x.

1964   Committee of inquiry into certain matters concerning the port transport industry
1st report
Session 1964-65 Cmnd. 2523 xxi.

1965   Final report
Session 1964-65 Cmnd. 2734 xxi.

1966   Committee of inquiry into the wages structure and level of pay for dock workers. Report
Session 1966-67 Cmnd. 3104 xxvi.

1976   Evidence of identification in criminal cases. Report of the departmental committee
Session 1975-76 HC. 338 xix.

DEVONSHIRE, E. W. S., Duke of

1945   Post-war training for the colonial service. Report of the committee
Colonial Office

Cocoa research conference held at the Colonial Office, May to June 1945. Report and proceedings
Colonial Office

DEWDNEY, Duncan A. C.

1966   Production planning and control. Report of the Mechanical Engineering Economic Development Committee conference. 2nd ed., 1968
N.E.D.O.

DIAMOND, John, Lord

1975   Royal Commission on the Distribution of Income and Wealth
Report, No. 1: Initial report on the standing reference
Session 1974-75 Cmnd. 6171 xxxii.

Report, No. 2: Income from companies and its distribution
Session 1974-75 Cmnd. 6172 xxxii.

1976   Report, No. 3: Higher incomes from employment
Session 1975-76 Cmnd. 6383 xli.

Report, No. 4: Second report on the standing reference
Session 1975-76 Cmnd. 6626 xlii.

Selected evidence submitted to the Commission for report No. 1
R. Commission

Selected evidence submitted to the Commission for report No. 2
R. Commission

Selected evidence submitted to the Commission for report No. 3
R. Commission

1977   Report, No. 5: Third report on the standing reference
Session 1977-78 Cmnd. 6999 xlix.

1978   Report, No. 6: Lower incomes
Session 1977-78 Cmnd. 7175 xlix.

Low incomes. Evidence to the Royal Commission on the Distribution of Income and Wealth. (Supplementary benefits administration paper No. 6)
D. of Health and Social Security

DIAMOND, A. L.

1975   Liability for defective products. (Law Commission working paper No. 64; Scottish Law Commission memorandum No. 20)
Law Commission

DICK, G. C.

1978   Discounted air fares. Report of the working party
D. of Trade

DICK, John A.

1965   Hydroelectric schemes. Report of the public inquiry into the North of Scotland Hydroelectric Board's constructional scheme, No. 39 (Fada/Fionn project) and constructional scheme No. 38 (Laidon project)
Scottish Development D.

DICKINSON, Fiona

1978   In and out of work; a study of unemployment, low pay and income maintenance services
North Tyneside Community Development Project

DICKMAN, J. H.

1974   Kwik Save Discount Group, Ltd. Report of investigations under the Companies Act
D. of Trade

DICKSON, G. R.

1977   Agricultural exports; the role of the breed societies and their national associations
Advisory Council for Agriculture and Horticulture in England and Wales

DICKSON, John A.

1969   Pulpwood supply and the paper industry. Report of a conference of the British paper and board makers' association, 12 June, 1968. (Forest record No. 68)
Forestry Commission

DIGNEY, N.

1975   Wash water storage scheme feasibility study. Report on the economic and social studies by the economic and social aspects working party
Central Water Planning Unit, D. of the Environment

DINSDALE, D. H.

1960   Costs and efficiency in the milk production. Report of the national investigation into the economics of milk production, 1955-57
M. of Agriculture, Fisheries and Food

DINWIDDY, Robert

1977   Effects of certain social and demographic changes on income distribution (background paper No. 3)
Royal Commission on the Distribution of Income and Wealth

DIPLOCK, William John Kenneth, Lord

1959   Boundary Commission for England. Report with respect to the areas comprised in the constituencies of Ilford North, Ilford South, Woodford, Liverpool, West Derby, Crosby, Huyton, Ormskirk, Preston South, Fylde, Leeds North East, Leeds East, York, Barkston Ash, Oxford, Henley, Gloucester, Stroud, Grimsby, Louth, Lincoln, Grantham, Gateshead East, Gateshead West, Reading, Newbury, Wokingham, Coventry East, Coventry North, Coventry South, Meriden, Rugby, Warwick and Leamington, Wandsworth, Putney, Kingston-upon-Thames, Richmond (Surrey), Portsmouth, Langstone, Petersfield, North Somerset, and Wells
Session 1958-59 HC.255 ix.

1960   Boundary Commission for England. Report with respect to the areas comprised in the constituencies of Walsall North, Walsall South, Middlesbrough East, Middlesbrough West, Barnsley and Wakefield
Session 1959-60 HC. 60 ix.

1972   Legal procedures to deal with terrorist activities in Northern Ireland. Report of the commission
Session 1972-73 Cmnd. 5185 xxvi.

1973   Security Commission. Report, May 1973
Session 1972-73 Cmnd. 5362 xxxiii.

Security Commission. Report, July 1973
Session 1972-73 Cmnd. 5367 xxxiii.

1976   Recruitment of mercenaries. Report of the committee of Privy Counsellors
Session 1975-76 Cmnd. 6569 xxi.

DIXON, P. J.
See DICKSON, J. A.

DIXON, S. Gurney-, Sir
See GURNEY-DIXON, S., Sir

DOBB, J. P. B.

1969   Agricultural valuation. 3rd report of the committee
M. of Agriculture, Fisheries and Food
See also HOOPER, L. J., WARE, E. S.

1969   Farm dairy buildings. Report of a working party
M. of Agriculture, Fisheries and Food

DOBBS, E. S.

1971   Music and the young school leaver: problems and opportunities. Report of the working party. (Working paper, 35)
Schools Council

DOBRY, G.

1974   Control of demolition
D. of the Environment

Review of the development control system. Interim report
D. of the Environment

1975   Review of the development control system. Final report
D. of the Environment

DOBSON, A. T. A.

1947   International overfishing conference. Final report of the Standing Advisory Committee, London, 16-19 April, 1947
Session 1947-48 Cmd. 7387 xxvii.

DOLL, Richard

1977   Breast cancer screening trials working group. Interim report, rev. ed. with addendum
D. of Health and Social Security

DONALD, K. W.

1978   The provision of hyperbaric facilities in Scotland. Report by the advisory group on health care aspects of industrial developments in the North Sea
Scottish Health Service

DONALD, Kenneth W.

1969   Uses and dangers of oxygen therapy. Report of a sub-committee of the standing medical advisory committee. Scottish Health Services Council
Scottish Home and Health D.

DONALDSON OF KINGSBRIDGE, J. G. S., Lord

1968   Report of the committee on herbage seed supplies
Session 1967-68 Cmnd. 3748 xxiii.

1970   Report of the committee on boy entrants and young servicemen
Session 1970-71 Cmnd. 4509 vi.

DONALDSON OF KINGSBRIDGE, J. G. S., Lord
(continued)

1973   Financial control of catering in the services. Report of the committee of inquiry
M. of Defence

1975   Accommodation for the lower priced market. Hotel and Catering E.D.C.
N.E.D.O.

DONALDSON, John Francis, Sir

1978   Commercial court committee. Report on arbitration
Session 1977-78 Cmnd. 7284 xxii.

DONKIN, S. B.

See VAUGHAN-LEE, A. G.

DONNELLY, H. H.

1956   Qualifications of teachers in schools holding the Teacher's Technical Certificate. Report of the committee
Scottish Education D.

1959   Basis of remuneration of part-time further education teachers. Report of working party
Scottish Education D.

1962   Appointment of teachers to education committees. Report of the working party on the appointment of teachers in the employment of education authorities in Scotland to the education committees of the authorities
Scottish Education D.

        Pensions for teachers' widows. Report of the working party on pensions for widows, widowers, children and other dependants of teachers in Scotland
Scottish Education D.

DONNISON, David V.

1970   Public Schools Commission. 2nd report
        Vol. 1: Report on independent day schools and direct grant grammar schools
        Vol. 2: Appendices
        Vol. 3: Scotland
D. of Education and Science

See also NEWSOM, J., Sir, for the first report

DONOVAN, T. N., Lord

1965   Court of Criminal Appeal. Report of the interdepartmental committee
Session 1964-65 Cmnd. 2755 xiii.

1968   Royal Commission on Trade Unions and Employers' Associations. Report
Session 1967-68 Cmnd. 3623 xxxii.

DOUGHTY, Charles, Sir

1941   Industrial Court Act 1919. Trade dispute apprehended at Briggs Motor Bodies Ltd., Dagenham. Report of the court of inquiry
Session 1940-41 Cmd. 6284 iv.

1943   Industrial Courts Act 1919. Dispute between the Clerical and Administrative Workers' Union and certain colliery companies in South Wales and Monmouthshire. Report by court of inquiry
Session 1943-44 Cmd. 6493 iv.

1947   Industrial Courts Act 1919. Industrial unrest in the wire and wire rope industry. Report of a court of inquiry
Session 1946-47 Cmd. 7097 xiv.

1951   Industrial Courts Act 1919. Causes and circumstances of a dispute between the Electrical Trade Union and the London Electricity Board. Report of a court of inquiry
Session 1950-51 Cmd. 8232 xvi.

DOUGLAS, J.

1976   Parliaments across frontiers; a short history of the Inter-Parliamentary Union
House of Commons

DOUGLAS, J. B., Sir

1944   Land settlement in Scotland. Scottish Land settlement committee report
Session 1944-45 Cmd. 6577 v.

1959   Presenting costs. Report of the Scottish committee
D. of Health for Scotland

DOUGLAS, K. G.

1953   Position of the enrolled assistant nurse within the National Health Service. Report of the standing nursing advisory committee of the Central Health Services Council
M. of Health

1959   Design of nurses' uniforms. Report of a subcommittee of the standing nursing advisory committee of the Central Health Services Council
M. of Health

DOUGLAS, W., Sir

1952   Southern Rhodesia, Northern Rhodesia and Nyasaland. Draft federal scheme. Report of the civil service preparatory commission
Session 1951-52 Cmd. 8673 ix.

DOUGLAS, W. S., Sir

1951   Purchase tax/utility committee report
Session 1951-52 Cmd. 8452 xviii.

DOUGLAS-HOME, A., Sir

1958   Basutoland. Report on constitutional discussions held in London in November and December, 1958
Session 1958-59 Cmnd. 637 ix.

DOW, Alistair

1974   Review Body on Doctors' and Dentists' remuneration. Supplement to the fourth report, 1974
Session 1974-75 Cmnd. 5849 xxxii.

See also HALSBURY, J. A. H. G., Earl

DOW, Hugh, Sir

1955   East Africa Royal Commission. Report
Session 1955-56 Cmd. 9475 xiii.

DOW, R. C. Scott-

See SCOTT-DOW, R. C.

DOWER, John

1945   National parks in England and Wales. Report
Session 1944-45 Cmd. 6628 v.

DOWNEY, William G.

1969   Development cost estimating. Report of the steering group
        Vol. 1: Report
        Vol. 2: Handbook of procedures—programming, estimating and control of development projects
M. of Technology

DOWSE, D. S.

1976   Milkmen; their recruitment, selection and training, a manager's guide, by the joint working party
Milk Marketing Board

DOYLE, Thomas A.

1974   Law enforcement commission report
Session 1974 Cmnd. 5627 xiii.

DRAKE, Madeline

1978   Policy and provision for the single homeless; a position paper by M. Drake and T. Biebuych
Personal Social Services Council

DRAPER, Paul

1977   Creation of the DoE (Civil service studies, 4)
Civil Service D.

DREW, Arthur

1978   Framework for a system for museums. Report of a working party
Standing Commission on Museums and Galleries

DROGHEDA, H. C. P., Earl of

1950   Cinematograph Films Council. Distribution and exhibition of cinematograph films. Report of the committee of inquiry
Board of Trade

1954   Overseas information services. Summary of the report of the independent committee of inquiry (Miscellaneous No. 12, 1954)
Session 1953-54 Cmd. 9138 xxxi.

1957   Imprisonment. Alternatives to short terms of imprisonment. Advisory Council on the Treatment of Offenders report
Home Office

DRUMMOND, G. G.

1975   Schools/industry liaison in the highlands and islands; an independent working party report
Highlands and Islands Development Board

DUBISSON, Peter William Grostete

1978   Land and General Development Ltd., Napet Securities Ltd. Interim and final reports of investigations under the Companies Act
D. of Trade

DUCE, Alan R.

1978   Human rights in prison
Home Office

DUDLEY, W. H. E., Earl of

1944   Design of dwellings. Report of the sub-committee of the central housing advisory committee and report of a study group on site planning and layout in relation to housing
M. of Health

DUKE-ELDER, Herbert, Sir

1956   Trial case lenses. Report of a committee
M. of Health

DUNBAR, J. G.

1975   Stirling House
Royal Commission on the Ancient and Historical Monuments of Scotland

DUNCAN, Joseph

1949   Land drainage (Scotland) committee report
Session 1950 Cmd. 7948 xii.

DUNCAN, J. N. Val, Sir

1969   Overseas representation. Report of the review committee (Miscellaneous No. 24, 1969)
Session 1968-69 Cmnd. 4107 xliv.

DUNHAM, Kingsley, Sir

1973   Mining and economic geology. Report of the working party. In Research in the geological sciences (publications series, No. 7)
National Environment Research Council

DUNSTER, H. J.

1971   Handbook of radiological protection, part 1. Data prepared by a panel of the radioactive substances advisory committee
D. of Employment *and* D. of Health and Social Security

DUNLOP, John

1958   Organisation of laboratory services. Report of a committee appointed by the Scottish Health Services Council
D. of Health for Scotland

        Mental health legislation. Report by a committee appointed by the Scottish Health Services Council
D. of Health for Scotland

1959   Mental health legislation. 2nd report by a committee appointed by the Scottish Health Services Council
D. of Health for Scotland

1962   Visiting patients in hospital. Report of a committee appointed by the Scottish Health Services Council
Scottish Home and Health D.

DUNNE, Laurence R., Sir

1945   Bethnal Green. Report on an inquiry into the accident at Bethnal Green Tube Station shelter on March 3, 1943
Session 1944-45 Cmd. 6583 iv.

DUNNET, G. M.

1976   Terrestrial biological surveillance working party report (Publications series B, No. 18)
Natural Environment Research Council

1977   Ecological research on seabirds. Report of the working group (Publications series C, No. 18)
National Environment Research Council

DUNNETT, James, Sir

1961   Shipbuilding advisory committee. Report of the sub-committee on prospects
M. of Transport

1964   Nuclear power for ship propulsion. Report of the working group on marine reactor research
Session 1963-64 Cmnd. 2358 viii.

DUNNING, J.

1977   Assessment for all. Report of the committee to review assessment in the 3rd and 4th years of secondary education in Scotland
Scottish Education D.

DUNPARK, Alistair McPherson Johnston, Lord

1977   Reparation by the offender to the victim in Scotland. Report by the committee
Session 1976-77 Cmnd. 6802 xviii.

DUNROSSIL, W. S., Viscount

1954   Boundary commission for England. 1st periodical report
Session 1953-54 Cmd. 9311 ix.

1954   Boundary Commission for Scotland. 1st periodical report
Session 1953-54 Cmd. 9312 ix.

        Boundary Commission for Wales. 1st periodical report
Session 1953-54 Cmd. 9313 ix.

DUNROSSIL, W. S., Viscount *(continued)*
    Boundary Commission for Northern Ireland. 1st periodical report
    Session 1953-54 Cmd. 9314 ix.

DU PARCQ, Herbert, Baron
1948   Royal Commission on Justices of the Peace. Report
    Session 1947-48 Cmd. 7463 xii.

DURAND, Victor
1960   Disturbances at the Carlton Approved School on 29 and 30 August, 1959. Report on an inquiry
    Session 1959-60 Cmnd. 937 ix.

DURBAN, D. D.
1976   Hotels prospects to 1985. Updating standing committee of the Hotels and Catering E.D.C.
        Summary and recommendations
        Research findings
    N.E.D.O.

DUTHIE, J. H.
1970   Primary school survey, a study of the teacher's day. A report by Dr. J. H. Duthie
    Scottish Education D.
1973   Lower limb modular prostheses. Report of an international conference on specification, Ascot, Berks., 1972
    D. of Health and Social Security
1975   Auxiliaries in the classroom
    Scottish Education D.

EADY, Nora M. E.
1978   Policy issues in residential care, a discussion document. Report to the P.S.S.C. from an advisory group
    Personal Social Services Council

EASTHAM, T.
1946   Clatworthy. Enquiry into the case of Arthur Alfred Clatworthy. Report
    Session 1945-46 Cmd. 6736 xiv.

EASTHAM, T. M.
1976   Vehicle and General Insurance Co. Ltd. Report of investigations under the Companies Act
    D. of Trade

EASTWOOD, C. G.
1948   Colonial primary products. Interim report of the committee
    Colonial Office
1949   British African land utilization conference. Final report, Jos, Nigeria, 5-17 November, 1949
    Colonial Office

EASTWOOD, Eric, Sir
1977   Future of radio astronomy in the U.K. Report of the review panel
    Science Research Council

EBERLIN, Richard
1978   Facilities for yachting. First report of the Royal Yachting Association facilities committee
    Sports Council

EBOR (Archbishop of York)
    See
    TEMPLE, William, 1929-42
    GARBETT, Cyril Forster, 1942-56

RAMSEY, Arthur Michael, 1956-61
COGGAN, Frederick Donald, 1961-74
BLANCH, Stuart Yarworth, 1974-

ECCLES, David McAdam, Viscount
1977   The library of the House of Lords. Report of the working group
    Session 1976-77 HL. 84

ECCLES, John D.
1975   Necessary partnership; reconciling conflicting objectives in the supply of process plant. Report of a working group of the Process Plant Working Party
    N.E.D.O.

EDE, A. Y.
1972   Advantages of the metric system, a study
    Metrication Board

EDE, J. Chuter-, Lord
    See CHUTER-EDE, J., Lord

EDEN, Anthony
1952   Britain's place in the world. (Britain and the free world, a series broadcast by the B.B.C.)
    Central Office of Information

EDEN, E. N.
1977   Metrological control systems. Report of the working party
    Session 1976-77 Cmnd. 6805 xix.

EDINBURGH, Prince Philip, Duke of
1965   Queen's award to industry. Report by a committee
    Prime Minister's Office
1975   Queen's award to industry. Report of the 1975 review committee
    D. of Industry

EDMOND, Andrew Durward
1962   Complaints made by the Scottish wool trades consultative committee. Report of the committee of investigation for G.B. under the British Wool Marketing Scheme, 1950
    D. of Agriculture and Fisheries for Scotland

EDMUND-DAVIES, Lord
    See DAVIES, Herbert Edmund, Lord

EDWARDS, Amy
1978   The prison system in England and Wales, 1878-1978
    Home Office

EDWARDS, F. L.
1953   Exchequer equalisation grants. Report of the committee
    M. of Housing and Local Government
1962   Rate deficiency grants in England and Wales. Report of the working party
    M. of Housing and Local Government

EDWARDS, H. J.
1966   The certificate of secondary education trial examinations: oral English. Report of the steering committee. (Examinations bulletin No. 11)
    Schools Council

EDWARDS, H. J. *(continued)*

1967 The certificate of secondary education trial examinations: written English. Report of the steering committee (Examinations bulletin No. 16)
Schools Council

EDWARDS, Hunt T.

1953 Wales and Monmouthshire. 2nd memorandum by the Council for Wales and Monmouthshire on its activities
Session 1952-53 Cmd. 8844 xxiv.

1954 South Wales ports. Report by the Council for Wales and Monmouthshire
Session 1954-55 Cmd. 9359 vii.

1956 Wales and Monmouthshire. 3rd memorandum by the Council for Wales and Monmouthshire on its activities
Session 1956-57 Cmnd. 53 xxvi.

EDWARDS, J. G., Sir

1960 Ancient monuments of central Caernarvonshire. 12th interim report of the Royal Commission on the Ancient and Historical Monuments of Wales and Monmouthshire
Session 1959-60 Cmnd. 1138 xvii.

1964 Ancient Monuments of West Caernarvonshire. 13th interim report of the Royal Commission on the Ancient and Historical Monuments and Constructions of Wales and Monmouthshire
Session 1964-65 Cmnd. 2551 xvii.

EDWARDS, Lawrence, Sir

1950 Ship repairing facilities on Merseyside. Report of a working party
Admiralty *and* M. of Transport

EDWARDS, L. John

1947 Publicity for Local government. Interim report of the consultative committee
M. of Health

EDWARDS, R. M. Wynne-, Sir
See **WYNNE-EDWARDS, R. M., Sir**

EDWARDS, R. W.

1972 Research in freshwater biology. Report of the sub-committee and its working groups. (Publications series B, No. 3)
Natural Environment Research Council

EDWARDS, Ronald S., Sir

1968 British air transport in the seventies. Report of the committee of enquiry into civil air transport
Session 1968-69 Cmnd. 4018 xxv.

EDWARDS, S. L.

1977 Tourism in the south west region; methodological report
South West Economic Planning Council
See also **BAYLISS, B. T.**

EDWARDS, Sam, Sir

1975 Postgraduate training. Working party report
Science Research Council

EGERTON, Alfred, Sir

1946 Heating and ventilation of dwellings. Report of a committee of the Building Research Board. (Post-war building studies No. 19)
M. of Works

1947 Heating and ventilation of schools. Report of the committee of the Building Research Board.

(Post-war building studies, No. 27)
M. of Works

1952 District heating. Report of a committee of the Building Research Board
Part 1: General report
Part 2: Survey of district heating practice abroad
Part 3: Memorandum on suggested district heating scheme for the Duddeston and Nechells redevelopment area of Birmingham
Part 4: Memorandum on district heating as applied to small housing estates
Part 5: Heat pump, with particular reference to district heating scheme with hot water distribution (the basic scheme)
M. of Works

ELDER, N. C. M.

1973 Regionalism and the publicity principle in Sweden (Research paper no. 3)
Commission on the Constitution

ELDER, S., DUKE-, Sir
See **DUKE-ELDER, S., Sir**

ELEY, J. L.

1972 E. J. Austin International Ltd. Report of investigations under the Companies Act
D. of Trade and Industry

1976 E. J. Austin International Ltd. Final report of investigations under the Companies Act
D. of Trade

ELLEN, R. J.

1974 National youth employment council. Final triennial report
D. of Employment

ELLES, R. J.

1974 Unqualified, untrained and unemployed. Report of a working party set up by the national youth employment council
D. of Employment

ELLIOT OF HARWOOD, K., Baroness

1963 Staffing of local authority children's departments. A report by the Scottish Advisory Council on Child Care
Scottish Home and Health D.

ELLIOT, Walter E.

1943 Committee on voluntary aid detachments. Report
Session 1942-43 Cmd. 6448 iv.

1944 Committee on the herring industry. Report
Session 1943-44 Cmd. 6503 iii.

1945 Commission on higher education in West Africa. Report
Session 1944-45 Cmd. 6655 v.

Wool marketing committee. Report
M. of Agriculture and Fisheries

ELLIOTT, J.
See **JOLLY, J. C.**

ELLIOTT, R. A.

1963 Technical committee on storm overflows and the disposal of storm sewage. Interim report
M. of Housing and Local Government

ELLIOTT, R. A. *(continued)*

1966   Working party on the design and construction of underground pipe sewers. 1st interim report
M. of Housing and Local Government

1967   Working party on the design and construction of underground pipe sewers
Notes of guidance on practical considerations in the structural design and the construction of small-diameter sewers and drains
Second report
M. of Housing and Local Government

1970   Technical committee on storm overflows and the disposal of storm sewage. Final report
M. of Housing and Local Government
See also H. W. COALES and G. S. WELLS

ELLIOTT, S.

1975   Northern Ireland border poll, 1973
Northern Ireland Office

ELLIOTT-BINNS, Edward Usher Elliott

1969   Suggestions and complaints in hospitals. Report of the working party
Scottish Home and Health D.

ELLIS, A. W. M.

1950   Papers of the Royal Commission on population, vol. 4: Reports of the biological and medical committee
Royal Commission on Population

ELLIS, R. W. B.

1961   Remand homes. Report of a special committee of the Scottish advisory council on child care
Session 1961-62 Cmnd. 1588 xxiii.

ELSON, M. J.

1977   Study of informal recreation in South East England
Countryside Commission

ELSTUB, St. John de Holt

1969   Productivity of the national aircraft effort. Report of a committee
M. of Technology

ELTON, G. A. H.

1971   Survey of mercury in food. 1st report by the working party on the monitoring of foodstuffs for mercury and other metals
M. of Agriculture, Fisheries and Food

1972   Survey of lead in food. 2nd report by the working party on the monitoring of foodstuffs for heavy metals
M. of Agriculture, Fisheries and Food

1973   Survey of mercury in food. 3rd report. A supplementary report by the working party on the monitoring of foodstuffs for heavy metals
M. of Agriculture, Fisheries and Food

Survey of cadmium in food. 4th report by the working party on the monitoring of foodstuffs for heavy metals
M. of Agriculture, Fisheries and Food

ELVIN, H. L.

1960   Social development through family and home. Report of a conference held at St. Hugh's College, Oxford, September 7 to 25, 1959
Colonial Office

ELY HOSPITAL INQUIRY
See HOWE, R. E. G.

EMERY, D.

1961   Special hospitals. Report of the working party
M. of Health

EMMERSON, Harold C., Sir

1949   Advisory council on building research and development. 1st report
M. of Works
See also GATER, G. H., Sir

1966   London Government Staff Commission. Report
M. of Housing and Local Government

EMMET OF AMBERLEY, E. V. E., Baroness

1970   Report of the advisory committee on the better provision of legal advice and assistance
Session 1969-70 Cmnd. 4249 xvii.

EMSLIE, George Carlyle, Lord

1961   Report on the local inquiry in the matter of a review of rents of council houses in Dunbarton
D. of Health for Scotland

1972   Penalties for homicide. Report of the committee
Session 1972-73 Cmnd. 5137 xiv.

ENGHOLM, B. C.

1957   Transactions in seeds. Report of the committee
Session 1957-58 Cmnd. 300 vii.

1960   Plant breeders' rights. Report of the committee on transactions in seeds
Session 1959-60 Cmnd. 1092 viii.

ENGLEDOW, F. L., Sir

1945   Farm buildings. Report by a committee (Post-war building studies No. 17)
M. of Agriculture, Fisheries and Food

1958   Technical problems of Welsh agriculture. Report of a committee appointed by the Agricultural Improvement Council for England and Wales
M. of Agriculture, Fisheries and Food

ENGLISH, Cyril

1971   Support for school science and technology. Report of the working party (Working paper No. 38)
Schools Council

EPSON, Eric

1971   Aircraft noise: flight routeing near airports. Noise Advisory Council working group
D. of the Environment

1974   Aircraft noise: review of aircraft departure routeing policy. Report by a working group
Noise Advisory Council

ERROLL OF HALE, Frederick James, Lord

1972   Liquor licensing. Report of the departmental committee
Session 1972-73 Cmnd. 5154 xiv.

ESHER, L. G. B., Viscount

1969   York; a study in conservation. Report by the preservation policy group
M. of Housing and Local Government

EVANS OF HUNGERSHALL, B. Ifor, Lord

1957   National Insurance (Claims and Payments) Amendment Regulations, 1957. Report of the National Insurance Advisory Committee
Session 1956-57 HC. 136 xv.

EVANS OF HUNGERSHALL, B. Ifor, Lord *(continued)*

Part-time employment. Report of the National Insurance Advisory Committee
Session 1956-57 Cmnd. 206 xv.

1957   National Insurance (Married Women) Amendment Regulations, 1957, Draft. Report of the National Insurance Advisory Committee
Session 1956-57 HC. 201 xv.

National Insurance (Contributions) Amendment Regulations, 1957. Report of the National Insurance Advisory Committee
Session 1956-57 HC. 237 xv.

National Insurance (Widow's Benefit and Retirement Pensions) Amendment Regulations, 1957. Report of the National Insurance Advisory Committee
Session 1956-57 HC. 239 xv.

National Insurance (Guardians' Allowances) Amendment Regulations, 1957. Report of the National Insurance Advisory Committee
Session 1956-57 HC. 291 xv.

National Insurance (Determination of Claims and Questions) Amendment Regulations, 1957. Report of the National Insurance Advisory Committee
Session 1956-57 HC. 246 xv.

National Insurance (Child's Special Allowance) Regulations, 1957. Report of the National Insurance Advisory Committee
Session 1956-57 HC. 290 xv.

National Insurance (Annulled Marriages) Regulations, 1957. Report of the National Insurance Advisory Committee
Session 1956-57 HC. 253 xv.

National Insurance (Unemployment and Sickness Benefit) Amendment Regulations, 1957. Report of the National Insurance Advisory Committee
Session 1956-57 HC. 244 xv.

National Insurance (Claims and Payments) Amendment (No. 2) Regulations, 1957. Report of the National Insurance Advisory Committee
Session 1956-57 HC. 247 xv.

National Insurance (Overlapping Benefits) Amendment Regulations, 1957. Report of the National Insurance Advisory Committee
Session 1957-58 HC. 5 xv.

National Insurance (Hospital In-patients) Amendment Regulations, 1957. Report of the National Insurance Advisory Committee
Session 1957-58 HC. 2 xv.

National Insurance (Unemployment and Sickness Benefit) Amendment (No. 2) Regulations, 1957. Report of the National Insurance Advisory Committee
Session 1957-58 HC. 3 xv.

National Insurance (General Benefit) Amendment Regulations, 1957. Report of the National Insurance Advisory Committee
Session 1957-58 HC. 4 xv.

National Insurance (Widow's Benefit and Retirement Pensions) Amendment (No. 2) Regulations 1957. Report of the National Advisory Committee
Session 1957-58 HC. 12 xv.

National Insurance (New Entrants' Transitional) Amendment (No. 2) Regulations, 1957. Report of the National Insurance Advisory Committee
Session 1957-58 HC. 25 xv.

National Insurance (General Benefit) Amendment (No. 2) Regulations, 1957. Report of the National Insurance Advisory Committee
Session 1957-58 HC. 26 xv.

National Insurance (Increase of Benefit and Miscellaneous Provisions) Amendment Regulations, 1957. Report of the National Insurance

Advisory Committee
Session 1957-58 HC. 33 xv.

National Insurance (Death Grant, Consequential Provisions) Regulations, 1957. Report of the National Insurance Advisory Committee
Session 1957-58 HC. 37 xv.

National Insurance (Classification) Amendment Regulations, 1957. Report of the National Insurance Advisory Committee
Session 1957-58 HC. 35 xv.

National Insurance (Contributions) Amendment (No. 2) Regulations, 1957. Report of the National Insurance Advisory Committee
Session 1957-58 HC. 36 xv.

1958   National Insurance (Mariners) Amendment Regulations, 1958. Report of the National Insurance Advisory Committee
Session 1957-58 HC. 257 xv.

National Insurance (New Entrants Transitional) Amendment Regulations, 1958. Reports of the National Insurance Advisory Committee
Session 1957-58 HC. 258 xv.

National Insurance (Determination of Claims and Questions) Amendment Regulations, 1958. Report of the National Insurance Advisory Committee
Session 1957-58 HC. 184 xv.

National Insurance (Residents and Persons Abroad) Amendment Regulations, 1958. Report of the National Insurance Advisory Committee
Session 1957-58 HC. 230 xv.

National Insurance (New Entrants Transitional) Amendment (No. 2) Regulations, 1958. Report of the National Insurance Advisory Committee
Session 1958-59 HC. 37 xvi.

National Insurance and Industrial Injuries (Collection of Contributions) Amendment Regulations, 1958. Report of the National Insurance Advisory Committee
Session 1958-59 HC. 74 xvi.

1959   Draft of the National Insurance (Earnings) Regulations, 1959. Report of the National Insurance Advisory Committee
Session 1958-59 HC. 99 xvi.

Draft of the National Insurance (Mariners) Amendment Regulations, 1959. Report of the National Insurance Advisory Committee
Session 1958-59 HC. 121 xvi.

National Insurance (Unemployment and Sickness Benefit) Amendment Regulations, 1959. Report of the National Insurance Advisory Committee
Session 1958-59 HC. 142 xvi.

National Insurance (Contributions) Amendment Regulations, 1959, and National Insurance (Determination of Claims and Questions) Amendment Regulations, 1959. Report of the National Insurance Advisory Committee
Session 1958-59 HC. 192 xvi.

National Insurance (Overlapping Benefits) Amendment Regulations, 1959. Report of the National Insurance Advisory Committee
Session 1958-59 HC. 264 xvi.

National Insurance (Unemployment and Sickness Benefit) Amendment (No. 2) Regulations 1959. Report of the National Insurance Advisory Committee
Session 1958-59 HC. 265 xvi.

National Insurance (Contributions) Amendment (No. 2) Regulations, 1959. Report of the National Insurance Advisory Committee
Session 1959-60 HC. 4 xvii.

National Insurance (Non-Participation Benefits and Scheme) Regulations, 1959. Report of the National Insurance Advisory Committee
Session 1959-60 HC. 19 xvii.

EVANS OF HUNGERSHALL, B. Ifor, Lord (continued)

National Insurance (Non-Participation Certificates) Regulations, 1959. Report of the National Insurance Advisory Committee
Session 1959-60 HC. 20 xvii.

National Insurance (Non-Participation Appeals and References) Regulations, 1959. Report of the National Insurance Advisory Committee
Session 1959-60 HC. 49 xvii.

1960   Draft of the National Insurance (Earnings) Regulations, 1960. Report of the National Insurance Advisory Committee
Session 1959-60 HC. 59 xvii.

Long-term hospital patients. Report of the National Insurance Advisory Committee
Session 1959-60 Cmnd. 964 xvii.

National Insurance (Classification) Amendment Regulations, 1960. Report of the National Insurance Advisory Committee
Session 1959-60 HC. 193 xvii.

National Insurance (Unemployment and Sickness Benefit) Amendment Regulations, 1960, and National Insurance (Contributions) Amendment Regulations, 1960. Report of the National Insurance Advisory Committee
Session 1959-60 HC. 183 xvii.

National Insurance (Assessment of Graduated Contributions) Regulations, 1960. Report of the National Insurance Advisory Committee
Session 1959-60 HC. 213 xvii.

National Insurance (Collection of Graduated Contributions) Regulations, 1960. Report of the National Insurance Advisory Committee
Session 1959-60 HC. 214 xvii.

National Insurance (Non-Participation Assurance of Equivalent Pension Benefits) Regulations, 1960. Report of the National Insurance Advisory Committee
Session 1959-60 HC. 236 xvii.

National Insurance (Non-Participation Benefits and Schemes) Amendment Regulations, 1960. Report of the National Insurance Advisory Committee
Session 1959-60. HC. 237 xvii.

National Insurance (Graduated Contributions and Non-Participating Employments Miscellaneous Provisions) Regulations, 1960. Report of the National Insurance Advisory Committee
Session 1959-60 HC. 265 xvii.

Draft of the National Insurance (Married Women) Amendment Regulations, 1960. Report of the National Insurance Advisory Committee
Session 1959-60 HC. 282 xvii.

Doctors' and Midwives' Certificates for National Insurance Purposes. Report of the National Insurance Advisory Committee
Session 1959-60 Cmnd. 1021 xvii.

National Insurance (General Benefit) Amendment Regulations, 1960. National Insurance (Contributions) Amendment (No. 2) Regulations, 1960. Report of the National Insurance Advisory Committee
Session 1959-60 HC. 275 xvii.

National Insurance (Hospital In-Patients) Amendment Regulations, 1960. Report of the National Insurance Advisory Committee
Session 1959-60 HC. 276 xvii.

National Insurance (Unemployment and Sickness Benefit) Amendment (No. 2) Regulations, 1960. Report of the National Insurance Advisory Committee
Session 1959-60 HC. 277 xvii.

Draft of the National Insurance (Mariners) Amendment Regulations, 1960. Report of the National Insurance Advisory Committee
Session 1960-61 HC. 21 xviii.

1961   National Insurance (Non-Participation Benefits and Schemes) Amendment Regulations, 1961. Report of the National Insurance Advisory Committee
Session 1960-61 HC. 44 xviii.

National Insurance (Non-Participation, Continuity of Employment) Regulations, 1961. Report the National Insurance Advisory Committee
Session 1960-61 HC. 45 xviii.

National Insurance (Classification) Amendment Regulations, 1961. Report of the National Insurance Advisory Committee
Session 1960-61 HC. 139 xviii.

National Insurance (Graduated Retirement Benefit and Consequential Provisions) Regulations, 1961. Report of the National Insurance Advisory Committee
Session 1960-61 HC. 156 xviii.

National Insurance (Collection of Graduated Contributions) Amendment Regulations, 1961. Report of the National Insurance Advisory Committee
Session 1960-61 HC. 157 xviii.

National Insurance (Contributions) Amendment Regulations, 1961. Report of the National Insurance Advisory Committee
Session 1960-61 HC. 203 xviii.

Pensions increments for wives and widows. Report of the National Insurance Advisory Committee
Session 1960-61 Cmnd. 1384 xviii.

National Insurance (Non-Participation Assurance of Equivalent Pension Benefits) Amendment Regulations, 1961. Report of the National Insurance Advisory Committee
Session 1960-61 HC. 266 xviii.

National Insurance (Non-Participation certificates) Amendment Regulations, 1961. Report of the National Insurance Advisory Committee
Session 1961-62 HC. 12 xvii.

National Insurance (Members of the Forces) Amendment Regulations, 1961. Report of the National Insurance Advisory Committee
Session 1961-62 HC. 33 xvii.

Draft of the National Insurance (Married Women) Amendment Regulations, 1961. Report of the National Insurance Advisory Committee
Session 1961-62 HC. 24 xvii.

National Insurance (General Benefit) Amendment Regulations, 1961. Report of the National Insurance Advisory Committee
Session 1961-62 HC. 37 xvii.

1962   National Insurance (Contribution) Amendment Regulations, 1962. Report of the National Insurance Advisory Committee
Session 1961-62 HC. 107 xvii.

National Insurance (Contribution) Amendment (No. 2) Regulations, 1962. Report of the National Insurance Advisory Committee
Session 1961-62 HC. 200 xvii.

National Insurance (Assessment of Graduated Contributions) Amendment Regulations, 1962. Report of the National Insurance Advisory Committee
Session 1961-62 HC. 261 xvii.

National Insurance (Collection of Graduated Contributions) Amendment Regulations, 1962. Report of the National Insurance Advisory Committee
Session 1962-63 HC. 1 xx.

1963   Draft of the National Insurance (Earnings) Regulations, 1963. Report of the National Insurance Advisory Committee
Session 1962-63 HC. 163 xx.

National Insurance (Contributions) Amendment Regulations, 1963; National Insurance (New Entrants Transitional) Amendment Regulations, 1963. Report of the National Insurance Advisory Committee
Session 1962-63 HC. 165 xx.

1964   National Insurance (Claims and Payments) Amendment Regulations, 1964. Report of the National Insurance Advisory Committee
Session 1963-64 HC. 281 xv.

National Insurance (Unemployment and Sickness Benefit) Amendment Regulations, 1964. Report of the National Insurance Advisory Committee
Session 1963-64 HC. 282 xv.

Time limits for claiming sickness benefit. Report of the National Insurance Advisory Committee
Session 1963-64 Cmnd. 2400 xv.

National Insurance (Continental Shelf) Regulations, 1964. Report of the National Insurance Advisory Committee
Session 1963-64 HC. 23 xv.

1967   National Insurance (Determination of Claims and Questions) Amendment Regulations, 1967. Report of the National Insurance Advisory Committee
Session 1966-67 HC. 343 xxxviii.

National Insurance (Overlapping Benefits) Amendment Regulations, 1967. Report of the National Insurance Advisory Committee
Session 1966-67 HC. 411 xxxviii.

National Insurance (Determination of Claims and Questions) Amendment (No. 2) Regulations, 1967. Report of the National Insurance Advisory Committee
Session 1966-67 HC. 412 xxxviii.

National Insurance (Mariners) Amendment Regulations, 1967. Report of the National Insurance Advisory Committee
Session 1966-67 HC. 439 xxxviii.

National Insurance (Earnings) Regulations, 1967. Report of the National Insurance Advisory Committee
Session 1966-67 HC. 441 xxxviii.

National Insurance (Residence and Persons Abroad) Amendment Regulations, 1967. Report of the National Insurance Advisory Committee
Session 1966-67 HC. 491 xxxviii.

National Insurance (Claims and Payments) Amendment Regulations, 1967. Report of the National Insurance Advisory Committee
Session 1966-67 HC. 602 xxxviii.

Earnings limit for retirement pensions. Report of the National Insurance Advisory Committee
Session 1966-67 Cmnd. 3197 xxxviii.

National Insurance (Computation of Earnings) Regulations, 1967. Report of the National Insurance Advisory Committee
Session 1966-67 Cmnd. 3288 xxxviii.

1968   National Insurance (Members of the Forces) Regulations, 1968. Report of the National Insurance Advisory Committee
Session 1967-68 HC. 267 xxv.

Conditions for unemployment benefit and contributions credits for occupational pensioners. Report of the National Insurance Advisory Committee
Session 1967-68 Cmnd. 3545 xxv.

National Insurance (Classification) Amendment Regulations, 1968. Report of the National Insurance Advisory Committee
Session 1967-68 Cmnd. 3798 xli.

Time limits for obtaining payments of benefit. Report of the National Insurance Advisory Committee
Session 1967-68 Cmnd. 3591 xxv.

1969   National Insurance (Claims and Payments) Amendment (No. 2) Regulations, 1969. Report of the National Insurance Advisory Committee
Session 1968-69 HC. 190 xxxv.

1970   National Insurance (Classification) Amendment Regulations, 1970. Report of the National Insurance Advisory Committee
Session 1969-70 HC. 150 xxvii.

National Insurance and Industrial Injuries (Stamps) Regulations, 1970. Report of the National Insurance Advisory Committee
Session 1969-70 HC. 202 xxvii.

National Insurance (Occupational Pensioners) (Unemployment Benefit) Regulations, 1970. Report of the National Insurance Advisory Committee
Session 1969-70 HC. 211 xxvii.

National Insurance (Classification) Amendment (No. 2) Regulations, 1970. Report of the National Insurance Advisory Committee
Session 1970-71 HC. 163 xlix.

National Insurance (Collection of Graduated Contributions) Regulations, 1970. Report of the National Insurance Advisory Committee
Session 1970-71 HC. 179 xlix.

1971   National Insurance (Married Women) Amendment Regulations, 1971. Report of the National Insurance Advisory Committee
Session 1970-71 HC. 337 xlix.

National Insurance (Unemployment and Sickness Benefit) Amendment Regulations, 1971. Report of the National Insurance Advisory Committee
Session 1970-71 HC. 394 xlix.

National Insurance and Industrial Injuries (Collection of Contributions) Amendment Regulations, 1971. Report of the National Insurance Advisory Committee
Session 1970-71 HC. 447 xlix.

National Insurance (General Benefit) Amendment Regulations, 1971. Report of the National Insurance Advisory Committee
Session 1970-71 HC. 452 xlix.

National Insurance (Classification) Amendment Regulations, 1971. Report of the National Insurance Advisory Committee
Session 1971-72 HC. 6 xxxviii.

EVANS, A. M.
1974   Shiftworking in the motor industry; detailed study and assessment. Report of the manpower working party of the Motor Manufacturing E.D.C.
N.E.D.O.

Shiftworking in the motor industry; summary report
N.E.D.O.

EVANS, B. M.
1967   Investigation into a difference between the Film Artistes' Association and the Film Production Association of Great Britain over the operation

EVANS, B. M. (*continued*)

of the employment agency for crowd artistes known as Central Castings Ltd. Report of a Committee
M. of Labour

EVANS, F. J.

1967   Cairngorm area. Report of the technical group on the Cairngorm area of the eastern highlands of Scotland. Repr. 1969
Scottish Development D.

1972   Trossachs study. The Trossachs report
Countryside Commission for Scotland

EVANS, Geoffrey, Sir

1948   British Guiana and British Honduras. Report of the settlement commission
Session 1948 Cmd. 7533 i.

EVANS, Myrddin-, G., Sir

See MYRDDIN-EVANS, G., Sir

EVANS, H. J.

1974   Service to sport; the story of the C.C.P.R.. 1935-1972
Sports Council

EVANS, I., Sir

See EVANS OF HUNGERSHALL, B. I., Lord

EVANS, K. W.

1978   Common land; preparations for comprehensive legislation. Report of an interdepartmental working party, 1975-77
D. of the Environment

EVANS, Timothy John

See BRABIN, D. J., Sir and HENDERSON, J. S.

EVE, M. T., Sir

See SILSOE, M. T., Lord

EVERSHED, F. Raymond, Lord

1945   Port transport industry. Report of a committee on investigation on a difference between employers and workpeople regarding the national minimum wage and the pieceworkers' minimum guarantee
M. of Labour and National Service

1945   Cotton spinning industry. Report of a commission set up to review the wages arrangements and methods of organisation of work
M. of Labour and National Service

1946   Cotton spinning industry. Supplement: Appendix IV—mule-spinners' wages. Report by the chairman of the commission
M. of Labour and National Service

1947   Cotton textile machinery industry. Committee of investigation
Interim report
Second and final report
M. of Supply

1949   Supreme Court practice and procedure. Interim report of the committee
Session 1948-49 Cmd. 7764 xiv.

1951   Supreme Court practice and procedure. 2nd interim report
Session 1950-51 Cmd. 8176 xvi.

1952   Supreme Court practice and procedure. 3rd interim report: Durham Palatine Court
Session 1951-52 Cmd. 8617 xvi.

1953   Supreme Court practice and procedure. Final report
Session 1952-53 Cmd. 8878 xiv.

1954   London Docks. Court of inquiry into a dispute in London Docks
Interim report
Session 1953-54 Cmd. 9302 xv.
Final report
Session 1953-54 Cmd. 9310 xv.

EVERSLEY, David Edward C.

1976   Growth of planning research since the early 1960s
Social Science Research Council

EXETER, D. G. B., Marquis of

1954   United Kingdom industrial delegation to Burma. Report
Board of Trade

EXETER, R. C., Bishop of

See MORTIMER, R. C., Bishop of Exeter

EXTON-SMITH, A. N.

1970   Nutrition of the elderly. Report by the panel (Reports on public health and medical subjects No. 123)
D. of Health and Social Security

1972   Nutrition survey of the elderly. Report by the panel (Reports on health and social subjects, No. 3)
D. of Health and Social Security
See also BROTHERSON, J. H. F.

EYERS, B. J.

1977   Dairy herd management; the cost of handling manure. Report of the farm waste committee, West Midland Region
M. of Agriculture, Fisheries and Food

FABER, Oscar

1943   Reinforced concrete structures. Report by a committee. (Post-war building studies No. 8)
M. of Works

FAIRLIE, H.

1969   Pupils' progress record. Report of a working party
Scottish Education D.

1974   Communication and implementation of aims in secondary education. Report of a working party
Scottish Education D.

FAIRWEATER, Hubert M.

1946   Codes of practice. Civil engineering, public works building and constructional work. Report of the committee. 3rd report.
M. of Works, published 1948

See also HINDLEY, Clement, Sir

FALK, Roger, Sir

1977   Agriculture into the 1980s: land use. Report of the land use group of the Agriculture E.D.C.
N.E.D.O.

FALVEY, D. J.
1968   Market—the world. A study of success in export-ing. Report of a working party of the Mechani-cal Engineering E.D.C.
N.E.D.O.

FARINGDON, A. G., Lord
1947   Appearance of housing estates. Report of a sub-committee of the Central Housing Advisory Committee
M. of Health

FARLEIGH HOSPITAL INQUIRY
See WATKINS, T.

FARQUAHARSON-LANG, W. M.
1966   Administrative practice of hospital boards in Scotland. Report of a committee of the Health Services Council
Scottish Home and Health D.

FARRER, M. I.
1968   Relieving nurses of non-nursing duties in general and maternity hospitals. Report by the sub-com-mittee of the Standing Nursing Advisory Com-mittee. Central Health Services Council
D. of Health and Social Security

FARRER-BROWN, Leslie
1968   Committee on research and development in modern languages. 1st report
D. Education and Science
1971   Committee on research and development in modern languages. 2nd report.
D. of Education and Science

FAULKNER, P., Sir
1953   Prevention of pollution of the sea by oil. Report of the committee
M. of Transport
1959   Safety of nuclear-powered merchant ships. Report of the committee
Session 1959-60 Cmnd. 958 xix.

FAULKS, Neville, Sir
1974   Defamation. Interim report of the committee
Session 1974 Cmnd. 5571 vii.
1975   Defamation. Report of the committee
Session 1974-75 Cmnd. 5909 xv.

FAY, Edgar Stewart
1960   Report of the investigation into the affairs of General London Urban Properties Ltd.
Board of Trade
1968   Report of inquiry in respect of the objections to the proposed amalgamation of the police areas of the County of Essex and the County Borough of Southend-on-Sea
Session 1967-68 Cmnd. 3500 xxx.
1977   Committee of inquiry into the circumstances which led to the Crown Agents requesting finan-cial assistance from the Government in 1974. Report
Session 1977-78 HC. 48 viii.

FEATHERSTONE, J. M.
1977   Trading with Europe; through transport and the total export concept. Through transport study group of the International Freight Movement E.D.C.
N.E.D.O.

FEDDEN, A. H. Roy, Sir
1974   A college of aeronautics. Report of the inter-departmental committee on the establishment of a school of aeronautical science
M. of Aircraft Production

FEILDEN, G. B. R.
1963   Engineering design. Report of a committee appointed by the Council for Scientific and Industrial Research to consider the present stand-ing of mechanical engineering design
D. of Scientific and Industrial Research

FENTEM, P. H.
1978   The case for exercise
Sports Council

FERGUSON, I., Sir
    See BRIDGES, E., Lord, 1962

FERGUSON, Thomas
1950   Monocular blindness. Report of a sub-committee of the Scientific Advisory Committee
D. of Health for Scotland
1968   The carcinogenic action of mineral oils; a chemical and biological study. Carcinogenic Action of Mineral Oils Committee. (Special report series No. 306)
Medical Research Council

FERGUSON, W. K.
1968   Modern studies for school leavers; suggestions for courses other than those leading to the Scot-tish Certificate of Education. (Consultative com-mittee on the curriculum papers No. 3)
Scottish Education D.

FERGUSSON, Donald
1942   Agricultural improvement council for England and Wales. 1st report
M. of Agriculture and Fisheries

FEVERSHAM, C. W. S., Earl of
1960   Human artificial insemination. Report of the departmental committee
Session 1959-60 Cmnd. 1105 ix.

FFORDE, Arthur, Sir
1946   Cement costs. Report by the committee
M. of Works

FIDDES, R. G.
1972   Data transmission; the future. The development of data transmission to meet future users' needs
N.E.D.O.

FIELD, F. E.
1962   Control of public expenditure in Grenada during 1961 and subsequently. Report of the commission of inquiry
Session 1961-62 Cmnd. 1735 xi.

FIELD-FISHER, T. G.
1974   Care and supervision provided in relation to Maria Colwell. Report of the committee of inquiry
D. of Health and Social Security

FIGGURES, Frank, Sir
1973   Industrial review to 1977; motors. Motor industry review group
N.E.D.O.

    Anomalies arising out of the pay standstill of November 1972. (Pay Board advisory report No.1)
Session 1972-73 Cmnd. 5429 xxx.

FIGGURES, Frank, Sir (continued)

1974   Problems of pay relativities. (Pay Board advisory report No. 2)
Session 1973-74 Cmnd. 5535 x.

Relative pay of mineworkers. (Pay Board special report)
Session 1974 Cmnd. 5567 xiv.

Criteria and methods for determining the pay of the science group in the Civil Service. (Pay Board advisory report, 3)
Session 1974. Cmnd. 5602 xiv.

London weighting. (Pay Board advisory report, 4)
Session 1974 Cmnd. 5660 xiv.

FINCH, J. C. Wynne-
See WYNNE-FINCH, J. C.

FINCH, S.
See MORTON-WILLIAMS, R., 1968

FINER, M.

1974   One-parent families. Report of the committee. 2 vols.
Session 1974 Cmnd. 5629 xiv.

FINLAY-MAXWELL, D.

1971   Cost of labour turnover in the wool textile industry. Wool Textile E.D.C.
N.E.D.O.

FISH, Hugh

1977   Desalination, 1977. Report of the standing technical committee on water treatment. (Standing technical committee reports No. 6)
D. of the Environment

FISHER, Geoffrey Francis, Archbishop of Canterbury, 1945-61

1945   Episcopal Pensions Measure. 92nd report by the Ecclesiastical Committee
Session 1944-45 HC. 79 iv; HL. 30

Incumbents (Disability) Measure. 93rd report by the Ecclesiastical Committee
Session 1944-45 HC. 81 iv; HL. 32

1946   Benefices (Suspension of Presentation) Measure. 94th report by the Ecclesiastical Committee
Session 1945-46 HC. 120 x; HL. 75

Ecclesiastical Commissioners (Curate Grants) Measure. 95th report by the Ecclesiastical Committee
Session 1945-46 HC. 122 x; HL. 77

Clergy Pensions (Supplementary Pensions) Measure. 96th report by the Ecclesiastical Committee
Session 1945-46 HC. 124 x; HL. 79

Incumbents (Discipline) Measure. 97th report by the Ecclesiastical Committee
Session 1945-46 HC. 174 x; HL. 131

Church Commissioners Measure. 98th report by the Ecclesiastical Commission
Session 1946-47 HC. 3 x; HL. 7

1947   Parsonages (Amendment) Measure. 99th report by the Ecclesiastical Committee
Session 1946-47 HC. 95 x; HL. 67

Clergy Pensions Measure. 100th report by the Ecclesiastical Committee
Session 1947-48 HC. 22 x; HL. 34

1949   Parochial Church Councils (Powers) (Amendment) Measure. 101st report by the Ecclesiastical Committee
Session 1948-49 HC. 97 xii; HL. 59

Church Dignitaries (Retirement) Measure. 102nd report by the Ecclesiastical Committee
Session 1948-49 HC. 99 xii; HL. 61

Pastoral Reorganisation Measure. 103rd report by the Ecclesiastical Committee
Session 1948-49 HC. 119 xii; HL. 73

Benefices (Suspension of Presentation) Measure, 1946 (Amendment) Measure. 104th report by the Ecclesiastical Committee
Session 1948-49 HC. 226 xii; HL. 161

Reorganisation Areas Measure, 1944 (Amendment) Measure. 105th report by the Ecclesiastical Committee
Session 1948-49 HC. 295 xii; HL. 210

1950   Incumbents (Discipline) Measure, 1947 (Amendment) Measure. 106th report by the Ecclesiastical Committee
Session 1950 HC. 115 vii; HL. 81

1951   Ecclesiastical Dilapidations Measures, 1923 to 1929 (Amendment) Measure. 109th report by the Ecclesiastical Committee
Session 1950-51 HC. 167 x; HL. 52

Cathedrals (Appointed Commissions) Measure. 110th report by the Ecclesiastical Committee
Session 1950-51 HC. 169 x; HL. 54

Benefices (Stabilisation of Incomes) Measure. 111th report by the Ecclesiastical Committee
Session 1950-51 HC. 171 x; HL. 56

1952   Church of England Pensions Board (Powers) Measure. 112th report by the Ecclesiastical Committee
Session 1951-52 HC. 127 viii; HL. 37

Union of Benefices (Disused Churches) Measure. 113th report by the Ecclesiastical Committee
Session 1952-53 HC. 9 viii; HL. 4

1953   Diocesan Stipends Funds Measure. 114th report by the Ecclesiastical Committee
Session 1952-53 HC. 120 viii; HL. 38

Incumbents (Discipline) and Church Dignitaries (Retirement) Amendment Measure. 115th report by the Ecclesiastical Committee
Session 1952-53 HC. 122 viii; HL. 40

Archdeaconries (Augmentation) Measure. 116th report by the Ecclesiastical Committee
Session 1952-53 HC. 173 viii; HL. 68

Benefices (Suspension of Presentation) Measure. 117th report by the Ecclesiastical Committee
Session 1952-53 HC. 293 viii; HL. 125

1954   New Housing Areas (Church Buildings) Measure. 118th report by the Ecclesiastical Committee
Session 1953-54 HC. 84 x; HL. 45

Reorganisation Areas Measure, 1944 (Amendment) Measure. 119th report by the Ecclesiastical Committee
Session 1953-54 HC. 86 x; HL. 47

Cathedrals (Grants) Measure. 120th report by the Ecclesiastical Committee
Session 1953-54 HC. 88 x; HL. 49

Clergy Pensions Measure. 121st report by the Ecclesiastical Committee
Session 1953-54 HC. 214 x; HL. 144

Inspection of Churches Measure. 122nd report by the Ecclesiastical Committee
Session 1954-55 HC. 10 iv; HL. 5

1955   Diocesan Education Committees Measure. 123rd report by the Ecclesiastical Committee
Session 1955-56 HC. 130 xi; HL. 130

Representation of the Laity Measure. 124th report by the Ecclesiastical Committee
Session 1955-56 HC. 276 xi; HL. 115

1956   Parochial Church Councils (Powers) Measure. 125th report by the Ecclesiastical Committee
Session 1955-56 HC. 278 xi; HL. 117

FISHER, Geoffrey Francis, Archbishop of Canterbury *(continued)*

1957   Channel Islands (Church Legislation) Measure, 1931 (Amendment) Measure. 126th report by the Ecclesiastical Committee
Session 1956-57 HC. 185 ix; HL. 84

Church Schools (Assistance by Church Commissioners) Measure. 127th report by the Ecclesiastical Commission
Session 1957-58 HC. 45 viii; HL. 23

Church Funds Investment Measure. 128th report by the Ecclesiastical Committee
Session 1957-58 HC. 46 viii; HL. 25

1959   Truro Cathedral Measure. 129th report by the Ecclesiastical Committee
Session 1958-59 HC. 84 ix; HL. 62

Vacancies in Sees Measure. 130th report by the Ecclesiastical Committee
Session 1958-59 HC. 111 ix; HL. 72

Guildford Cathedral Measure. 131st report by the Ecclesiastical Committee
Session 1958-59 HC. 110 ix; HL. 74

1960   Church Property (Miscellaneous Provisions) Measure. 132nd report by the Ecclesiastical Committee
Session 1959-60 HC. 159 ix; HL. 71

Farnham Castle Measure. 133rd report by the Ecclesiastical Committee
Session 1960-61 HC. 18 ix; HL. 12

1961   Baptismal Registers Measure. 134th report by the Ecclesiastical Committee
Session 1960-61 HC. 228 ix; HL. 97

FISHER, H.

1973   Abuse of social security benefits. Report of the committee
Session 1972-73 Cmnd. 5228 xxxiii.

FISHER, Henry, Sir

1977   Inquiry into circumstances leading to the trial of three persons on charges arising out of the death of Maxwell Confait and the fire at 27 Doggett Road, London SE6. Report
Session 1977-78 HC. 90 xx.

FISHER, M. G.

1952   Scottish local government law. Consolidation committee
         1st report. Session 1952-53 Cmd. 8729 xv.
         2nd report. Session 1952-53 Cmd. 8751 xv.
         3rd report. Session 1953-54 Cmd. 8993 xvi.

FISHER, Nigel T. L.

1963   Report of the Bahamas constitutional conference, held in London, May 1963
Session 1962-63 Cmnd. 2048 x.

FISHER, P.

1975   Management training in industrial relations. Report of the working group of the Management Education, Training and Development Committee. N.E.D.O.

FISHWICK, F.

1974   Shiftworking in the motor industry; detailed study and assessment. Motor Manufacturing Economic Development Committee
N.E.D.O.

FITZGERALD, J.

1958   " Crush hour " travel in central London. Report of the first year's work of the committee for staggering of working hours in central London
M. of Transport and Civil Aviation

FITZGERALD, Maurice

1939   Valuation for rates. Report of the departmental committee. August 1939, published 1944
M. of Health

FITZGERALD, T.

1948   Civil services of Northern Rhodesia and Nyasaland, 1947. Part 1
Crown Agent
Civil services of Northern Rhodesia and Nyasaland, 1947. Part 2
Colonial Office

FITZGERALD, W. J., Sir

1950   Disorders in the Eastern provinces of Nigeria. Report of the commission of inquiry
Colonial Office

FLANDERS, Allan D.

1964   Report of an inquiry into the causes and circumstances of a difference over the appointment of dock foremen at Southampton Docks
M. of Labour

1965   Report of a committee of investigation into the Bristol and Avonmouth docks dispute
M. of Labour

FLECK, Alexander, Lord

1955   National Coal Board. Report of the Advisory committee on organisation
National Coal Board

1957   Atomic Energy. Report of the committee appointed to examine the organisation of certain parts of the United Kingdom Atomic Energy Authority
Session 1957-58 Cmnd. 338 vii.

Atomic Energy Authority. Report of the committee appointed to examine the organisation for control of health and safety in the United Kingdom Atomic Energy Authority
Session 1957-58 Cmnd. 342 vii.

1958   Windscale piles. Final report of the committee appointed to make a technical evaluation of information relating to the design and operation of the Windscale piles and to review the factors involved in the controlled release of Wigner energy
Session 1957-58 Cmnd. 471 vii.

1960   Fishing industry. Report of the committee of inquiry
Session 1960-61 Cmnd. 1266 xv.

1965   Radio astronomy. Report of the committee
Science Research Council

FLEMING, Arthur P. M., Sir

1948   Technical and scientific register. Present and future supply and demand for persons with professional qualifications in electrical engineering. Electrical engineering panel of the engineering sub-committee. Report
M. of Labour and National Service

FLEMING, D. P., Lord

1943   Abolition of tuition fees in grant-aided secondary schools. Special report of the committee on public schools
Board of Education

1944   Public schools and the general educational system. Report of the committee
M. of Education

FLETCHER, B. A.

1951   Youth leaders and community centre wardens.

FLETCHER, B. A. *(continued)*

2nd report of the national advisory council on the training and supply of teachers
M. of Education

FLOWERS, Brian Hilton, Sir

1966 Report of a joint working group on computers for research
Session 1965-66 Cmnd. 2883 v.

1974 Pollution control; progress and problems. 4th report of the Royal Commission on Environmental Pollution
Session 1974-75 Cmnd. 5780 ix.

1976 Air pollution control; an integrated approach. 5th report of the Royal Commission on Environmental Pollution
Session 1975-76 Cmnd. 6371 xii.

Nuclear power and the environment. 6th report of the Royal Commission on Environmental Pollution
Session 1975-76 Cmnd. 6618 xii.

FOGARTY, S. W.

1978 Lead pollution in Birmingham. Report of the working party (Pollution paper No. 14)
Central Unit on Environmental Pollution

FONTAINE, B. L. S.

1969 Management training in the distributive trades. Distributive Trades Economic Development Committee
N.E.D.O.

FOOT, M. R. D.

1976 S.O.E. in France; an account of the work of the British Special Operations Executive in France. 1940-1944
Cabinet Office

FORBES, A. F., Sir

1955 Development in the iron and steel industry, 1953-1958. Report of the Iron and Steel Board
Session 1954-55 HC. 49 vi.

1957 Development in the iron and steel industry. Special report by the Iron and Steel Board
Session 1956-57 HC. 214 xv.

FORBES, H.

1972 The registration of builders. Report of an inquiry.
D. of the Environment

FORESTIER-WALKER, G. F., Sir

See LLEWELYN-DAVIES, R., Lord

FORSTER OF HARRABY, John, Lord

Coal mining industry. Committee on the recruitment of juveniles
1942   First report
1943   Supplemental report
M. of Fuel and Power

1946 Omnibus industry. Report by a court of inquiry into a difference between the two sides of the National Council for the Omnibus Industry on the trade union application for a national wages and conditions agreement
Session 1945-46 Cmd. 6796 xiv.

Trawler fishing industry. Report of a court of inquiry into the circumstances and causes of the stoppage of work in the trawler fishing industry
Session 1945-46 Cmd. 6882 xii.

Smithfield market. Report of a court of inquiry set up to inquire whether there are future causes of industrial unrest amongst the workers concerned likely to affect the smooth and efficient running of Smithfield Market
Session 1945-46 Cmd. 6932 xiii.

Port Transport industry. Report of an inquiry
M. of Labour and National Service

1947 Report by a court of inquiry into the difference that has arisen between the Shipbuilding Employers' Federation and the Confederation of Shipbuilding and Engineering Unions' claim for a 40-hour week of five days
Session 1946-47 Cmd. 7036 xiv.

Savoy Hotel Ltd. Report of a court of inquiry into the causes and circumstances of a dispute between the Savoy Hotel and members of the National Union of General and Municipal Workers
Session 1947-48 Cmd. 7266 xiv.

1948 Report of a court of inquiry into disputes between the National Coal Board and the National Union of Colliery Winding Enginemen
Session 1947-48 HC. 47 x.

Report of a court of inquiry appointed to inquire into a dispute between the Engineering and Allied Employers' National Federation and the Confederation of Shipbuilding and Engineering Unions
Session 1947-48 Cmd. 7511 xi.

British Broadcasting Corporation and Musicians' Union. Report of the independent committee on minimum fees for casual studio broadcasts and to examine and make recommendations on certain other questions
M. of Labour and National Service

1949 Railways conciliation and salaried grades. Report of the board of conciliation
M. of Labour and National Service

Railway shopmen. Report of a board of conciliation
M. of Labour and National Service

1950 Catering Wages Commission. Report of an inquiry into the operations of the Catering Wages Act, 1943, in the hotel industry
Session 1950 Cmd. 8004 vi.

1952 Association football. Report of a committee of investigation into a difference regarding the terms and conditions of Association Football players
M. of Labour and National Service

Report of a court of inquiry into a dispute between D. C. Thomson & Co. Ltd., and certain workpeople, members of the National Society of Operative Printers and Assistants
Session 1951-52 Cmd. 8607 xv.

1953 Report of a court of inquiry into the dispute between the Austin Motor Co. Ltd., and certain workpeople, members of the National Union of Vehicle Builders
Session 1952-53 Cmd. 8839 xiii.

1955 Report of a court of inquiry into a dispute between members of the Newspaper Proprietors' Association and members of the Amalgamated Engineering Union and the Electrical Trades Union
Session 1954-55 Cmd. 9439 v.

1956 Report of a court of inquiry into the causes and circumstances of disputes between the London Master Printers' Association and the London Typographical Society and the Association of the Correctors of the Press
Session 1955-56 Cmd. 9717 xxi.

1961 Port transport industry. Objections made to the draft Dock Workers (Regulations of Employment) (Amendment) Order, 1961. Report
M. of Labour

FOSTER, Christopher

1978   Road haulage operators' licensing. Report of the independent committee of inquiry
D. of Transport

FOSTER, John G., Sir

1971   Inquiry into the practice and effects of Scientology
Session 1971-72 HC. 52 xxxvi.

FOSTER, W.

1947   Apprenticeship for coal face workers. Report of the departmental committee
M. of Fuel and Power

FOSTER-SUTTON, Stafford W. P., Sir

1956   Nigeria. Report of the tribunal appointed to inquire into allegations reflecting on the official conduct of the premier of, and certain persons holding ministerial and other public offices in, the eastern region of Nigeria
Session 1956-57 Cmnd. 51 x.

1961   Disturbances in Zanzibar. Report of a commission of inquiry (Colonial No. 353)
Colonial Office

1962   Kenya. Report of the regional boundaries commission
Session 1962-63 Cmnd. 1899 x.

Kenya. Report of the constituencies delimitation commission
Session 1962-63 Cmnd. 1921 x.

FOWLER, R. F.

1951   Cost of living committee. Report of the technical committee
Session 1951-52 Cmd. 8481 ix.

1971   Proposals for retail prices indices for regions. Reports of the retail prices advisory committee and the technical committee on regional prices indices
Session 1970-71 Cmnd. 4749 xlvi.

FOX, W. M.

1977   Leisure and the quality of life; a report on four local experiments
2 volumes
D. of the Environment

FOXELL, J. T.

1952   Monarchs of all they surveyed, the story of the Post Office surveyors
Post Office

FRANCIS, H. E.

1971   Rent Acts. Report of the committee
Session 1970-71 Cmnd. 4609 xxiii.

FRANKLIN, H. W. F.

1951   Prisons, borstal institutions, approved schools and remand homes. Report of a committee to review punishments

        Parts I and II Prisons and borstal institutions
Session 1950-51 Cmd. 8256 xviii.

        Parts III and IV: Approved schools and remand homes
Session 1951-52 Cmd. 8429 xviii.

FRANKLIN, Reginald, Sir

1952   Grain drying and storage in Great Britain. Report of the working party
M. of Agriculture and Fisheries

1953   Quality milk production. Report of the working party
M. of Agriculture and Fisheries

FRANKLYN, Harold, Sir

    Battles, actions and engagements. Official names of the battles, actions and engagements fought by the land forces of the Commonwealth during the 2nd World War, 1939-45. Battles nomenclature committee

1955   Report
1958   Final Report
War Office

FRANKS OF HEADINGTON, Oliver S., Lord

1956-57 Administrative tribunals and enquiries
Report of the committee
Session 1956-57 Cmnd. 218 viii.
Minutes of evidence. 27 days; February 6, 1956-February 21, 1957
Home Office

1972   Section 2 of the Official Secrets Act, 1911. Report of the departmental committee
Vol. 1: Report
Session 1971-72 Cmnd. 5104 xxxvii.
Vol. 2: Written evidence
Vol. 3. Oral evidence
Vol. 4: Oral evidence
Home Office

1977   Register of dependants. Report of the Parliamentary group on the feasibility and usefulness of a register of dependants [of immigrants]
Session 1976-77 Cmnd. 6698 xlii.

FRASER, D. Kennedy

1957   Welfare needs of mentally handicapped persons. Report by a committee of the Scottish council on the welfare of handicapped persons
D. of Health for Scotland

FRASER, Hugh, Sir

1961   Report of the Leeward Islands and Windward Islands constitutional conference held in London in June 1961
Session 1960-61 Cmnd. 1434 x.

       See also MAUDLING, R., 1962

FRASER, John, Sir

1943   Venereal diseases. Report by the medical advisory committee (Scotland)
Session 1943-44 Cmd. 6518 iv.

1946   Laboratory services. Report of the medical advisory committee (Scotland)
D. of Health for Scotland

FRASER, M. W. K.

1974   Handling of complaints against the police. Report of the working group for Scotland
Session 1974-75 Cmnd. 5583 xiv.

1975   Special constables. Report of the working party of the police advisory board for Scotland
Scottish Home and Health D.

FRASER, R. P.

1971   Fowl Pest. Newcastle diseases epidemic, 1970-71. Report of the review panel
Session 1970-71 Cmnd. 4797 v.

1975   Making work more satisfying, prepared by the tripartite steering group on job satisfaction
D. of Employment

FREEMAN, F. L.

1954   Art examinations. Report of the national advisory committee
M. of Education

1957   Art examinations. Report of the national advisory committee on proposed changes in art examinations and the length of the diploma course
M. of Education

FREEMAN, J. C.

1974   Community councils. Report of the committee
Scottish Development D.

FREESON, Reg

1976   Study group on programmes of social ownership and renovation of council dwellings
D. of the Environment

FRENCH, Henry, Sir

1945   Conference on the post-war loaf. Report
Session 1945-46 Cmd. 6701 xii.

1949   Cost of home information services. Report of the committee
Session 1948-49 Cmd. 7836 xxiv.

FRODSHAM, A. F.

1977   Machine tools; the employees' view of the industry. Machine Tools Economic Development Committee
N.E.D.O.

FRYER, R. M.

1977   Training and development of administrators. Preliminary report by the national staff committee for administrative and clerical staff
D. of Health and Social Security

FULLWOOD, N.

1967   Teaching of classics in schools. A report of the working party on the curriculum in Latin and Greek
Scottish Education D.

FULTON OF FALMER, J. S., Lord

1962   Demand and supply of teachers, 1960-1980. 7th report of the National Advisory Council on the Training and Supply of Teachers
M. of Education

Future pattern of the education and training of teachers. 8th report of the National Advisory Council on the Training and Supply of Teachers
M. of Education

1968   The Civil Service
Vol. 1: Report of the committee
Session 1967-68 Cmnd. 3638 xviii.
Vol. 2: Report of a management consultancy group
Vol. 3(1): Surveys and investigations; social survey of the civil service
Vol. 3(2): Surveys and investigations; evidence submitted to the committee, 1966-68
Vol. 4: Factual, statistical and explanatory papers
Vol. 5 (2 parts): Proposals and opinions
Treasury

FYFE, G. Matthew

1957   Mental deficiency in Scotland. Report of the mental health sub-committee
D. of Health for Scotland

FYFE, William Hamilton, Sir

1943   Compulsory day continuation classes. 4th report of the advisory council on education in Scotland
Scottish Education D.

1944   Technical education. Interim report of a special committee of the advisory council on education in Scotland
Session 1944-45 Cmd. 6593 v.

1946   Scottish technical education. Report of a special committee of the advisory council on education in Scotland
Session 1945-46 Cmd. 6786 xi.

Primary education. Report of the advisory council on education in Scotland
Session 1946-47 Cmd. 6973 xi.

FYFE, W. S.

1973   Geochemistry (pure and applied). Report of the working party. In Research in the geological sciences. (Publication series B, No. 7)
Natural Environment Research Council

GAITSKELL, Hugh

1944
and
1946   Survey of international cartels and internal cartels. 2 vols.
D. of Trade, published in 1976

GANE, Dilys

1978   Wool textile industry scheme. An assessment of the effects of selective assistance under the Industry Act, 1972
D. of Industry

GANN, A. S.

1974   Vocational courses in art and design. Report of the working group
D. of Education and Science

GARBETT, Cyril Forster, Archbishop of York, 1942-56

1944   Reorganisation Areas Measure. 90th report by the Ecclesiastical Committee
Session 1943-44 HC. 45 iii; HL. 15

Emergency Legislation Measure. 91st report by the Ecclesiastical Committee
Session 1944-45 HC. 5 iv; HL. 3

1950   Bishops (Retirement) Measure. 108th report by the Ecclesiastical Committee
Session 1950-51 HC. 35 x; HL. 19

Diocesan Education Committees Measure, 1943 (Amendment) Measure. 107th report by the Ecclesiastical Committee
Session 1950-51 HC. 37 x; HL. 20

GARCIA, J. L. B.

1974   Safety of scaffolding. Report
D. of Employment

GARDINER, G. A., Lord

1975   Report of a committee to consider, in the context of civil liberties and human rights, measures to deal with terrorism in Northern Ireland
Session 1974-75 Cmnd. 5874 xxviii.

GARDINER, Thomas, Sir

1951   Organisation, structure and remuneration of the works group of professional civil servants. Report of the committee
Treasury

1952   Organisation, structure and remuneration of the professional accountant class in the civil service. Report of the committee
Treasury

GARDOM, J. W.

See HARVEY, B. H.

GARLICK, J.

See KINGS NORTON, H. R., Lord

GARNER, F. H.

1962   Irrigation in Great Britain. A report by the natural resources (technical) committee
Office of the Minister for Science

GARNER, M. A.

1976   Relationships of government and public in France, West Germany and Sweden. (A study of U.K. nationalised industries background paper No. 2)
N.E.D.O.

GARRETT, A. Wilfred, Sir

1942   Suppression and removal of dust containing silica in the tile-making and electrical porcelain fittings section of the pottery industry. Committee appointed to consider methods. Report
M. of Labour and National Service

1946   Brick industry. Committee on amenities in the brick industry. Report
M. of Works

1950   Tuberculosis and other communicable diseases in relation to nurses and other health workers. Report of the Industrial Injuries Advisory Council
Session 1950-51 Cmd. 8093 xvi.

1952   Time limits. Report of the Industrial Injuries Advisory Council on the time limits for claiming and obtaining payment of benefits under the National Insurance (Industrial Injuries) Act, 1946
Session 1951-52 Cmd. 8511 xv.

1953   Pneumoconiosis. Report of the Industrial Injuries Advisory Council on the method of prescribing pneumoconiosis under the National Insurance (Industrial Injuries) Act, 1946
Session 1952-53 Cmd. 8866 xiv.

1954   Reynaud's phenomenon. Report of the Industrial Injuries Advisory Council on the question whether Reynaud's phenomenon should be prescribed under the National Insurance (Industrial Injuries) Act, 1946
Session 1954-55 Cmd. 9347 vi.

GARRETT, D.

1972   E. H. Austin International Ltd. Report of investigations under the Companies Act
D. of Trade and Industry

1976   E. H. Austin International Ltd. Final report of investigations under the Companies Act
D. of Trade

GARRETT, S. D.

1976   Research in terrestrial microbiology. Report of the working party. (Publications series B, No. 13)
Natural Environment Research Council

GASKIN, Maxwell

1969   North east Scotland; a survey of its development potential
Scottish Development D.

1971   Freight rates and prices in the islands. Report of a study of the impact of freight charges on prices and development in the Western Isles and the Orkney and Shetland Islands
Highlands and Islands Development Board

1976   Scottish construction into the early 1980s. Building and Civil Engineering Economic Development Committee
N.E.D.O.

1978   Economic impact of North Sea oil on Scotland. Final report
Scottish Office

GATER, George H., Sir

1948   Film studio committee. Report
Board of Trade

Building apprenticeship; recruiting and training. Special report of the Building Apprenticeship and Training Council
M. of Works

Recruitment of masons. Special report of the Building Apprenticeship and Training Council
M. of Works

1949   Film production costs. Report of the working party
Board of Trade

1952   Building; training for management. 4th special report of the Building Apprenticeship and Training Council
M. of Works

1953   Building research and development. 2nd report of the advisory council
M. of Works
See also EMMERSON, H., Sir

1956   Methods used by universities of contracting and of recording and controlling expenditure. Report of the sub-committee of the University Grants Committee
Session 1956-57 Cmnd. 9 xix.

GATHERER, W. A.

1967   English in the secondary school—early stages. (Central committee on English bulletin No. 1)
Scottish Education D.

1968   Teaching of literature. (Central committee on English bulletin No 2)
Scottish Education D.

1970   English for the young school leaver. (Central committee on English bulletin No. 3)
Scottish Education D.

1971   English in the secondary school—later stages. (Central committee on English bulletin No. 4)
Scottish Education D.

1972   The teaching of English language. (Central committee on English bulletin No. 5)
Scottish Education D.

GAULD, M. B.

1978   An aims and objectives approach to the teaching of history in SI and SII. Report of the working party of the consultative committee on the curriculum. (Bulletin, 4)
Scottish Education D.

GEDDES, R. C., Lord

1965   Carriers' licensing. Report of the committee
M. of Transport

GEDDES, R. M.

1966   Shipbuilding inquiry committee. Report
Session 1965-66 Cmnd. 2937 vii.

GEDGE, M. L.

Shares of no par value

1954   Minutes of evidence; April 14, 1953 to June 30, 1953
Board of Trade
Report of the committee
Session 1953-54 Cmd. 9112 xix.

GEE, H. G.
1953   Electricity sub-committee of the joint consultative committee. Report
M. of Labour and National Service

GENTLEMAN, Hugh
1971   Scotland's travelling people; problems and solutions. Report by H. Gentleman and S. Swift
Scottish Development D.

GEORGE, T. Neville
1973   Palaeonotology and stratigraphy. Report of the working party. In Research in the geological sciences. (Publications series B, No. 7)
Natural Environment Research Council

GERRARD, A. D.
1952   Murder of Beatrice Alice Rimmer. Inquiry into certain matters arising subsequent to the conviction at Liverpool Assizes on February 27, 1952, of Edward Francis Devlin and Alfred Burns of her murder
Session 1951-52 Cmd. 8522 xxv.

GIBBENS, Edward Brian
1967   Administration of punishment at Court Lees Approved School. Report of inquiry
Session 1966-67 Cmnd. 3367 xxvi.

1968   National Health Service. Findings and recommendations following enquiries into allegations concerning the care of elderly patients in certain hospitals, II: Cowley Road Hospital, Oxford
Session 1967-68 Cmnd. 3687 xxviii.

Report of the public inquiry into the accident at Hixon level crossing on January 6, 1968
Session 1967-68 Cmnd. 3706 xvi.

GIBBON, Michael
1976   Aberconway. Special community review draft proposals
Local Government Boundary Commission for Wales

1978   Borough of Newport. Special community review report and proposals
Local Government Boundary Commission for Wales

Borough of Yns Mon—Isle of Anglesey. Special community review report and proposals
Local Government Boundary Commission for Wales

Carmarthen; special community review draft proposals
Local Government Boundary Commission for Wales

City of Swansea. Special community review report and proposals
Local Government Boundary Commission for Wales

Cynon Valley. Special community review [supplement]
Local Government Boundary Commission for Wales

Dinefwr. Special community review draft proposals
Local Government Boundary Commission for Wales

District of Preseli and the District of South Pembrokeshire. Boundary review report and proposals
Local Government Boundary Commission for Wales

District of South Pembrokeshire and the District of Carmarthen. Boundary review report and proposals
Local Government Boundary Commission for Wales

Islwyn. Special community review draft proposals
Local Government Boundary Commission for Wales

Lliw Valley. Special community review draft proposals
Local Government Boundary Commission for Wales

Preseli. Special community review draft proposals
Local Government Boundary Commission for Wales

Rhymney Valley. Special community review draft proposals
Local Government Boundary Commission for Wales

South Pembrokeshire. Special community review draft proposals
Local Government Boundary Commission for Wales

Torfaen. Special community review draft proposals
Local Government Boundary Commission for Wales

GIBBS, N. H.
1976   History of the Second World War. Grand strategy, vol. 1: Rearmament policy
Cabinet Office

GIBSON, C. W.
1949   Selection of tenants and transfers and exchanges. 3rd report of the housing management sub-committee of the Central Housing Advisory Committee
M. of Health

GIBSON, Donald, Sir
1965   Assessment of new building products. Report of the committee on agreement
M. of Public Building and Works

GIBSON, J. P.
1974   Technology for exploiting offshore oil and gas. Interim report of the working party
D. of Energy

GILBERT, Dennis
1976   Bath environmental capacity study
D. of the Environment

GILL, C. Lovett
1945   Walls, floors and roofs. Report by a committee convened by the Royal Institute of British Architacts. (Post-war building studies No. 15)
M. of Works

GILLENDER, H.
1967   The use of headlamps. Report of the working party on the lighting of motor vehicles
M. of Transport

GILLIATT, W., Sir
  See HOLLAND, E., Sir

GILLIE, Annis
1963   Field work of the family doctor. Report of the sub-committee of the standing medical advisory committee. Central Health Services Council
M. of Health

GILLIE, Blaise

1959   Wales and Monmouthshire. Report on developments and government action for the period July 1, 1957 to December 31, 1958
Session 1958-59 Cmnd. 684 xix.

GILLORAN, J. L.

1973   Community medicine in Scotland. Report of a sub-group of the joint working party on the integration of medical work
Scottish Home and Health D.

    Sexually transmitted diseases. Report of the joint sub-committee of the Scottish Health Services Council
Scottish Home and Health D.

GIRDWOOD, J. G.

    Cost of house-building. Report of the committee of inquiry
1948   1st report
    M. of Health
1950   2nd report
    M. of Health
1952   3rd report
    M. of Health

1953   Cost of house maintenance. Report of the committee of inquiry
M. of Housing and Local Government

GITTINS, C. E.

1968   Primary education in Wales. A report of the Central Advisory Council for Education (Wales)
D. of Education and Science

GLEN, Alexander, Sir

1970   Short sea shipping. The report by the working party of the Movement of Exports Economic Development Committee
N.E.D.O.

GLENNIE, J. F.

    See McLELLAN, A. G.

GLOSSOP, R.

1973   Engineering geology. Report of the working party. In Research in the geological sciences (Publications series B, No. 7)
Natural Environment Research Council

GLOVER, Ian

1978   Manufacturing and management
D. of Industry

GODBER, George E., Sir

1967   Organisation of medical work in hospitals. 1st report of the joint working party
M. of Health

1969   Responsibilities of the consultant grade. Report of the working party
D. of Health and Social Security

1971   All in a working day. A management services (N.H.S.) study
D. of Health and Social Security

    Organisation of the work of junior hospital doctors. A management services (N.H.S.) study commissioned by the joint working party on the organisation of medical work in hospitals
D. of Health and Social Security

1972   Organisation of medical work in hospitals. 2nd report of the joint working party
D. of Health and Social Security

1973   General medical services. Report of the joint working party
D. of Health and Social Security

1974   Organisation of medical work in hospitals. 3rd report of the joint working party
D. of Health and Social Security

1975   Laboratory use of dangerous pathogens. Report of the working party
D. of Health and Social Security

    Nutrition survey of pre-school children, 1967-68. Report by the committee on medical aspects of food policy (Reports on health and social subjects No. 10)
D. of Health and Social Security

GODDARD, R., Lord

1943   Hereford juvenile court inquiry. Report of the tribunal
Session 1942-43 Cmd. 6485 iv.

1945   Longton, Stoke-on-Trent. Procedure at a case heard before two justices at Longton, Stoke-on-Trent. Report of an inquiry into the case of Cecil Basil Whelan
Home Office

1953   Law of civil liability for damage done by animals. Report of the committee
Session 1952-53 Cmd. 8746 xiv.

GODFREY, P.

1973   Rolls-Royce Ltd. Report of investigations under the Companies Act
D. of Trade and Industry

GOLD, D. J.

1974   Shop steward education and training. Report of a working party
Scottish Education D.

GOODALE, Ernest W., Sir

1953   British Industries Fair. Report of the sub-committee to review the present arrangements for the British Industries Fair
Session 1953-54 Cmd. 9013 x.

GOODE, A. P.

1976   A study of some methods of traffic restraint. Report prepared by a DoE working group (Research report, 14)
D. of the Environment

GOODENOUGH, William, Sir

1944   Medical Schools. Report of the inter-departmental committee
M. of Health

GOODISON, R. R.

1962   Aviation kerosene and wide-cut gasoline. Report of the working party (C.A.P. 177)
M. of Aviation

GOODMAN, A. A., Lord

1965   Committee on the London Orchestras. Report
Arts Council

1969   Opera and ballet in the U.K., 1966-69. Report
Arts Council

GOODMAN, N. M.

1959   Convalescent treatment. Report of a working party
M. of Health

GORDON, I. R.
1975   Retirement industry in the south west, a survey
South West Economic Planning Council

GORDON, Mrs. J. Wolridge-
    See **WOLRIDGE-GORDON, Mrs. J.**

GORDON, K.
1947   Petroleum and synthetic oil industry of Germany.
Report by a mission (B.I.O.S. overall report, No. 11)

GORDON-BROWN, A. D.
1974   Handling of complaints against the police. Report of the working group for England and Wales
Session 1974-75 Cmnd. 5582 xiv.

GORELL, R., Lord
1947   Regent's Park Terraces. Report of the committee
Session 1946-47 Cmd. 7094 xiv.

GORELL-BARNES, W. L., Sir
1956   African land tenure in East and Central Africa.
Report of the conference
Colonial Office

GORMAN, William
1946   Printing trades dispute. Report of a court of inquiry into the nature and circumstances of a dispute between the British Federation of Master Printers and the Printing and Kindred Trades Federation
Session 1945-46 Cmd. 6912 xiv.

GOSLING, Arthur H., Sir
1968   Footpaths. Report of the committee
M. of Housing and Local Government

GOSPEL, H.
1972   Employers organisations and industrial relations. (Study No. 1)
Comm.ssion on Industrial Relations

GOULD, Robert M., Sir
    Electricity sub-committee of the joint consultative committee
1947   Report. May 12
1948   Report. June 15
1949   Report, June 23
1950   Report. May 13
1951   Report. August 1
1952   Report. July 1
M. of Labour and National Service

    Cost of living advisory committee
1947   Interim report
Session 1946-47 Cmd. 7077 x.
1951   Interim report
Session 1950-51 Cmd. 8328 xi.

1952   Working of the interim index of retail prices.
Report of the cost of living advisory committee
Session 1951-52 Cmd. 8481 ix.

GOWERS, Ernest A., Sir
1947   Closing hours of shops. Scottish Home Department committee of inquiry
Session 1946-47 Cmd. 7105 xiv.

1949   Health, welfare and safety in non-industrial employment, hours of employment of juveniles.
Report of the committee of inquiry
Session 1948-49 Cmd. 7664 xv.

1950   Houses of outstanding historical or architectural interest. Report of the committee
Treasury

1952   Capital punishment. Royal Commission on Capital Punishment
    Report
    Session 1952-53 Cmd. 8932 vii.
    Minutes of Evidence, 1st to 31st days
    Memoranda and replies to a questionnaire received from foreign and commonwealth countries. 1: Commonwealth countries; 2: United States of America; 3: Europe
Royal Commission on Capital Punishment

1954   Foot-and-mouth disease. Report of the departmental committee
Session 1953-54 Cmd. 9214 xiii.

GRAHAM, A.
1959   Safety, health and welfare conditions in non-ferrous foundries. 2nd report of the joint standing committee: Technical sub-committee report
M. of Labour

GRAHAM, N. W.
1969   Consultative committee on the curriculum. 1st report
Scottish Education D.

GRAHAM HALL, Miss J.
    See **HALL, Miss J. Graham**

GRAHAM-HARRISON, F. L. T.
1965   Police cadets. Report of a working party
Home Office

1974   Bail procedures in magistrates' courts. Report by the working party
Home Office

GRAHAM-WHITE, G. H.
1944   Seamen's welfare in ports. Report of the committee
M. of Labour and National Service

GRAINGER-STEWART, T.
    Supply of teachers in Scotland. Reports of the departmental committee
1950   1st report
    Session 1950-51 Cmd. 8123 xi.
1953   2nd report
    Session 1952-53 Cmd. 8721 ix.
1957   3rd report
    Session 1956-57 Cmnd. 196 x.
    See also: RODGER, A. G.

1954   Structure of further education salaries. Report of a working party
Session 1954-55 Cmd. 9365 iv.

1958   Pensions for the widows, children and dependants of teachers in Scotland. Report of the working party
Session 1957-58 Cmnd. 527 x.

GRANT, Frederick
1953   Purchase tax. Report of the purchase tax (valuation) committee
Session 1952-53 Cmd. 8830 xvi.

GRANT, R. A.
1976   Local housing needs and strategies; case study of the Dundee sub-region
Scottish Development D.

GRANT, W., Lord
1967   The Sheriff Court. Report by the committee
Session 1966-67 Cmnd. 3248 xlviii.

GRAVES, F. C.

1978   Construction for industrial recovery. The role of building and civil engineering in promoting the efficiency of British manufacturing industry. Building and Civil Engineering Economic Development Committee
N.E.D.O.

GRAY, F., Sir

1957   Passage of smolts and kelts through passes. Salmon research committee pass investigation sub-committee report
Scottish Home D.

GRAY, J. Neville

1951   Report on the advisability of extending compulsory registration of title on sale to the County of Surrey
Lord Chancellor's D.

GRAY, P. G.

1960   Rent Act, 1957. Report of inquiry by P. G. Gray and E. Parr
Session 1960-61 Cmnd. 1246 xx.

GRAY, S. M.

1978   The supply of petroleum and petroleum products to Rhodesia
Foreign and Commonwealth Office

GREEN, J.

1974   Waymarking for footpath and bridleway. Report of the waymarking study group
Countryside Commission

GREEN, M. E.

1978   Unemployment benefit; fortnightly attendance and payment. Report by the joint working party
D. of Employment

GREEN, Stephen Lycett, Sir

1963   Recruitment, training and promotion of administrative and clerical staff in the hospital service. Report of the committee of inquiry
M. of Health

GREENE, W. A., Lord

    Coal mining industry. Reports of the board of investigation
1942   Report into the immediate wages issue
1942   Output bonus supplemental report
1943   3rd report
1944   4th and final report: scheme for an output bonus
    M. of Labour and National Service
1943   Wages and machinery for determining wages and conditions of employment in the coal mining industry
M. of Labour and National Service

GREENWOOD OF ROSSENDALE, A. W. J., Lord

1977   Local government staff commission for England. Report
D. of Employment

GREENWOOD, John

1972   Wage payment systems in the clothing industry. Manpower working party
N.E.D.O.

GREGORY, H. S.

1952   Copyright committee. Report
Session 1951-52 Cmd. 8662 ix.

GREGORY, Janet

1978   Parents' attitudes to the hospital service (Research paper, 5)
Royal Commission on the National Health Service

GRESTY, Colin

1956   Drying of moulds by portable dryers. Report of the technical sub-committee of the Joint Standing Committee on conditions in iron foundries
M. of Labour and National Service

GREVE, John

1978   Low incomes in Sweden (Background paper No. 6)
Royal Commission on the Distribution of Income and Wealth

GRIFFITHS, J. T.

1978   Industrial strategy: electronic consumer goods sector working party progress report
N.E.D.O.

GRIFFITHS, W. E. B.

1965   Report of the United Kingdom altimeter committee (CAP 231)
M. of Aviation

1968   Safety performance of United Kingdom airline operators: special review
Board of Trade

GRIFFITHS, W. H.

1968   Collapse of flats at Ronan Point, Canning Town. Report of the inquiry
M. of Housing and Local Government

1970   Disruption of operations and industrial relations at Heathrow (London) Airport. Committee of inquiry
    First report
    Session 1970-71 Cmnd. 4405 xxv.
    Final report
    Session 1970-71 Cmnd. 4449 xxv.
    See also ROBERTSON, D. J.

GRIFFITHS, William, Sir

1950   Technical and scientific register. Present and future supply and demand for persons with professional qualifications in metallurgy. Metallurgists' sub-committee. Report
M. of Labour and National Service

GRIGG, James, Sir

1954   Departmental records. Report of the committee
Session 1953-54 Cmd. 9163 xi.

1958   Recruiting. Report of the advisory committee
Session 1958-59 Cmnd. 545 viii.

GRIMES, William Francis

1976   Pre-Norman ancient monuments of Glamorgan. 14th interim report of the Royal Commission on Ancient and Historical Monuments in Wales
Session 1975-76 Cmnd. 6455 xv.

GRIMMIT, H. W.

1958   Nuclear power station at Trawsfynydd. Report of the public inquiry, held on February 12-14, 1958, by H. W. Grimmit and C. D. Buchanan
M. of Power

GRINLING, J.

1978 Distilling: Scotch whisky. Report of the distilling sector working group
N.E.D.O.

GRINT, Edmund Thomas Charles

1969 Report of a court of inquiry into a dispute at the British Broadcasting Corporation
Session 1969-70 Cmnd. 4240 xiv.

GROSS, W. D.

See WOLFENDEN, J., Sir

GROSSET, J. B.

1966 The hospital pharmaceutical service in Scotland. Report of a committee of the standard pharmaceutical advisory committee. Scottish Health Services Council
Scottish Home and Health D.

GROVES, R.

1960 Report on bread and flour. Food standards committee
M. of Agriculture, Fisheries and Food

1961 Report on mineral oil in food. Food standards committee
M. of Agriculture, Fisheries and Food

1962 Report on hard, soft and cream cheeses. Food standards committee
M. of Agriculture, Fisheries and Food

Report on dried milk. Food standards committee
M. of Agriculture, Fisheries and Food

Report on canned meat. Food standards committee
M. of Agriculture, Fisheries and Food

1963 Report on meat pies. Food standards committee
M. of Agriculture, Fisheries and Food

GUEST, C. W. Graham, Lord

1957 Building legislation in Scotland. Report of the committee
Session 1956-57 Cmnd. 269 ix.

1960 Boundary Commission for Scotland. Report with respect to the area comprised in the following constituencies: West Fife and Dunfirmline Burghs, West Renfrewshire and Greenock, Midlothian and Edinburgh, Pentlands
Session 1959-60 HC. 73 ix.

Scottish licensing law
1960 1st report of the committee
Session 1960-61 Cmnd. 1217 xviii.
1963 2nd report by the committee
Session 1962-63 Cmnd. 2021 xx.

GUILLEBAUD, C. W.

1947 Railway companies. Report of a court of inquiry into application by the trade unions representing the employees of the railway companies for improvement in wages and reductions in weekly hours of work
Session 1946-47 Cmd. 7161 xiv.

1951 Report of a court of inquiry into application for an improvement in wages and salaries made to the Railway Executive by the National Union of Railwaymen, the Associated Society of Locomotive Engineers and Firemen, and the Railway Clerks Association
Session 1950-51 Cmd. 8154 xiii.

1953 Report of a court of inquiry into an apprehended dispute affecting the National Society of Operative Printers and Assistants, the Printing Machine Managers Trade Society, Associated Newspapers, Ltd., and the Newspaper Proprietors Association
Session 1952-53 Cmd. 8931 xiii.

1955 National Health Service. Report of the committee of inquiry into the cost of the National Health Service
Session 1955-56 Cmd. 9663 xx.

GUINDEY, M.

1948 European economic co-operation. Committee on payments agreements. Final report
Foreign Office

GUITON, Nick

1975 The farmer as co-operative director
Central Council for Agricultural and Horticultural Co-operation

1976 Communications in co-operatives
Central Council for Agricultural and Horticultural Co-operation

GUMLEY, C. S.

1961 Hospital Catering (Scotland). Report of a joint committee of the standing medical advisory committee and the standing advisory committee on hospital and specialist services
Scottish Home and Health D.

GURNEY-DIXON, Samuel, Sir

1954 Early leaving. Report of the central advisory council for education (England)
M. of Education

GUTHRIE, H. W., Lord

1949 Tenure of shops and business premises in Scotland
Interim report
Session 1948-49 Cmd. 7603 xii.
Final report
Session 1950 Cmd. 7903 xiv.

1952 Scottish leases. Report of the committee
Session 1951-52 Cmd. 8656 xvi.

1960 Legal aid in criminal proceedings. Report by a committee
Session 1959-60 Cmnd. 1015 xvii.

GWYNN, E. H.

1964 Organisation of the prison medical service. Report of the working party
Home Office

HACKETT, Maurice, Sir

1967 A strategy for the south-east. A first report by the South-East Economic Planning Council
D. of Economic Affairs

HAGENBUCH, Walter

1970 Report of a committee of inquiry into the difference between Newlyn Pier and Harbour Commissioners and the Transport and General Workers Union over the reinstatement of former employees
D. of Employment and Productivity

HAILEY, W. M., Lord

1943 Colonial research committee. Progress report
Session 1942-43 Cmd. 6486 ix.

HAINING, B. W.

1972 Training for marketing. Report by the sales/marketing sub-committee of the committee for commercial and administrative training
D. of Employment

HALCROW, William, Sir

1955   Volta River project, vol. 3: Engineering report of the preparatory commission
Board of Trade
See also VAUGHAN-LEE, A. G.

HALDANE, R. A.

1966   The protection afforded to wild life in Scotland; a short review
Nature Conservancy

HALE, A. R.

1972   A review of the industrial accident research literature. Research papers for the committee on safety and health at work
D. of Health and Social Security

HALE, Edward, Sir

1960   Superannuation of university teachers. Report of a committee of the University Grants Committee
Treasury

1963   The use of vacations by students. Interim report of the committee on university teaching methods of the University Grants Committee
Treasury

1964   University teaching methods. Report of the committee of the University Grants Committee
D. of Education and Science

HALE, M.

1972   A review of the industrial accident research literature. Research paper for the committee on safety and health at work
D. of Health and Social Security

HALL, Jean Graham

1968   Statutory maintenance limits. Report of the committee
Session 1967-68 Cmnd. 3587 xxxii.

HALL, Lady Margaret

1975   Profitability and liquidity in the distributive trades; an examination of financial data in selected sectors. Profits and liquidity steering group of the Distributive Trades Economic Development Committee
N.E.D.O.

HALL, Noel F., Sir

1957   Hospital service. Report on the grading structure of administrative and clerical staff
M. of Health

1970   Hospital pharmaceutical service. Report of the working party
D. of Health and Social Security

HALL, Robert, Sir

1962   Economy of Northern Ireland. Report of the joint working party
Session 1961-62 Cmnd. 1835 xix.

1963   Transport needs of Great Britain in the next twenty years. Report of a group
M. of Transport

HALLIDAY, J. M.

1966   Conveyancing legislation and practice. Report by a committee
Session 1966-67 Cmnd. 3118 xxvi.

HALSBURY, J. A. H., Earl of

1963   Decimal currency. Report of the committee of inquiry
Session 1962-63 Cmnd. 2145 xi.

1971   The preservation of technological material. Report and recommendations
Standing Commission on Museums and Galleries

Review Body on Doctors' and Dentists' Remuneration

1971   Report
Session 1971-72 Cmnd. 4825 xxxiv.

1972   Report
Session 1971-72 Cmnd. 5010 xxxiv.

1973   Third report
Session 1972-73 Cmnd. 5353 xxx.
Supplement to the third report
Session 1972-73 Cmnd. 5377 xxx.
Second supplement to the third report
Session 1973-74 Cmnd. 5517 x.

1974   Fourth report
Session 1974 Cmnd. 5644 xv.
Supplement to the fourth report
Session 1974-75 Cmnd. 5849 xxxii.
See also WOODROOFE, E., Sir

Pay and related conditions of service of nurses and midwives

1974   Report of the committee of inquiry
1975   Supplement
D. of Health and Social Security

1975   Pay and related conditions of service of the professions supplementary to medicine and speech therapists. Report of the committee of inquiry
D. of Health and Social Security

HALSEY, A. H.

1972   Educational priority, vol. 1: E.P.A. problems and policies
D. of Education and Science

HALSEY, Brian

1968   Growing your own sales staff—21 golden rules. A guide to the selection and training of sales staff in the smaller shop. Distributive Trades Economic Development Committee
N.E.D.O.

1970   From facts to fortunes. The independent shopkeeper's guide to bigger profits. Distributive Trades Economic Development Committee
N.E.D.O.

1973   Finding the better way; a wholesaler's guide to imroved labour utilisation. Distributive Trades Economic Development Committee
N.E.D.O.

HAMILTON, D., Duke

1963   Pilot training. Report of the committee. (CAP 194)
M. of Aviation

HAMILTON OF DALZELL, J. d'H., Lord

1973   Legal aid and advice. Interim report; comments and recommendations of the Advisory Committee of the Law Society
Session 1972-73 HC. 76 xiii.

1977   Advisory Committee on Legal Aid. Evidence to the Royal Commission on Legal Services
Lord Chancellor's Office

HAMLIN, A. G.

See LLEWELYN, G. I. W.

HAMMER, J. D. G.

1975   Safety at the reel-up on board making machines. 3rd report of the joint standing committee for paper mills
D. of Employment

HAMMER, J. D. G. *(continued)*

1976   Causes and prevention of break-out during vertical semi-continuous and continuous casting of aluminium alloys. 2nd report of the joint standing committee on health, safety and welfare in foundries
Health and Safety Executive

1976   A warning and control system for continuous casting (as applied to copper alloys). 3rd report of the joint standing committee on health, safety and welfare in foundries
Health and Safety Executive

HAMMOND, Rob

1977   Race and local authority housing, information on ethnic groups. Report by a working party of the London Housing Research Group
Community Relations Commission

HAMP, Stanley

1944   Business buildings. Report by a committee. (Post-war building studies No. 16)
M. of Works

HANBURY, Harold Greville

1954   Report of a court of inquiry into a dispute between employers represented by the employers' side and trade unions represented by the trade union side of the National Council for the Omnibus Industry
Session 1953-54 Cmd. 9093 xv.

HANBURY, J.

1976   The organisation of the in-patients' day. Report of a committee of the central health services council
D. of Health and Social Security

HANBURY-WILLIAMS, J. C.

1946   Egypt, British goodwill trade mission. Report
Board of Trade

HANCOCK, Ernest

1946   Assessment of disablement due to specified injuries. Report of the interdepartmental committee
Session 1946-47 Cmd. 7076 x.

HANCOCK, F., Dame

     See MARKHAM, V., Miss

HANCOCK, H. D.

1961   Local government Commission for England
Report No. 1: South western general review area. Report and proposals and maps A-F; also separate maps 1-7
Report No. 2: West midlands general review area. Report and proposals and maps A-C; also separate maps 1-3
Report No. 3: East midlands general review area. Report and proposals with maps A-F; also separate maps 1-4

1963   Report No. 5: Tyneside special review area. Report and proposals and maps A-D, and separate maps 1-4
Report No. 6: North eastern general review area. Report and maps and separate maps 1-4

1964   Report No. 7: West Yorkshire special review area. Report and proposals and maps A-C; also separate maps 1-12
M. of Housing and Local Government

HANCOCK, T.

1966   Expansion of Peterborough. Consultants' proposals for designation
M. of Housing and Local Government

HANDFORD, John, Sir

1953   Slaughterhouses (Scotland). Interdepartmental committee reports
Interim report
Session 1953-54 Cmd. 9060 xix.

1954   Report
Session 1954-55 Cmd. 9376 vii.

HANKEY, M. P. A., Lord

1943   Report on the Imperial Agricultural Bureaux by a committee
Imperial Agricultural Bureau

1944   Higher appointments. Report of the committee
Session 1944-45 Cmd. 6576 iv.
Television committee. Report, 1943
Privy Council Office

1948   Technical and scientific register. Present and future supply and demand for persons with professional qualifications in physics. Physicists' sub-committee report
M. of Labour and National Service

1949   Technical and scientific register. Present and future supply and demand for persons with professional qualifications in chemistry. Chemists' sub-committee report
M. of Labour and National Service
Present and future supply and demand for persons with professional qualifications in architecture. Report by the architects' sub-committee
M. of Labour and National Service
Present and future supply and demand for persons with professional qualifications in electrical engineering. Report by the electrical engineering panel of the engineering sub-committee
M. of Labour and National Service
Present and future supply and demand for persons with professional qualifications in geology. Report by the geologists' sub-committee
M. of Labour and National Service

1950   Present and future supply and demand for persons with professional qualifications in valuation and estate management. Report by the surveyors panel (valuation and estate management) of the building and civil engineering sub-committee
M. of Labour and National Service
Present and future supply and demand for persons with professional qualifications in mechanical engineering. Report by the mechanical engineering sub-committee
M. of Labour and National Service
Present and future supply and demand for persons with professional qualifications in civil engineering. Report by the civil engineers' panel of the engineering sub-committee
M. of Labour and National Service
Present and future supply and demand for persons with professional qualifications in chemical engineering. Report by the chemical engineers sub-committee
M. of Labour and National Service
Present and future supply and demand for persons with professional qualifications in building and quantity surveying. Report by the building and civil engineers sub-committee
M. of Labour and National Service
Present and future supply and demand for persons with professional qualifications in biology, agriculture and related sciences. Report by the biologists and agriculturalists sub-committee
M. of Labour and National Service

1951   Present and future supply and demand for persons with professional qualifications in metallurgy. Report by the metallurgists sub-committee
M. of Labour and National Service

HANLON, John A. T.

1978   Industrial relations in the coaching industry. Report of a committee of inquiry. (Report No. 16)
Advisory, Conciliation and Arbitration Service

HANNIGAN, J. E.

1977   Study group on programmes of social ownership and renovation of council dwellings. 1st report
D. of the Environment

1978   Lead pollution in Britain. Report of the working party. (Pollution paper No. 14)
Central Unit on Environmental Pollution

HANRATTY, James

See HAWSER, C. Lewis

HARDIE, J. Blair

See BLAIR HARDIE, J.

HARDIE, S. J. L.

1947   Jute. Working party report
Board of Trade

HARDMAN, D. R.

1947   Education administration in Wales. Report of the working party to investigate the need for a Welsh Joint Education Committee
M. of Education

Education for industry and commerce. Working party report
M. of Education

HARDMAN, Henry, Sir

1971   Report of the committee appointed by the Post Office and Union of Post Office Workers to inquire into the circumstances of a dispute arising out of the Union's claim for pay increases and shortening of incremental scales
D. of Employment

Dispersal of government work from London. Report
Session 1972-73 Cmnd. 5322 vi.

HAREWOOD, G. H. H. L., Earl of

1969   A report on opera and ballet in the United Kingdom, 1966-69
Arts Council

HARGREAVES, W. S.

1966   The Certificate of Secondary Education trial examinations: home economics. Report of the steering committee (Examinations bulletin No. 9)
Schools Council

HARKER, R. Bramley

See BRAMLEY-HARKER, R.

HARLING, C. J.

1974   Shiftworking in the motor industry; detailed study and assessment. Motor Manufacturing Economic Development Committee
N.E.D.O.

HARMAN, C. E., Sir

1958   Rights of light. Report of the committee on the law relating to rights of light
Session 1957-58 Cmnd. 473 xvii.

1960   Chancery Chambers and the Chancery Registrars' Office. Report of the committee
Session 1959-60 Cmnd. 967 xvii.

HARPER, J.

1969   Forensic psychiatry. Report of a sub-committee of the standing medical advisory committee. Scottish Health Services Council
Scottish Home and Health D.

HARRAGIN, W., Sir

1946   Civil services of British West Africa. Report of the commission (Colonial No. 209)
Colonial Office

HARRIS, G. S.

1978   Salmon propagation in England and Wales. Report by the Association of River Authorities/ National Water Council working party
National Water Council

HARRIS, M. R.

1975   John Willment Automobiles Ltd. Report of investigations under the Companies Act
D. of Trade

HARRIS, N. D.

1978   Materials handling; an introduction
D. of Industry

HARRIS, Sidney, Sir

1948   Grants for the development of marriage guidance. Report of the departmental committee
Session 1948-49 Cmd. 7566 xvii.

HARRIS, William G.

1968   Contracting in civil engineering since Banwell. A survey of the implementation of the recommendations of the committee on the placing and management of contracts. A report by the working party of the Civil Engineering Economic Development Committee
N.E.D.O.
See also POTTS, P. G.

HARRISON, D. B.

1972   Traffic noise; the vehicle regulations and their enforcement. Report by a working group of the Noise Advisory Council.
D. of the Environment

1978   Noise implications of the transfer of freight from road to rail. Report by a working group of the Noise Advisory Council
D. of the Environment

HARRISON, F. L. T. Graham-

See GRAHAM-HARRISON, F. L. T.

HARRISON, M., Miss

See REDCLIFFE-MAUD, J. P., Lord

HARTWELL, B. J.

1958   After-care and supervision of discharged prisoners. Report of the sub-committee of the Advisory Council on the Treatment of Offenders
Home Office

1963   Organisation of after-care. Report of the Advisory Council on the Treatment of Offenders
Home Office

HARVARD DAVIS, R.

1971   The organisation of group practice. Report of a sub-committee of the standing medical advisory committee. Central Health Services Council
D. of Health and Social Security

HARVEY, Brian H.

Guarding of foundry machinery. Report of the sub-committee on machinery safety of the joint standing committee on health, safety and welfare in foundries

1971   First report
1973   Second report
       D. of Employment
       See also WATSON, C. E.

HARVEY, R. J. P.

1955   Mobile radio committee report
       Post Office

HARVEY, W. H. G.

1975   Public lending right; an account of an investigation of technical and cost aspects
       D. of Education and Science

HARVIE, D. E.

1974   Mentally handicapped children in residential care. Report of a study group
       D. of Health and Social Security

HASLEGRAVE, Herbert L.

1969   Technician courses and examinations. Report of the committee of the National Advisory Council on Education for Industry and Commerce
       D. of Education and Science

HASELGROVE, D. C.

1957   Child cyclists. Report of the working party
       M. of Transport and Civil Aviation

Road safety, Slough experiment. Report on a large-scale experiment into the effectiveness of road safety measures conducted in the Borough of Slough from April 2, 1955 to March 31, 1957
M. of Transport and Civil Aviation

HAWSER, C. Lewis

1975   The case of James Hanratty
       Session 1974-75 Cmnd. 6021 xv.

HAWTHORNE, William R., Sir

1975   Advisory council on energy conservation. (Energy paper No. 3)
       D. of Energy

1976   Policy statement by the Trades Union Congress. Advisory council on energy conservation. (Energy paper No. 6)
       D. of Energy

1977   Freight transport; short and medium term considerations. Advisory council on energy conservation paper 6. (Energy paper No. 24)
       D. of Energy

1978   Energy for transport; long term possibilities. Advisory council on energy conservation. (Energy paper No. 26)
       D. of Energy

HAWTON, John, Sir

1964   The future of the waterways. Interim report
       British Waterways Board

HAXBY, P.

1972   Training for transport and physical distribution. Report by the distribution and transport sub-committee
       D. of Employment

HAY, John A.

1960   Department road safety committee. Report on the results of the experimental introduction of a 40 m.p.h. speed limit in the London traffic area
       Session 1959-60 HC. 144 xx.

HAYCOCKS, N.

1975   Training of teachers for further education. Report of the sub-committee of the advisory committee on the supply and training of teachers
       D. of Education and Science

1977   Training of adult education and part-time further education teachers. Report of the advisory committee on the supply and training of teachers sub-committee
       D. of Education and Science

1978   Training teachers for education management in further and adult education; a discussion paper by the sub-committee of the advisory committee on the supply and training of teachers
       D. of Education and Science

HAYES, F. C.

1972   Training for the management of human resources. Report by the personnel management sub-committee of the J.I.T.B. committee for commercial and administrative training
       D. of Employment

HAYTER, G. C. H. C., Lord

1977   Trading with Europe; through transport and the total export concept. International Freight Movement Economic Development Committee
       N.E.D.O.

1975   United Kingdom air cargo, prepared for the air cargo working party of the International Freight Movement Economic Development Committee
       N.E.D.O.

HAYTER, William, Sir

1961   Oriental, Slavonic, east European and African studies. Report of the sub-committee. University Grants Committee
       Treasury

HAYWARD, R.

1975   National health service staff commission report, 1972-75
       D. of Health and Social Security

HAYWARD, Richard A.

1967   Administration of the wage stop. Report of the Supplementary Benefits Commission
       M. of Social Security

HAZAN, J. B. R.

1976   Hartley Baird Ltd. Report of investigation under the Companies Act
       D. of Trade

HAYZELDEN, J. E.

1978   Electoral register. Report of the working party
       Home Office

HEATH, J. B.

1973   Inflation and company accounts in mechanical engineering. Report of the company liquidity and investment working party. Mechanical Engineering Economic Development Committee
       N.E.D.O.

HEATON, C. Henniker-

       See HENNIKER-HEATON, C.

HEATON, D.

       See HAYZELDEN, J. E.

HEGGIE, J. F.

1972   Safety in pathology laboratories. A handbook prepared by a working party
D. of Health and Social Security

Safety in the post-mortem room. A handbook prepared by a working party
D. of Health and Social Security

HEILBRON, R.

1978   Kuehne and Nagel Ltd. Report of investigation under the Companies Act
D. of Trade

HEILBRON, Rose

1975   Advisory group on the law of rape. Report
Session 1975-76 Cmnd. 6352 xx.

HEILPERN, G.

See DAVIES, J. M.

HELMORE, W.

1948   Civil aircraft. Report of the committee on certification of civil aircraft and approval of equipment
Session 1948-49 Cmd. 7705 xi.

HENDERSON, George, Sir

1956   Medical superintendents' and medical staff committees. Report of the sub-committee of the standing advisory committee on hospital and specialist services. Scottish Health Services Council
D. of Health for Scotland

HENDERSON, Hubert Douglas, Sir

1949   Royal Commission on Population. Report
Session 1948-49 Cmd. 7695 xix.

1950   Royal Commission on Population papers, vol 5. Memoranda presented to the Royal Commission
Royal Commission on Population

HENDERSON, John Scott

1951   Cruelty to wild animals. Report of the committee
Session 1950-51 Cmd. 8266 viii.

1952   Broadmoor. Report of the Broadmoor inquiry committee
1951-52 Cmd. 8594 xviii.

1953   Mrs. Beryl Evans and Geraldine Evans. Report of an inquiry into certain matters arising out of their deaths, and out of the conviction of Timothey John Evans, of the murder of Geraldine Evans
Session 1952-53 Cmd. 8896 ix.

1953   The case of Timothy John Evans. Supplementary report
Session 1952-53 Cmd. 8946 ix.

HENDERSON, P.

1959   Standards of normal weight in infancy. Report. (Public health and medical subjects report No. 99)
M. of Health

1976   School health service, 1907-1974
D. of Education and Science

HENDERSON, T. G.

1975   Catering in Scottish Schools. Report by a working party
Scottish Education D.

HENDERSON, W. Craig

Retail trade committee reports

1941   Interim report on the opening of new shops and the restriction on categories of goods sold in existing shops

1942   Second interim report: the impact of the war on the retail trades on goods other than food

1942   Third report. Concentration in the retail non-food trades
Board of Trade

HENDRY, N. G. C.

1973   Organisation of a medical advisory structure. Report of the sub-group of the joint working party on integration of medical work
Scottish Home and Health D.

HENDRY, R.

1975   English department in the Scottish secondary school. Scottish central committee on English
Scottish Education D.

HENEAGE, Arthur P., Sir

1948   Public access to afforestation and agriculture on gathering grounds. Report of a sub-committee of the central advisory water committee
M. of Health

1950   Land drainage in England and Wales. Report of the land drainage legislation sub-committee of the central advisory water committee
M. of Agriculture and Fisheries

HENIG, Mark, Sir

1969   Opportunity in the East Midlands. East Midlands Economic Planning Council
D. of Economic Affairs

HENNIKER-HEATON, C.

1964   Day release. The report of the committee
D. of Education and Science

HENRY, G. L. F.

1969   Scheme for the introduction and operation of registration of title to land in Scotland. Report by a committee
Session 1968-69 Cmnd. 4137 xxxvi.

HENSTRIDGE, E. J.

1978   Industrial relations training. Report of the working party
Civil Service College

HEPBURN, H. A.

1949   Safety in the use of power presses. Report of the proceedings of the joint standing committee. 1st report
M. of Labour and National Service

1950   Fumes from oil-bonded cores. Technical report on practical methods of reducing the amount of fumes from oil-bonded cores by the joint standing committee on conditions in iron foundries
M. of Labour and National Service

1951   Milling machines. 2nd report of the committee on the safeguarding of milling machines
M. of Labour and National Service

Dust in steel foundries. 2nd report of a committee to consider methods of preventing the production of and inhalation of dust and the possibility of reducing the use of materials containing free silica in steel foundries
M. of Labour and National Service

Fencing of hydraulic presses. Report of the joint standing committee on safety in the use of power presses
M. of Labour and National Service

1953   Prevention of accidents in paper mills. Joint standing committee. 2nd report: machinery accidents
M. of Labour and National Service

HERBECQ, John

1978   Interchange between the home civil service and the diplomatic service. Report of a working group
Civil Service D.

HERBERT, Edwin Savoury, Sir

1949   Intermediaries. Report of the committee
Session 1950 Cmd. 7904 xii.

1955   Electricity supply industry. Report of the committee of inquiry
Session 1955-56 Cmd. 9672 xv.

1956   Port Said. Damages and casualties in Port Said. Report on investigation into the effects of the military action in October and November, 1956
Session 1956-57 Cmnd. 47 xviii.
Royal Commission on Local Government in Greater London

1958   Memoranda of evidence from government departments (written)

1959   Minutes of Evidence, 1st to 70th day; 5 March, 1959 to 2 February 1960
Appendix 1

1960   Appendix 2
Report
Session 1959-60 Cmnd. 1164 xviii.
Royal Commission on Local Government in Greater London

HERBERT, R.

1953   Slaughterhouses. Interdepartmental committee
Interim report
Session 1953-54 Cmd. 9060 xix.

1955   Report
Session 1955-56 Cmd. 9542 xxvii.

HERON, Conrad F.

1971   Hotel and catering industry. Part 1: hotels and restaurants (Commission on Industrial Relations report No. 23)
Session 1970-71 Cmnd. 4789 xxv.

British Home Stores (Commission on Industrial Relations report No. 24)
Session 1970-71 Cmnd. 4791 xxv.

Commission on Industrial Relations. 2nd general report (Report No. 25)
Session 1971-72 Cmnd. 4803 xviii.

See also WOODCOCK, George

See also NEAL, L. F.

HETHERINGTON, Hector J. W., Sir

1943   Post-war hospital problems in Scotland. Report of the committee
Session 1942-43 Cmd. 6472 iv.

Domestic help. Committee on minimum rates of wages and conditions of employment in connection with special arrangements for domestic help
Session 1942-43 Cmd. 6481 iv.

1944   Workmen's compensation. Royal Commission report
Session 1944-45 Cmd. 6588 vi.

1947   Port transport industry. Report of an inquiry into the amount and basis of calculation of the guaranteed wage to be made to dock workers under the dock workers (regulation of employment) scheme, 1947
M. of Labour and National Service

HETHERINGTON, Roger, Sir

1949   Technical and scientific register. Present and future supply and demand of persons with professional qualifications in civil engineering. Report of the civil engineers' panel of the engineering sub-committee
M. of Labour and National Service

HEYMAN, A.

1976   Lonrho Ltd. Report of investigations under the Companies Act
D. of Trade

HEYWORTH, Geoffrey, Lord

1945   The gas industry. Report of a committee of inquiry
Session 1945-46 Cmd. 6699 xii.

1961   Council on prices. Productivity and Incomes. 4th report
Council on Prices, Productivity and Incomes

1965   Report of the committee on social studies
Session 1964-65 Cmnd. 2660 xxii.

1964   University appointments board. Report by the University Grants Committee
D. of Education and Science

HICKS, Donald

1967   Grit and dust emissions. Report of the working party
M. of Housing and Local Government

HIGGINS, P. B.

1972   Operational safety during vertical semi-continuous casting of aluminium. 1st report of the sub-committee on continuous castings and high speed melting of the joint standing committee of health, safety and welfare in foundries
D. of Employment

1977   A study of the causes of molten metal and water explosions. Further report of the sub-committee on continuous casting and speed melting of the joint standing committees of health, safety and welfare in foundries
Health and Safety Executive

Study of the causes of molten metal and water explosions. 4th report of the sub-committee on continuous casting and high speed melting of the joint standing committees of health, safety and welfare in foundries
Health and Safety Executive

HILDITCH, T. P.

1954   Vaporising liquid extinguishing agents. Report of a committee. (Fire research technical paper No. 2)
D. of Scientific and Industrial Research

HILL, A. Bradford, Sir

1954   Measurement of morbidity. Report of the statistics sub-committee of the Registrar General's advisory committee on medical nomenclature and statistics
General Register Office

HILL, Douglas W.

1945   Mule spinners' cancer and automatic wiping down motions. Interim report of the joint advisory committee on the cotton industry
M. of Labour and National Service

1952   Mule spinners' cancer. 2nd interim report of the joint advisory committee of the cotton industry
M. of Labour and National Service

HILL, F. G.

1950   Deterioration of cast iron and spun iron pipes. Report of the departmental committee. Interim report
M. of Health

1954   Sewage sludge. Report of an informal working party on the treatment and disposal of sewage sludge
M. of Housing and Local Government

1960   Pollution of water by tipped refuse. Report of the technical committee on the experimental disposal of house refuse in wet and dry pits
M. of Housing and Local Government

HILL, J. Dennis N., Sir

1968   Hospital treatment of acute poisoning. Report of the joint sub-committee of the standing medical advisory committees. Central and Scottish Health Services Councils
D. of Health and Social Security

HILL, R. J. C.

1973   Packing for profit. Report of the port traffic working group.
    Vol. 1: Economic advantages of unitising break-bulk cargo
    Vol. 2: Practical guide to unitising break-bulk cargo
N.E.D.O.

HILL, SAMUEL & CO. LTD.

1971   Shipbuilding on the Upper Clyde
Session 1971-72 Cmnd. 4918 xxxvii.

HILL WATSON, L., Lord

1954   Drainage of trade premises. Report of the committee
Session 1953-54 Cmd. 9117 xi.

HILLIER, R.

1964   Report of the joint advisory committee for the cutlery and silverware trades in Sheffield and district
M. of Labour

HIMSWORTH, Harold P., Sir

Hazards to man of nuclear and allied radiations. Report by a committee of the Medical Research Council

1956   1st report
Session 1955-56 Cmd. 9780 xi.

1960   2nd report
Session 1960-61 Cmnd. 1225 ix.

Report of the enquiry into the medical and toxicological aspects of C.S. (Orthochlorobenzylidene malononitrile)

1969   Part 1: Enquiry into the medical situation following the use of C.S. in Londonderry on 13th and 14th August 1969
Session 1968-69 Cmnd. 4173 xxviii.

1971   Part 2: Enquiry into toxicological aspects of C.S. and its use for civil purposes
Session 1970-71 Cmnd. 4775 xxi.

HINCHINBROOKE, A. V. E. P., Viscount
    See MONTAGU, A. V. E. P.

HINCHLIFFE, Henry, Sir

Committee on the cost of prescribing
1958   Interim report
1959   Final report
M. of Health

HINDLEY, Clement, Sir

1943   Codes of practice committee for civil engineering, public works, buildings and constructional work
1st report
2nd report
M. of Works

See also FAIRWEATHER, H. W.

HINES, J. G.

1978   Industrial corrosion monitoring. Committee on corrosion working party
D. of Industry

HIRST, C. D.

First Re-investment Trust Ltd., Nelson Financial Trust Ltd., English and Scottish Unit Trust Holdings, Ltd.

1974   Interim report of investigations under the Companies Act

1975   Second and final report of investigations under the Companies Act
D. of Trade

HITCHMAN, Alan, Sir

1956   Agricultural Improvement Council for England and Wales. 3rd report, 1950-56
M. of Agriculture, Fisheries and Food

HOAR, T. P.

1971   Survey of corrosion and protection in the United Kingdom. Report of the committee on corrosion and protection
D. of Trade and Industry

HOBDAY, S. R.

1949   Prevention of river pollution. Report of the rivers pollution prevention sub-committee of the Central Advisory Water Committee
M. of Health

HOBHOUSE, Arthur, Sir

1943   Rural housing. 3rd report of the rural housing sub-committee of the Central Housing Advisory Committee
M. of Health

1947   National Parks (England and Wales). Report of the committee
Session 1946-47 Cmd. 7121 xiii.

Footpaths and access to the countryside. Special committee report
Session 1946-47 Cmd. 7207 x.

HOBSON, D. C.

1976   London and County Securities Group Ltd. Report of investigations under the Companies Act
D. of Trade

HOBSON, J. L.

1974   Safety recommendations. Report of the joint standing committee on safety in the cotton and allied fibres weaving industry
D. of Employment

HOCKEY, L.

1978   District nursing in Scotland. Report of a working party
Scottish Home and Health D.

HODGES, M. W.

1973   School transport. Report of the working party
D. of Education and Science

HODGSON, Derek

1972　Codification of the criminal law; general principles: Parties, complicity and liability for the acts of another. Report of a working party. (Working paper, No. 43)
Law Commission

Codification of the criminal law; general principles. Criminal liability of corporations. (Working paper No. 44)
Law Commission

1973　Codification of the criminal law; general principles. Inchoate offences; conspiracy, attempt and incitement. Report of a working party. (Working paper No. 50)
Law Commission

1974　Codification of the criminal law; general principles. Defences of general application. Report of a working party. (Working paper No. 55)
Law Commission

Codification of the criminal law; conspiracies relating to morals and decency. Report of a working party. (Working paper No. 57)
Law Commission

1975　Codification of the criminal law; conspiracies to effect a public mischief and to commit a civil wrong. Report of a working party. (Working paper No. 63)
Law Commission

HODGSON, E. W.

1967　Power press and drop stamping problems in the cutlery and silverware trades in Sheffield and District. Report of the working party representing the joint standing committee on safety in the use of power presses in the cutlery and silverware trades in Sheffield and district
M. of Labour

1968　Power press toolsetting and tool design. 6th report of the joint standing committee on safety in the use of power presses
M. of Labour

1969　Safety in the use of press brakes. 7th report of the joint standing committee of safety in the use of power presses
D. of Employment and Productivity

1970　Electro-sensitive safety devices for friction-clutch press brakes. 8th report of the joint standing committee on safety in the use of power presses
D. of Employment and Productivity

HODGSON, Edward H., Sir

1950　Weights and measures legislation. Report of the committee
Session 1950-51 Cmd. 8219 xx.

HODSON, D.

See BOTTINI, R.

HODSON, F. C. L., Lord

1959　Conflicts of jurisdiction affecting children. Report of the committee
Session 1958-59 Cmnd. 842 xvi.

HOFFERT, W. H.

1948　Sludging and corrosion in benzole absorption plants. Report on the investigations of the benzole technical committee
M. of Fuel and Power

HOLE, G. V.

1963　Air freight working party. Report (CAP 192)
M. of Aviation

1964　Third London airport. Report of the interdepartmental committee (CAP 193)
M. of Aviation

HOLLAND, Eardley, Sir

1949　Neonatal mortality and morbidity. Report by a joint committee of the Royal College of Obstetricians and Gynaecologists and the British Paediatric Association. (Reports on public health and medical subjects No. 94)
M. of Health

Royal Commission on Population. Vol. 1: Family limitation and its influence on human fertility during the past 50 years. An investigation carried out by the council of the Royal College of Obstetricians and Gynaecologists
Royal Commission on Population

HOLLAND, E. Milner, Sir

1954　Savoy Hotel Ltd. and Berkeley Hotel Co. Ltd. Report of investigation under the Companies Act
Board of Trade

1965　Housing in Greater London. Report of the committee
Session 1964-65 Cmnd. 2605 xvii.

HOLLAND, G.

1977　Young people and work. Report by the working party on the feasibility of a new programme of opportunities for unemployed young people
Manpower Services Commission

HOLLAND-MARTIN, Deric E., Sir

Trawler safety. Committee of inquiry
1968　Interim report
Session 1967-68 Cmnd. 3773 xxxiii.
1969　Final report
Session 1968-69 Cmnd. 4114 xlvi.

HOLLOWAY, A.

1962　Manufacture and inspection of welded structures for aircraft engine parts. Report by the gas turbine collaboration committee, welding and fabricated structures panel. 2nd ed.
M. of Aviation

HOLMAN, J. F.

1974　Strategic settlement pattern for the south west. Report of the South West Economic Planning Council
D. of Environment

HOLMES, Maurice G., Sir

1947　Examinations in secondary schools. Secondary schools examinations council report
M. of Education

1948　Civil Services of Kenya, Tanganyika, Uganda and Zanzibar. Report of the commission
Colonial Office

1949　British Caribbean area. Unification of public services. Report of the commission
Colonial Office

1955　Public Trustee Office. Report of the committee of inquiry
Session 1955-56 Cmd. 9755 xxvii.

HOLMES, W.

1977　Evaluation of the first importation into Great Britain in 1970-71 of Limousin bulls from France and Simmental bulls from Germany and Switzerland. Report of the Limousin and Simmental tests steering committee
M. of Agriculture, Fisheries and Food

HOLROYD, R., Sir

1970　Fire service. Report of the departmental committee
Session 1969-70 Cmnd. 4371 xii.

HOMAN, J. R. S.

1974   Industrial review to 1977: textiles. Joint textile committee
N.E.D.O.

HOME, A., Earl of
See DOUGLAS-HOME, A., Sir

HONEYMAN, George G., Sir

1947   The hairdressing trade. Report of a commission of inquiry on an application for the establishment of a wages council
M. of Labour and National Service

The retail bookselling, news agency, stationery, tobacco and confectionery trades. Report of a commission of inquiry on the question whether a wages council should be established
M. of Labour and National Service

The retail drapery, outfitting and footwear trades. Report of a commission of inquiry on an application for the establishment of a wages council
M. of Labour and National Service

The retail food trades. Report of a commission of inquiry on an application for the establishment of a wages council
M. of Labour and National Service

The retail furnishing and allied trades. Report of a commission of inquiry on an application for the establishment of a wages council
M. of Labour and National Service

1948   The retail drapery, outfitting and footwear trades. Report of a commission of inquiry on a draft order for the establishment of a wages council
M. of Labour and National Service

The retail food trades (Scotland). Report of a commission of inquiry on a draft order for the establishment of a wages council
M. of Labour and National Service

The retail furnishing and allied trades. Report of a commission of inquiry on a draft order for the establishment of a wages council
M. of Labour and National Service

Revision of the building regulations. Report of the inquiry with respect to the draft code in relation to safety, health and welfare
M. of Labour and National Service

1960   Examination of steam boilers in industry. Report of the advisory committee
Session 1959-60 Cmnd. 1173 xiv.

1961   Draft Construction (Lifting Operations) Regulations and the Construction (General Provisions) Regulations. Report by the commission of inquiry
M. of Labour

Sugar confectionery and food preserving wages council (Great Britain). Report of the commission of inquiry
M. of Labour

1965   Report of the arbitral body on salaries of teachers in primary and secondary schools, England and Wales
D. of Education and Science

1966   The Draft Construction (Working Places) Regulations and the draft Construction (Health and Welfare) Regulations. Report by the commission of inquiry
M. of Labour

Port transport industry. Report of an inquiry held under the Dock Workers (Regulation of Employment) Act, 1946.
M. of Labour

1967   Report of a court of inquiry into the causes and circumstances of a dispute at the tube works of Stewarts and Lloyds Ltd. at Corby
Session 1966-67 Cmnd. 3260 xxxvii.

Report of the arbitral body on salaries of teachers in primary and secondary schools, England and Wales
D. of Education and Science

1968   Report of the arbitral body on the payment of teachers in primary and secondary schools, London area
D. of Education and Science

Report of the arbitral body on salaries for teachers in establishments for further education
D. of Education and Science

1969   Report of the arbitral body on salaries for teachers in establishments for further education. (Remuneration of Teachers Act 1965)
D. of Education and Science

Salaries of registered teachers in primary and secondary schools and teachers in further education centres. Report of the arbitral body for Scotland
Scottish Education D.

HOOD, S. W.

1950   Manufactured meat products. Report of the working party
M. of Food

HOOKWAY, H. T.

1972   Public lending right. Report of the working party
D. of Education and Science

1973   Scope for automatic data processing in the British Library. Report of a study into the feasibility of applying A.D.P. to the operations and service of the British Library. 2 vols.
D. of Education and Science

HOOPER, Frederick, Sir

1959   Resettlement advisory board. Progress report
Session 1958-59 Cmnd. 789 viii.
See also WOLFENDEN, J., Sir

HOOPER, L. J.

1977   Agricultural valuation. 4th report of the committee
M. of Agriculture, Fisheries and Food
See also DOBB, E. S., WARE, R. R.

HOPKINS, Richard V. N., Sir

1946   Census of distribution committee. Report
Session 1945-46 Cmd. 6764 x.

1952   Cotton import committee report
Session 1951-52 Cmd. 8510 ix.

1953   Cotton import (review). Report of the committee
Session 1952-53 Cmd. 8861 ix.

HOPKINSON, Henry

1953   Report of the West African forces conference, Lagos, April 20 to 24, 1953. (Colonial No. 304)
Colonial Office

HORNE, F. R.

1950   Qualitative control of seeds. Report of the committee
M. of Agriculture and Fisheries

HORTON, C. E.

1950   Centimetric aerials for marine navigational radar. Proceedings of a conference held June 15-16, 1950 in London
M. of Transport

HORTON, J. W.

1966   The Certificate of Secondary Education experimental examinations: music. Report of the steering committee. (Examinations bulletin No. 10)
Schools Council

HORTON, M.
See REDCLIFFE-MAUD, J. P., Lord

HOSEGOOD, J. P.

Housing finance in Wales. Reports of the working party
1977   1st report
1978   2nd report
Welsh Office

HOUGHTON OF SOWERBY, A. L. N. D., Lord

1974   Pay of non-university teachers. Report of the committee of inquiry
Session 1974-75 Cmnd. 5848 xxxi.

1976   Financial aid to political parties. Report of the committee
Session 1975-76 Cmnd. 6601 xiii.

Cabinet document security. Report of the committee of Privy Counsellors
Session 1976-77 Cmnd. 6677 xi.

HOUGHTON, A.

1978   Study of returnable and non-returnable containers. An interim report of the waste management advisory council's packaging and containers working group
D. of Industry

HOUGHTON, William F., Sir

1968   Training for office supervision. A report by the commercial and clerical training council. Central Training Council
M. of Labour

Training of export staff. A report by the commercial and clerical training council. Central Training Council
D. of Employment and Productivity

1970   Adoption of children. Working paper containing the provisional proposals of the departmental committee
Home Office
See also STOCKDALE, F. A.

HOUSE, D. V.

1963   Shipping services to Northern Ireland. Report of the committee
M. of Transport

HOUSTON, H. R.

1967   Ignitions of firedamp in the machine cut. Report by the working party on frictional sparking
National Coal Board

HOWE, R. E. Godfrey

1969   Report of the committee of inquiry into allegations of ill-treatment of patients and other irregularities at the Ely Hospital, Cardiff
Session 1968-69 Cmnd. 3975 xxxiii.

HOWELL, Denis

1969   Youth and community work in the 70s. Proposals by the youth service development council
D. of Education and Science

1975   Working party on crowd behaviour. Recommendations to British teams competing in European competitions
D. of the Environment

1976   Working party on crowd behaviour. Circular for 1976-77 season
D. of the Environment

HOWES, R.

1972   Mid-Wales; an assessment of the impact of the Development Commission factory programme
Development Commission

HOWIE, James

1978   Codes of practice for the prevention of infection in clinical laboratories and post-mortem rooms, by a working party of expert representatives
D. of Health and Social Security

HOWITT, Harold, Sir

1945   Rhodesian Railways Ltd. Report on state ownership. (Dominions No. 3)
Dominions Office

Pay and organisation of civil service medical staffs
1950   Interim report of the committee. December 1950
1951   Interim report of the committee. April 1951
1951   Report. August 1951
Treasury

1955   Pig production. Development of pig production in the U.K. Report of the advisory committee
Session 1955-56 Cmd. 9588 xxvi.

1956   Defence contracts. Report of the committee of inquiry on the powers of the Crown to authorise the use of unpatented inventions and unregistered designs in connection with defence contracts
Session 1955-56 Cmd. 9788 xiv.

1957   British Transport Commission. Report on the purchasing procedure
Session 1956-57 Cmnd. 262 xix.

HOWLETT, J.

Computer networks. Reports of the national committee
1977   Interim report
1978   Report
D. of Industry

HOWLETT, R.

1966   Nutrional standard of the school dinner. Report of the departmental working party
D. of Education and Science

HUBBARD, A. W.

1975   Survey of lead in food. 1st supplementary report to the fifth report of the working party on the monitoring of foodstuffs for heavy metals
M. of Agriculture, Fisheries and Food

1978   Surveillance of food contamination in the U.K. 1st report of the steering group on food surveillance (Food surveillance paper No. 1)
M. of Agriculture, Fisheries and Food

HUCKLE, J. R. D.

1974   Strategic choice for East Anglia. Report by the East Anglia Regional Strategy Team
D. of the Environment

HUDSON, D.
See BOTTINI, R.

HUDSON, Edmund P., Sir

1971   Technician courses and examinations in Scotland. Scottish technical education consultative council
Scottish Education D.

HUDSON, J. A.

1972   Central arrangements for promoting educational technology in the U.K. Report of the working party
D. of Education and Science

1975   Catering in schools. Report of the committee
D. of Education and Science

HUDSON, R. J., Sir

1952   Southern Rhodesia, Northern Rhodesia and Nyasaland. Draft federal scheme. Report of the judicial commission
Session 1951-52 Cmd. 8671 ix.

HUGHES, Alan

1978   Competition policy including a research annex: competition policy and economic performance in the U.K.
N.E.D.O.

HUGHES, H. D.

1976   Adult literacy. The adult literacy resource agency's management committee report for 1975-76
D. of Education and Science

HUGHES, R. Moelwyn

1946   Bolton Wanderer's football ground. Inquiry into the disaster at the Bolton Wanderer's football ground on March 9, 1946. Report
Session 1945-46 Cmd. 6846 x.

1947   Catering Wages Commission. Report on an inquiry under the Catering Wages Act into alleged overcharging for holiday accommodation
M. of Labour and National Service

Catering Wages Commission. Report recommending variation of the field of operation of the catering wages board in regard to canteens provided by dock authorities
Session 1946-47 Cmd. 7191 x.

Catering Wages Commission. Employment agencies serving the catering industry. Report of an enquiry
M. of Labour and National Service

Catering Wages Commission. The problems affecting the remuneration of catering workers which result from the practice of giving tips. Report of an inquiry
M. of Labour and National Service

1948   Greater London water supplies. Report of a departmental committee
M. of Health

1949   Cotton Manufacturing Commission. Report of an inquiry into wages arrangements and methods of organisation of work in the cotton manufacturing industry. Final report. 4 parts
M. of Labour and National Service

HUGHES, T. P.

1971   Design and construction of underground pipe sewers. 3rd report of the working party
D. of the Environment

1975   Sewers and water mains. First report of the working party
D. of the Environment

HULL, H., Sir

1953   Transport tribunal. In the matter of the application of the British Transport Commission (1953 No. 134) to confirm the British Transport Commission (Passenger) Charges Scheme, 1953
M. of Transport

HUMBLE, Stephen

1977   Neighbourhood councils in England
D. of the Environment; published by the University of Birmingham Institute of Local Government Studies

HUME, A. B.

1960   Use of short sentences of imprisonment by the courts. Report of the Scottish advisory council committee on the treatment of offenders
Scottish Home D.

HUMPHRYS, H. J.

1942   Barnborough Main Colliery, South Yorkshire. Report on the causes and circumstances attending the upheaval of floor which occurred on 24 April 1942
Session 1942-43 Cmd. 6414 vi.

1948   Hazards connected with shotfiring in rippings. A summary of the first progress report by the committee on shotfiring in Yorkshire
M. of Fuel and Power

HUNT, H. C. J., Lord

1967   Immigrants and the youth service. Report of a committee of the youth service development council
D. of Education and Science

1968   Nigeria. British relief advisory mission
Session 1967-68 Cmnd. 3727 xxxix.

1969   Police in Northern Ireland. Report of the advisory committee
Home Office

1970   Nigeria. The problem of relief in the aftermath of the Nigerian civil war. Report of the mission
Session 1969-70 Cmnd. 4275 viii.

HUNT, F. W.

1946   Jute industry factory advisory committee. Final report
M. of Labour and National Service

HUNT, J. W.
See ASTLEY, I. D.

HUNT, Joseph A., Sir

1966   Training for commerce and the office. Report by the Central Training Council's commercial and clerical training committee
M. of Labour

1967   An approach to the training and development of managers. A report by the Central Training Council's management training and development committee
M. of Labour

1969   The intermediate areas. Report of a committee
Session 1968-69 Cmnd. 3998 xxxv.

1970   Report of an inquiry into the pattern and organisation of the college year by the committee on the effective use of technical college resources
D. of Education and Science

See also PILKINGTON, W. H., Lord

HUNT, T.

1967   The West Midlands; patterns of growth. A first report by the West Midlands Economic Planning Council
D. of Economic Affairs

HUNTER, J., Sir

1965   Central Training Council. Report to the minister
Session 1964-65 H.C. 352 xvii.

HUNTER, J. O. M., Lord

Scottish salmon and trout fisheries
1963   1st report
Session 1962-63 Cmnd. 2096 xvii.
1965   2nd report
Session 1964-65 Cmnd. 2691 xv.

HUNTER, J. O. M., Lord *(continued)*

1972   Town and Country Planning (Scotland) Bill. Report on the consolidation of certain enactments. (Scot. Law Com. No. 24)
Session 1971-72 Cmnd. 4949 xxii.

Family law. Report on jurisdiction in consistorial causes affecting matrimonial status (Scot. Law Com. No. 25)
Session 1971-72 HC. 488 xxii.

Draft Statute Law (Repeals) Bill. Statute law revision, 4th report. (Law Com. No. 49) (Scot. Law Com. No. 26)
Session 1971-72 Cmnd. 5108 xxii.

1973   Second programme of consolidation and statute law revision. (Scot. Law Com. No. 27)
Session 1972-73 HC. 180 xiv.

Scottish Law Commission. 7th annual report, 1971-72. (Scot. Law Com. No. 28)
Session 1972-73 HC. 136 xiv.

Third programme of law reform. (Scot. Law Com. No. 29)
Session 1972-73 HC. 283 xiv.

Liability for antenatal injury. (Scot. Law Co. No. 30)
Session 1972-73 Cmnd. 5371 xiv.

Report on the law relating to damages for injuries causing death. (Scot. Law Com. No. 31)
Session 1972-73 HC. 393 xiv.

Statute law revision; fifth report. Draft Statute Law (Repeals) Bill. (Law. Com. No. 57) (Scot. Law Com. No. 32)
Session 1973-74 Cmnd. 5493 iv.

1974   Scottish Law Commission. 8th annual report 1972-73. (Scot. Law Com. No. 33)
Session 1974 HC. 84 vii.

Report on presumption of death. (Scot. Law Com. No. 34)
Session 1974 HC. 225 vii.

Friendly Societies Bill. Report on the consolidation of the Friendly Societies Acts, 1896 to 1971. (Law Com. No. 59) (Scot. Law Com. No. 35)
Session 1974 Cmnd. 5634 vii.

Statute law revision. 6th report: draft Statute Law (Repeals) Bill. (Law Com. No. 63) (Scot. Law Com. No. 36)
Session 1974-75 Cmnd. 5792 xvii.

Scottish Law Commission, 9th annual report. (Scot. Law Com. No. 37)
Session 1974-75 HC. 183 xvii.

1975   Supply Powers Bill. Report on the consolidation of certain enactments. (Law Com. No. 66) (Scot. Law Com. No. 38)
Session 1974-75 Cmnd. 5850 xvii.

Exemption clauses second report. (Scot. Law Com. No. 39)
Session 1974-75 HC. 605 xvii.

Statute law revision, 7th report. Draft Statute Law (Repeals) Bill. (Law Com. No. 70) (Scot. Law Com. No. 40)
Session 1975-76 Cmnd. 6303 xx.

Scottish Law Commission. 10th annual report, 1974-75. (Scot. Law Com. No. 41)
Session 1975-76 HC. 93 xxi.

1976   Family law. Report on liability for adultery and enticement of a spouse. (Scot. Law Com. No. 42)
Session 1975-76 HC. 497 xxi.

1977   Scottish Law Commission. 11th annual report, 1975-76. (Scot. Law Com. No. 43)
Session 1976-77 HC. 111 xix.

Statute law revision, 8th report. Draft Statute Law (Repeals) Bill. (Law Com. No. 80) (Scot. Law Com. No. 44)
Session 1976-77 Cmnd. 6719 xix.

Liability for defective products. (Law Com. No. 82) (Scot. Law Com. No. 45)
Session 1976-77 Cmnd. 6831 xix.

1978   Third programme of consolidation and statute law revision. (Scot. Law Com. No. 46)
Session 1977-78 HC. 192 xxiii.

Scottish Law Commission. 12th annual report, 1976-77. (Scot. Law Com. No. 47)
Session 1977-78 HC. 211 xxiii.

Statute law revision, 5th report. Draft Statute Law (Repeals) Bill. (Law Com. No. 87) (Scot. Law Com. No. 48)
Session 1977-78 Cmnd. 7189 xxiii.

Electricity (Scotland) Bill. Report on the consolidation of certain enactments. (Scot. Law Com. No. 49)
Session 1977-78 Cmnd. 7178 xxiii.

Adoption (Scotland) Bill. Report on the consolidation of certain enactments. (Scot. Law Com. No. 50)
Session 1977-78 Cmnd. 7187 xxiii.

Damages for personal injuries. Report on (1) admissibility of claims for services (2) admissible deductions. (Scot. Law Com. No. 51)
Session 1977-78 HC. 557 xxiii.

Married Women's Policies of Assurance (Scotland) Act. 1880. Report. (Scot. Law Com. No. 52)
Session 1977-78 Cmnd. 7245 xxiii.

Interpretation Bill. Report on the Interpretation Act, 1889 and certain other enactments relating to the construction and operation of acts of Parliament and other instruments. (Law Com. No. 90) (Scot. Law Com. No. 53)
Session 1977-78 Cmnd. 7235 xxiii.

Customs and Excise Management Bill. Report on the consolidation of certain enactments. (Law Com. No. 93) (Scot. Law Com. No. 54)
Session 1978-79 Cmnd. 7418
See also DIAMOND, A. L.

1973   Boundary Commission for Scotland. Report
Session 1972-73 HC. 140 vi.

1975   Crime and the prevention of crime. A memorandum by the Scottish Council on Crime
Scottish Home and Health D.

HUNTER, Laurence C.

1971   Report of an inquiry into a difference between members of the Association of Scientific, Technical and Managerial Staffs and Courtaulds Ltd. over the termination of employment at Spennymoor of certain members of the Association
D. of Employment

1975   Panel of investigation into current difficulties affecting the T & GWU at the Dagenham Cold Store and F. J. Robertson Ltd. and also the effect on employers of registered dock labour in the London area. (Report No. 2)
Advisory Conciliation and Arbitration Service

1978   Labour shortages and manpower policy. (Manpower studies, 1978/2)
Manpower Services Commission

HUNTER, R. B.

1972   Medical administrators. Report of the working party
D. of Health and Social Security

1975   Tobacco substitute and additives in tobacco products; their testing and marketing in the U.K. First report of the independent scientific committee on smoking and health
D. of Health and Social Security

HURST, Gerald, Sir

1954   Adoption of children. Report of the departmental committee
Session 1953-54 Cmd. 9248 viii.

HUSKISSON, R. A.

1976   Hotel prospects in 1988; a summary and recommendations by the Hotels and Catering Economic Development Committee
N.E.D.O.

HUTCHESON, G. A.

1971   Training for work study practice. Report prepared and presented to the Department of Employment by a joint committee of industrial training boards
D. of Employment

HUTCHESON, J. C.
    See SINGLETON, J. E.

HUTCHINSON, A. S., Sir

1947   Transfer of members of the national fire service to fire brigades. Interim report of the Central Fire Brigades Advisory Council (England and Wales) committee
Home Office

HUTCHISON, James H.

1968   The medical care of epilepsy in Scotland. Report of a sub-committee of the Standing Medical Advisory Committee
Scottish Home and Health D.

HUTCHISON, William

1968   Higher police training in Scotland. Report of a working party of the Police Advisory Board for Scotland
Scottish Home and Health D.

HUTSON, Lockhart W.

1946   Labour requirements in the brick industry. 1st report of the national brick advisory council technical committee
M. of Works

1953   Increase in the cost of maintaining houses. Report by a sub-committee of the Scottish building costs committee
D. of Health for Scotland

HUTTON, H. R.

1972   The Public Trustee Office. Report of the committee of inquiry
Session 1971-72 Cmnd. 4914 xxii.

HUTTON, Maurice, Sir

1953   Tax-paid stocks. Report of the committee
Session 1952-53 Cmd. 8784 xvii.

HUXLEY, J. S.

1947   Conservation of nature in England and Wales. Wildlife conservation special committee report
Session 1946-47 Cmd. 7122 xiv.

HYAM, J.
    See WHITLEY, R. L.

HYDE, W. N.

1976   The feasibility of an experiment in the tape-recording of police interrogations. Report of a committee
Session 1975-76 Cmnd. 6630 xxxix.

HYTMER, B. Alan

1976   Roadships Ltd. (formerly known as Ralph Hilton Transport Services, Ltd.). Report of investigations under the Companies Act
D. of Trade

ILCHESTER, G. S. H., Earl of

1952   Ancient monuments of the western part of the County of Dorset. 20th interim report of the Royal Commission on Ancient and Historical Monuments and Constructions of England
Session 1951-52 Cmd. 8670 xv.

ILIFF, Neil A.

1970   Printing in a competitive world. Report of the Printing and Publishing E.D.C.s joint mission to printing firms in five countries
N.E.D.O.

INCE, Godfrey H., Sir

1945   Juvenile employment service. Report of the committee
M. of Labour and National Service

1948   Joint consultation, training within the industry, works information and personnel management. Report of the conference
M. of Labour and National Service

1956   Welsh broadcasting. Report of a committee of inquiry
Session 1956-57 Cmnd. 39 ix.

1955   Effects of national service on the education and employment of young men. Report of the inquiry
M. of Labour and National Service

INGALL, D. H.

1958   Training of district nurses. Report of the advisory committee
M. of Health

INGLEBY, O., Viscount

1960   Children and young persons. Report of the committee
Session 1959-60 Cmnd. 1191 ix.

INGLIS, Charles, Sir
    Railway (London plan) committee
1946   Report
1948   Final report
    M. of Transport

INGLIS, James C., Sir
    Higher education in the colonies. Inter-university council
1946   Report
    Session 1944-45 Cmd. 6647 iv.
1948   Report
    Session 1947-48 Cmd. 7331 xi.
1949   2nd report
    Session 1948-49 Cmd. 7801 xiii.
1951   3rd report
    Colonial Office

INGRAM, J. T.

1967   Nomenclature of fungi pathogenic to man and animals. Medical mycology committee. (Memorandum No. 23) 3rd ed.
Medical Research Council

INSALL, D. W.

1969   Chester; a study in conservation. Report of the preservation policy group
M. of Housing and Local Government

INSKIP, J. H.

1974   South Ockendon Hospital. Report of the committee of inquiry
Session 1974 HC. 124 v.

IRELAND, F. W.

1970 Report on a fatal accident in a factory at Southport, Lancashire on April 10, 1968
Home Office

IRESON, Richard

1978 International input-output tables for Wales and the rest of the U.K., 1968
Welsh Office

IRVINE, Ian Alexander Noble

1976 Roadships Ltd. (formerly known as Ralph Hilton Transport Services Ltd.). Report of investigations under the Companies Act
D. of Trade

IRVINE, James, Sir

1944 West Indies committee of the commission on higher education in the colonies. Report
Session 1944-45 Cmd. 6654 v.

IRVING, Edmund, Sir

1971 British research in the Antarctic. Report of the Antarctic committee. (Publications series B, No. 1)
Natural Environment Research Council

1976 Navigation of the River Mersey, 1975. Report on the state of navigation
D. of Transport

IZARD, C. G.

1948 Compensation and superannuation of staffs of approved societies. Statement by the minister of national insurance and final report of the staffing advisory committee
M. of National Insurance

JABSON, M.

1950 Home committee of the Scottish Advisory Council on Child Care. Report
Scottish Home D.

JACK, D. T., Sir

1957 Report of a court of inquiry into the causes and circumstances of a dispute between the British Overseas Airways Corporation and the Merchant Navy and Airline Officers' Association
Session 1956-57 Cmnd. 105 xiv.

Report of a court of inquiry into a dispute between employers who are members of the Engineering and Allied Employers' National Federation and workmen who are members of trade unions affiliated to the Confederation of Shipbuilding and Engineering Unions
Session 1956-57 Cmnd. 159 xiv.

Report of a court of inquiry into a dispute between employers who are members of the Shipbuilding Employers' Federation and workmen who are members of trade unions affiliated to the Confederation of Shipbuilding and Engineering Unions
Session 1956-57 Cmnd. 160 xiv.

1958 Report of a court of inquiry into the causes and circumstances of a dispute at London Airport existing between employers and unions represented on the National Joint Council for Civil Air Transport
Session 1958-59 Cmnd. 608 xvi.

1961 Rural bus services. Report of the committee
M. of Transport

1963 Report of a court of inquiry into the causes and circumstances of a dispute between the Ford Motor Company Ltd., Dagenham and members of the trade unions represented on the trade union side of the Ford National Joint Negotiating Committee
Session 1962-63 Cmnd. 1999 xx.

1964 Report of the committee of inquiry into the dispute at the Spitalfields, Borough, Stratford, Brentford and King's Cross Markets
M. of Labour *and* M. of Agriculture, Fisheries and Food

1965 Report of the committee on scales of salaries for the teaching staff of colleges of education, England and Wales
D. of Education and Science

Report of the committee on scales of salaries for teachers in establishments for further education, England and Wales
D. of Education and Science

Report of the committee on scales of salaries for the teaching staff of farm institutes and for teachers of agriculture (including horticultural) subjects, England and Wales
D. of Education and Science

JACKSON OF BURNLEY, Willis, Lord

1968 Television advisory committee. Report, 1967
Post Office

JACKSON, C. H. Ward-

See WARD-JACKSON, C. H.

JACKSON, E. J. W.

1949 Youth leaders and community centre wardens. Report of the committee on recruitment, training and conditions of service
M. of Education

JACKSON, G. O.

1978 Design and export, the better use of design resources for meeting the needs of U.K. clients and earning foreign currency. Report of the steering committee, Civil Engineering Economic Development Committee
N.E.D.O.

JACKSON, H. B.

1977 Morecambe Bay, Dee estuary and Wash feasibility studies of estuarial water storage in the U.K.
Central Water Planning Unit

JACKSON, R. A.

1955 Volta River project. Vol. 1: report of the preparatory commission
Board of Trade

JACKSON, R. D.

See TULLY, J.

JACKSON, W., Sir

1957 Supply and training of teachers for technical colleges. Report of the special committee
M. of Education

1966 Committee on manpower resources for science and technology. Report on the 1965 triennial manpower survey of engineers, technologists, scientists and technical supporting staff
Session 1966-67 Cmnd. 3103 xxxix.

JACOB, G. H. Lloyd-

See LLOYD-JACOB, G. H.

JAMES OF RUSHOLME, E. J. F., Lord

1972 Teacher education and training. Report by a committee of inquiry
D. of Education and Science

JAMES, Arthur, Lord

1975 Distribution of criminal business between the crown court and magistrates courts. Report of the interdepartmental committee
Session 1975-76 Cmnd. 6323 xix.

JAMES, A. E., Sir

1965 Report of inquiry into the circumstances in which it was possible for detective sergeant Harold Gordon Challoner of the Metropolitan Police to continue on duty at a time when he appears to have been affected by the onset of mental illness
Home Office

1972 Report of the tribunal appointed to inquire into certain issues in relation to the circumstances leading up to the cessation of trading by the Vehicle and General Insurance Co. Ltd.
Session 1971-72 HC. 133 ix.

JAMES, K. G.

1976 Prospects for the plastics packaging industry. Report based on a study of past performance, future investment requirements and constraints to profitable growth by the plastics packaging investment study panel
N.E.D.O.

JAMESON, William Wilson, Sir

1956 An inquiry into health visiting. Report of a working party on the field of work, training and recruitment of health visitors
M. of Health

1947 Psychologists and psychiatrists in the services. Report of an expert committee on their work
Privy Council Office

JAUNCEY, C. E.

1972 Report on the local inquiry in relation to the implementation by Falkirk Town Council of parts II and IV of the Housing (Financial Provisions) (Scotland) Act
Scottish Development D.

1975 Report of the committee of inquiry into the consideration given and steps taken towards securing the welfare of Richard Clark by Perth Town Council and other bodies or persons concerned
Scottish Education D.

JAY, Peggy

1976 Mental handicap nursing and care. Progress report of the committee of inquiry
D. of Health and Social Security

JEFFERY, John, Sir

1943 Local government and public health consolidation (Scotland) committee 1st report, August 1939
Session 1942-43 Cmd. 6476 v.

JEFFREYS, J.

1973 Distributive trades in the common market. Report by the working group

JEGER, Lena M.

1970 Taken for granted. Report of the working party on sewage disposal
M. of Housing and Local Government

JELLICOE, G. P. J. R., Earl of

1963 Conference on water resources in the North-West
M. of Housing and Local Government

JENKINS, D. L., Lord

1950 Leasehold committee. Final report
Session 1950 Cmd. 7982 xii.

1953 Law reform committee. 1st report: Statute of Frauds and section 4 of the Sale of Goods Act. 1893
Session 1952-53 Cmd. 8809 xiv.

1954 Law reform committee. 2nd report: Innkeepers' liability for property of travellers, guests and residents
Session 1953-54 Cmd. 9161 xvi.

Law reform committee. 3rd report: Occupiers' liability to invitees, licensees and trespassers
Session 1953-54 Cmd. 9305 xvi.

1956 Law reform committee. 4th report: Rule against perpetuities
Session 1956-57 Cmnd. 18 xv.

1957 Law reform committee. 5th report: Conditions and exceptions in insurance policies
Session 1956-57 Cmnd. 62 xv.

Law reform commission. 6th report: Courts' power to sanction variation of trusts
Session 1957-58 Cmnd. 310 xv.

1958 Law reform committee. 7th report: Effect of tax liabilities on damages
Session 1957-58 Cmnd. 501 xv.

1959 Law reform committee. 8th report: Sealing of contracts made by bodies corporate
Session 1958-59 Cmnd. 622 xvi.

1960 Law reform committee. 9th report: Liability in tort between husband and wife
Session 1960-61 Cmnd. 1268 xviii.

1962 Law reform committee. 10th report: Innocent misrepresentation
Session 1961-62 Cmnd. 1782 xviii.

1963 Law reform committee. 11th report. Loss of service
Session 1962-63 Cmnd. 2017 xx.

Company law committee
1960-1 Minutes of evidence. 1st-20th days, 23 September 1960-24th March 1961
1962 Report
Session 1961-62 Cmnd. 1749 xii.
Board of Trade

JENNINGS, W. Ivor, Sir

Royal Commission on Common Land
1956-7 Minutes of evidence. 1st to 49th days, 7th and 8th March 1956 to 2nd May 1957
Appendix to minutes of evidence
Index to minutes of evidence
Report
Session 1957-58 Cmnd. 462 x.

JENOUR, Maynard, Sir

1961 The problems of communication. Proceedings of a conference on science and industry
D. of Scientific and Industrial Research

JEPHCOTT, Harry, Sir

Synthetic detergents
1954 Interim report of the committee
1955 Report of the committee
M. of Housing and Local Government

Department of Scientific and Industrial Research. Report of a committee of inquiry
Session 1955-56 Cmd. 9734 xxvii.

JESSUP, F. W.

1968 A report on the supply and training of librarians. Library Advisory Council (England) and Library Advisory Council (Wales)
D. of Education and Science

JOBSON, Margaret

1950 Report of the homes committee of the Scottish advisory council
Scottish Home D.

JOHNSON, B. F. H.

1973 Training for professional accountants in industry, commerce and public services. Report by the joint committee of industrial training boards on the training of accountants
D. of Employment

JOHNSON, D. P. Croom-

See CROOM-JOHNSON, D. P.

JOHNSON, F. C., Sir

1946 Witnesses allowances order. Departmental committee report
Home Office

1952 Police pensions. Report of the working party of the Police Council
Home Office

JOHNSON, N.

1973 Federalism and decentralisation in the Federal Republic of Germany (research papers No. 1)
Commission on the Constitution

JOHNSON-MARSHALL, P.

See MATTHEW, R. H., Sir
See also WATSON, J. W.

JOHNSTON, Alexander, Sir

1972 The Berrow's Organisation Ltd. and the County Express Group. A report by the Monopolies Commission on the proposed transfer of four newspapers to the Berrow's Organisation Ltd.
Session 1971-72 HC. 224 xxii.

1973 Report on the proposed transfer of 18 newspapers to Westminster Press, Ltd. Monopolies Commission report
Session 1972-73 HC. 460 xv.

1974 Courier Printing and Publishing Co. Ltd. and Associated Newspapers Group Ltd. A report on the proposed transfer of five newspapers to Associated Newspapers Group Ltd.
Session 1974 HC. 108 viii.

1975 G. and A. N. Scott Ltd. and the Guardian and Manchester Evening News Ltd. A report on the proposed transfer of four newspapers to the Guardian and Manchester Evening News by the Monopolies and Mergers Commission
Session 1974-75 HC. 349 xvii.

1976 Indirect electrostatic reprographic equipment. A report on supply by the Monopolies and Mergers Commission
Session 1976-77 HC. 47 xx.

Barristers' services. Report on the supply by Her Majesty's counsel alone of their services by the Monopolies and Mergers Commission
Session 1975-76 HC. 512 xxii.

Advocates' services. Report on the supply by senior counsel alone of their services by the Monopolies and Mergers Commission
Session 1975-76 H.C. 513 xxi.

Services of solicitors in England and Wales. Report on supply of services in relation to restrictions on advertising, by the Monopolies and Mergers Commission
Session 1975-76 HC. 557 xxii.

Frozen foodstuffs. Report on supply in the U.K. of frozen foodstuffs for human consumption by the Monopolies and Mergers Commission

Session 1975-76 HC. 674 xxii.
See also ROSKILL, A., Sir

JOHNSTON, K.

1962 Industrial designs. Report of the departmental committee
Session 1961-62 Cmnd. 1808 xx.

JOHNSTON, K. S.

1967 Exports by air. A report by a working party of the Movement of Exports Economic Development Committee
N.E.D.O.

JOHNSTON, T. L.

1972 The demand for private houses in Scotland. A report for the Scottish housing advisory committee
Scottish Development D.

JOHNSTONE, C.

1968 Report on a fatal accident in a blast furnace at Scunthorpe, Lincolnshire on 17 July, 1965
Home Office

JOHNSTONE, D.

1975 A tax shall be charged. (Civil service studies No. 1)
Civil Service D.

JOLLY, John Catterall

1946 John Elliott. Inquiry into the case of John Elliott
Session 1945-46 Cmd. 6933 xiv.

1947 Ware inquiry. Report of an inquiry into the confession made by David John Ware of the murder of Olive Balchin in respect of which murder Walter Graham Rowland was convicted at Manchester Assizes on December 16, 1946
Session 1946-47 Cmd. 7049 xiv.

1948 Inquiry into the proposed compulsory amalgamation of the police forces of the County of Cheshire and the City and County Borough of Chester, held at the Town Hall, Chester on July 21 and 22, 1948. Report
Home Office

JONES, Edward, Sir

1974 County courts and magistrates' courts in Northern Ireland. Report of the committee
Session 1974-75 Cmnd. 5824 xv.

JONES, Aubrey

1965 Road haulage rates. National Board for Prices and Incomes report No. 1
Session 1964-65 Cmnd. 2695 xix.

Wages, costs and prices in the printing industry. National Board for Prices and Incomes report No. 2
Session 1964-65 Cmnd. 2750 xix.

Prices of bread and flour. National Board for Prices and Incomes report No. 3
Session 1964-65 Cmnd. 2760 xix.

Prices of household and toilet soaps, soap powders and soap flakes and soapless detergents. National Board for Prices and Incomes report No. 4
Session 1964-65 Cmnd. 2791 xix.

Remuneration of administrative and clerical staff in the electricity supply industry. National Board for Prices and Incomes report No. 5
Session 1964-65 Cmnd. 2801 xix.

Salaries of Midland Bank staff. National Board for Prices and Incomes report No. 6
Session 1965-66 Cmnd. 2839 vi.

Electricity and gas tariffs, London Electricity Board and Scottish, South Western and Wales gas

boards. National Board for Prices and Incomes report No. 7
Session 1965-66 Cmnd. 2862 vi.

1966   Pay and conditions of service of British Railways staff (conciliation, salaried and workshop grades). National Board for Prices and Incomes report No. 8
Session 1965-66 Cmnd. 2873 vi.

Wages in the bakery industry. National Board for Prices and Incomes report No. 9 (interim)
Session 1965-66 Cmnd. 2878 vi.

Armed forces pay. National Board for Prices and Incomes report No. 10
Session 1965-66 Cmnd. 2881 vi.

Pay of the higher civil service. National Board for Prices and Incomes report No. 11
Session 1965-66 Cmnd. 2882 vi.

Coal prices. National Board for Prices and Incomes report No. 12
Session 1965-66 Cmnd. 2919 vi.

Costs, prices and profits in the brewing industry. National Board for Prices and Incomes report No. 13
Session 1966-67 Cmnd. 2965 xlii.

Road haulage charges (final report). National Board for Prices and Incomes report No. 14
Session 1966-67 Cmnd. 2968 xlii.

Scottish teachers' salaries. National Board for Prices and Incomes report No. 15
Session 1966-67 Cmnd. 3005 xlii.

Pay and conditions of busmen. National Board for Prices and Incomes report No. 16
Session 1966-67 Cmnd. 3012 xlii.

Wages in the bakery industry. National Board for Prices and Incomes report No. 17
Session 1966-67 Cmnd. 3019 xlii.

Pay of industrial civil servants. National Board for Prices and Incomes report No. 18
Session 1966-67 Cmnd. 3034 xlii.

General report, 1965-66. National Board for Prices and Incomes report No. 19
Session 1966-67 Cmnd. 3087 xlii.

Reports 20 and 21. **See MARQUAND, H. A.**

Rate of interest on building society mortgages, National Board for Prices and Incomes report No. 22
Session 1966-67 Cmnd. 3136 xlii.

Productivity and pay during the period of severe restraint. National Board for Prices and Incomes report No. 23
Session 1966-67 Cmnd. 3167 xlii.

Wages and conditions in the electrical contracting industry. National Board for Prices and Incomes report No. 24
Session 1966-67 Cmnd. 3127 xlii.

1967   Pay of workers in agriculture in England and Wales. National Board for Prices and Incomes report No. 25
Session 1966-67 Cmnd. 3199 xlii.

Prices of standard newsprint. National Board for Prices and Income report No. 26
Session 1966-67 Cmnd. 3210 xlii.

Pay of workers in the retail drapery, outfitting and footwear trades. National Board for Prices and Incomes report No. 27
Session 1966-67 Cmnd. 3224 xlii.
Statistical supplement
Session 1966-67 Cmnd. 3224-I xlii.

Prices of compound fertilisers. National Board for Prices and Incomes report No. 28
Session 1966-67 Cmnd. 3228 xlii.

The pay and conditions of manual workers in local authorities, the National Health Service, gas and water supply (with) statistical supplement. National Board for Prices and Incomes report No. 29
Session 1966-67 Cmnd. 3230, Cmnd. 3230-I xlii.

Pay and conditions of limbfitters employed by J. E. Hanger & Co. National Board for Prices and Incomes report No. 30
Session 1966-67 Cmnd. 3245 xliii.

Distribution costs of fresh fruit and vegetables. National Board for Prices and Incomes report No. 31
Session 1966-67 Cmnd. 3265 xliii.

Fire service pay. National Board for Prices and Incomes report No. 32
Session 1966-67 Cmnd. 3287 xliii.

Remuneration of milk distributors (interim report). National Board for Prices and Incomes report No. 33
Session 1966-67 Cmnd. 3294 xliii.

Bank charges. National Board for Prices and Incomes report No. 34
Session 1966-67 Cmnd. 3292 xliii.

Pay and conditions of merchant navy officers. National Board for Prices and Incomes report No. 35
Session 1966-67 Cmnd. 3302 xliii.

Productivity agreements. National Board for Prices and Incomes report No. 36
Session 1966-67 Cmnd. 3311 xliii.

Costs and charges in the motor repairing and servicing industry. National Board for Prices and Incomes report No. 37
Session 1966-67 Cmnd. 3368 xliii.

Portland cement prices. National Board for Prices and Incomes report No. 38
Session 1966-67 Cmnd. 3381 xliii.

Costs and prices of aluminium semi-manutactures. National Board for Prices and Incomes report No. 39
Session 1966-67 Cmnd. 3378 xliii.

2nd general report. National Board for Prices and Incomes report No. 40
Session 1966-67 Cmnd. 3394 xliii.

Salaries of staff employed by the General Accident Fire and Life Assurance Corporation Ltd. National Board for Prices and Incomes report No. 41
Session 1966-67 Cmnd. 3398 xliii.

Pay of electricity supply workers. National Board for Prices and Incomes report No. 42
Session 1966-67 Cmnd. 3405 xliii.

Costs and revenue of national daily newspapers. National Board for Prices and Incomes report No. 43
Session 1966-67 Cmnd. 3435 xliii.

London weighting in the non-industrial Civil Service. National Board for Prices and Incomes report No. 44
Session 1967-68 Cmnd. 3436 xxvii.

Pay of chief and senior officers in local government service and in the Greater London Council. National Board for Prices and Incomes report No. 45
Session 1967-68 Cmnd. 3473 xxvii.

The remuneration of milk distributors (final report). National Board for Prices and Incomes report No. 46
Session 1967-68 Cmnd. 3477 xxvii.

Prices of fletton and non-fletton bricks. National Board for Prices and Incomes report No. 47
Session 1967-68 Cmnd. 3480 xxvii.

Charges, costs and wages in the road haulage industry. National Board for Prices and Incomes

report No. 48
Session 1967-68 Cmnd. 3482 xxvii.
Statistical supplement
Session 1967-68 Cmnd. 3482-I xxvii.

Pay and conditions of service of engineering workers (first report on the engineering industry) National Board for Prices and Incomes report No. 49
Session 1967-68 Cmnd. 3495 xxvii.
Statistical Supplement
Session 1967-68 Cmnd. 3495-I xxvii.

Productivity agreements in the bus industry. National Board for Prices and Incomes report No. 50
Session 1967-68 Cmnd. 3498 xxvii.

1968 Pay and productivity of industrial employees of the United Kingdom Atomic Energy Authority. National Board for Prices and Incomes report No. 51
Session 1967-68 Cmnd. 3499 xxvii.

Costs and charges in the radio and television rental and relay industry. National Board for Prices and Incomes report No. 52
Session 1967-68 Cmnd. 3520 xxvii.

Flour prices. National Board for Prices and Incomes report No. 53
Session 1967-68 Cmnd. 3522 xxvii.

Remuneration of solicitors. National Board for Prices and Incomes report No. 54
Session 1967-68 Cmnd. 3529 xxvii.

Distributors' margins in relation to manufacturers' recommended prices. National Board for Prices and Incomes report No. 55
Session 1967-68 Cmnd. 3546 xxvii.

Proposals by the London Transport Board and British Railways Board for fare increases in the London area. National Board for Prices and Incomes report No. 56
Session 1967-68 Cmnd. 3561 xxvii.

Gas prices (first report). National Board for Prices and Incomes report No. 57
Session 1967-68 Cmnd. 3567 xxvii.

Post Office charges. National Board for Prices and Incomes report No. 58
Session 1967-68 Cmnd. 3574 xxvii.

The bulk supply tariff of the Central Electricity Board. National Board for Prices and Incomes report No. 59
Session 1967-68 Cmnd. 3575 xxvii.

Pay of nurses and midwives in the National Health Service. National Board for Prices and Incomes report No. 60
Session 1967-68 Cmnd. 3585 xxvii.

Prices of secondary batteries. National Board for Prices and Incomes report No. 61
Session 1967-68 Cmnd. 3597 xxvii.

Increases in rents of local authority housing (with) statistical supplement. National Board for Prices and Incomes report No. 62
Session 1967-68 Cmnd. 3604, Cmnd. 3604-I xxvii.

Pay of municipal busmen. National Board for Prices and Incomes report No. 63
Session 1967-68 Cmnd. 3605 xxvii.

Increase in prices of mercury hearing-aid batteries manufactured by Mallory Batteries Ltd. National Board for Prices and Incomes report No. 64
Session 1967-68 Cmnd. 3625 xxviii.

Payment by result systems (with) supplement. National Board for Prices and Incomes report No. 64
Session 1967-68 Cmnd. 3627, Cmnd. 3627-I xxviii.

Price of Butyl rubber. National Board for Prices

and Incomes report No. 66
Session 1967-68 Cmnd. 3626 xxviii.

Passenger fares and freight charges of the North of Scotland, Orkney and Shetland Shipping Co. Ltd. National Board for Prices and Incomes report No. 67
Session 1967-68 Cmnd. 3631 xxviii.

Agreement made between certain engineering firms and the Draughtmen's and Allied Technicians' Association. National Board for Prices and Incomes report No. 68
Session 1967-68 Cmnd. 3632 xxviii.

Pay and conditions of busmen employed by the corporations of Belfast, Glasgow and Liverpool. National Board for Prices and Incomes report No. 69
Session 1967-68 Cmnd. 3646 xxviii.

Standing reference on the pay of the armed forces, 1st report. National Board for Prices and Incomes report No. 70
Session 1967-68 Cmnd. 3651 xxviii.

Architects' costs and fees. National Board for Prices and Incomes report No. 71
Session 1967-68 Cmnd. 3653 xxviii.

Proposed increases by British Railways Board in certain country-wide fares and charges. National Board for Prices and Incomes report No. 72
Session 1967-68 Cmnd. 3656 xxviii.

The prices of Hoover Domestic Appliances. National Board for Prices and Incomes report No. 73
Session 1967-68 Cmnd. 3671 xxviii.

Agreements relating to terms and conditions of employment of staff employed by the Prudential Assurance Co. Ltd. and the Pearl Assurance Co. Ltd. National Board for Prices and Incomes report No. 74
Session 1967-68 Cmnd. 3674 xxviii.

Costs and prices of the chocolate and sugar confectionery industry. National Board for Prices and Incomes report No. 75
Session 1967-68 Cmnd. 3694 xxviii.

Increase in rental charges for equipment hired from IBM United Kingdom Ltd. National Board for Prices and Incomes report No. 76
Session 1967-68 Cmnd. 3699 xxviii.

3rd annual report, 1967-68. National Board for Prices and Incomes report No. 77
Session 1967-68 Cmnd. 3715 xxviii.

Award relating to terms and conditions of employment in the Road Passenger Transport Department of Rochdale County Borough Council. National Board for Prices and Incomes report No. 78
Session 1967-68 Cmnd. 3723 xxviii.

Electricity supply industry national guidelines covering productivity payments. National Board for Prices and Incomes report No. 79
Session 1967-68 Cmnd. 3726 xxviii.

Distributors' margins on paint, children's clothing, household textiles and proprietary medicines. National Board for Prices and Incomes report No. 80
Session 1967-68 Cmnd. 3737 xxviii.

Pay awards made by the City and County of Bristol to staff employed in its dock undertaking. National Board for Prices and Incomes report No. 81
Session 1967-68 Cmnd. 3752 xxviii.

Report on an agreement relating to the pay of sawyers and woodcutting machinists in the saw milling industry. National Board for Prices and Incomes report No. 82
Session 1967-68 Cmnd. 3768 xxviii.

JONES, Aubrey (continued)

Hours of work, overtime and shiftworking. National Board for Prices and Incomes report No. 161
Session 1970-71 Cmnd. 4554 xlv.
Supplement
Session 1970-71 Cmnd. 4554-I xlv.

See also PEDDIE, J. M., Lord

1973   Seat prices. Report of the committee of inquiry
Arts Council

JONES, Austin

County court procedure
1948   1st interim report of the committee
Session 1947-48 Cmd. 7468 xi.
1949   Final report of the committee
Session 1948-49 Cmd. 7668 xiii.

JONES, B.

1965   Audio-visual aids in higher scientific education. Report of the committee of the University Grants Committee
D. of Education and Science

1971   Assessment of children. Report of a study group of the Social Work Services Group
Scottish Education D.

JONES, B. R.

1976   Preservation of sterility in ophthalmic preparations used in the treatment of eye cases. Report of the working party
D. of Health and Social Security

JONES, Ben G.

1975   Welsh Language in nursery education
Council for the Welsh Language

1978   A future for the Welsh Language
Council for the Welsh Language

Publishing in the Welsh Language
Council for the Welsh Language

JONES, C. Bryner, Sir

1950   Malltraeth Marsh investigation. Welsh agricultural land sub-commission. Report
M. of Agriculture and Fisheries

Borth Bog investigation. Report of the Welsh agricultural land sub-commission
M. of Agriculture and Fisheries

JONES, Clement W., Sir

1948   Technical and scientific register. Present and future demand and supply for persons with professional qualifications in geology. Report of the geologists' sub-committee
M. of Labour and National Service

1948   West Indian shipping services. Report
Commonwealth Shipping Committee

JONES, Deborah

1972   Education for management and study of resources, a report. Management, Education. Training and Development Committee
N.E.D.O.

JONES, Ewart, Sir

1978   Information transfer and use in chemistry. Final report of the chemical information review committee. (Research and Development Report No. 5385)
British Library

JONES, E. M. KEMP-, Mrs.

See KEMP-JONES, E. M.

JONES, F. E.

1967   The brain drain. Report of the working group on migration of the committee on manpower resources for science and technology
Session 1966-67 Cmnd. 3417 xxxix.

1974   Summary of findings and recommendations of the industrial review to 1977. Mechanical Engineering Economic Development Office
N.E.D.O.

JONES, F. Llewellyn-

1965   Science in education in Wales today. Report of the Central Advisory Council for Education (Wales)
D. of Education and Science

JONES, G. I.

1950   Basutoland medicine murder. Report on the recent outbreak of " Diretlo " murders in Basutoland
Session 1950-51 Cmd. 8209 x.

JONES, H.

1973   Industrial review to 1977: chemicals. Chemicals Economic Development Committee
N.E.D.O.

JONES, J. D.

1965   Piccadilly Circus. Report of the working party
M. of Housing and Local Government

JONES, J. Harry

1945   Road accidents report
M. of Transport

JONES, J. Morgan

1960   Welsh Agricultural college. Report of a working party
M. of Agriculture, Fisheries and Food

JONES, N. H.

Wool textile industry; spacing of certain machinery; processes subsequent to carding. Joint factory advisory committee
1946   Interim report
1948   Final report
M. of Labour and National Service

JONES, Richard M.

1971   Absenteeism. (Manpower papers No. 4)
D. of Employment

JONES, S. Lloyd

1962   London Government. The London boroughs. Report
M. of Housing and Local Government

JONES, T. L.

1977   Assessment of housing requirements. Report of the housing services advisory group
D. of the Environment

Tenancy agreements. Report by the housing services advisory group
D. of the Environment

1978   Allocation of council housing. Housing services advisory group
D. of the Environment

Client role in public sector house-building. Report of the housing services advisory group
D. of the Environment

Housing of one-parent families. Report of the

JONES, T. L. (*continued*)

housing services advisory group
D. of the Environment

Organising a comprehensive housing service. Report of the housing service advisory group
D. of the Environment

JONES, T. P.

1977   Energy strategy. Report of the working group. (Paper No. 2)
Energy Commission

JONES, William

1944   Coal miners. Report of the advisory committee on the treatment and rehabilitation of coal miners in the Wales region suffering from pneumoconiosis
M. of Fuel and Power

JONES, W. L., MARS-

See MARS-JONES, W. L.

JONES, W. R.

1946   China clay. Report of the working committee
Session 1945-46 Cmd. 6748 x.

Ball-clay industry inquiry report
Board of Trade

JUKES, J. A.

Water services; economic and financial policies
1973   1st report
1974   2nd report
            3rd report
D. of the Environment

Water services; economic and financial policies: social report
D. of the Environment

JUPP, K. G.

1975   Fairfield Home, Edwalton, Nottinghamshire of 15 December 1974. Report of the committee of inquiry into the fire
Session 1974-75 Cmnd. 6149 x.

KARMEL, D.

1961   Truck acts. Report of the committee
M. of Labour

1962   British Wool Marketing Scheme, 1950. Complaints made by the Scottish wool trades consultative committee. Report of the committee of investigation for Great Britain
D. of Agriculture and Fisheries for Scotland

KARN, V. A.

See CULLINGWORTH, J. B.

KAUFMAN, M.

1975   Education and training for the 16-18-year-olds. 1st report of the study group
Rubber and Plastics Processing Industry Training Board

1976   School curricula for a changing world. 2nd report of the study group
Rubber and Plastics Processing Industry Training Board

KAUSMAN, M. A.

1973   Regional strategy for water recreation. Zone 1: Great Ouse and its associated waterways. Report of the committee. 3 vols.
Sports Council, Eastern Region

KAY, A.

1977   Cardiac surgery. A report by a programme planning group of the Scottish Health Service Planning Council
Scottish Home and Health D.

KAY, J. B.

1967   Allocating council houses. Report of the sub-committee of the Scottish Housing Advisory Committee
Scottish Development D.

KEANEY, M. D. W.

1976   Scottish literature in the secondary school. Report of the sub-committee of the Scottish central committee on English
Scottish Education D.

KEDDIE, J. A. Grant

1945   Congenital deaf-mutism in Scotland. Report
D. of Health for Scotland

KEEN, B. A., Sir

1946   Vegetable oil and oil seeds produced in the West African colonies. Report of the mission appointed to inquire into production and transport
Colonial Office

KEITH OF AVONHOLM, J., Lord

1963   Accommodation needs of the Scottish Record Office, Registrar-General's Office and Lyon Office. Report of a committee
Scottish Home and Health D.

KEITH, James

1945   The needs of youth in these times. A report of the Scottish youth advisory committee
Scottish Education D.

1946   The recruitment and training of youth leaders and organisers. A report of the Scottish youth advisory committee
Scottish Education D.

KEITH, Kenneth A.

1968   East Anglia: a study. 1st report by the East Anglia Planning Council
D. of Economic Affairs

KELHAM, R. Langdale

1957   Rehabilitation of amputees. General principles drawn up by a sub-committee of the Brussels Treaty Organisation
M. of Health

KELLY, M.

1972   Small firms in the manufacturing sector (Committee of inquiry on small firms research report No. 3)
D. of Trade and Industry

KEMP-JONES, E. M.

1971   Employment of women in the civil service. Report of a departmental committee (C.S.D. management studies No. 3)
Civil Service D.

KENDREW, John C.

1968   Molecular biology. Report of the working group of the Council for Scientific Policy
Session 1967-68 Cmnd. 3675 xxxi.

KNOX, T. Malcolm, Sir

1945   Development of the catering, holiday and tourist services. Report of an inquiry by the Catering Wages Commission
M. of Labour and National Service

Staggering of holidays. Report by the Catering Wages Commission
M. of Labour and National Service

Training for the catering industry. Report of an inquiry by the Catering Wages Commission
M. of Labour and National Service

1957   Teachers. Measures to improve the supply of teachers in Scotland. Special committee of the Advisory Council on Education in Scotland
Interim report
Session 1956-57 Cmnd. 202 x.

1958   Report
Session 1958-59 Cmnd. 644 xi.

1960   Post-fourth year examination structure in Scotland. Report of a special committee of the Advisory Council on Education in Scotland
Session 1959-60 Cmnd. 1068 xii.

1961   Transfer from primary to secondary education. Report of a special committee of the Advisory Council on Education in Scotland
Session 1961-62 Cmnd. 1538 xiii.

KOGAN, M.

1977   Health and health policy; priorities for research. Report of the advisory panel
Social Science Research Council

LACEY, G.

1948   East African rice mission report. (Colonial No. 246)
Colonial Office

LAIDLAW, G. P., Sir

1948   Scottish building costs. Report of the committee
D. of Health for Scotland

LAMBERT, H. G.

1953   Bulk handling of home-grown grain. Report of the working group
M. of Agriculture and Fisheries

LANE, E. K.

1974   Abortion Act. Committee on the working of the Act
Vol. 1: Report
Session 1974-75 Cmnd. 5579 vi.
Vol. 2: Statistical volume
Vol. 3: Survey of abortion patients
D. of Health and Social Security

LANG, Cosmo Gordon, Archbishop of Canterbury, 1928-1942

1940   Benefice Buildings (Postponement of Inspections and Repayment of Loans) Measure. 82nd report of the Ecclesiastical Commission
Session 1939-40 HC. 143 iv; HL. 61-I

Ecclesiastical Dilapidations (Chancel Repairs) Measure. 83rd report of the Ecclesiastical Commission
Session 1939-40 HC. 145 iv; HL. 61-II

1941   Diocesan Reorganisation Committee Measure. 84th report of the Ecclesiastical Commission
Session 1940-41 HC. 30 iv; HL. 30

1942   Ecclesiastical Commissioners (Powers) Measure. 85th report of the Ecclesiastical Commission
Session 1941-42 HC. 70 iv; HL. 16

LANG, John G., Sir

Pricing of Ministry of Aviation contracts
1964   1st report of the inquiry
Session 1963-64 Cmnd. 2428 xvi.

1965   2nd report of the inquiry
Session 1964-65 Cmnd. 2581 xix.

1969   Crowd behaviour at football matches. Report of the working party
M. of Housing and Local Government

LANGDON, R. N. D.

First Re-investment Trust Ltd., Nelson Financial Trust Ltd., English and Scottish Unit Trust Holdings Ltd.

1974   Interim report of investigations under the Companies Act

1975   2nd and final report of investigations under the Companies Act
D. of Trade

LANSDOWNE, G. J. C., Marquess of

1963   Malaysia. Report of the intergovernmental committee
Session 1962-63 Cmnd. 1954 x.

LATEY, J. B.

1967   Age of majority. Report of the committee
Session 1966-67 Cmnd. 3342 xxi.

LAW, D.

1972   Mid-Wales; an assessment of the impact of the development factory programme
Development Commission

LAWRENCE, Dennis

1977   Co-operative development agency. Report of the working group
Session 1976-77 Cmnd. 6972 viii.

LAWRENCE, F. Geoffrey, Sir

1963   Scottish plumbers' and the Scottish builders' agreements of 1962. Report of the National Incomes Commission
Session 1962-63 Cmnd. 1994 xxi.

Report on the agreements of February-March 1963 in electrical contracting, in heating, ventilating and domestic engineering, and in exhibition contracting. National Incomes Commission report No. 2
Session 1962-63 Cmnd. 2098 xxi.

1964   Remuneration of academic staff in universities and colleges of advanced technology. National Incomes Commission report No. 3
Session 1963-64 Cmnd. 2317 xvii.

Report of the committee on the remuneration of ministers and members of parliament
Session 1964-65 Cmnd. 2516 xix.

1965   Agreements of November-December 1963 in the engineering and shipbuilding industries. National Incomes Commission report No. 4
Interim report
Session 1963-64 Cmnd. 2380 xviii.
Final report
Session 1964-65 Cmnd. 2583 xix.

LAWSON, Neil

1970   Codification of the criminal law; general principles: the mental element in crime. Report of a working party (working paper No. 31)
Law Commission

1971   Transfer of land. Appurtenant rights. First programme, item IX. Report of the working group (working paper No. 36)
Law Commission

LAWSON, William, Sir
1970   Review Board for Government Contracts. Report on the interim review
Review Board for Government Contracts

LAYBOURNE, K.
1970   " Cross'd with adversity "; the education of socially disadvantaged children in secondary schools. Report of the working party (working paper No. 27)
Schools Council

LAYFIELD, F. H. B.
1973   Greater London development plan. Report of the panel of inquiry. 2 vols.
D. of the Environment

1976   Local government finance. Report of the departmental committee [with] 9 appendices
Session 1975-76 Cmnd. 6453 xxi.

LAYTON, D. N.
1977   Corrosion control, a profitable technology. Committee on corrosion
D. of Industry

LEACH, C.
1976   Measurement of labour efficiency in retail stores. Working party on pay and efficiency in retail distribution
N.E.D.O.

LEACH, E. B.
1969   Better delivery; how to make delivery promises more reliable; reduce delivery times; and improve profitability. Report of a working party of the Mechanical Engineering Economic Development Committee
N.E.D.O.

LEACH, K. M.
1967   Future demand for process plant. A report by the process plant working party
N.E.D.O.

Investment by the process industries. 2nd report by the process plant working party
N.E.D.O.

1968   The process and allied industries investment. 3rd report by the process plant working party
N.E.D.O.

LEACH, R. G.
1963   Milk Marketing Scheme, 1933 (as amended). Report by the Consumers' Committee for England and Wales
M. of Agriculture, Fisheries and Food

1972   Pergamon Press, Ltd. Further interim report of investigations under the Companies Act
D. of Trade and Industry

1973   Maxwell Scientific International (Distribution Services) Ltd., Robert Maxwell & Co. Ltd., and final report of investigations under the Companies Act on Pergamon Press Ltd.
D. of Trade and Industry

LEDINGHAM, John, Sir
1942   Report of the committee on bed-bug infestation, 1935-40 (Special report series No. 45)
Medical Research Council

LEE, A. G.
1947   Absorption of staffs of approved societies. Statement by the Minister and interim report of a staffing advisory committee
M. of National Insurance

LEE, A. G. Vaughan-
See VAUGHAN-LEE, A. G.

LEE, M. C.
1978   Housing for people. Report of the housing services advisory sub-group on the allocation of council housing
D. of the Environment

LEES, D. S.
1972   National Insurance (Earnings-Related Benefit) Amendment Regulations, 1972. Report of the National Insurance Advisory Committee
Session 1971-72 HC. 322 xxxviii.

National Insurance (Non-Participation—Benefits and Schemes) Amendment Regulations, 1972. Report of the National Insurance Advisory Committee
Session 1971-72 HC. 377 xxxviii.

1973   National Insurance and Industrial Injuries (Collection of Contributions) Regulations. Report of the National Insurance Advisory Committee
Session 1972-73 HC. 337 xxxiii.

National Insurance (Graduated Contributions) Amendment Regulations, 1973. Report of the National Insurance Advisory Committee
Session 1972-73 HC. 203 xxxiii.

National Insurance (Members of the Forces) Amendment Regulations, 1973. Report of the National Insurance Advisory Committee
Session 1972-73 HC. 246 xxxiii.

National Insurance (Overlapping Benefits and Miscellaneous Amendments) Regulations, 1973. Report of the National Insurance Advisory Committee
Session 1972-73 Cmnd. 5420 xxxiii.

1974   National Insurance (Classification) Amendment Regulations, 1974. Report of the National Insurance Advisory Committee
Session 1973-74 HC. 101 xii.

National Insurance (Health Service Reorganisation Consequential Amendments) Regulations. Report of the National Insurance Advisory Committee
Session 1974 HC. 32 xvi.

1975   Vibration syndrome. Report by the Industrial Injuries Advisory Council
Session 1974-75 Cmnd. 5965 viii.

Viral hepatitis. Report by the Industrial Injuries Advisory Council
Session 1974-75 Cmnd. 6257 viii.

1976   Vinylchloride monomer. Report by the Industrial Injuries Advisory Committee
Session 1975-76 Cmnd. 6620 xi.

Social Security (Contributions) Amendment Regulations, 1976. Report of the National Insurance Advisory Committee
Session 1975-76 HC. 138 xlv.

Social Security (Invalid Care Allowance) Regulations, 1976. Report of the National Insurance Advisory Committee
Session 1975-76 HC. 271 xlv.

Social Security (Medical Evidence) Regulations, 1976. Report of the National Insurance Advisory Committee
Session 1975-76 HC. 349 xlv.

Social Security (Northern Ireland Reciprocal Arrangements) Regulations, 1976. Report of the National Insurance Advisory Committee
Session 1975-76 HC. 527 xlv.

1977   Social Security (Claims and Payments) Amendment (No. 2) Regulations. Report of the National Insurance Advisory Committee
Session 1976-77 Cmnd. 6924 xlv.

LEES, D. S. (*continued*)

Social Security (Benefit) (Married Women and Widows Special Provisions) Amendment Regulations. Report of the National Insurance Advisory Committee
Session 1976-77 Cmnd. 6929 xlv.

Social Security Benefit (Persons Abroad) Amendment Regulations, 1977. Report of the National Insurance Advisory Committee
Session 1976-77 Cmnd. 6967 xlv.

Social Security (Claims and Payments) (Unemployment Benefit Transitory Provisions, Regulations, 1977 and the Social Security (Claims and Payments) Amendment Regulations, 1977. Report of the National Insurance Advisory Committee
Session 1976-77 Cmnd. 6897 xlv.

Social Security (Non-contributory Invalidity Pension) Amendment Regulations, 1977. Report of the National Insurance Advisory Committee
Session 1976-77 Cmnd. 6900 xlv.

Social Security (Hospital In-patients) Amendment Regulations, 1977. Report of the National Insurance Advisory Committee
Session 1976-77 Cmnd. 6973 xlv.

Regulation 11(2)(a) of the Employment Protection (Recoupment of Unemployment Benefit and Supplementary Benefit) Regulations, 1977. Report of the National Insurance Advisory Committee
Session 1976-77 HC. 311 xlv.

Social Security (Categorisation of Earners) Amendment Regulations, 1977. Report of the National Insurance Advisory Committee
Session 1976-77 HC. 418 xlv.

Social Security (Unemployment, Sickness and Invalidity Benefit) (Amendment) Regulations, 1977. Report of the National Insurance Advisory Committee
Session 1977-78 Cmnd. 6976 lii.

Seasonal workers. Report of the National Insurance Advisory Committee
Session 1977-78 Cmnd. 6991 lii.

Social Security (Contributions) Miscellaneous Amendments Regulations, 1977. Report of the National Advisory Committee
Session 1977-78 Cmnd. 7008 lii.

Social Security (Categorisation of Earners and Contributions) Amendment Regulations. Report of the National Insurance Advisory Committee
Session 1977-78 HC. 109 lii.

1978   Occupational deafness. Report by the Industrial Injuries Advisory Committee
Session 1977-78 Cmnd. 7266 lii.

Social Security (Graduated Retirement Benefit) Regulations, 1978. Report of the National Insurance Advisory Committee
Session 1977-78 HC. 290 lii.

Social Security (Miscellaneous Amendments) Regulations, 1978. Report of the National Insurance Advisory Committee
Session 1977-78 HC. 314 lii.

Social Security (Contributions) Amendment Regulations, 1978. Report of the National Insurance Advisory Committee
Session 1977-78 HC. 308 lii.

Social Security (Contributions) Amendment (No. 2) Regulations, 1978. Report of the National Insurance Advisory Committee
Session 1977-78 HC. 363 lii.

Social Security (Contributions) Amendment (No. 2) Regulations, 1978. Report of the National Insurance Advisory Committee
Session 1977-78 HC. 502 lii.

Mobility allowance (Mobility Payment Arrangements) Regulations, 1978. Report of the National

Insurance Advisory Committee
Session 1977-78 Cmnd. 7307 lii.

Social Security (Unemployment, Sickness and Invalidity Benefit) Amendment (No. 3) Regulations, 1978. Report of the National Insurance Advisory Committee
Session 1977-78 Cmnd. .321 lii.

Social Security (Claims and Payments) (Unemployment Benefit Transitory Provisions) Amendment Regulations, 1978. Report of the National Insurance Advisory Committee on the draft regulations
Session 1977-78 Cmnd. 7296 lii.

Social Security (Overlapping Benefit) Amendments (No. 2) Regulations, 1978. Report of the National Insurance Advisory Committee
Session 1978-79 Cmnd. 7379

Social Security (Categorisation of Earners) Amendment Regulations, 1978. Report of the National Insurance Advisory Committee
Session 1978-79 Cmnd. 7393

Social Security (Non-Contributory Invalidity Pension) Amendment (No. 2) Regulations, 1978. Report of the National Insurance Advisory Committee
Session 1978-79 Cmnd. 7427

Unemployment Benefit for Students. Report of the National Insurance Advisory Committee
Session 1978-79 Cmnd. 7384

Social Security (Contributions) Amendment (No. 3) Regulations, 1978. Report of the National Insurance Advisory Committee
Session 1978-79 HC. 76

Social Security (Contributions) (Mariners) Amendment Regulations, 1978. Report of the National Insurance Advisory Committee
Session 1978-79 HC. 86

See also ANDERSON, W. C.

LEGG, Charles

1976   Administration of the rent rebate and rent allowance schemes
D. of the Environment

LEGGATT, A.

1976   Fircroft College. Report of the committee of inquiry
Session 1975-76 HC. 319 xi.

LEGGATT, A. P.

1976   London and County Securities Group Ltd. Report of investigations under the Companies Act
D. of Trade

LEGGATT, T. W.

1972   The training of British managers; a study of need and demand. Management Education, Training and Development Committee
N.E.D.O.

LEGGETT, Frederick W., Sir

1951   Unofficial stoppages in the London docks. Report of a committee of inquiry
Session 1950-51 Cmd. 8236 xvi.

1956   Building apprenticeship and training council. Final report
M. of Works

LEICESTER, C.

1972   Britain 2001 A.D. An analysis of economic activity, work and leisure time at the turn of the century
Post Office

LEIGH-BREESE, P. L.

1954   Residential qualifications. Housing management sub-committee of the Central Housing Advisory Committee. 5th report
M. of Housing and Local Government

1955   Unsatisfactory tenants. Housing management sub-committee of the Central Housing Advisory Committee. 6th report
M. of Housing and Local Government

LEIGHTON, Alan

1977   " Out of Work? " A guide for men and women who have become unemployed
Manpower Services Commission

LEITCH, George, Sir

1977   Trunk road assessment. Report of the advisory committee
D. of Transport

LEMON, Ernest, Sir

1949   Standardization of engineering products. Report of the committee
M. of Supply

LENNON, K. J.

See STARITT, J.

LENNOX-BOYD, A. T.

See BOYD OF MERTON, A. T., Viscount

LE QUESNE, J. G.

1976   Eurocanadian Shipholdings Ltd. and Furness, Withy and Co. Ltd. and Manchester Liners Ltd. Report on the existing and proposed mergers by the Monopolies and Mergers Commission
Session 1975-76 HC. 639 xxii.

Services of Solicitors in Scotland. Report of the Monopolies and Mergers Commission
Session 1975-76 HC. 558 xxii.

1977   British Petroleum Ltd. and Century Oils Group Ltd. A report on the proposed merger by the Monopolies and Mergers Commission
Session 1976-77 Cmnd. 6827 xix.

Diazo copying materials. Report on supply by the Monopolies and Mergers Commission
Session 1976-77 HC. 165 xx.

Babcock and Wilcox Ltd. and Herbert Morris Ltd. Report on the existing and proposed mergers by the Monopolies and Mergers Commission
Session 1976-77 HC. 175 xix.

Flour and bread. Report on supply in the U.K. of wheat flour and of bread made from wheat flour, by the Monopolies and Mergers Commission
Session 1976-77 HC. 412 xx.

Architects' services. Report of the Monopolies and Mergers Commission
Session 1977-78 HC. 4 xxiv.

Surveyors' services: Report by the Monopolies and Mergers Commission
Session 1977-78 HC. 5 xxiv.

The Fruehauf Corporation and Crane Fruehauf. Report on the proposed merger by the Monopolies and Mergers Commission
Session 1976-77 Cmnd. 6906 xx.

1978   Smith Brothers Ltd. and Bisgood, Bishop and Co. Ltd. A report on the proposed merger by the Monopolies and Mergers Commission
Session 1977-78 HC. 242 xxiv.

Rockware Group Ltd., United Glass Ltd., Redfearn National Glass Ltd. A report on the proposed mergers by the Monopolies and Mergers Commission
Session 1977-78 HC. 431 xxiv.

Ceramic sanitaryware. Report on the supply in the U.K. and export from the U.K. of ceramic sanitaryware by the Monopolies and Mergers Commission
Session 1977-78 Cmnd. 7327 xxiv.

Wholesaling of newspapers and periodicals. A report on the wholesale supply of national newspapers and periodicals in England and Wales and in Scotland in relation to refusal to supply and participating in retailing. Monopolies and Mergers Commission
Session 1977-78 Cmnd. 7214 xxiv.

See also ROSKILL, A., Sir
JOHNSTON, A., Sir
RICHARDS, E. L.

LESLIE, H. R.

See BIRDSAY, H. R., Lord

LEVY, R. F.

1958   Imported timber. Report on whether and to what extent the recommendation of the Monopolies Commission has been complied with
Session 1957-58 HC. 274 xvi.

1959   Anthrax. Report of the committee on inquiry
Session 1959-60 Cmnd. 846 xxxvi.

Chemical fertilizer. Report on supply by the Monopolies Commission
Session 1958-59 HC. 267 xvii.

1961   Supply of cigarettes and tobacco and of cigarette and tobacco machinery. Report by the Monopolies Commission
Session 1960-61 HC. 218 xix.

1963   Supply of electrical equipment for mechanically propelled land vehicles. Report by the Monopolies Commission
Session 1963-64 HC. 59 xvi.

1964   Supply of wallpaper. Report by the Monopolies Commission
Session 1963-64 HC. 21 xvi.

1965   Supply of petrol to retailers in the U.K. A report by the Monopolies Commission
Session 1964-65 HC. 264 xix.

1966   The British Motor Corporation Ltd. and the Pressed Steel Co. Ltd. A report on the merger by the Monopolies Commission
Session 1965-66 HC. 46 xxix.

LEWES, F. M. M.

1970   The holiday industry of Devon and Cornwall. Southwest Economic Planning Council
M. of Housing and Local Government

LEWIN, Walpole S.

1971   Organisation and staffing of operating departments. Report of a joint sub-committee on the standing medical and nursing advisory committees
M. of Health and Social Security

LEWIS, A. D.

1978   Standards of care of mentally ill and mentally handicapped patients in hospital. Report of the working party
Welsh Office

LEWIS, J. P.

1974   Study of the Cambridge sub-region
D. of the Environment

LEWIS, M. M.

1968   The education of deaf children; the possible place of finger spelling and signing. Report of the committee
D. of Education and Science

LEWIS, R

1976   Prospects for the plastics packaging industry. Plastics Steering Committee N.E.D.O.

LEWIS, W. H. P., Sir

1948   Army and Air Force courts-martial. Report of the committee Session 1948-49 Cmd. 7608 xiv.

LEYLAND, N. H.

1970   Effect of the milk marketing scheme on consumers. Report of the Consumers' Committee for England and Wales M. of Agriculture, Fisheries and Food

LILLEY, G. M.

1977   Concorde noise levels. Report by a working group Noise Advisory Council

LILLICRAP, H. G.

1967   Mobile Radio Committee. 5th report Post Office

LINDLEY, John

1945   The cotton spinning industry. Report of a commission set up to review the wages arrangements and methods of organisation of work and to make recommendations M. of Labour and National Service

LINDOP, Norman, Sir

1978   Data protection. Report of the committee Session 1978-79 Cmnd. 7341

LINDSAY OF BIRKER, A. D., Lord

1947   Expenses of members of local authorities. Report of the interdepartmental committee Session 1946-47 Cmd. 7126 xiii.

LINDSAY, Humphrey Brown, Sir

1950   Prevention of pollution of rivers and other waters. Report of the sub-committee of the Scottish Waters Advisory Committee Session 1950-51 Cmd. 8111 xix.

1951   What local authorities can do to promote health and prevent disease. Report of the standing advisory committee on local authority services D. of Health for Scotland

The general practitioner and the hospital service. Report by a joint sub-committee of the medical, hospital and specialist services and general practitioner services standing advisory committees D. of Health for Scotland

LINSTEAD, Hugh, Sir

1955   Hospital pharmaceutical service. Report of the sub-committee of the Central Health Services Council M. of Health

LISHMAN, W. A.

1977   Senile and presenile dementias; a report of the M R C. sub-committee Medical Research Council

LISTON, D. J.

1973   Education and training for overseas trade British Overseas Trade Board

LITTLER, S.

1978   Home Office local radio working party. 1st report Home Office

See also TREVELYAN, D. J.

LITTLEWOOD, F. D.

See JONES, S. L.

LITTLEWOOD, Sydney, Sir

1965   Experiments on animals. Report of the departmental committee Session 1964-65 Cmnd. 2641 xv.

LIVESEY, L.

1974   Fencing and spacing of shuttleless weaving machines. Report by the joint standing committee for the wool textile industry D. of Employment

LLEWELLIN, J. J., Lord

1952   Ports Efficiency Committee. 1st and 2nd reports M. of Transport

LLEWELLYN-JONES, F.

See JONES, F. L.

LLEWELYN, G. I. W.

1971   Technology and the garment industry. A report by the programmes analysis unit on the role of machinery in the garment industry. Clothing Economic Development Committee N.E.D.O.

LLEWELYN-DAVIES, R., Lord

1971   Buildings for mentally handicapped people D. of Health and Social Security

LLOYD OF HAMPSTEAD, D., Lord

1967   National film school. Report of a committee to consider the need for a national film school D. of Education and Science

LLOYD, A. D. F., Lord

1955   Movements of persons within a British Caribbean federation. Report of the conference held in Port of Spain, Trinidad, 14-17 March, 1955 Colonial Office

LLOYD, G.

1974   Earnings in the building industry; a survey of operatives' earnings and hours in May 1973. Employment problems working party N.E.D.O.

LLOYD, Selwyn

1973   Boundary Commission for Scotland. Report with respect to (various) areas Session 1972-73 HC. 140 vi.

Conference on electoral law. Letter dated 20 June 1973 Session 1972-73 Cmnd. 5363 xi.

LLOYD-DAVIES, Trevor A.

1968   Problems arising from the use of asbestos: memorandum of the senior medical inspector's advisory panel M. of Labour

1971   Respiratory disease in foundrymen. Report of a survey D. of Employment

LLOYD JACOB, G. H. L., Sir

1949   Resale price maintenance. Report of the committee Session 1948-49 Cmd. 7696 xx.

LLOYD JONES, S.

See JONES, S. L.

LLOYD THOMAS, R.
    See THOMAS, R. L.

LLOYD-WILLIAMS, Hugh
1959   Cold store undertakings. Report of inquiry held under the schedule to the Dock Workers (Regulation of Employment) Act, 1946
M. of Labour and National Service

1960   Ocean shipowners' tally clerks. Report of a committee to consider the difficulties which have arisen in the Port of London
M. of Labour

Dock Workers (Regulation of Employment) Scheme. I: list of ports; II: timber and pitwood. Report of the inquiry
M. of Labour

LOCKE, G. M. L.
1970   Census of woodlands, 1965-67. A report on Britain's forest resources
Forestry Commission

LOCKHART, J. M. B.
1976   Business Education Council. 1st policy statement
Business Education Council

1977   Initial guidelines on the implementation of policy
Business Education Council

LOCKWOOD, John F., Sir
1960   General Certificate of Education and 6th form studies. 3rd report of the Secondary Schools Examinations Council
M. of Education

1961   Examinations in secondary schools. Certificate of Secondary Education proposed for new school leaving certificate other than the G.C.E. 4th report of the Secondary School Examinations Council
M. of Education

1962   Examinations in secondary schools. Certificate of Secondary Education; notes for the guidance of regional examining bodies. 5th report of the Secondary Schools Examination Council
M. of Education

Sixth form studies and university entrance requirements. 6th report of the Secondary School Examinations Council
M. of Education

1963   Scope and standards of the Certificate of Secondary Education. 7th report of the Secondary School Examinations Council
M. of Education

1964   Examining of English language. 8th report of the Secondary School Examinations Council
D. of Education and Science

Schools' curricula and examinations. Report of the working party
M. of Education

LOCOCK, Guy, Sir
1952   Wood flour. Report of the standing committee appointed under the Merchandise Marks Act
Session 1952-53 Cmd. 8796 xv.

1955   Oil burning apparatus. Standing committee report
Session 1955-56 Cmd. 9686 xxiii.

LOFTHOUSE, J. A.
Efficiency in road construction. Civil Engineering Economic Development Committee
1966   Report of the working party
1967   2nd report of the working party
N.E.D.O.

LONG, R. L.
1974   Industrial review to 1977. Iron and steel castings. Iron and steel advisory committee
N.E.D.O.

LONGFORD, F. A.
1946   Flying-boat base committee report (M.C.A.P. 13)
M. of Civil Aviation

LONGSTRETH THOMPSON, F.
1944   Merseyside plan, 1944. A report prepared in consultation with the technical committee of the Merseyside advisory joint planning committee
M. of Town and Country Planning
    See also DAVIES, C.

LORAINE, P.
1955   National stud policy and methods of organisation. Report of the committee
M. of Agriculture, Fisheries and Food

LOUGHLIN, Charles
1970   Maintenance manuals for buildings. Committee on building maintenance (R. & D. bulletins)
M. of Public Building and Works

LOUTIT, J. F.
1975   Criteria for controlling radiation doses to the public after accidental escape of radioactive material. Committee on protection against ionising radiations
Medical Research Council

LOVEDAY, Thomas
1944   Veterinary education in Great Britain. 2nd report of the committee
Session 1943-44 Cmd. 6517 iv.

1945   Agricultural employment. The provision in secondary schools of courses preparatory to agricultural employment. Report of the advisory committee
M. of Education

Higher agricultural education in England and Wales. Report of the committee
Session 1945-46 Cmd. 6728 x.

1947   Agricultural and horticultural institutes. Interim report of the advisory committee
M. of Agriculture and Fisheries

1949   Agriculturalists, horticulturists and domestic producers. Report on the provision of part-time instruction by local education authorities by the advisory committee
M. of Agriculture and Fisheries

LOVELUCK, P. E.
A Welsh rate support grant system
1977   1st report of the joint working party
1978   2nd report of the joint working party
Welsh Office

LOWE, Douglas G. A.
1968   Friern Hospital. National Health Service findings and recommendations following inquiries into allegations concerning the care of elderly patients in certain hospitals, III
Session 1967-68 Cmnd. 3687 xxviii.

LOWRY, Robert, Sir
1973   Civil and criminal jurisdiction in Northern Ireland. Interim report of the joint committee
Session 1972-73 Cmnd. 5431 xiv.

1974   Law enforcement commission report
Session 1974 Cmnd. 5627 xiii.

1975   Northern Ireland constitutional convention. Report
Session 1975-76 HC. 1 xxxvii.

LUCAS, A. H. S.

1976   Materials handling; tackling the job. Committee for materials handling
D. of Industry

LUCAS, S.

1974   Survey of abortion patients (for the committee on the working of the Abortion Act)
D. of Health and Social Security

LUCAS OF CHILWORTH, G. W., Lord

1947   Working of the Agricultural Marketing Acts. Report of the committee (economic series No. 48)
M. of Agriculture and Fisheries

LUXMOORE, F., Sir

1943   Committee on post-war agricultural education in England and Wales. Report
Session 1942-43 Cmd. 6433 iv.

LYCETT GREEN, S., Sir

See GREEN, S. L., Sir

LYDDON, W. D. C.

See CAMPBELL, A. D.

LYNN, C. W.

1949   Agricultural extension and advisory work with special reference to the colonies. A report on a tour made in 1947 in east and west Africa, England, Canada and the United States of America and Puerto Rico. (Colonial No. 241)
Colonial Office

LYNSKEY, G. J., Sir

1949   Tribunal of inquiry into allegations reflecting on the official conduct of Ministers of the Crown and of other public servants
Report
Session 1948-49 Cmd. 7616 xviii.
Proceedings with minutes of evidence. November to December 1949
Home Office

LYTHGOE, J., Sir

1945   Nurses and midwives salaries committees (England and Scotland). Report of the joint superannuation sub-committee
Session 1944-45 Cmd. 6603 v.

LYTTLETON, O.

See CHANDOS, O., Viscount

MABANE, W., Lord

    Publicity and recruitment for the civil defence and allied services (advisory committee)
1952   1st report
Session 1952-53 Cmd. 8708 viii.
1954   2nd report
Session 1953-54 Cmd. 9131 x.

McARTHUR, I.

1966   Private legislation (Scotland) procedure. Report of the committee
Scottish Office

McBOYLE, J.

1963   Prevention of neglect of children. Report of the committee of the Scottish advisory council on child care
Session 1962-63 Cmnd. 1966 ix.
1967   Local authority records. Report by a committee
Scottish Home and Health D.

McCAFFERTY, J.

1978   Economics in S. I and S. II; a feasibility study. Report of the working party to the Scottish central committee on social subjects. (Consultative committee on the curriculum bulletin No. 3)
Scottish Education D.

McCALL, P.

1975   Water services staff commission. Report
D. of the Environment

McCANN, P. T.

1975   Secondary education of physically handicapped children in Scotland. Report of the committee
Scottish Education D.

McCARTHY, W. E. J., Lord

1969   Dispute between the Durham local education authority and the National Association of Schoolmasters. Report of the committee of inquiry
Session 1968-69 Cmnd. 4152 xxviii.

1976   Making Whitley work; a review of the operation of the National Health Service Whitley Council system
D. of Health and Social Security

McCLELLAND, William

1948   Visual and aural aids. Reports of the advisory
&   council on education in Scotland
1950   Session 1950-51 Cmd. 8102 xi.
1949   Pupils who are defective in hearing. Report of the advisory council on education in Scotland
Session 1950 Cmd. 7866 ix.

    Pupils who are defective in vision. Report of the advisory council on education in Scotland
Session 1950 Cmd. 7885 ix.
1950   Pupils with physical disabilities. Report of the advisory council on education in Scotland
Session 1950-51 Cmd. 8211 xi.

    Libraries, museums and art galleries. Report of the advisory council on education in Scotland
Session 1950-51 Cmd. 8229 xi.
1951   Pupils handicapped by speech disorders. Report of the advisory council on education in Scotland
Session 1951-52 Cmd. 8426 x.

    Pupils who are maladjusted because of social handicap. Report of the advisory council on education in Scotland
Session 1951-52 Cmd. 8428 x.

    Pupils with mental or educational disabilities. Report of the advisory council on education in Scotland
Session 1951-52 Cmd. 8401 x.

    Administration of education for handicapped pupils. Report of the advisory council on education in Scotland
Session 1951-52 Cmd. 8432 x.

    Further education. Report of the advisory council on education in Scotland
Session 1951-52 Cmd. 8454 x.

McCOWAN, P. K.

1962   Medical services for child guidance. Report by a sub-committee of the standing medical advisory committee
Scottish Home and Health D.

McCONNELL, P. L.

1969   Recruitment, selection and training. A report by the manpower working party of the Clothing Economic Development Committee
N.E.D.O.

McCONNELL, P. L. (*continued*)

1971 Work study in the clothing industry. Clothing Economic Development Committee
N.E.D.O.

1972 Wage payment systems in the clothing industry. Manpower working party of the Clothing Economic Development Committee
N.E.D.O.

1973 Investment appraisal for the clothing industry. A report for the Clothing Economic Development Committee
N.E.D.O.

1974 Employment practices in E.E.C. clothing industries. Report and appendices by the European study group, Clothing Economic Development Committee. 2 vols.
N.E.D.O.

McCORQUODALE, OF NEWTON, M. S., Lord

1965 Assessment of disablement. Report of the committee
Session 1965-66 Cmnd. 2847 vi.

McCOWAN, P. K.

1962 Medical services for child guidance. Report by a sub-committee of the standing medical advisory committee. Central Health Services Council
Scottish Home and Health D.

McCREADIE, C. M.
See TULLY, J.

MacCRINDLE, R. A.

1973 Rolls-Royce Ltd. Report of investigations under the Companies Act
D. of Trade and Industry

McCULLOUGH, T. W.

1956 Conditions in iron foundries. 1st report of the joint standing committee
M. of Labour and National Service

1957 Power presses. 3rd report of proceedings of the joint standing committee on safety in the use of power presses
M. of Labour and National Service

MACDERMOTT, J. C., Lord

1970 Supreme Court of Judicature of Northern Ireland. Report of the committee
Session 1969-70 Cmnd. 4292 xvii.

MACDONALD, A. G., Lord

1964 The young chronic sick. Report of a sub-committee of the Scottish health services council
Scottish Home and Health D.

McDONALD, I. D.
See BEACH, S. T.

MacDONALD, Ian

1972 Report on the local inquiry in relation to the implementation by Glasgow corporation of parts II and IV of the Housing (Financial Provisions) (Scotland) Act, 1972
Scottish Development D.

1973 Report of the local inquiry in relation to the implementation by Midlothian County Council of parts II and IV of the Housing (Financial Provisions) (Scotland) Act, 1972
Scottish Development D.

MacDONALD, R.

1978 A curricular approach to religious education. (Scottish committee on religious education bulletin No. 1)
Scottish Education D.

MACDONALD, R. H., Lord

1970 " No folks of their own ". A report on one aspect of community care of the mentally handicapped
Scottish Home and Health D.

1972 A duty to care; an account of the Mental Welfare Commission for Scotland between 1962-1972
Scottish Home and Health D.

1975 " No place to go ". Report of the Mental Welfare Commission for Scotland
Scottish Home and Health D.

1977 Report of a court of inquiry into a trade dispute at Dyce Airport, Aberdeen between Bristow Helicopters Ltd., and members of the British Airline Pilots Association
D. of Employment

McELHONE, Frank

1977 Football crowd behaviour. Report of the working group.
Scottish Education D.

McFADYEN, Edward

1971 Voluntary group trading; 6 case studies compiled on behalf of the voluntary group advisory panel, Distributive Trades Economic Development Committee
N.E.D.O.

McFADZEAN, W. H., Lord

1970 Queen's award to industry. Report of the 1970 review committee
D. of Trade

McFADZEAN, Frank

1976 British Airways Board. 4th report on organisation
Session 1975-76 HC. 722 ix.

See also NICOLSON, D. L.

MACGREGOR, Alexander S. M., Sir

1943 The freezing point (Hortvet) test of milk. Report of a sub-committee of the scientific advisory committee
D. of Health for Scotland

1946 Neo-natal deaths due to infection. Report of the sub-committee of the scientific advisory committee
D. of Health for Scotland

1948 Control of midges. 2nd report of the sub-committee of the scientific advisory committee
D. of Health for Scotland

See also CREW, F. A. E.

1949 Tuberculosis meningitis treated with streptomycin. Interim report of a sub-committee of the scientific advisory committee
D. of Health for Scotland

MACGREGOR, Alistair G.

1967 Definition of drugs (borderline substances). Report of the standing joint committee on the classification of proprietary preparations. Central and Scottish health services control
M. of Health

1968 Revision of the classification system. Report of the standing joint committee on the classification of proprietary preparations. Central and Scottish health services council
M. of Health

McGREGOR, Oliver Ross

Royal Commission on the Press
1976 National newspaper industry. Interim report
Session 1975-76 Cmnd. 6433 xli.

McGREGOR, Oliver Ross *(continued)*

1977   Final report and appendices
Session 1976-77 Cmnd. 6810, 6810-I xl.

1976   Industrial relations in the national newspaper industry, a report (research series No. 1)
Session 1976-77 Cmnd. 6680 xl.
Industrial relations in the provincial newspaper and periodical industries (research series No. 2)
Session 1976-77 Cmnd. 6810-II xl.
Attitudes to the press (research series No. 3)
Session 1976-77 Cmnd. 6810-III xli.
Analysis of newspaper content (research No. 4)
Session 1976-77 Cmnd. 6810-IV xli.
Concentration of ownership in the provincial press (research series No. 5)
Session 1976-77 Cmnd. 6810-V xli.
Periodicals and the alternative press (research series No. 6)
Session 1976-77 Cmnd. 6810-VI xli.

McHAFFIE, Isabel

1971   Before five. Report on pre-school education
Scottish Education D.

McINTOSH, Ronald, Sir

1976   A study of U.K. nationalised industries; their role in the economy and control in the future. 2 vols.
N.E.D.O.
Financial analysis. (A study of U.K. nationalised industries background paper No. 1)
N.E.D.O.
Relationships of government and public enterprises in France, West Germany and Sweden. (A study of U.K. nationalised industries background paper No. 2)
N.E.D.O.
Output, investment and productivity. (A study of U.K. nationalised industries background paper No. 3)
N.E.D.O.

1977   Manpower and pay trends. (A study of U.K. nationalised industries background paper No. 4)
N.E.D.O.
Price behaviour. (A study of U.K. nationalised industries background paper No. 5)
N.E.D.O.
Relationships with other sectors of the economy; the evidence of input-output analysis. (A study of U.K. nationalised industries background paper No. 6)
N.E.D.O.
Exports and imports. (A study of U.K. nationalised industries background paper No. 7)
N.E.D.O.
Engineering craftsmen; shortages and related problems. Report of the M.S.C./N.E.D.O. Committee on the supply and utilisation of skilled engineering manpower
N.E.D.O.

McINTOSH, Ronald Robert Duncan

1971   Proposals for retail price indices for regions. Retail prices index advisory committee
Session 1970-71 Cmnd. 4749 xlvi.

McINTYRE, J.

1977   Water safety. Report of the working party
Home Office

McINTYRE, J. G.

    See SORN, J. G., Lord

MacKAY, D. I.

1978   Economic impact of North Sea oil on Scotland. Final report
Scottish Office

McKECHNIE, Hector

1958   Diligence. Report of the committee
Session 1957-58 Cmnd. 456 xv.

MACKENZIE, C. H.

1962   Electricity in Scotland. Report of the committee on the generation and distribution of electricity in Scotland
Session 1962-63 Cmnd. 1859 xvii.

MACKENZIE, P. K.

1961   Milk powder. Prepared by the milk powder sub-committee of the milk and milk products technical advisory committee
M. of Agriculture, Fisheries and Food

MACKESON, H. R.

1953   Bilateral Trade Negotiations Committee report
Board of Trade

MACKIE, T. J.

1949   Hill farm research. Report of the Scottish Hill Farm Research Committee
D. of Agriculture for Scotland

McKINLAY, K. A.

1977   Edward Wood & Co. Ltd., Skibben Winton Construction Ltd. Report of investigations under the Companies Act
D. of Trade

MACKINLAY, W. M.

1960   Our children's teeth. Interim report by the Scottish standing committee on dental health education
D. of Health for Scotland

MACKINTOSH, C. M., Lord

1950   Law succession in Scotland. Report of the committee of inquiry
Session 1950-51 Cmd. 8144 xv.

MACKINTOSH, J. M.

1951   Social workers in the mental health services. Report of the committee
Session 1950-51 Cmd. 8260 xv.

1956   Moving from the slums. 7th report of the housing management sub-committee of the central housing advisory committee
M. of Housing and Local Government

McLAGAN, John

1950   Establishment of a customs union in the British Caribbean area. Report of the commission
Colonial Office

McLATCHIE, T.

1977   The management of local authority house building programmes. 1st report of the development management working group
D. of the Environment

McLAUGHLIN, P.

1974   Date marking of food. Steering group on food freshness. Interim report (SG FF/REP/1)
M. of Agriculture, Fisheries and Food

MACLEAN, A.

1951 Design and workmanship of non-traditional houses. Report by the Scottish Housing Advisory Committee on the arrangements for safeguarding the standard of design and workmanship of non-traditional houses
D. of Health for Scotland

Housing of special groups. Older people; one-person and two-person households; large households; disabled people; higher income group households; occupational groups. Reports by the Scottish Housing Advisory Committee
D. of Health for Scotland

MACLEAN, Fitzroy, Sir

1955 Territorial army. Report of the commission on the administration of the Territorial Army
Session 1955-56 Cmd. 9523 x.

McLELLAN, A. G.

Water resources in the North. Northern technical working party
1967   Interim report (publications No. 5)
1970   Report
Water Resources Board

MACLENNAN, Hector, Sir

1969 Advice from the advisory group on transplantation problems on the question of amending the Human Tissue Act, 1961. National Health Service
Session 1968-69 Cmnd. 4106 xlvi.

MACLEOD, Iain N.

1958 Industrial health survey in Halifax. Report by H.M. Factory Inspectorate and recommendations of the Industrial Health Advisory Committee
M. of Labour and National Service

1960 Kenya constitutional conference. Report of the conference held in London in January and February 1960
Session 1959-60 Cmnd. 960 x.

Nyasaland constitutional conference. Report of the conference held in London in July and August, 1960
Session 1959-60 Cmnd. 1132 xi.

1961 West Indies constitutional conference. Report of the conference held in London, May and June, 1961
Session 1960-61 Cmnd. 1417 xiii.

1959 Practices impeding the full and efficient use of manpower. Report of an inquiry undertaken by the national joint advisory council
M. of Labour and National Service

MACLURE, J. S.
See BULLOCK, A.

McMEEKING, J. G.

1958 Further education for commerce. Report of the advisory committee. National advisory council on education for industry and commerce
M. of Education

MACMICHAEL, Harold, Sir

1946 Malaya. Report on a mission to Malaya. (Colonial No. 194)
Colonial Office

Malta. Report of the constitutional commissioner. (Colonial No. 207)
Colonial Office

McMILLAN, E. L.

1973 Remedial professions. Report by a working party
D. of Health and Social Security

MACMILLAN, Hugh Pattison, Lord

1948 Land registration in Scotland 1st report
Session 1947-48 Cmd. 7451 xiii.

Tudor IV aircraft. Report of the court of investigation of the accident to the Tudor IV aircraft "Star Tiger" G-AHNP on January 30, 1948 held under the Air Navigation (Investigation of Accidents) Regulations, 1922
Session 1948 Cmd. 7517 ii.

McNAIR, Arnold D., Lord

1944 Teachers and youth leaders. Report of the committee to consider the supply, recruitment and training of teachers and youth leaders
M. of Education

1946 Palestine. The system of education of the Jewish community in Palestine. Report of the commission of inquiry
Colonial Office

1956 Dental profession. Report of the committee on recruitment to the dental profession
Session 1955-56 Cmd. 9861 xiv.

Teachers' salaries. Scales of salaries for teachers in primary and secondary schools maintained by local education authorities, England and Wales, 1956. Report of the Burnham Committee
M. of Education

Teachers' salaries. Report of the committee representing local education authorities and teachers on scales of salaries for the teaching staff of farm institutes and teachers of agricultural (including horticultural) subjects, England and Wales
M. of Education

Teachers' salaries. Report of the committee representative of associations of local education authorities, training college authorities and of the Association of Teachers in Colleges and Departments of Education on scales of salaries for the teaching staff of training colleges, England and Wales
M. of Education

Teachers' salaries. Scales of salaries for teachers in establishments for further education maintained by local education authorities, England and Wales. Report of the Burnham committee
M. of Education

McNAIR, W. L., Sir

1944 Limitation of actions and bills of exchange committee report
Session 1944-45 Cmd. 6591 v.

McNAIRN, E. S.

1972 Rating of plant and machinery. Report of the committee
D. of the Environment

McNEE, J. W., Sir

1947 Cerebro-spinal fever. Report by the infectious diseases sub-committee of the Scientific Advisory Committee on a comparison of penicillin and sulphonamide treatments of meningococcal meningitis in young children
D. of Health for Scotland

1948 A comparison of diptheria in inoculated and uninoculated persons in a partly inoculated population. Report of the infectious diseases sub-committee of the Scientific Advisory Committee
D. of Health for Scotland

MACONOCHIE, Robert H.

1949 Poaching and illegal fishing of salmon and trout in Scotland. Report of the committee
Session 1950 Cmd. 7917 xi.

1954 Close seasons for deer in Scotland. Report of the committee (with a minority report)
Session 1953-54 Cmd. 9273 x.

McPHAIL, R. T. M.

1976   Vehicle and General Insurance Co. Ltd. **Report of investigations under the Companies Act**
D. of Trade

McPHERSON, D. G.

1972   Management arrangement for the reorganised national health service in Wales
Welsh Office

McQUAIL, D.

1976   Review of sociological writing on the press (working paper No. 2)
Royal Commission on the Press

MACRAE, A. K. M.

1965   Alcoholics. Report on health services for their treatment and rehabilitation
Scottish Home and Health D.

MACWALTER, R. J.

1969   Dairy effuents. Report of the sub-committee of the milk and milk products technical advisory committee
M. of Agriculture, Fisheries and Food

MacWILLIAM, C. G.

1978   Roads and transport with particular reference to rural areas. Policy committee report
Highlands and Islands Development Board

MADDEX, George, Sir

1968   University teachers' superannuation. Report of the working party
D. of Education and Science

MADDOCK, Ieuan

1970   Maintenance engineering. Report by the working party
M. of Technology

MAIDEN, A.

1972   Health services in new towns. Working group 1: general medical services in new towns and similar communities
D. of Health and Social Security

MAIR, Alex

1972   Medical rehabilitation; the pattern for the future. Report of a sub-committee of the standing medical advisory committee. Scottish Health Service Council
Scottish Home and Health D.

MALLABAR, John F., Sir

1971   Government industrial establishments. Report of the committee
Session 1970-71 Cmnd. 4713 x.

MALLABY, H. George C.

1967   Staffing of local government. Report of the committee
M. of Housing and Local Government

MALTMAN, W.

See MACLEAN, A.

MANGUT, D. S.

1974   Kwik Save Discount Group Ltd. Report of investigations under the Companies Act
D. of Trade

MANKTELOW, Richard, Sir

1961   Report of the inquiry into the draft of the Skelmersdale New Town (Designation) Order, 1961
M. of Housing and Local Government

1963   Federation of East Caribbean territories. Report of the Civil Service Commission
Vol. 1: Report
Vol. 2: Tables B, D, L-Z and AA
Session 1962-63 Cmnd. 1992 x.

MANN, Jack

1978   The Birmingham and Midland Canal Carrying Co. Ltd. Report of investigations under the Companies Act
D. of Trade

MANNERS, E. G.

1954   Work of nurses in hospital wards. Report by the standing nursing and midwifery committee on the " Job Analysis of the Work of Nurses in Hospital Wards " prepared by the Nuffield Provincial Hospitals Trust
D. of Health for Scotland

1955   State enrolled assistant nurses in the National Health Service. Report by the standing nursing and midwifery advisory committee. Scottish Health Services Council
D. of Health for Scotland

MANNSELL, G.

See CHANTLER, P.

MARCHANT, E. C.

1966   The Certificate of Secondary Education experimental examinations: geography. Report of the steering committee (examinations bulletin No. 14)
Schools Council

MARKHAM, Violet

1942   Amenities and welfare conditions in the three women's services. Report of the committee
Session 1941-42 Cmd. 6384 iv.

1944   Post-war organisation of private domestic employment. Report by Miss V. Markham and Miss F. Hancock
Session 1944-45 Cmd. 6550 v.

MARQUAND, H. A.

1966   Laundry and dry cleaning charges. National Board for Prices and Incomes report No. 20
Session 1966-67 Cmnd. 3093 xlii.

Coal distribution costs. National Board for Prices and Incomes report No. 21
Session 1966-67 Cmnd. 3094 xlii.

See also JONES, Aubrey

MARQUAND, J. M.

1976   Uniform accounting for local authority waste paper salvage schemes. Report of the working group
D. of the Environment

MARRE, Alan S., Sir

1964   Selection and training of supervisors. Progress report
M. of Labour

Sick pay schemes. Report of a committee of the national joint advisory council
M. of Labour

1968   A report of the cost of living advisory committee
Session 1967-68 Cmnd. 3677 xix.

1978   Thalidomide. 'Y' list inquiry report
D. of Health and Social Security

MARRIOTT, G. W.

1977   Footwear industry study steering group report
D. of Industry

MARS-JONES, W. L.

1964 Report of inquiry into the inquiries made into the case of Thomas Halloran and Patrick Joseph Cox and the cases of Patrick Albert Tisdall, Thomas Alfred Kingston and Sidney Hill-Burton
Session 1964-65 Cmnd. 2526 xxi.

1967 Report of inquiry in respect of the objections to the proposed compulsory amalgamation of the police areas of the County of Berkshire, the County of Buckinghamshire, the County of Oxfordshire, the City of Oxford and the Borough of Reading
Session 1966-67 Cmnd. 3343 xlvi.

MARSH, Norman

See HODGSON, Derek

MARSH, Richard

1972 British Railways Board. Second report of the Board on organisation
Session 1971-72 HC. 223 xxxix.

MARSHALL, Arthur H.

1970 Highway maintenance. Report of the committee
D. of the Environment

See also REDCLIFFE-MAUD, J. P., Lord

MARSHALL, F., Sir

See BAINS, M. A.

MARSHALL, Frank Shaw, Sir

1978 The Marshall inquiry on Greater London. Report
Greater London Council

MARSHALL, J. S.

1971 Outburst of coal and firedamp at Cynheidre/ Pentremawr Colliery, Carmarthenshire on 6 April, 1971
Session 1971-72 Cmnd. 4804 viii.

MARSHALL, P. J.-

See MATTHEW, R. H., Sir
See WATSON, J. W.

MARSHALL, Robert, Sir

1977 Environmental Board. 1st progress report
D. of the Ennvironment

MARSLAND, E. C.

1975 Principles of local exhaust ventilation. 1st report of the sub-committee on dust and fumes, of the joint standing committee on health, safety and welfare in foundries
D. of Employment

Foundry dust control; fettling benches and small adjustable hoods. 2nd report of the sub-committee on dust and fumes of the joint standing committee on health and welfare in foundries
D. of Employment

1977 Some aspects of pneumoconiosis in a group of mechanised iron foundries. 3rd report of the sub-committee on dust and fumes of the joint standing committee on health, safety and welfare in foundries
Health and Safety Executive

1978 Noise in foundries. 1st report of the sub-committee on foundry noise
Health and Safety Executive

MARTIN, Andrew

See HODGSON, Derek
HOLLAND-MARTIN, D. E., Sir

MARTIN, L. C. J.

1960 Assistance with the cost of boarding education. Report of the working party
M. of Education

MASON, E. A.

1977 Materials in medical engineering. Report by the working party of the materials science and technology committee
Science Research Council

MASSEY, Harrie S. W., Sir

1966 Science policy. Report of the council for scientific policy
Session 1966-67 Cmnd. 3007 xlviii.

1971 Support of scientific research in the universities Report of a study by the Council for Scientific Policy
Session 1970-71 Cmnd. 4798 xlvii.

1977 Future of X-ray astronomy in the U.K. Report of the review panel. Astronomy Space and Radio Board
Science Research Council

MASSEY, Vincent

1945 Museums and galleries. Report of the committee on the functions of the National Gallery and Tate Gallery and respect of paintings of the Victoria and Albert Museum, together with a memorandum thereon by the Standing Commission on Museums and Galleries
Session 1945-46 Cmd. 6827 xiii.

MASTERMAN, J. C., Sir

1949 Political activities of civil servants. Report of the committee
Session 1948-49 Cmd. 7718 xii.

MASTON, Charles J.

1969 Hours of employment of women and young persons employed in factories. Report of a working party of the national joint advisory council on part VI of the Factories Act 1961 and associated legislation
D. of Employment and Productivity

MATHYS, H. R.

1974 British trade mark law practice. Report of the committee
Session 1974 Cmnd. 5601 xiv.

MATTHEW, R. H., Sir

1967 Central Lancashire; study for a city. Consultant's proposals for designation by Matthew, Johnson-Marshall & Partners
M. of Housing and Local Government

Report of a public inquiry into the future use or uses of the Broad Sanctuary site, City of Westminster
M. of Housing and Local Government

1968 The Grangemouth/Falkirk regional survey and plan. Prepared for the area joint planning advisory committee. 2 vols.
Scottish Development D.

1972 New life in old towns
D. of the Environment

See also ABERCROMBIE, P., Sir

MATTHEWS, John C.

1973 Assessment of attainment in sixth-form science. A report by the working party. (Examinations bulletin, No. 27)
Schools Council

MATTHEWS, J. D.

1971 Tree, forest and woodland research. Report of the forestry and woodland research committee. (Publications series B No. 2)
Natural Environment Research Council

MATTHEWS, P. J.

1976   Inventory of U.K. research on land disposal of sewage sludge. Sub-committee of the standing committee on disposal of sewage sludge (water engineering research and development division technical note No. 5)
D. of the Environment

MATTHEWS, R. O. C.

Transmitted deprivation. Joint working party
1974   1st report
1975   2nd report
Social Science Research Council

See also ROBINSON, D.

MAUD, J. P. R., Sir

See REDCLIFFE-MAUD, J. P., Lord

MAUDE, E. John, Sir

1953   Sanitary inspectors. Report of the working party on the recruitment, training and qualification of sanitary inspectors
M. of Health

MAUDE, John Cyril

1947   Standon Farm Approved School. Report of the committee of inquiry into the conduct of Standon Farm Approved School and the circumstances connected with the murder of a master at the school on 15 February 1947
Session 1946-47 Cmd. 7150 xiv.

MAUDLING, Reginald

1962   Zanzibar constitutional conference. Report. Held in London, March and April 1962
Session 1961-62 Cmnd. 1699 xi.

Kenya constitutional conference. Report
Session 1961-62 Cmnd. 1700 xi.

Kenya coastal strip conference. Report
Session 1961-62 Cmnd. 1701 xi.

East Caribbean Federation conference. Report
Session 1961-62 Cmnd. 1746 xi.

Uganda independence conference. Report
Session 1961-62 Cmnd. 1778 xi.

Trinidad and Tobago conference. Report
Session 1961-62 Cmnd. 1757 xi.

MAXWELL, Alexander, Sir

1953   Discharged prisoners' aid societies. Report of the committee
Session 1952-53 Cmd. 8879 ix.

Central criminal court in South Lancashire. Report of the departmental committee
Session 1952-53 Cmd. 8955 xiv.

MAXWELL, P.

1972   Report on the local inquiry in relation to the implementation by Kirkcaldy Town Council of parts II and IV of the Housing (Financial Provisions) (Scotland) Act, 1972
Scottish Development D.

MAYBRAY-KING, H., Lord

1969   Boundary Commission for England. 2nd periodical report
Session 1968-69 Cmnd. 4084 xxvi.

Boundary Commission for Scotland. 2nd periodical report
Session 1968-69 Cmnd. 4085 xxvi.

Boundary Commission for Wales. 2nd periodical report
Session 1968-69 Cmnd. 4086 xxvi.

Boundary Commission for Northern Ireland. 2nd periodical report
Session 1968-69 Cmnd. 4087 xxvi.

MAYACH, R. B.

1977   Joint working party of the remedial and nursing professions. Report
D. of Health and Social Security

MAYCOCK, W. d'A.

1972   Testing for the presence of Australia (hepatitis associated) antigen and its antibody. Revised report of the advisory group
D. of Health and Social Security

1976   Testing for the presence of hepatitis B surface antigen and its antibody. Second report of the advisory group
D. of Health and Social Security

MAYNARD, Alan

1978   Doctor manpower, 1975-2000; alternative forecasts and their resource implications. (Research paper No. 4)
Royal Commission on the National Health Service

MEDLIK, S.

1974   Hotels and government policy. Parity treatment study group of the Hotels and Catering Economic Development Committee
N.E.D.O.

MEE, A. J.

1969   Science for general education: for the first two years and the early school leaver. Report of the working party on secondary school science. (Curriculum papers No. 7)
Scottish Education D.

MEEKS, G.

1976   Financing of quoted companies in the U.K. (Background paper No. 1)
Royal Commission on the Distribution of Income and Wealth

MELVILLE, Charles

1973   Training of staff for centres for the mentally handicapped. Report of the committee
Scottish Education D.

MENSFORTH, Eric, Sir

1971   The means of authenticating the quality of engineering products and materials. Report of a committee
D. of Trade and Industry

MERRISON, Alexander W.

Inquiry into the basis for design and method of erection of steel box-girder bridges. Committee of inquiry
1971   Interim report (abridged version)
1973   Report (abridged version)
    Appendix 1: interim design and workmanship rules
1973   Parts 1 and 2
1974   Part 3
1973   Part 4
    D. of the Environment
1976   The task of the Commission
Royal Commission on the National Health Service

MERTHYR, W. B. C., Lord
1946 Report of the interdepartmental committee on the Rag Flock Acts
Session 1945-46 Cmd. 6866 xiv.
1955 Hedgerow and farm timber. Report of the committee
Forestry Commission

MESSER, Frederick, Sir
1952 Co-operation between hospital local authority and general practitioner services. Report of the committee of the Central Health Services Council
M. of Health

Hospital supplies. Central Health Services Council committee
1956 Interim report
1958 Final report
M. of Health

METHVEN, M. J.
1976 Review of the Trade Descriptions Act, 1968. Report
Session 1975-76 Cmnd. 6628 ix.

MILES DAVIES, A. E.
See DAVIES, A. E. M.

MILLAR, E. L. M.
Ambulance training and equipment. Report by the working party
1966 Part 1: Training
1967 Part 2: Equipment and vehicles
M. of Health

MILLAR, H. J.
1975 Report on the effect on consumers of the Scottish Milk Marketing Scheme, Aberdeen and District Marketing Scheme, and the North of Scotland Milk Marketing Scheme
D. of Agriculture and Fisheries for Scotland

MILLAR, William Malcolm
1970 Services for the elderly with mental disorder. Report of a sub-committee of the standing medical advisory committee. Scottish Health Services Council
Scottish Home and Health D.
1972 Moral and religious education in Scottish schools. Report of a committee
Scottish Education D.

MILLBOURN, P. Eric, Sir
1950 Increased mechanisation in the U.K. ports. Report of the working party
M. of Transport
1957 London airport development committee. Report
M. of Transport and Civil Aviation

MILLER, Bernard, Sir
1970 Urban models in shopping studies. Distributive Trades Economic Development Committee
N.E.D.O.
1971 Future pattern of shopping. Shopping capacity sub-committee of the Distributive Trades Economic Development Committee

MILLER, C.
1961 Commercial court users' conference report
Session 1961-62 Cmnd. 1616 xii.

MILLER, James M., Sir
1970 Council house communities: A policy for progress. Report of the sub-committee on amenity and social character of local authority housing schemes
Scottish Development D.

MILLER, Keith
1978 Domestic electrical appliances sector working party. Progress report
N.E.D.O.

Productivity, industrial relations and the working environment in the U.K. domestic electrical appliances industry. Report of the domestic electrical appliances sector working party
N.E.D.O.

MILLER, O. Bernard, Sir
1971 Future pattern of shopping. Report by the shopping capacity sub-committee of the Distributive Trades Economic Development Committee
N.E.D.O.

MILLER, Paul H. L.
1974 Anatomy of purchasing clothing machinery. Machinery purchasing attitudes survey group of the Clothing Economic Development Committee
N.E.D.O.

MILLETT, P. J.
1975 John Willment Automobiles Ltd. Report of investigations under the Companies Act
D. of Trade

MILNE, David, Sir
1950 Scottish local government manpower committee
1st report
Session 1950 Cmd. 7951 xiii.
1952 2nd report
Session 1951-52 Cmd. 8658 xiv.
1964 Aberdeen typhoid outbreak, 1964. Report of the departmental committee of inquiry
Session 1964-65 Cmnd. 2542 xvii.

MILNE, G. F., Lord
1943 River boards. 3rd report of the Central Water Advisory Committee
Session 1942-43 Cmd. 6465 vi.

MILNER HOLLAND, E., Sir
See HOLLAND, E. M., Sir

MISSELBROOK, B. Desmond
1971 New homes in the cities; the role of the private developer in urban renewal in England and Wales. Building Economic Development Committee
N.E.D.O.
1974 Field-work staffing (Scotland). Summary of a report by a committee of the Advisory Council on Social Work
Scottish Education D., Social Work Services Group

MITCHELL, Craig
1963 Water services in central Scotland. Report of the Scottish Water Advisory Committee
Scottish Development D.
1966 Water service in Scotland. Final report of the Scottish Water Advisory Committee
Session 1966-67 Cmnd. 3116 li.

MITCHELL, D. S.

1976   Materials-handling costs; a new look at manufacture. Report by a working party of the committee for materials handling
D. of Industry

MITCHELL, J. A. M.

1976   Social work services in the Scottish health service. Report of the working party
Scottish Education D.

1977   Relationship between health boards and local authorities. Report of the working party
Scottish Home and Health D.

MITCHELL, Miles E., Sir

1946   Standards of fitness for habitation. Report by the sub-committee of the Central Housing Advisory Committee
M. of Health

1950   Housing for special purposes; supplement to the housing manual, 1949. Report of the housing manual sub-committee of the Central Housing Advisory Committee
M. of Local Government and Planning

MITCHELL, Ross G.

1968   Child care in Scotland, 1967. A report. Social Work Services Group
Session 1967-68 Cmnd. 3682 xvii.

1970   Handicapped children in care of local authorities and voluntary organisations. Report of the committee of the Scottish Advisory Committee on Child Care
Scottish Education D., Social Work Services Group

MITCHELL, Steuart, Sir

1960   Machine tool industry. Report by the sub-committee of the Machine Tool Advisory Council
Board of Trade

MITTLER, Peter

1977   Mental handicap; planning together (National development group for the mentally handicapped pamphlet No. 1)
D. of Health and Social Security

Mentally handicapped children; a plan for action. (National development group for the mentally handicapped pamphlet No. 2)
D. of Health and Social Security

Helping mentally handicapped school leavers. (National development group for the mentally handicapped pamphlet No. 3)
D. of Health and Social Security

Residental short-term care for mentally handicapped people; suggestions for action. (National development group for the mentally handicapped pamphlet No. 4)
D. of Health and Social Security

Day services for mentally handicapped adults. (National development group for the mentally handicapped pamphlet No. 5)
D. of Health and Social Security

1978   Helping mentally handicapped people in hospital. Report of the national development group for the mentally handicapped
D. of Health and Social Security

MOCATTA, A. A., Sir

1956   Cheque endorsement. Report of the committee
Session 1956-57 Cmnd. 3 ix.

MOLE, Charles J., Sir

1952   Economy of building materials. Report by the heads of the works directorates of the service departments and the Ministry of Works
M. of Works

MOLLISON, P. L.

See SQUIRE, J. R.

MOLONY, J. T., Sir

1962   Consumer protection reports of the committee
Interim report
Session 1959-60 Cmnd. 1011 xii.
Final report
Session 1961-62 Cmnd. 1781 xii.

MOLSON, A. H. E., Lord

1954   Road safety. Report of the committee on massed start cycle racing
M. of Transport and Civil Aviation

1956   Child cyclists. Report of the committee on road safety
M. of Transport and Civil Aviation

1962   Uganda. Report of a commission of Privy Counsellors on a dispute between Buganda and Bunyora
Session 1961-62 Cmnd. 1717 xi.

MONCKTON OF BRENCHLEY, Walter, Viscount

Workmen's compensation (contributory negligence). Departmental committee

1944   Interim report on alternative remedies
Session 1944-45 Cmd. 6580 vi.

1945   2nd interim report on alternative remedies
Session 1944-45 Cmd. 6642 vi.

1946   Final report
Session 1945-46 Cmd. 6860 xiii.

1960   Review of the constitution of Rhodesia and Nyasaland. Report of the advisory commission (with) appendices I-VIII
Session 1959-60 Cmnd. 1148, Cmnd. 1149, Cmnd. 1150 xi.

MONTAGU OF BEAULIEU, E. J. B., Lord

1976   Control of motor rallies. Report of the advisory committee
D. of the Environment

MONTAGU, A. V. E. P.

1955   Works of art in the House of Commons. Report of an advisory committee
M. of Works

MONTAGU, Ewen E. S.

1953   Cadet entry into the Royal Navy. Report of the committee on cadet entry into the executive, engineering and supply and secretariat branches of the Royal Navy
Session 1952-53 Cmd. 8845 xvi.

MONTEITH, J. L.

1976   Research in applied and world climatology. Report of a working party on applied climatology. (Publications series B No. 17)
Natural Environment Research Council

MONTGOMERY, G. L.

1959   Maternity services in Scotland. Report of a committee of the Scottish Health Services Council
M. of Health

MOORE, H. R.

1976 Regional chairmen's inquiry into the working of the D.H.S.S. in relation to regional health authorities
D. of Health and Social Security

MOORE, J. M.

1978 Administration trainee review committee report.
Civil Service D.

MOORE-BRABAZON, J. T. C.

See BRABAZON OF TARA, J. T. C., Lord

MOOS, S.

1972 Aspects of monopoly and restrictive practice legislation to small firms. (Committee of inquiry on small firms report No. 13)
D. of Trade and Industry

MORAN, C. McM., Lord

1949 Scientific results of German medical war crimes Report of an inquiry of a committee
Foreign Office

MORE, N. E. A.

1973 Decimalisation of Britain's currency
Treasury

MORGAN, A. M.

1966 Preservation of pension rights on change of employment. Report of a committee of the national joint advisory council
M. of Labour

MORIARTY, M. J.

1978 Review of the criminal injuries compensation scheme. Report of an interdepartmental working party
Home Office

MORISON, Alastair M.

1971 Report on the local inquiry in the matter of review of rents of council houses in Coatbridge
Scottish Development D.

MORISON, Ronald, Sir

1961 Probation service. Report of the departmental committee
Session 1961-62 Cmnd. 1650 xxiii.

1962 Probation service. 2nd report of the departmental committee
Session 1961-62 Cmnd. 1800 xxiii.

MORPETH, Douglas

1976 Current cost accounting; proposed statement of standard accounting practice prepared by the inflation accounting steering group of the Accounting Standards Committee
D. of Trade

MORRIS OF BORTH-Y-GEST, John W., Lord

1941 Requisitioning and compensation. Report of the requisitioning of land and buildings and the operation of the Compensation (Defence) Act, 1939
Session 1940-41 Cmd. 6313 iv.

1944 War damaged licensed premises and reconstruction. Report of the committee
Session 1943-44 Cmd. 6504 iv.

Selling price of houses. Report of the interdepartmental committee
Session 1945-46 Cmd. 6670 x.

1954 Report of a court of inquiry into a dispute between employers who are members of the Shipbuilding Employers' Federation and workmen who are members of the trades unions affiliated to the Confederation of Shipbuilding and Engineering Unions
Session 1953-54 Cmd. 9085 xv.

Report of a court of inquiry into a dispute between employers who are members of the Engineering and Allied Employers' National Federation and workmen who are members of trades unions affiliated to the Confederation of Shipbuilding and Engineering Unions
Session 1953-54 Cmd. 9084 xv.

1965 Jury service. Report of the departmental committee
Session 1964-65 Cmnd. 2627 xviii.

MORRIS OF GRASMERE, Charles R., Lord

1966 Higher education mission to the South Pacific appointed by agreement between the governments of Britain and New Zealand with the co-operation of the government of Australia. Report of the mission
M. of Overseas Development

MORRIS, G. I.

1960 Planning of helicopter stations in the London area. Report of the committee. (CAP 173)
M. of Aviation

MORRIS, Harold, Sir

1940 H.M. prisons and borstal institutions (female nursing staff—scales of pay). Board of arbitration award
M. of Labour

Prison service (hours of duty). Board of arbitration award
M. of Labour

1943 Report by the court of inquiry into the wages and hours of work in the woolcombing section of the wool textile industry in Yorkshire
Session 1943-44 Cmd. 6499 iv.

MORRIS, Ivor R.

1961 Sheep recording and progeny testing. Report of the committee
M. of Agriculture, Fisheries and Food

MORRIS, J. D. O.

1974 Housing and social work, a joint approach. The interim report on links between housing and social work
Scottish Development D.

1975 Housing and social work, a joint approach. Report of the committee on links between housing and social work
Scottish Development D.

MORRIS, John
1967 Railway policy
Session 1967-68 Cmnd. 3439 xxxix.

MORRIS, Malcolm
1968 Findings and recommendations following inquiries into allegations concerning the care of elderly patients in certain hospitals. I: Banstead Hospital
Session 1967-68 Cmnd. 3687 xxviii.

MORRIS, Parker, Sir
1961 Homes for today and tomorrow. Report of a sub-committee of the Central Housing Advisory Committee
M. of Housing and Local Government

MORRIS, Philip, Sir

1951   Training and supply of teachers. 1st report of the national advisory council covering the period 1949 to 1951
M. of Education

1953   Graduate teachers of mathematics and science. Report of the National Advisory Council on the Training and Supply of Teachers
M. of Education

1954   Training and supply of teachers of handicapped pupils. 4th report of the National Advisory Council on the Training and Supply of Teachers
M. of Education

1956   Three years' training for teachers. 5th report of the National Advisory Council on the Training and Supply of Teachers
M. of Education

1957   Teacher training; scope and content of the three-year course of teacher training. 6th report of the National Advisory Council on the Training and Supply of Teachers
M. of Education

1959   Report of the Commonwealth Education Conference
Session 1958-59 Cmnd. 841 xi.

MORRISON, Charles M.

1974   Educational priority, vol. 5: E.P.A.—a Scottish study
Scottish Education D.

MORRISON, W. S.

See DUNROSSIL, W. S., Viscount

MORSE, Chandler

1960   Basutoland, Bechuanaland Protectorate and Swaziland. Report of an economic survey mission (with maps)
Commonwealth Relations Office

MORSE, Jeremy

1978   Investment reserve schemes. Report of a working party
N.E.D.O.

MORTIMER, J. E.

1976   Engineering construction performance. Report of the comparative construction performance working party of the Mechanical and Electrical Engineering economic development committees
N.E.D.O.

Accurist Watches Ltd. and the Transport and General Workers Union (report No. 5)
Advisory, Conciliation and Arbitration Service

W. Ball (Woodworkers) Ltd. and the Furniture, Timber and Allied Trades Unions (report No. 6)
Advisory, Conciliation and Arbitration Service

1977   Scottish and Newcastle Breweries Ltd. Report of an inquiry into industrial relations in the transport activities of the company's north-east region (report No. 9)

Advisory, Conciliation and Arbitration Service
Retail Wages Councils. Report of an inquiry concerning draft orders abolishing nine retail wages councils and establishing in their place two new wages councils (report No. 10)
Advisory, Conciliation and Arbitration Service

1978   Button Manufacturing Wages Council (report No. 11)
Advisory, Conciliation and Arbitration Service

Royal Commission on the National Health Service: ACAS evidence. An assessment of ACAS involvement in National Health Service industrial relations (report No. 12)

Advisory, Conciliation and Arbitration Service
Toy Manufacturing Wages Council (report No. 13)
Advisory, Conciliation and Arbitration Service
St. Stephen's Parliamentary Press (H.M.S.O.). Inquiry into industrial relations (report No. 14)
Advisory, Conciliation and Arbitration Service

MORTIMER, R. C., Bishop of Exeter

1962   Preventive detention. Report of the advisory council on the treatment of offenders
Home Office

1970   Safety of natural gas as a fuel. Report of the inquiry
M. of Technology

MORTON OF HENRYTON, F. D., Lord

1951   Law of intestate succession. Report of the committee
Session 1950-51 Cmd. 8310 xvi.

1952   Marriage and Divorce, Royal Commission on Minutes of evidence. 37 days

1955   Royal Commission on Marriage and Divorce Report
Session 1955-56 Cmd. 9678 xxiii.

MORTON, Frank A.

1970   Safety of natural gas as a fuel. Report of the enquiry
M. of Technology

MORTON, R. A.

1975   Research in marine biochemistry. Report of the working party (publications series B No. 10)
Natural Environment Research Council

MORTON, Richard A.

1965   Cyclamates. Report of the Food Additives and Contaminants Committee
M. of Agriculture, Fisheries and Food

Solvents. Report of the Food Additives and Contaminants Committee
M. of Agriculture, Fisheries and Food

1967   Aldrin and dieldrin residues in food. Report of the Food Additives and Contaminants Committee
M. of Agriculture, Fisheries and Food

Cyclamates. 2nd report of the Food Additives and Contaminants Committee
M. of Agriculture, Fisheries and Food

1968   Azodicarbonamide. Report of the Food Additives and Contaminants Committee
M. of Agriculture, Fisheries and Food

Further classes of food additives. Report of the Food Additives and Contaminants Committee
M. of Agriculture, Fisheries and Food

1970   Leaching of substances from packaging materials into food. Report of the Food Additives and Contaminants Committee
M. of Agriculture, Fisheries and Food

MORTON-WILLIAMS, Roma

1968   Young school leavers. Report of an inquiry carried out for the Schools Council by the Government Social Survey
Schools Council

MOSS, J.

1953   Child migration to Australia
Home Office

MOSS, L.

See REDCLIFFE-MAUD, J. P., Lord

MOTT, Neville, Sir

1966   The educational role of the Ministry of Aviation establishments. Report of the working party of the Electronics Research Council
M. of Aviation

MOUNTBATTEN OF BURMA, L. F. A. V. N., Earl

1947   South-East Asia, 1943-45. Report to the combined chiefs of staff
War Office

1966   Prison escapes and security. Report of the inquiry
Session 1966-67 Cmnd. 3175 xlvii.

1969   Post surrender tasks. Section E of the report to the combined chiefs of staff
M. of Defence

MOYNE, W. E., Lord

1944   West India Royal Commission. Statement of action taken on recommendations
Session 1944-45 Cmd. 6656 x.

MUDIE, Francis, Sir

1956   British Caribbean federal capital commission. Report
Colonial Office

MUIR, W. A. Gordon

1977   Training for tomorrow; an action plan for Scottish housing. Report of a sub-committee of the Scottish Housing Advisory Committee
Scottish Development D.

MUKHERJEE, S.

1974   There's work to be done; unemployment and manpower policies
Manpower Services Commission

MUMFORD, A. C.

1971   Survey on management training and development. Central Training Council training survey unit report
D. of Employment

MUNDY, J. A.

1978   Materials handling; an introduction
D. of Industry

MUNN, J.

1977   Structure of the curriculum in the third and fourth years of the Scottish secondary schools. Consultative committee on the curriculum
Scottish Education D.

MUNRO, Alison

1973   Children's footwear. Report of the committee
Session 1972-73 Cmnd. 5243 x.

MUNSTER, G. W. R. H., Earl of

1944   Welfare of troops in India and South-East Asia Commands. Report
Session 1944-45 Cmd. 6578 iv.

MURDOCH, R. D.

1975   Work restructuring projects and experiments in the U.K. (Work Research Unit report No. 2)
D. of Employment

1976   Work restructuring projects and experiments in the U.S.A. (Work Research Unit report No. 3)
D. of Employment

MURGATROYD, F. B.

1972   Reclaiming the 70s; the future for the low-cost woollen sector. Wool Textile Economic Development Committee
N.E.D.O.

MURRANT, Ernest, Sir

1952   Ports Efficiency Committee. 1st and 2nd reports
M. of Transport

1956   Ports Efficiency Committee. 3rd report
M. of Transport and Civil Aviation

MURRAY, David King, Sir

1944   Scottish coalfields. Report of the committee
Session 1944-45 Cmd. 6575 iv.

MURRAY, Keith, Sir

1963   First employment of university graduates. Report of the University Grants Committee
Treasury

MYERS, G. M. P.

1969   Formulæ methods of price adjustment on building contracts. Report by the steering group on price fluctuations formulæ. Building Economic Development Committee
N.E.D.O.

MYRDDIN-EVANS, Guildhaume, Sir

1952   Human relations in industry. Report of a conference held at the Institution of Civil Engineers, London, 18-20 March 1952
M. of Labour and National Service

1963   Local Government Commission for Wales. Report and proposals for Wales. Maps 1-36
M. of Housing and Local Government

NAISBY, John V.

1970   Sight tests for seafarers. Report of the committee to review the Board of Trade sight test standards for persons serving or intending to serve in the Merchant Navy or in the fishing fleet
Board of Trade

NASH, T. A. M.

1948   Tsetse flies in British West Africa. Report
Colonial Office

NATHAN, H. L., Lord

1952   Charitable trusts. Report of the committee on the law and practice relating to charitable trusts
Session 1952-53 Cmnd. 8710 viii.

NEAL, L.

1947   Estate development and management in war-damaged areas. Central Advisory committee report
M. of Town and Country Planning

NEAL, L. F.

1971   Engelhard Industries Ltd. (report No. 26)
Commission on Industrial Relations

The hotel and catering industry, part 2: industrial catering (report No. 27)
Commission on Industrial Relations

1972   John Bamber Engineering Ltd. (report No. 28)
Commission on Industrial Relations

Alcan Smelter Site (report No. 29)
Commission on Industrial Relations

NEAL, L. F. *(continued)*

Approved closed shop agreement. British Shipping Federation/National Union of Seamen (report No. 30)
Commission on Industrial Relations

Disclosure of information (report No. 31)
Commission on Industrial Relations

C. A. Parsons & Co. Ltd. and associated companies (report No. 32)
Commission on Industrial Relations

Industrial relations training (report No. 33)
Commission on Industrial Relations

The role of management in industrial relations (report No. 34)
Commission on Industrial Relations

1973   Williams & Glyn's Bank Ltd. (report No. 35)
Commission on Industrial Relations

Hotel and catering industry, part 3: public houses, clubs and other sectors (report No. 36)
Commission on Industrial Relations

Annual report for 1972 (report No. 37)
Commission on Industrial Relations

Allied Breweries (U.K.) Ltd. (report No. 38)
Commission on Industrial Relations

Communications and collective bargaining (report No. 39)
Commission on Industrial Relations

Approved closed shop in theatre, independent television and films
(report No. 40)
Commission on Industrial Relations

National Coal Board bulk terminal, Immingham (report No. 41)
Commission on Industrial Relations

Coventry Economic Building Society (report No. 42)
Commission on Industrial Relations

Horizon Holidays Ltd. and associated companies (report No. 43)
Commission on Industrial Relations

Connor & Forbes Ltd. (report No. 44)
Commission on Industrial Relations

Walter Alexander & Company (Coachbuilders) Ltd. (report No. 45)
Commission on Industrial Relations

Coffin Furniture and Cerement Making Wages Council (report No. 46)
Commission on Industrial Relations

Hollow Ware Wages Council (report No. 47)
Commission on Industrial Relations

Keg and Drum Wages Council (report No. 48)
Commission on Industrial Relations

Pin Hook and Eye Snap Fastener Wages Council (report No. 49)
Commission on Industrial Relations

Stamped or Pressed Metal-Wares Wages Council (report No. 50)
Commission on Industrial Relations

Boot and Floor Polish Wages Council (Great Britain) (report No. 51)
Commission on Industrial Relations

General Accident Fire and Life Assurance Corporation Ltd., 2nd report (report No. 52)
Commission on Industrial Relations

Con-Mech (Engineers) Ltd. (report No. 53)
Commission on Industrial Relations

G. Clancey Ltd. (report No. 54)
Commission on Industrial Relations

1974   Pan American World Airways Incorporated (report No. 55)
Commission on Industrial Relations

Edinburgh Corporation Transport Department (report No. 56)
Commission on Industrial Relations

Bridgwater Building Society (report No. 57)
Commission on Industrial Relations

Barclays Bank International Ltd. (report No. 58)
Commission on Industrial Relations

Messrs. Gordon Nunns (report No. 59)
Commission on Industrial Relations

NAAFI (report No. 60)
Commission on Industrial Relations

Pfizer Ltd. (report No. 61)
Commission on Industrial Relations

Lesney Products & Co. Ltd. (report No. 62)
Commission on Industrial Relations

William Hill Organisation (report No. 63)
Commission on Industrial Relations

Seymour & Story Group (report No. 64)
Commission on Industrial Relations

Annual report for 1973 (report No. 65)
Commission on Industrial Relations

Airline Engineering Ltd. (report No. 66)
Commission on Industrial Relations

Colvern Ltd. (report No. 67)
Commission on Industrial Relations

Associated Octel Co. Ltd., 2nd report (report No. 68)
Commission on Industrial Relations

Small firms and the code of industrial relations practice (report No. 69)
Commission on Industrial Relations

Davenports Brewery (Holdings) Ltd. (report No. 70)
Commission on Industrial Relations

John Joyce Ltd. (report No. 71)
Commission on Industrial Relations

Ken Hailes Ltd. (report No. 72)
Commission on Industrial Relations

Messrs. Roland Jones (report No. 73)
Commission on Industrial Relations

Ken Munden (Turf Accountant) Ltd.; Ken Munden (Racing) Ltd. (report No. 74)
Commission on Industrial Relations

Temperance Permanent Building Society (report No. 75)
Commission on Industrial Relations

Mansfield Hosiery Mills (report No. 76)
Commission on Industrial Relations

Clothing Wages Councils (report No. 77)
Commission on Industrial Relations

Lloyds Bank Ltd. (report No. 78)
Commission on Industrial Relations

Anglia Building Society (report No. 79)
Commission on Industrial Relations

Rubery Owen and Co. Ltd. and associated companies (report No. 80)
Commission on Industrial Relations

Hector MacDonald Ltd. (report No. 81)
Commission on Industrial Relations

Norwich Union Insurance Group (report No. 82)
Commission on Industrial Relations

Paper Box Wages Council (report No. 83)
Commission on Industrial Relations

Lombard North Central Ltd. (report No. 84)
Commission on Industrial Relations

NEAL, L. F. (*continued*)

Industrial relations in multi-plant undertakings (report No. 85)
Commission on Industrial Relations

Building societies (report No. 86)
Commission on Industrial Relations

Professional football (report No. 87)
Commission on Industrial Relations

Imperial Chemical Industries Ltd. (report No. 88)
Commission on Industrial Relations

Retail distribution (report No. 89)
Commission on Industrial Relations

Final report (report No. 90)
Commission on Industrial Relations

NEDEN, Wilfred J., Sir

Electricity sub-committee of the joint consultative committee
1954   Report
1955   Report
M. of Labour and National Service

Index of retail prices. Report on proposals for a new index by the cost of living advisory committee
Session 1955-56 Cmd. 9710 xiii.

NELSON, George H., Sir

1945   Census of production committee report
Session 1945-46 Cmd. 6687 x.

NELSON, H. I.

1958   Police forces of the County of Carmarthen and the County of Cardigan. Report of inquiry into the proposed compulsory amalgamation
Session 1957-58 Cmnd. 374 xvii.

NETHERTHORPE, J., Lord

1962   Antibiotics in animal feeding. Report of the joint committee
Agricultural Research Council *and* Medical Research Council

NEUBERGER, A.

1974   Food and nutrition research. Report of the joint committee
Agricultural Research Council *and* Medical Research Council

NEWBY, F.

See PRICE, C.

NEWSAM, Frank, Sir

1946   Higher training for the police service in England and Wales. Report
Session 1946-47 Cmd. 7070 xiii.

Police post-war committee
1946   2nd report
         3rd report
1947   4th report
Home Office

NEWSAM, J. H., Sir

1963   Half our future. Report of the central advisory council for education (England)
M. of Education

1968   Public Schools Commission. 1st report (with) appendices. 2 vols.
D. of Education and Science

See also DONNISON, D. V.

NEWSON-SMITH, Frank, Sir

1945   Training for business administration committee report
Session 1945-46 Cmd. 6673 x.

NEWTON, C. M.

1948   Civil aviation accident investigation procedure. Report of the committee of the national civil aviation consultative council
Session 1948-49 Cmd. 7564 xi.

NIBLETT, W. R.

1957   Halls of residence. Report of the University Grants Committee sub-committee
Treasury

NICHOLS, R. W.

1969   Pressure vessels. Report of the committee of inquiry
         Vol. 1: report
         Vol. 2: appendices of evidence
M. of Technology

NICHOLSON, P. B.

1977   The Somerset wetlands project. Report by a working party
Nature Conservancy Council

NICOL, A. J.

1967   Efficient use of manpower. Report of a study group composed of directors and senior managers of well-known firms in the Midlands
M. of Labour

NICOLL, E. H.

1977   Storm sewage separation and disposal. Report of the working party
Scottish Development D.

NICOLSON, David L.

British Airways Board
1972   1st report on organisation
         Session 1971-72 HC. 386 viii.
         2nd report on organisation
         Session 1972-73 HC. 74 vi.
1973   3rd report on organisation
         Session 1973-74 HC. 31 iii.

See also McFADZEAN, F.

NIND, P. F.

1970   The supply of teachers for management education. 1st report by the Management Education, Training and Development Committee
N.E.D.O.

1972   Supply of teachers for management education. 2nd report by the Management Education, Training and Development Committee
N.E.D.O.

NIVEN, J. F.

1973   New Scottish local authorities organisation and management structures. Report of the working group
Scottish Development D.

NOBLE, Kenneth

Fresh Food Reference
1974   Report for September 1973 to February 1974
         Session 1974 HC. 74 xiv.

NOBLE, Kenneth *(continued)*

Marketing of eggs. 2nd report on the reference
Session 1974 HC. 329 xiv.

Report for January to July 1974
Session 1974-75 HC. 25 xxxii.

Prices, margins and channels of distribution for fruit and vegetables. Interim report
Price Commission

1975   Prices, margins and channels of distribution for fruit and vegetables. Report No. 5 (final)
Price Commission

NOBLE, T. A. F.

1966   Report on the work of the Probation and After-Care Department, 1962-65
Session 1966-67 Cmnd. 3107 xlvii.

NOEL-BAKER, Philip

1944   Road safety. Interim report of a committee
M. of War Transport

See also CALLAGHAN, James; STRAUSS, G. R.

NORMAND, W. G., Lord

1943   Utilisation of land in the rural areas of Scotland. Report of a committee
Session 1942-43 Cmd. 6440 v.

NORRIS, G. A.

1973   Financial management for the smaller garage. Motor Vehicle Distribution and Repair Economic Development Committee
N.E.D.O.

NORRIS, W. H.

1968   Metric units with reference to water, sewage and related subjects. Report of a working party
M. of Housing and Local Government

NORTH, George, Sir

1948   Social and economic research. Report of the interdepartmental committee
Session 1948 Cmd. 7537 ii.

1950   Social and economic research. Report of the interdepartmental committee
Session 1950-52 Cmd. 8091 xix.

1956   Social and economic research. Report of the interdepartmental committee
Lord President's Office *and* H.M. Treasury

NORTH, J. J.

1977   Economics of irrigation. Report of the working party
Agricultural Development and Advisory Service

NORTHUMBERLAND, H. A., Duke of

1953   Slaughter of horses. Report of the committee of inquiry
Session 1952-53 Cmd. 8925 xvii.

1964   Recruitment for the veterinary profession. Report of the departmental committee of inquiry
Session 1963-64 Cmnd. 2430 xx.

1969   Foot-and-mouth disease, 1968. Report of the committee of inquiry
Part 1
Session 1968-69 Cmnd. 3999 **xxx.**
Part 2
Session 1969-70 Cmnd. 4225 v.

See also REID, J.

1977   The ownership of land by agricultural landlords in England and Wales. Agricultural Economic Development Committee
N.E.D.O.

NORTON, A.

See REDCLIFFE-MAUD, J. P., Lord

NORWOOD, C., Sir

1943   Curriculum and examinations in secondary schools. Report of the committee of the secondary school examinations council. Repr. 1946
Board of Education

NOURSE, Martin Charles

1978   Land and General Developments, Ltd., Napet Securities, Ltd. Interim and final reports of investigation under the Companies Act
D. of Trade

NUGENT OF GUILDFORD, G. R. H., Lord

1957   Motor cyclists. Committee on road safety. Report on the minimum age for motor cyclists
M. of Transport and Civil Aviation

1959   London roads. Report of the committee
Session 1958-59 Cmnd. 812 xix.

1973   Defence lands committee. Report
M. of Defence

OAKE, G. R.

1951   Meat inspection. Report of the interdepartmental committee
M. of Food

OAKES, Gordon J.

1978   Management of higher education in the maintained sector. Report of the working party
Session 1977-78 Cmnd. 7130 x.

OAKLEY, F. W.

1968   Memorandum on the diploma in management studies. Committee for the Diploma in Management Studies. 2nd ed.
D. of Education and Science

OAKSEY, G., Lord

See TREVETHIN AND OAKSEY, G., Lord

OASTLER, E. G.

1963   Bronchitis. Report of a sub-committee of the standing medical advisory committee. Scottish Health Services Council
Scottish Home and Health D.

O'BRIEN, L. K., Lord

1974   Export of animals for slaughter. Report of the committee
Session 1974 Cmnd. 5566 iii.

O'BRIEN, F. W. F.

1973   Local inquiry in relation to the implementation by Clydebank Town Council of parts II and IV of the Housing (Financial Provisions) (Scotland) Act, 1972. Report
Scottish Development D.

O'BRIEN, R.

1969   Manpower productivity comparison. A report prepared by the wool (and allied) textile employers' council's management services centre. Wool and Textiles Economic Development Committee
N.E.D.O.

O'BRIEN, R. *(continued)*

1977   Training for skills; a programme for action. Report by the vital skills task group
Manpower Services Commission, Training Services Agency

O'CONNOR, F. B.

1977   Otters, 1977. 1st report of the joint otter group
Nature Conservancy Council

O'CONOR, May

1951   Deaf-blind persons. Report of the committee on the welfare of the deaf and on their special welfare needs
M. of Health

O'DELL, Alan

1977   Mobile homes in England and Wales, 1975. Report of surveys
D. of the Environment

OFFORD, R. S.

See CHANTLER, P.

OGDEN, George, Sir

1973   New water industry; management and structure. Report of the committee
D. of the Environment

OGDEN, W. M.

1964   Depopulation in mid-Wales. Report of a committee
M. of Housing and Local Government

OLDFIELD-DAVIES, Alun B.

1953   Arts in education. Music in the schools of Wales. Report of the Central Advisory Council for Education (Wales)
M. of Education

1954   Arts in education. Drama in the schools of Wales. Report of the Central Advisory Council for Education (Wales)
M. of Education

1955   Arts in education. Arts and crafts in the schools of Wales. Report of the Central Advisory Council for Education (Wales)
M. of Education

1960   Education in rural Wales. Report of the Central Advisory Council for Education (Wales)
M. of Education

        Technical education in Wales. Report of the Central Advisory Council for Education (Wales)
M. of Education

OLIVER, D. A.

1952   Metals economy. Advisory committee report
M. of Supply

OLIVER, G. H.

1946   Electoral registration. Report of the committee on electoral registration
Session 1946-47 Cmd. 7004 xi.

OLIVER, R.

1943   Detention barracks. Report of the Prime Minister's committee of inquiry
Session 1942-43 Cmd. 6484 iv.

O'NEILL, Denis E.

1949   Fire prevention and fire fighting in ships in port. Report of the working party
M. of Transport

OPPE, T. E.

1974   Present-day practice in infant feeding. Report of the working party (report on health and social subjects, No. 9)
D. of Health and Social Security

1977   The composition of mature human milk. Report of a working party of the committee on medical aspects of food policy (report on health and social subjects No. 12)
D. of Health and Social Security

1978   Breast feeding. Report of the committee on medical aspects of food policy, panel on child nutrition
D. of Health and Social Security

ORDE-BROWNE, G. St. J., Sir

1943   Labour conditions in Ceylon, Mauritius and Malaya. Report
Session 1942-43 Cmd. 6423 ix.

1945   Labour conditions in east Africa. Report (Colonial No. 193)
Colonial Office

O'RIORDAN, Timothy

1978   Sharing rivers and canals; a study of the views of course anglers and boat users on selected waterways (study No. 16)
Sports Council

ORMISTON, J. H.

1973   Moray Firth; an agricultural study (special report No. 9)
Highlands and Islands Development Board

ORMROD, Roger

1971   Legal education. Report of the committee
Session 1970-71 Cmnd. 4595 x.

ORR, Alan Stewart, Sir

1977   Law reform committee. 21st report: final report on limitation of actions
Session 1976-77 Cmnd. 6923 xix.

ORR, I. B.

1943   Infant mortality in Scotland. Report of a sub-committee of the scientific advisory committee
D. of Health for Scotland

ORR, J. BOYD, Lord

See BOYD ORR, J., Lord

OSBORNE, H. E.

1976   Passenger transport; short and medium term considerations. (Advisory Council on Energy Conservation paper No. 2) (Energy paper No. 10)
D. of Energy

1978   Energy for transport; long-term possibilities. Report of the transport working group. (Advisory Council on Energy Conservation paper No. 8) (Energy paper No. 26)
D. of Energy

OSBORNE, J. G.

1974   Description of the indices for use with the N.E.D.O. price adjustment formula for building works. Building Economic Development Committee
N.E.D.O.

        Price adjustment formulae for building contracts; a guide to the practical application of the formulae. Building Economic Development Committee
N.E.D.O.

OSMOND, S. P.

1972   Recording court proceedings. Report of a working party
Lord Chancellor's Office

O'SULLIVAN, D. N.

1951   Disposal of internal restitution claims in the British zone of Germany. Report of the committee on progress made, with appendices
Foreign Office

O'SULLIVAN, P. E.

1978   Working group on buildings. Report to the Advisory Council on Energy Conservation on session January to October 1977 (Energy paper No. 25)
D. of Energy

O'SULLIVAN, R.

1958   Operation of the British Wool Marketing Scheme, 1950. Report of the committee of investigation for Great Britain
M. of Agriculture, Fisheries and Food

OTTON, G. J.

1974   Social work support for the health service. Report of the working party
D. of Health and Social Security

OWEN, Lloyd O.

1961   Water resources of Wales. Report of the Welsh advisory water committee
Session 1960-61 Cmnd. 1331 xxi.

OWEN, R. A.

1972   Management arrangements for the reorganised National Health Service in Wales. Report of the steering committee and the study group
Welsh Office

P-E CONSULTING GROUP LTD.
See TROWBRIDGE, G. W.
SHANKS, M. J.

PACK, D. C.

1977   Truancy and indiscipline in schools in Scotland. Report of committee of inquiry
Scottish Education D.

PADMORE, T., Sir
See DUNNETT, J., Sir

PAGE, Harry, Sir

1973   National savings. Report of the review committee
Session 1972-73 Cmnd. 5273 xxxi.

PAGET, Gregg

1978   Sharing rivers and canals; a study of the views of course anglers and boat users on selected waterways (study No. 16)
Sports Council

PAKENHAM, F. A., Lord
See LONGFORD, F. A., Lord

PALACHE, Albert

1944   Tendencies to monopoly in the cinematograph film industry. Report of a committee
Board of Trade

PALMER, William, Sir

1953   Iron and steel consumer's council. Report for the final period
Session 1952-53 HC. 224 xiv.

PALMER, W.
See PERCIVAL-PRESCOTT, W.

PARCQ, H., Baron Du
See DU PARCQ, H., Baron

PARISH, David E. Woodbine

1964   Building research and information services. Report of a working party
M. of Public Building and Works

1970   Hospital building maintenance. Report of the committee
D. of Health and Social Security

PARKER OF WADDINGTON, Hubert Lister P., Lord

1957   Bank rate. Proceedings of the tribunal of inquiry into allegations that information about the raising of bank rate was improperly disclosed, with minutes of evidence
Home Office

1958   Bank rate. Report of the tribunal of inquiry into allegations that information about the raising of bank rate was improperly disclosed
Session 1957-58 Cmnd. 350 viii.

1972   Authorised procedures for the interrogation of persons suspected of terrorism. Report of the committee of Privy Councillors
Session 1971-72 Cmnd. 4901 xviii.

PARKER, K. A. L.

1961   Higher police training. Report of the committee of the Police Council
Home Office

1963   Higher police training; supplementary report on the special course at the Police College by a committee of the Police Council
Home Office

PARKER, P.

1972   The eleven billion mark market. A study of the market for ladies' outerwear in West Germany. Clothing Economic Development Committee
N.E.D.O.

Wage payment systems in the clothing industry (newsletter No. 15) Clothing Economic Development Committee
N.E.D.O.

1973   Employees' attitudes and their effect on labour turnover in the clothing industry. Clothing Economic Development Committee
N.E.D.O.

1974   Anatomy of purchasing clothing machinery. Clothing Economic Development Committee
N.E.D.O.

Employment practices in E.E.C. clothing industries. Clothing Economic Development Committee
N.E.D.O.

Low-cost work aids for the clothing and garment industries. Clothing Economic Development Committee
N.E.D.O.

1975   Unlocking productivity potential; the experience of seven firms in the clothing industry. Clothing Economic Development Committee
N.E.D.O.

PARKER, Roger Jocelyn
1975   Flixborough disaster. Report of the court of inquiry
        D. of Employment
1978   Windscale inquiry. Report and annexes. 3 vols
        D. of the Environment
        Windscale inquiry. Index to the transcript of the hearings. 4 microfiches
        D. of Industry Library Services

PARKER, S. R.
        See REDCLIFFE-MAUD, J. P., Lord

PARKER MORRIS, Sir
        See MORRIS, P., Sir

PARKES, Dennis
1978   Terotechnology handbook. Committee for terotechnology
        D. of Industry

PARR, E.
        See GRAY, P. G.

PARRY, David Hughes, Sir
1965   Legal status of the Welsh language. Report of the committee
        Session 1964-65 Cmnd. 2785 xxii.

PARRY, H. Wynn, Sir
        See WYNN PARRY, H., Sir

PARRY, J. H.
1965   Latin American studies. Report of the committee of the University Grants Committee
        D. of Education and Science

PARRY, Thomas
1967   Libraries. Report of the committee
        University Grants Committee

PART, U. R.
1977   How to write metric; a style guide for teaching and using SI units. Working group on metrication
        Metrication Board

PARTHASARATHI, G.
1955   Cambodia international commission for supervision and control in Cambodia
            1st progress report
            Session 1954-55 Cmd. 9458 xix.
            2nd progress report
            Session 1955-56 Cmd. 9534 xliv.
            3rd interim report
            Session 1955-56 Cmd. 9579 xliv.
            4th interim report
            Session 1955-56 Cmd. 9671 xliv.

PASSMORE, R.
1969   Recommended intakes of nutrients for the U.K. Report of the panel on recommended allowances of nutrients (reports on public health and medical subjects No. 120)
        D. of Health and Social Security

PATERSON, I. V.
1973   New Scottish local authorities; organisation and management structures. Report of a working party
        Scottish Development D.
        See also NIVEN, J. F.

PATERSON, Thomas
1949   Choosing council tenants. Report by the Scottish Housing Advisory Committee on local authorities' methods of allocating tenancies
        D. of Health for Scotland
        See also MACLEAN, A.

PATON, Thomas A. L.
1970   Large industrial sites. Report of the working party
        N.E.D.O.

PATTERSON, C. C.
1944   The lighting of buildings. Report by the lighting committee of the Buildings Research Board. (Post-war building studies No. 12)
        M. of Works

PAULA, F. C., de
1977   Agriculture into the 1980s: finance. Agriculture Economic Development Committee
        N.E.D.O.
        Agriculture into the 1980s: the impact of taxation. Agriculture Economic Development Committee
        N.E.D.O.

PAYNE, J.
1974   Educational priority, vol. 2: E.P.A. surveys and statistics
        D. of Education and Science

PAYNE, R. W.
1969   Enforcement of judgement debts. Report of the committee
        Session 1968-69 Cmnd. 3909 xxxvi.

PAYNE, Robert, Sir
1972   Whittingham Hospital. Report of the committee of inquiry. National Health Service
        Session 1971-72 Cmnd. 4861 xvi.

PAYNTER, T. W.
1975   Difficulties affecting London docks. Report of the panel of investigation. (Report No. 2)
        Advisory, Conciliation and Arbitration Service

PEACOCK, A. T.
        See CROWTHER OF HEADINGLY, Lord

PEACOCK, Alan
1970   Orchestral resources in Great Britain. Report of the committee
        Arts Council

PEACOCKE, G. J.
1974   Report on a fatal accident in an explosives factory at South Normanton, Derbyshire on 23 March 1971
        Home Office

PEARCE, E. H., Lord
1972   Commission on Rhodesia opinion. Report. (Miscellaneous No. 19, 1972)
        Session 1971-72 Cmnd. 4964 viii.

PEARCE, A. W.
1976   Industry group report. (Advisory Council on Energy Conservation paper No. 4) (Energy paper No. 15)
        D. of Energy

PEARSON, Colin Hargreaves, Lord

1959   Funds in court. Report of the committee
Session 1958-59 Cmnd. 818 xiii.

1966   Transfer of title to chattels. 12th report of the
Law Reform Committee
Session 1966-67 Cmnd. 2958 xxxix.

Hearsay evidence in civil proceedings. 13th report
of the Law Reform Committee
Session 1966-67 Cmnd. 2964 xxxix.

Acquisition of easements and profits by pres-
cription. 14th report of the Law Reform
Committee
Session 1966-67 Cmnd. 3100 xxxix.

1967   Final report of the court on inquiry into certain
matters concerning the shipping industry
Session 1966-67 Cmnd. 3211 xxxvi.

The rule in Hollington v. Hewthorn. 15th report
of the Law Reform Committee
Session 1966-67 Cmnd. 3391 xxxiv.

Privilege in civil proceedings. 16th report of the
Law Reform Committee
Session 1967-68 Cmnd. 3472 xxv.

1968   Report of court of inquiry into the dispute
between the British Overseas Airways Corporation
and the British Air Line Pilots Association
Session 1967-68 Cmnd. 3551 xxiii.

Report of a court of inquiry into the dispute
between the British Steel Corporation and certain
of their employees
Session 1967-68 Cmnd. 3754 xxiii.

1970   Report of a court of inquiry into a dispute
between the parties represented on the National
Joint Council for the Port Transport Industry
Session 1970-71 Cmnd. 4429 xxv.

Evidence of opinion and expert evidence. 17th
report of the Law Reform Committee
Session 1970-71 Cmnd. 4489 xxxi.

1971   Conversion and detinue. 18th report of the Law
Reform Committee
Session 1970-71 Cmnd. 4774 xxxi.

Salaries of teachers in primary and secondary
schools. Report of the arbitral body
D. of Education and Science

1973   Interpretation of wills. 19th report of the Law
Reform Committee
Session 1972-73 Cmnd. 5301 xiv.

1977   Royal Commission on civil liability and compensation for personal injury. Report, statistics and
costings, overseas systems of compensation. 3 vols.
Session 1977-78 Cmnd. 7054 I-III xxi, xxii.

See also ORR, A. S., Lord

PEART, Thomas Frederick

1969   Marine science and technology. Report
Session 1968-69 Cmnd. 3992 xxxix.

PEDDIE, J. M., Lord

1964   Co-operatives overseas. Report of the committee
on co-operatives
Session 1963-64 Cmnd. 2257 x.

1971   Coal prices, 2nd report. National Board for
Prices and Incomes report No. 153, supplement
No. 1
Session 1970-71 Cmnd. 4455-I xlv.

Coal prices, 2nd report. National Board for
Prices and Incomes report No. 153, supplement
No. 2
Session 1970-71 Cmnd. 4455-II xlv.

1970   Standing reference on the pay of the armed forces,
5th report: separation allowance. National Board
for Prices and Incomes report No. 158
Session 1970-71 Cmnd. 4529 xlv.

London Transport fares. National Board for
Prices and Incomes report No. 159
Session 1970-71 Cmnd. 4540 xlv.

Costs, prices and profitability in the ice-cream
manufacturing industry. National Board for
Prices and Incomes report No. 160
Session 1970-71 Cmnd. 4548 xlv.

1971   Costs, charges and productivity of the National
Freight Corporation. National Board for Prices
and Incomes report No. 162
Session 1970-71 Cmnd. 4569 xlvi.

Costs and charges in the motor repairing and
servicing industry. National Board for Prices and
Incomes report No. 163
Session 1970-71 Cmnd. 4590 xlvi.

Standing reference on the remuneration of
solicitors, 2nd report. National Board for Prices
and Incomes report No. 164
Session 1970-71 Cmnd. 4624 xlvi.

Prices, profits and costs in food distribution.
National Board for Prices and Incomes report
No. 165
Session 1970-71 Cmnd. 4645 xlvi.

Pay and conditions of service of ancillary workers
in the National Health Service. National Board
for Prices and Incomes report No. 166
Session 1970-71 Cmnd. 4644 xlvi.

The pay and conditions of service of workers in
the laundry and dry cleaning industry. National
Board for Prices and Incomes report No. 167
Session 1970-71 Cmnd. 4647 xlvi.

Pay and conditions in the contract cleaning
trade. National Board for Prices and Incomes
report No. 168
Session 1970-71 Cmnd. 4637 xlvi.

General problems of low pay. National Board
for Prices and Incomes report No. 169
Session 1970-71 Cmnd. 4648 xlvi.

Fifth and final general report (with) supplement.
National Board for Prices and Incomes report
No. 170
Session 1970-71 Cmnd. 4649-I xlvi.

See also JONES, Aubrey

1970   Views and recommendations of the Post Office
Users' National Council on the Post Office proposed charges in telecommunications tariffs
(report No. 1)
Post Office Users' National Council

Report on proposals for increased postal tariffs
(report No. 2)
Post Office Users' National Council

1972   Report of the Post Office proposals for increased
postal tariffs (report No. 3)
Post Office Users' National Council

How good is our postal service? Report on a
monitoring exercise on the delivery of first-class
mail
Post Office Users' National Council

Report on the Post Office proposals for increased
telephone connection charges (report No. 5)
Post Office Users' National Council

Report on the Post Office proposals for increased
Giro tariffs (report No. 6)
Post Office Users' National Council

1973   Proposals for increased postal tariffs and charges
in remittance services. Report and recommendations by the Post Office Users' National Council
(report No. 7)
Post Office Users' National Council

Report on the Post Office proposals for tariff
changes in the inland and international telecommunications services (report No. 8)
Post Office Users' National Council

PEDDIE, J. M., Lord (*continued*)

1974 Efficiency of the Post Office telephone metering and billing systems. Report by the Post Office Users' National Council (report No. 9)
Post Office Users' National Council

Post Office proposals for increased postal, remittance services, and telecommunications tariffs. Report by the Post Office Users' National Council (report No. 10)
Post Office Users' National Council

1975 Post Office proposals for increased postal, telecommunications and Giro remittance service charges. Report by the Post Office Users' National Council (report No. 11)
Post Office Users' National Council

Post Office proposals for increased postal, telecommunications and Giro remittance service charges. Report by the Post Office Users' National Council (report No. 12)
Post Office Users' National Council

1976 Post Office proposals for increased postal charges. Report by the Post Office Users' National Council (report No. 13)
Post Office Users' National Council

Report on sub-Post Offices (report No. 14)
Post Office Users' National Council

1976 Evidence submitted to the Post Office review committee
Post Office Users' National Council

1977 Report on Post Office proposals for increased Giro tariffs (report No. 15)
Post Office Users' National Council

Report on Post Office proposals for increased inland postal charges (report No. 16)
Post Office Users' National Council

PEECH, N. M.

1960 Solid smokeless fuels. Report of the committee
Session 1959-60 Cmnd. 999 ix.

PEEL, Denys F.

1971 Fire and rescue operations following an aircraft accident at Heathrow Airport. Report of the working party (CAP 556)
D. of Trade and Industry

PEEL, John, Sir

1970 Domiciliary midwifery and maternity bed needs. Report of the sub-committee of the standing maternity and midwifery advisory committee.
Central Health Services Council
D. of Health and Social Security

1972 Use of fetuses and fetal material for research. Report of the advisory group
D. of Health and Social Security

PELHAM, Henry, Sir

1945 Teachers' salaries. Scales of salaries for the teaching staffs of training colleges, England and Wales. Report of the committee
M. of Education

PEMBERTON, Frances, Sir

1976 The Wash; water shortage scheme; report on the feasibility study
Water Resources Board

PENMAN, A. D. M.

1969 A selection of technical reports submitted to the Aberfan tribunal
Welsh Office

See also DAVIES, H. E., Sir

PENMAN, William

1948 Differences in dispensing practice between England, Wales and Scotland. Report by the working party
M. of Health

1949 Dental practitioners. Report of the working party on a chairside times taken in carrying out treatment by general dental practitioners in England, Wales and Scotland
M. of Health

Ophthalmic medical practitioners. Report by the working party on the average time taken to test sight by ophthalmic medical practitioners under the supplementary ophthalmic services to the National Health Service
M. of Health

1950 Ophthalmic opticians. Working party. Report on the average time taken to test by ophthalmic opticians and the average time taken by ophthalmic opticians and by dispensing opticians in fitting and supplying glasses
 Part 1. Report on the average time taken to test sight by ophthalmic opticians
 Part 2. Report on the average time taken by ophthalmic opticians and dispensing opticians in fitting and supplying glasses
M. of Health

PENN, Richard

1977 Upper Afan community development project. Final report. Home Office, published by the University of Wales Institute for Science and Technology

PEPPIATT, L. E., Sir

1960 Levy on betting on horse races. Report of the departmental committee
Session 1959-60 Cmnd. 1003 xvi.

PERCIVAL, Geoffrey

1978 Government's industrial estates in Wales, 1936-1975
Welsh Development Agency

PERCIVAL-PRESCOTT, W.

1953 Coronation chair (Note by W. Palmer based on a full report and examination of the chair by W. Percival-Prescott)
M. of Works

PERCY OF NEWCASTLE, Eustace, Lord

1945 Higher technological education. Report of a special committee
M. of Education

1954 Scales of salaries. Teachers in primary and secondary schools maintained by local education authorities, England and Wales, 1954. Report of the Burnham Committee
M. of Education

Scales of Salaries. Teaching of staff farm institutes and for teachers of agricultural (including horticultural) subjects to the staff local education authorities, England and Wales, 1954. Report of the committee
M. of Education

Scales of salaries. Teaching staff of training colleges, England and Wales, 1954. Report of the committee
M. of Education

Scales of salaries. Teachers in establishments for further education, including technical and commercial colleges and institutes, art colleges and schools maintained by local education authorities in England and Wales, 1954. Report of the Burnham Committee
M. of Education

PERCY OF NEWCASTLE, Eustace, Lord *(continued)*
Royal Commission on the law relating to mental illness and mental deficiency
1957   Report
Session 1956-57 Cmnd. 169 xvi.
1954   Minutes of evidence taken before the Royal Commission, 7 days
Royal Commission on the Law Relating to Mental Illness and Mental Deficiency

PERCY, T. R.
1963   Allegations of ill-treatment of prisoners in Her Majesty's prison, Durham. Report of an inquiry held by the visiting committee
Session 1962-63 Cmnd. 2068 xxiii.

PERKINS, D. C. W.
1970   Industrial training in the imported timber trade. Working party report
Furniture and Timber Trade Industry Training Board

PERKS, W.
1967   Criminal statistics. Report of the departmental committee
Session 1967-68 Cmnd. 3448 xix.

PERRIN, J. H.
1972   Management by objectives. Report of the working party
M. of Agriculture, Fisheries and Food

PERRIN, John
1978   Management of financial resources in the National Health Service (research paper No. 2)
Royal Commission on the National Health Service

PERRIN, M. W., Sir
1964   Colouring matters. Report on Food Standards Committee
M. of Agriculture, Fisheries and Food

Food labelling. Report of the Food Standards Committee
M. of Agriculture, Fisheries and Food
1965   Flavouring agents. Report of the Food Standards Committee
M. of Agriculture, Fisheries and Food

PETERS, Rudolph, Sir
1953   Vitamin C requirements of human adults. Vitamin C sub-committee of the accessory food factors committee report. (Special report series No. 280)
Medical Research Council

PETTER, G. S. V.
1957   Higher education in the British Caribbean. Report of the mission
Colonial Office

PETTIT, D. E. A.
1973   Lorries and the world we live in
D. of the Environment
1975   Profitability and liquidity in the distributive trades; an examination of financial data in selected sectors. Distributive Trades Economic Development Committee
N.E.D.O.
1976   Physical distribution management. Distributive Trades Economic Development Committee
N.E.D.O.
1977   Direct distribution; an initial assessment of the market and the need for special facilities
Lorries and the Environment Committee

Freight complexes; an appraisal of the role of freight complexes and possible approaches to development of a number of complexes in the U.K.
Lorries and the Environment Committee

PHELPS BROWN, E. H.
See BROWN, E. H. P.

PHILIP, J. R., Sir
1948   Milk services, Scotland. Report of the committee
D. of Agriculture for Scotland
1952   National Museum of Antiquities of Scotland. Report of the Committee
Session 1951-52 Cmd. 8604 xvii.

PHILLIMORE, H. J., Lord
1974   Contempt of court. Report of the committee
Session 1974-75 Cmnd. 5794 xv.

PHILLIPS, Thomas W., Sir
1950   Building. Report of the working party on building operations
M. of Works
1954   Old age. Report of the committee on the economic and financial problems of the provision for old age
Session 1954-55 Cmd. 9333 vi.

PICKERING, George, Sir
1962   Post graduate medical education and the specialities, with special reference to the problems in London. Report by the University Grants Committee. (Reports on public health and medical subject No. 106)
M. of Health

PICTON, J. G.
1964   Licensed Residential Establishment and Licensed Restaurant Wages. Report of a commission of inquiry
M. of Labour
1965   Report of an inquiry into the difference in the South Wales coalfield
M. of Labour

PIERCY, W., Lord
1947   Hops. 2nd reorganisation commission for England. (Economic series No. 47)
M. of Agriculture and Fisheries
1951   Youth employment service. Report of the committee on the recruitment and training for the youth employment service
M. of Labour and National Service
1956   Disabled persons. Report of the committee of inquiry on the rehabilitation, training and resettlement of disabled persons
Session 1955-56 Cmd. 9883 xiv.

PILCHER, D.
1975   Commercial property development. 1st report of the advisory group
D. of the Environment

PILCHER, Gonne St. Claire, Sir
1950   Naval Discipline Act, 1950. Reports of the committee appointed to consider the administration of justice under the Act
1st report
Session 1950-51 Cmd. 8094 xvii.
2nd report
Session 1950-51 Cmd. 8119 xvii.

PILE, W. D.

1965   Family pension benefits for teachers in England and Wales. Report of the official working party on pensions for widows, widowers, children and other dependants of teachers in England and Wales
D. of Education and Science

PILKINGTON, W. Harry, Lord

1960   Royal Commission on Doctors' and Dentists' Remuneration
Report
Session 1959-60 Cmnd. 939 xii.

Minutes of Evidence, 1st to 23rd day, 5 December 1957 to 22 January 1959
Royal Commissions

Appendix to the minutes of evidence. Selection of witnesses' supplementary statements
Royal Commissions

Written evidence
Vol. 1. Factual memorandum by the Ministry of Health and the Department of Health for Scotland
Vol. 2. Memoranda of evidence of selected representative organisations
Royal Commissions

Index to oral and written evidence
Royal Commissions

Supplement to the report. Further statistical appendix
Session 1959-60 Cmnd. 1064 xii.

1962   Report of the committee on broadcasting, 1960
Session 1961-62 Cmnd. 1753 xvii.

The future of sound radio and television. A short version of the report of the committee
Post Office

1966   Agricultural education. Report of the advisory committee of the national advisory council on education for industry and commerce
D. of Education and Science

1968   The use of buildings and equipment. Report by the committee on the more effective use of technical college resources. National advisory council on education for industry and commerce
D. of Education and Science

1969   The use of costing and other financial techniques in technical colleges. Report by the committee on the more effective use of technical college resources. National advisory council on education for industry and commerce
D. of Education and Science

PIPPARD, A. J. S.

1961   Pollution of the tidal Thames. Report of the departmental committee on the effects of heated and other effluents and discharges on the condition of the tidal reaches of the River Thames
M. of Housing and Local Government

PITTAM, R. R.

      Legal aid in criminal proceedings
1962   1st report of the working party
1963   Final report of the working party
Home Office

PITTOM, L. A.

1974   Precautions in the use of asbestos in the construction industry. A report by the sub-committee of the joint advisory committee on safety and health in the construction industries
D. of Employment

PLANT, Arnold, Sir

1949   Cinematography films, distribution and exhibition of inquiry
Session 1948-49 Cmd. 7837 xii.

1955   Byssinosis. Report of the Industrial Injuries Advisory Council
Session 1955-56 Cmd. 9673 xxii.

Cadmium poisoning. Report of the Industrial Injuries Advisory Council
Session 1955-56 Cmd. 9674 xxii.

1956   Rules governing assessment of disablement in cases involving damage to an organ which in normal person is one of a pair. Report of the Industrial Injuries Advisory Council
Session 1955-56 Cmd. 9827 xxii.

1957   Review of the prescribed diseases schedule. Report of the Industrial Injuries Advisory Council
Session 1957-58 Cmnd. 416 xv.

1962   Fowl pest policy. Report of the committee
Session 1961-62 Cmnd. 1664 viii.

1964   Farmer's lung. Report by the Industrial Injuries Advisory Council
Session 1963-64 Cmnd. 2403 xv.

1965   Byssinosis in flax and hemp workers. Report by the Industrial Injuries Advisory Council
Session 1964-65 Cmnd. 2730 xviii.

PLANT, Cyril

1977   Law in Northern Ireland relating to divorce and homosexuality. Report of the standing advisory commission on human rights
Northern Ireland Office

Protection of human rights by law in Northern Ireland. Standing advisory commission of human rights
Session 1977-78 Cmnd. 7009 xlii.

PLATT, B. S.

1945   Nutrition in the British West Indies. Report. (Colonial No. 195)
Colonial Office

1968   Iron in flour. Report of the panel on iron in flour (Reports on public health and medical subjects No. 117)
D. of Health and Social Security

PLATT, Harry, Sir

1958   Welfare of children in hospital. Report of the committee of the Central Health Services Council
M. of Health

1962   Accident and emergency services. Report of a sub-committee of the standing medical advisory committee. Central Health Services Council
M. of Health

PLATT, J. W.

1962   Management studies in technical colleges. 1st report of the United Kingdom advisory council on education for management
M. of Education

PLATT, Robert, Lord

1960   Medical staffing structure in the hospital service. Report of the joint working party
M. of Health

PLAYFAIR, E. W., Sir

      See PROCTOR, P. D., Sir

PLIATZKY, Leo

1978   Accidents at sea causing oil pollution; review of contingency measures. Report by the steering group
D. of Trade

PLOWDEN, B. H., Lady

1967   Children and their primary schools. A report of the Central Advisory Council for Education (England)
          Vol. 1. The report
          Vol. 2. Research and surveys
D. of Education and Science

PLOWDEN, E. N., Lord

1961   Control of public expenditure report
Session 1960-61 Cmnd. 1432 xx.

1964   Representational services overseas. Report of the committee (Miscellaneous No. 5, 1964)
Session 1963-64 Cmnd. 2276 xi.

1965   Aircraft industry. Report of the committee of inquiry
Session 1965-66 Cmnd. 2853 vi.

1976   Structure of the electricity supply industry in England and Wales. Report of the committee of inquiry
Session 1975-76 Cmnd. 6388 xi.

PLOWMAN, H.

See JONES, S. L.

POCHIN, E. E.

1961   Introductory manual on the control of health hazards from radioactive materials. Committee on protection against ionizing radiations (Memorandum No. 39)
Medical Research Council

POLE, Felix J. C., Sir

1944   Private enterprise housing. Report of the private enterprise sub-committee of the Central Housing Advisory Committee
M. of Health

POLL, C.

See MORTON-WILLIAMS, R.

POLSON, Milson George

1968   Findings and recommendations following inquiries into allegations concerning the care of elderly patients in certain hospitals, VI: St. Lawrence's Hospital, Bodmin. National Health Service
Session 1967-68 Cmnd. 3687 xxviii.

PORCHESTER, H. G. R. M., Lord

1977   Study of Exmoor. Report
D. of the Environment

PORRITT, Arthur, Sir

1962   Medical aid to the developing countries. Report by a working party
D. of Technical Co-operation

PORTER, E.

1973   Pollution in four industrialised estuaries. Four case studies undertaken for the Royal Commission on Environmental Pollution
D. of the Environment

PORTER, S. L., Lord

1948   Law of defamation. Report of the committee
Session 1948 Cmd. 7536 i.

POSNER, Michael

1977   Energy topics in the social sciences. Report by the committee to the research initiatives board
Social Science Research Council

POSNETT, Richard N.

1978   Dominica; termination of association. Report (miscellaneous No. 20, 1978)
Session 1977-78 Cmnd. 7279 viii.

        St. Lucia constitutional conference, London, July 1978. Report. (Miscellaneous No. 23, 1978)
Session 1977-78 Cmnd. 7328 viii.

POTTER, H. V.

1944   Plastics. Report by a committee convened by the British Plastics Federation (Post-War building studies No. 3)
M. of Works

POTTS, P. G.

1967   Action on the Banwell report. A survey of the implementation of the recommendations of the committee on the placing and management of contracts. A report by a working party of the Building Economic Development Committee
N.E.D.O.
See also HARRIS, W. G.

POWELL, Muriel B., Dame

1961   Report of the sub-committee appointed to answer the pattern of the in-patients' day. Central Health Services Council
M. of Health

1966   The post-certificate training and education of nurses. Report by a sub-committee of the standing nursing advisory committee. Central Health Services Council
M. of Health

1972   Nurses in an integrated health service. Report of a working group
Scottish Home and Health D.

POYNTON, Hilton, Sir

1960   Public services conference held in the Colonial Office, London, 1-10 March 1960 (Colonial No. 347)
Colonial Office

PRAIN, A. M.

1966   Probation hostels in Scotland. Final report by the Scottish probation advisory and training council
Scottish Home and Health D.

PRESCOTT, W. Percival-

See PERCIVAL-PRESCOTT, W.

PRICE, C.

1971   Air structures; a survey commissioned by the Ministry of Public Buildings and Works
D. of the Environment

PRICE, Keith W., Sir

1948   Timber and plywood, 1949 to 1953. Report of the committee appointed to consider the U.K.'s probable requirements and supplies
Board of Trade

PRICE, P. Stanley-
      See STANLEY-PRICE, P.

PRIESTLEY, Raymond E., Sir
1955   Royal Commission on the Civil Service
        Report, minutes of evidence and appendices
        Session 1955-56 Cmd. 9613 xi.

PRIOR, Peter J.
1978   Motorway service areas. Report of the committee
        of inquiry (with) appendices. 2 vols.
        D. of Transport

PRITCHARD, E. S.
1973   Shoplifting and thefts by shop staff. Report of
        a working party on internal shop security
        Home Office

PRITCHARD, F. E., Sir
1959   Rating of charities and kindred bodies. Report
        of the committee
        Session 1958-59 Cmnd. 831 xix.

PRITCHARD, M.
1969   Rural studies in secondary schools. Report of
        the working party (working paper No. 24)
        Schools Council

PROCTER, F.
1967   Dairy floors. Report of the sub-committee of the
        milk and milk products technical advisory
        committee
        M. of Agriculture, Fisheries and Food

PROCTOR, P. D., Sir
        Local government manpower committee
1949   1st report
            Session 1950 Cmd. 7870 xiii.
1951   2nd report
            Session 1951-52 Cmd. 8421 xvi.
1954   Tate Gallery. Report by the Trustees
        Treasury

PROSSER, D. P.
1978   Glossary of terms used in measurement and
        control systems for the water industry. Report
        of the working party on control systems for the
        water industry. (Standing technical committee
        report No. 11)
        National Water Council

PROUDMAN, J.
1958   Information on water resources. Report of a
        sub-committee of the Central Advisory Water
        Committee
        M. of Housing and Local Government
1960   Growing demand for water. 2nd report of a sub-
        committee of the Central Advisory Water
        Committee
        M. of Housing and Local Government
1962   Growing demand for water. Final report of a
        sub-committee of the Central Advisory Water
        Committee
        M. of Housing and Local Government
1962   Oceanographic and meteorological research in
        relation to sea defence. 1st report of the advisory
        committee
        M. of Agriculture, Fisheries and Food

PROVAN, A. L.
1963   Antibiotics in milk in Great Britain. Report of
        the milk hygiene sub-committee of the milk and
        milk products technical advisory committee
        M. of Agriculture, Fisheries and Food

PUGH, I. V.
1965   Future of development plans. Report of the
        planning advisory group
        M. of Housing and Local Government

PURCHAS, Francis Brooks
1968   Report of an inquiry in respect of the objections
        to the proposed compulsory amalgamation of
        the police areas of the county of Northumber-
        land, the City of Newcastle upon Tyne and the
        County Borough of Tynemouth
        Session 1967-68 Cmnd. 3797 xxx.

QUARRELL, J. G.
1973   Training modules for qualified firemen. Report
        of the working party of the Central Fire Brigades
        Advisory Councils for England and Wales and
        for Scotland
        Home Office

QUESNE, J. G., Le
      See LE QUESNE, J. G.

QUIRK, Randolph
1972   Speech therapy services. Report of the committee
        D. of Education and Science

RADCLIFFE, Cyril John, Viscount
1948   British Film Institute. Report of the committee
        Session 1947-48 Cmd. 7361 x.

        Royal Commission on the Taxation of Profits
        and Income
1952-4   Minutes of evidence
            Royal Commission
1953   1st report
            Session 1952-53 Cmd. 8761 xviii.
1954   2nd report
            Session 1953-54 Cmd. 9105 xix.
            Final report
            Session 1955-56 Cmd. 9474 xxvii.

            See also COHEN, L. L., Lord

1956   Cyprus. Constitutional proposals for Cyprus
        report
        Session 1956-57 Cmnd. 42 x.

        Working of the monetary system
1959   Report of the committee
            Session 1958-59 Cmnd. 827 xvii.
1957-9   Minutes of evidence, 11 July 1957 to 30 April
            1959
1960   Principal memoranda of written evidence,
            vols. 1-3
        Treasury
1961   Security procedures in the public service. Report
        of the committee
        Session 1961-62 Cmnd. 1681 xxiii.
1963   Vassall case. Report of the tribunal appointed
        to inquire into the Vassall case and related
        matters
        Session 1962-63 Cmnd. 2009 xxiv.
1967   'D' notice matters. Report of the committee of
        inquiry
        Session 1966-67 Cmnd. 3309 xlviii.
1976   Ministerial memoirs. Report of the committee of
        Privy Councillors

RADLEY, W. G., Sir
1947   Hearing aids and audiometers. Report of the
        committee on electro-acoustics (special report
        No. 261)
        Medical Research Council

RADZINOWICZ, L.

1968   The regime for long-term prisoners in conditions
of maximum security. Advisory Council on the
Penal System
Home Office

RAISMAN, Jeremy, Sir

1952   Southern Rhodesia, Northern Rhodesia and
Nyasaland draft federal scheme. Report of the
fiscal commission
Session 1951-52 Cmd. 8672 ix.

1958   Nigeria. Report of the fiscal commission
Session 1957-58 Cmnd. 481 ix.

1961   East Africa. Report of the economic and fiscal
commission
Session 1960-61 Cmnd. 1279 x.

RALPHS, L.

1974   Dissemination and in-service training. Report of
the working party (pamphlet No. 14)
Schools Council

RAMPTON, Jack

1976   Automotive energy working group. Report
D. of Energy

RAMSAY, J. Douglas, Sir

1944   National parks, a Scottish survey. Report by the
Scottish national parks survey committee
Session 1944-45 Cmd. 6631 v.

1947   National parks and the conservation of nature
in Scotland. Report by the Scottish national
parks committee and the Scottish wild life conservation committee
Session 1947-48 Cmd. 7235 xiv.

1948   Nature reserves in Scotland. Final report by the
Scottish national parks committee and the Scot-
tish wild life conservation committee
Session 1948-49 Cmd. 7814 xviii.

RAMSDEN, E. J. S. H., Lord

1945   Exhibitions and fairs. Report of the committee
Session 1945-46 Cmd. 6782 xii.

**RAMSEY, Arthur Michael, Archbishop of Canterbury,
1961-1974**

1961   Clergy Pensions Measure. 135th report by the
Ecclesiastical Committee
Session 1960-61 HC. 256 ix; HL. 131

1962   Ecclesiastical Fees Measure. 136th report by the
Ecclesiastical Committee
Session 1961-62 HC. 195 x; HL. 78

1963   Ecclesiastical Jurisdiction Measure. 137th report
by the Ecclesiastical Committee
Session 1962-63 HC. 211 ix; HL. 74

        Cathedrals Measure. 138th report by the Eccle-
siastical Committee
Session 1962-63 HC. 261 ix; HL. 105

1964   Church Commissioners (Loan for Theological
Colleges and Training Houses) Measure. 139th
report by the Ecclesiastical Committee
Session 1963-64 HC. 72 ix; HL. 41

        Incumbents and Churchwardens (Trusts) (Meas-
ure. 140th report by the Ecclesiastical Committee
Session 1963-64 HC. 74 ix; HL. 43

        Churchwardens (Appointment and Registration)
Measure. 141st report by the Ecclesiastical
Committee
Session 1963-64 HC. 73 ix; HL. 45

        Holy Table Measure. 142nd report by the
Ecclesiastical Committee
Session 1963-64 HC. 127 ix; HL. 65

        Faculty Jurisdiction Measure. 143rd report by
the Ecclesiastical Committee
Session 1963-64 HC. 128 ix; HL. 66

        Clergy (Ordination and Miscellaneous Provisions)
Measure. 144th report by the Ecclesiastical Com-
mittee
Session 1963-64 HC. 200 ix; HL. 113

        Vestures of Ministers Measure. 145th report by
the Ecclesiastical Committee
Session 1963-64 HC. 257 ix; HL. 151-I

        Prayer Book (Miscellaneous Provisions) Measure.
146th report by the Ecclesiastical Committee
Session 1963-64 HC. 258 ix; HL. 152-I

        Church Commissioners Measure. 147th report by
the Ecclesiastical Committee
Session 1963-64 HC. 294 ix; HL. 193

1965   Prayer Book (Alternative and Other Services)
Measure. 148th report by the Ecclesiastical
Committee
Session 1964-65 HC. 91 xii; HL. 34

        Benefices (Suspension of Presentation) (Contin-
uance) Measure. 149th report by the Ecclesiastical
Committee
Session 1964-65 HC. 112 xii; HL. 47

        Prayer Book (Miscellaneous Provisions) Measure.
150th report by the Ecclesiastical Committee
Session 1964-65 HC. 236 xii; HL. 139

        Prayer Book (Versions of the Bible) Measure.
151st report by the Ecclesiastical Committee
Session 1965-66 HC. 7 iv; HL. 7

1967   Clergy Pensions (Amendment) Measure. 152nd
report by the Ecclesiastical Committee
Session 1966-67 HC. 359 xxiv; HL. 185

        Extra-Parochial Ministry Measure. 153rd report
by the Ecclesiastical Committee
Session 1966-67 HC. 510 xxiv; HL. 257

        Overseas and Other Clergy (Ministry and Ordina-
tion) Measure. 154th report by the Ecclesiastical
Committee
Session 1966-67 HC. 512 xxiv; HL. 258

1968   Pastoral Measure. 155th report by the Ecclesiastical Committee
Session 1967-68 HC. 175 xvii; HL. 81

        Prayer Book (Further Provisions) Measure.
156th report by the Ecclesiastical Committee
Session 1967-68 HC. 353 xvii; HL. 181
Reprinted Session 1968-69 HC. 8 xxvii.

        Prayer Book (Further Provisions) (No. 2)
Measure. 156th report by the Ecclesiastical
Committee
Session 1967-68 HC. 437 xvii; HL. 199

        Clergy Pensions (Amendment) Measure. 157th
report by the Ecclesiastical Committee
Session 1968-69 HC. 246 xxvii; HL. 82

1969   Synodical Government Measure. 158th report by
the Ecclesiastical Committee
Session 1968-69 HC. 282 xxvii; HL. 104

1970   Collegiate Churches (Capital Endowments)
Measure. 159th report by the Ecclesiastical
Committee
Session 1969-70 HC. 168 vii; HL. 61

        Sharing of Church Buildings Measure. 160th
report by the Ecclesiastical Committee
Session 1969-70 HC. 170 vii; HL. 59

        Synodical Government (Special Majorities)
Measure. 161st report by the Ecclesiastical
Committee
Session 1970-71 HC. 200 vii; HL. 61

        Church Commissioners Measure. 162nd report
by the Ecclesiastical Committee
Session 1970-71 HC. 198 vii; HL. 59

RAMSEY, Arthur Michael, Archbishop of Canterbury
(continued)

1971   Benefices Measure. 163rd report by the Ecclesiastical Committee
Session 1970-71 HC. 556 vii; HL. 225

1971   Admission to Holy Communion Measure. 164th report of the Ecclesiastical Committee
Session 1971-72 HC. 59 vii; HL. 33

Repair of Benefice Buildings Measure. 165th report of the Ecclesiastical Committee
Session 1971-72 HC. 61 vii; HL. 35

For 166th and 167th reports **see COGGAN, D.**

1974   Synodical Government (Amendment) Measure. 168th report of the Ecclesiastical Committee
Session 1974 HC. 48 iii; HL. 12

Ecclesiastical Jurisdiction (Amendment) Measure. 169th report by the Ecclesiastical Committee
Session 1974 HC. 50 iii; HL. 14

Church of England (Worship and Doctrine) Measure. 170th report of the Ecclesiastical Committee
Session 1974; HC. 256 iii; HL. 104

RANCE, Hubert, Sir

1949   British Caribbean standing closer association. Report of the committee. (Colonial No. 255)
Colonial Office

RANGELEY, W. R.

1976   Research on geomorphology of water-produced land forms. Report of the working party. (Publications series B no. 16)
Natural Environment Research Council

RANKIN, Andrew

1977   New Brighton Association Football and Athletic Club Co. Ltd. Report of investigations under the Companies Act
D. of Trade

RATCLIFFE, J. A.

1963   The effects of high altitude nuclear explosions on scientific experiments
Session 1962-63 Cmnd. 2029 xxiii.

RATCLIFFE, S.

1977   Preliminary study of long-term air traffic systems in Europe. Report of a study team. 3 vols.
D. of Industry

RAVENHILL, A. P.

1971   Standard system of catering accounting; an aid to achieving profits by the application of a uniform system of management accounting to catering operations. Report of the Advisory Committee on standard catering accounts. Hotels and Catering Economic Development Committee
N.E.D.O.

RAWSON, Stanley

1975   Unlocking productivity potential; the experience of seven firms in the clothing industry. Clothing Economic Development Committee
N.E.D.O.

RAY, H. A.

1968   Service in hotels; a study of the labour costs of providing personal services in hotels with suggestions for cost savings. Hotels and Catering Economic Development Committee
N.E.D.O.

RAYBOULD, J. G.

1973   Employment practices in E.E.C. textile industries. Report of the manpower working party of the Wool Textile Economic Development Committee
N.E.D.O.

RAYNER, Derek George

1971   Government organisation for defence procurement and civil aerospace. Report by a project team
Session 1970-71 Cmnd. 4641 xx.

READHEAD, D.

1978   Food purchasing advisory group. Meat sub-committee final report
D. of Health and Social Security

READING, G. R., Marquess of

1958   Highway law. Report of the committee on consolidation of highway law
Session 1958-59 Cmnd. 630 xvi.

READING, S., Dowager Marchioness of

1959   Councils and their houses. Management of estates. 8th report of the housing management sub-committee of the Central Housing Advisory Committee
M. of Housing and Local Government

1966   Residential provision for homeless discharged offenders. Report of the working party on the place of voluntary service in after-care
Home Office

1967   The place of voluntary service in after-care. 2nd report of the working party
Home Office

READY, A. W.

1952   Welsh language publishing. Report of the committee
Session 1951-52 Cmd. 8661 xviii.

REBBECK, Denis

1977   Marine pilotage. Report of the advisory committee on the content of future pilotage legislation
D. of Trade

REDCLIFFE-MAUD, J. P., Lord

1966   Committee on the management of local government. Interim report on the allowances of elected members of local authorities
M. of Housing and Local Government

1967   Committee on the management of local government
Vol. 1: Report of the committee
Vol. 2: Local government councillor, by L. Moss and S. R. Parker
Vol. 3: Local government elector, by M. Horton
Vol. 4: Local government administration abroad; an inquiry carried out by A. H. Marshall
Vol. 5: Local government administration in England and Wales; an inquiry carried out by M. Harrison and A. Norton
Main points of the committee
M. of Housing and Local Government

1969   Royal Commission on Local Government in England

REDCLIFFE-MAUD, J. P., Lord *(continued)*

Vol. I: Report
Session 1968-69 Cmnd. 4040 xxxviii.
Vol. II: Memorandum of dissent by Mr. D. Senior
Session 1968-69 Cmnd. 4040-I xxxviii.
Vol. III: Research appendices
Session 1968-69 Cmnd. 4040-II xxxviii.

Local government reform. Short version of the report of the Royal Commission on Local Government in England
Session 1968-69 Cmnd. 4039 xxxviii.

1974   Conduct in local government. Prime Minister's committee on local government rules of conduct
Vol. 1: Report
Session 1974-75 Cmnd. 5636 viii.
Vol. 2: Written evidence
Cabinet Office

REDDAWAY, William B.

1970   Effects of the Selective Employment Tax. 1st report: the distributive trades
Treasury

1972   Consulting engineering firms' costs and earnings. Report of the Reddaway inquiry
D. of the Environment

REDPATH, John T.

1968   Committee for the co-ordination of underground services on building sites. 1: the common trench (R&D bulletins)
M. of Public Building and Works

1969   Committee for the co-ordination of underground services on building sites. 2: Co-ordination management (R&D bulletins)
M. of Public Building and Works

1971   Commodity information for the construction industry; a survey of supply and demand. Working party on data co-ordination
D. of the Environment

Information system for the construction industry. Final report of the working party on data co-ordination
D. of the Environment

Winter building. A review of winter building techniques by the winter building advisory committee
D. of the Environment

REED, Derek

1977   Effects of certain social and demographic changes on income distribution (background paper No. 3)
Royal Commission on the Distribution of Income and Wealth

REES, Frederick, Sir

1946   Welsh slate industry. Report by the committee
M. of Works

1951   Night banking. Report of the committee
Session 1950-51 Cmd. 8378 xviii.

REES, J. Tudor

1950   County police forces of Leicestershire and Rutland. Proposed compulsory amalgamation. Report of the inquiry held at the Castle, Oakham, April 13 and 14, 1950
Home Office

REES, G. L.

1973   Survey of the Welsh economy (research papers No. 8)
Commission on the Constitution

REES-THOMAS, W.

1945   Mental nursing. Report of the sub-committee of the nursing services inter-departmental committee on mental nursing and the nursing of the mentally defective
M. of Health

REES-WILLIAMS, D. R.

1947   Burma. Frontier areas committee of inquiry report
Session 1946-47 Cmd. 7138 x.

REID, Charles Carlow

1945   Coal mining. Report of the technical advisory committee
Session 1944-45 Cmd. 6610 iv.

REID, John

1968   Origin of the 1967-68 foot-and-mouth disease epidemic. Report
Session 1967-68 Cmnd. 3560 xxxix.

See also NORTHUMBERLAND, H. A., Duke of

REID, J. J. A.

1970   People with epilepsy. Report of a joint sub-committee of the standing medical advisory committee and the advisory committee on the health and welfare of handicapped persons
D. of Health and Social Security

REID, J. S. C., Lord

1957   Malaya. Report of the Federation of Malaya constitutional commission (Colonial No. 330)
Colonial Office

1963   Registration of title to land in Scotland. Report by a committee
Session 1962-63 Cmnd. 2032 xx.

REID, R.

1977   State Hospital, Carstairs. Report of a public local inquiry into circumstances surrounding the escape of two patients on 30 November 1976 and into security and other arrangements at the hospital
Scottish Home and Health D.

REINERS, William J.

1969   Coding and data co-ordination; a short report prepared by the committee on the application of computers in the construction industry
M. of Public Building and Works

REITH, G.

1968   Community of interests. A report on the relationship between schools, youth service, community service, further education colleges, evening classes and sports organisations in the provision of social education and opportunities for recreation and leisure activities
Scottish Education D.

REITH, J. C. W., Lord

1946   New towns committee
Interim report
Session 1945-46 Cmd. 6759 xiv.
2nd interim report
Session 1945-46 Cmd. 6794 xiv.
Final report
Session 1945-46 Cmd. 6876 xiv.

RENNIE, E. M.

1967   Decimal currency, stage 1. Report of the sub-committee on decimalisation and metrication (Consultative committee on the curriculum, curriculum papers 1)
Scottish Education D.

1968   Decimal currency, stage 2. Report of the sub-committee on decimalisation and metrication (consultative committee on the curriculum, curriculum papers No. 1)
Scottish Education D.

Going metric; implications for the primary school. Report of the sub-committee on decimalisation and metrication (consultative committee on the curriculum, curriculum papers No. 4)
Scottish Education D.

Going metric; implications for secondary schools (consultative committee on the curriculum, curriculum papers No. 5)
2nd edition published 1974
Scottish Education D.

RENTON, David, Sir

1975   Preparation of legislation. Report of a committee
Session 1974-75 Cmnd. 6053 xii.

REYNOLDS, B. J.

1946   Approved schools and remand homes. Report of the committee on remuneration and conditions of service
Home Office

RICHARD, E. J.

1972   Aircraft noise; should the noise and number index be revised? A report by the research sub-committee
Noise Advisory Council

1974   Noise in the next ten years. Report by the panel on noise in the seventies
Noise Advisory Council

RICHARDS, E. L.

1974   Eagle Star Insurance Co. Ltd. and Bernard Sunley Investment Trust Ltd. and Grove-Wood Securities Ltd. Report by the Monopolies and Mergers Commission on the proposed merger
Session 1974 Cmnd. 5641 viii.

1975   Dentsply International Ltd. and A.D. International Ltd. A report on the proposed merger by the Monopolies and Mergers Commission
Session 1974-75 HC. 394 xvii.

1976   Services of solicitors in England and Wales. Report on the supply of services in relation to restrictions on advertising
Session 1975-76 HC. 558 xxii.

Barristers' services. Report of the supply of services in relation to restrictions on advertising
Session 1975-76 HC. 559 xxii.

Advocates' services. Report on the supply of services in relation to restrictions on advertising
Session 1975-76 HC. 560 xxii.

1977   Pilkington Brothers Ltd. and U.K.O. International Ltd. Report on the proposed merger by the Monopolies and Mergers Commission
Session 1976-77 HC. 267 xx.

See also ROSKILL, A., Sir

RICHARDS, James, Sir

1973   Planning and redevelopment in London's entertainment area, with special reference to the theatre
Arts Council

RICHARDS, R.

1956   Ancient monuments of East Caernarvonshire. 11th interim report of the Royal Commission on the Ancient and Historical Monuments and Constructions of Wales and Monmouthshire
Session 1955-56 Cmd. 9762 xxi.

RICHARDSON, Gordon

1964   Turnover taxation. Report of the committee
Session 1963-64 Cmnd. 2300 xix.

RICHARDSON, R. T.

1977   Mixed ability teaching in mathematics. Survey of recent practice by the working party
Schools Council, published by Evans/Methuen Educational

RIDLEY, F. F.

1973   French prefectoral system; an example of integrated administrative decentralisation. (Research papers No. 4)
Commission on the Constitution

RIDLEY, M., Viscount

1945   Rent control. Interdepartmental committee report
Session 1944-45 Cmd. 6621 v.

1952   Fuel and power resources. Report of the committee on a national policy for the use of fuel and power resources
Session 1951-52 Cmd. 8647 xii.

RIGBY, Norman L.

1970   Hosiery and knitwear in the 1970s; a study of the industry's future market prospects. A report prepared by Associated Industrial Consultants Ltd. for the Marketing Action Group of the Hosiery and Knitwear Economic Development Committee
N.E.D.O.

RIMAN, P. H.

1957   Manufacture and inspection of welded structures for aircraft engine parts. Report of the gas-turbine collaboration committee welding panel
M. of Supply

RIMMER, Beatrice Alice
See GERRARD, A. D.

RIPPON, G.

1973   A guide to noise units
Noise Advisory Council

RITCHIE, J.
See RAMSAY, J. D., Sir

RITSON, Edward H., Sir

1959   Rating of plant and machinery. Report of the committee
M. of Housing and Local Government

1962   East Midlands general review. Report of the inspector appointed to hear objections to the proposals that the administrative counties of Huntingdonshire and the Soke of Peterborough should be amalgamated to form a new administrative county to be known as Huntingdon and Peterborough and the administrative counties of Cambridgeshire and the Isle of Ely, which are already parts of the geographical county, should be amalgamated to form a single administrative county of Cambridge. Date of inquiry: 2 to 10 October, 1962
M. of Housing and Local Government

RITSON, Edward H., Sir *(continued)*

East Midlands general review area. Report of the inspector appointed to hear objections to the proposal to amalgamate Leicestershire and Rutland, and to the recommendation that the area of the present county of Rutland (subject to minor boundary adjustment) should form a single rural district. Date of inquiry: 17 to 26 July, 1962
M. of Housing and Local Government

ROBBINS, L. C., Lord

1955   Queen's Hall. Report of the committee to consider a new Queen's Hall
Session 1954-55 Cmd. 9467 vii.

1963   Higher education. Government statement on the report of the committee
Session 1963-64 Cmnd. 2165 xxvi.

Higher education
Report of the committee and appendices I, III, IV
Session 1962-63 Cmnd. 2154, Cmnd. 2154-I, Cmnd. 2154-III, Cmnd. 2154-IV xi, xii.

1964   Appendix II-A: Students and their education
Appendix II-B: Students and their education
Session 1962-63 Cmnd. 2154-II, Cmnd. 2154-II-1 xii.
Appendix 5: Higher education in other countries
Session 1963-64 Cmnd. 2154-V xii.
Evidence, part 1: Volumes A-F written and oral evidence received by the committee
Evidence, part 2: Documentary evidence submitted to the committee
Session 1962-63 Cmnd. 2154-VI to Cmnd. 2154-XII xii, xiii, xiv

London opera centre. Report of the committee appointed to investigate recent criticism of the centre
Arts Council

ROBENS OF WOLDINGHAM, A., Lord

1967   Malta. Report of the joint mission
Session 1966-67 Cmnd. 3366 xxv.

1972   Safety and health at work. Report of the committee
Vol. 1: Report
Session 1971-72 Cmnd. 5034 xii.
Vol. 2: Selected written evidence
D. of Employment

ROBERTS, J. E.

1975   Radiotherapy apparatus safety measures panel. Recommendations
D. of Health and Social Security

ROBERTS, Jean

1950   Boarding-out committee of the Scottish advisory council on child care. Report
Scottish Home D.

1966   Measures to secure a more equitable distribution of teachers in Scotland. Report
Scottish Education D.

ROBERTS, R. K.

1978   Carriage of dangerous goods in ships. Report of the standing advisory committee. 3rd ed.
D. of Trade

ROBERTS, S., Sir

1958   Structure of the public library services in England and Wales. Report of the committee
Session 1958-59 Cmnd. 660 xvi.

ROBERTS-WRAY, Kenneth O., Sir

1953   Native courts and native customary law in Africa. Judicial adviser's conference. Special supplement to the Journal of African Administration
Colonial Office

ROBERTSON OF OAKRIDGE, Brian H., Lord

1959   British Transport Commission. Report, re-appraisal of the plan for the modernisation and re-equipment of British Railways
Session 1958-59 Cmnd. 813 xvi.

ROBERTSON, A. P.

1976   Scottish national health service staff commission. Report
Scottish Home and Health D.

ROBERTSON, D. G.

1972   Technical education in secondary schools. Report of the working party (curriculum paper No. 10)
Scottish Education D.

ROBERTSON, Donald J.

1967   Report of an inquiry into a dispute between the Steel Company of Wales and the Amalgamated Union of Building Trade Workers
M. of Labour

Report of a court of inquiry into a dispute between the British Railways Board and the National Union of Railwaymen concerning guards and shunters
Session 1966-67 Cmnd. 3426 xxxvii.

1968   The Grangemouth/Falkirk regional survey and plan
Vol. 1: Economic and social issues
Vol. 2: Physical planning aspects
Prepared for the growth area joint planning advisory committee
Scottish Development D.

Report of a court of inquiry into a dispute at the Bromborough, Cheshire plant of Girling Ltd.
Session 1968-69 Cmnd. 3855 xxiii.

Report of the court of inquiry into a dispute at Rootes Motors Ltd., Linwood, Scotland
Session 1967-68 Cmnd. 3692 xxiii.

1969   Report of a court of inquiry into a dispute at the Port Talbot Works of the British Steel Corporation
Session 1968-69 Cmnd. 4147 xxxiii.

1970   Disruption of operations and industrial relations at Heathrow (London) Airport. 1st report of the committee of inquiry
Session 1970-71 Cmnd. 4485 xxx.

See also GRIFFITHS, W. H.

ROBERTSON, Ian M., Lord

1968   Scottish teachers' salaries memorandum
Scottish Education D.

1969   Standards for the public library service in Scotland. Report of a working party
Scottish Education D.

1970   Scottish teachers' salaries memorandum
Scottish Education D.

ROBERTSON, James W., Sir

1954   British Guiana constitutional commission. Report
Session 1953-54 Cmd. 9274 x.

1961   Kenya coastal strip. Report of the commissioner
Session 1961-62 Cmnd. 1585 xi.

ROBERTSON, R.

1965   Future recruitment and training of teachers for further education in Scotland. A report by the standing committee on the supply and training of teachers for further education
Scottish Education D.

ROBINSON, D.

1977   Transmitted deprivation. 3rd report of the joint working party
Social Science Research Council
See also MATTHEWS, R. O. C.

ROBINSON, Derek

1977   Remuneration of councillors. Report of the committee of inquiry into the system of remuneration of members of local authorities
Session 1977-78 Cmnd. 7010 xxiii.
Vol. 2. The survey of councillors and local authorities
D. of the Environment

ROBINSON, D. W.
See BURNS, W.

ROBINSON, H.

1978   Management accounting in the water industry; a research paper. Report from the multi-disciplinary group No. 3
National Water Council

ROBINSON, J.

1975   Accommodation for the lower-priced market. Low-priced accommodation study group. Hotels and catering Economic Development Committee
N.E.D.O.

ROBINSON, J. F.

1953   Survey of blackface sheep with special reference to their hardiness. A report to the Scottish Hill Farm Research Committee
D. of Agriculture for Scotland

ROBINSON, Kenneth

1972   Committee of inquiry into a dispute between employees of the Mansfield Hosiery Mills Ltd., Loughborough and their employer. Report
D. of Employment

ROBINSON, Leslie, Sir

1972   Electrical power in Europe; the plant suppliers and their customers. Electrical Engineering Economic Development Committee
N.E.D.O.

1974   Industrial review to 1977: electrical engineering. Electrical Engineering Economic Development Committee
N.E.D.O.

ROBINSON, Roy L., Sir

1943   Post-war forest policy. Report
Session 1942-43 Cmd. 6447 iv.

ROBINSON OF KIDDINGTON, Inga-Stina, Baroness
1976   Oral contraceptives. Report of the joint working group
D. of Health and Social Security

ROBSON, Thomas B., Sir

1958   Coal distribution costs in Great Britain. Report of the committee of inquiry
Session 1957-58 Cmnd. 446 viii.

ROCHDALE, J. D., Viscount

1962   Major ports of Great Britain. Report of the committee of inquiry
Session 1961-62 Cmnd. 1824 xx.

1970   Committee of inquiry into shipping. Report
Session 1969-70 Cmnd. 4337 xxvii.

ROCHE, A. A., Lord
1944   Justices' clerks. Departmental committee report
Session 1943-44 Cmd. 6507 iv.

RODGER, A. G.

1962   Supply of teachers in Scotland. 4th report of the departmental committee
Session 1961-62 Cmnd. 1601 xiii.
See also GRAINGER-STEWART, T.

1965   Conditions of service in further education in Scotland. Report
Scottish Education D.

1967   Ascertainment of children with hearing defects. Report of the working party
Scottish Education D.

1969   Ascertainment of children with visual handicaps. Report of the working party
Scottish Education D.

RODGERS, John

1954   Litter in the Royal parks. Report of the committee
M. of Works

ROGERS, H. R.

1944   Power presses. Report of the committee on safety in the use of power presses
M. of Labour and National Service

Bending brakes. Joint standing committee on the safety of heavy power presses
1944   Report
1949   Final report
M. of Labour and National Service

ROGERS, Philip, Sir

1972   Management arrangements for the reorganised National Health Service. Management study steering committee
D. of Health and Social Security

ROGERS, R. J.

1944   Gas installations. Report by a committee convened by the Institution of Gas Engineers. (Post-war building studies No. 6)
M. of Works

ROMNEY, D. H.
See WRIGHT, A. C. S.

ROOM, R. G.
1968   Costing your labour turnover. Rubber Economic Development Committee
N.E.D.O.

ROSE, G. N. G.
1971   Royal Commission on Assizes and Quarter Sessions. Report of the special statistical survey
Royal Commission on Assizes and Quarter Sessions
See also BEECHING, R., Lord

ROSE, Harold B.
1970   Management education in the 1970s; growth and issues. A report for the Management Education, Training and Development Committee
N.E.D.O.

ROSE, Hugh, Sir
1956   Employment of children in the potato harvest. Report of the committee
Session 1955-56 Cmd. 9738 xvii.

ROSEBERY, A. E. H. M. A., Earl of
1949   Export and slaughter of horses. Report of the departmental committee
Session 1950 Cmd. 7888 xii.

ROSENHEIM, M. L., Lord

1972 Heat sterilised fluids for parenteral administration. Interim report
Medicines Commission

Hepatitis and the treatment of chronic renal failure. Report of the advisory group
D. of Health and Social Security

1973 Prevention of bicrobial contamination of medicinal products. Report
Medicines Commission

ROSEVEARE, Martin P., Sir

1949 Women teachers. Report of the working party on the supply of women teachers
M. of Education

ROSKILL, Ashton, Sir

1966 Colour film. Report by the Monopolies Commission on the supply and processing of colour film
Session 1966-67 HC. 1 xli.

Films. Report by the Monopolies Commission on the supply of films for exhibition in cinemas
Session 1966-67 HC. 206 xli.

Aluminium semi-manufactures. A report by the Monopolies Commission concerning the supply of aluminium semi-manufactures
Session 1966-67 HC. 263 xl.

The Times Newspaper and the Sunday Times Newspaper. A report by the Monopolies Commission on the proposed transfer to a newspaper proprietor
Session 1966-67 HC. 273 xli.

1967 Infant milk foods. A report on the Monopolies Commission on the supply of infant milk foods
Session 1966-67 HC. 319 xli.

International motor insurance cards. A report by the Monopolies Commission on the provision of insurance in relation to the issue of the international motor insurance cards
Session 1966-67 HC. 487 xli.

British Insulated Callenders Cables Ltd. and Pyrotenax Ltd. A report by the Monopolies Commission on the proposed merger
Session 1966-67 HC. 490 xl.

Guest, Keen and Nettlefolds Ltd. and Birfield Ltd. A report by the Monopolies Commission on the merger
Session 1966-67 Cmnd. 3186 xli.

United Drapery Stores Ltd. and Montague Burton Ltd. A report by the Monopolies Commission on the proposed merger
Session 1966-67 Cmnd. 3397 xli.

1968 Thomson Newspapers Ltd. and Cursha and Son Ltd. A report by the Monopolies Commission on the proposed transfer of three weekly newspapers owned by Cursha and Son Ltd. to Thomson Newspapers Ltd.
Session 1967-68 HC. 66 xxvi.

Flat glass. A report by the Monopolies Commission on the supply of flat glass
Session 1967-68 HC. 83 xxvi.

Man-made cellulosic fibres. A report by the Monopolies Commission on the supply of man-made cellulosic fibres
Session 1967-68 HC. 130 xxvi.

Men's haircutting services. A report by the Monopolies Commission on a reference concerning the supply of haircutting services for men
Session 1967-68 HC. 263 xxvi.

Barclays Bank Ltd., Lloyds Bank Ltd., and Martins Bank Ltd. A report by the Monopolies Commission on the proposed merger
Session 1967-68 HC. 319 xxvi.

Thorn Electrical Industries Ltd. and Radio Rentals Ltd. A report by the Monopolies Commission on the proposed merger
Session 1967-68 HC. 318 xxvi.

Electric lamps. 2nd report by the Monopolies Commission on the supply of electric lamps. Parts 1 and 2
Session 1968-69 HC. 4 xl.

Clutch mechanisms for road vehicles. Report by the Monopolies Commission on the supply of clutch mechanisms for road vehicles
Session 1968-69 HC. 32 xl.

1969 Recommended resale prices. A report by the Monopolies Commission on the general effect on the public interest of the practice of recommending or otherwise suggesting prices to be charged on the resale of goods
Session 1968-69 HC. 100 xl.

Estate agents. A report by the Monopolies Commission on the supply of certain services by estate agents
Session 1968-69 HC. 216 xl.

Unilever Ltd. and Allied Breweries Ltd. A report on the proposed merger and general observations on mergers
Session 1968-69 HC. 297 xl.

The Rank Organisation Ltd., and the De La Rue Co. Ltd. A report by the Monopolies Commission on the proposed merger and general observations on mergers
Session 1968-69 HC. 298 xl.

Cigarette filter rods. A report by the Monopolies Commission on the supply and exports of cigarette filter rods
Session 1968-69 HC.335 xl.

1970 George Outram & Co. Ltd. and Hamilton Advertiser Ltd. and Baird & Hamilton Ltd. A report by the Monopolies Commission on the proposed transfer of six weekly newspapers owned by Hamilton Advertiser Ltd. and Baird & Hamilton Ltd. to George Outram & Co. Ltd.
Session 1969-70 HC.76 xviii.

Metal containers. A report by the Monopolies Commission on the supply of metal containers
Session 1970-71 HC.6 xxxii.

British Sidac Ltd and Transparent Paper Ltd. Report by the Monopolies Commission on the proposed merger
Session 1970-71 HC.154 xxxii.

Refusal to supply. A report by the Monopolies Commission on the general effect on the public interest of the practice of refusing to supply goods required for business purposes and of entering into certain exclusive supply agreements
Session 1970-71 Cmnd. 4372 xxxii.

A report on the general effect on the public interest of certain restrictive practices so far as they prevail in relation to the supply of professional services. Part 1: the report. Monopolies Commission
Session 1970-71 Cmnd. 4463 xxxii.

1971 Starch, glucoses and modified starches. A report by the Monopolies Commission on their supply
Session 1970-71 HC.615 xxxii.

1972 Connection charges for electricity and gas. Report by the Monopolies Commission
Session 1971-72 Cmnd. 5063 xxii.

Beecham Group Ltd. and Glaxo Group Ltd.; the Boots Co. Ltd. and Glaxo Group Ltd. A report by the Monopolies Commission on the proposed mergers
Session 1971-72 HC.341 xxii.

Fire insurance. Report of the Monopolies Commission
Session 1971-72 HC. 396 xxii.

ROSKILL, Ashton, Sir *(continued)*

1973   Breakfast cereals. Report by the Monopolies Commission on the supply of ready cooked breakfast cereal foods
Session 1972-73 HC.2 xv.

Asbestos and certain asbestos products. A report on supply by the Monopolies Commission
Session 1972-73 HC.3 xv.

Chlordiazepodics and diazepam. Report on supply by the Monopolies Commission
Session 1972-73 HC.197 xv.

Footwear machinery. Report on supply and exports by the Monopolies Commission
Session 1972-73 HC.215 xv.

Parallel pricing. Report on the general effect on the public interest by the Monopolies Commission
Session 1972-73 Cmnd. 5330 xv.

Wire and fibre ropes. A report on supply and exports by the Monopolies Commission
Session 1973-74 HC.2 iv.

1974   Plasterboard. Report on supply by the Monopolies Commission
Session 1973-74 HC.94 iv.

Cross-channel car ferry services. Report by the Monopolies Commission
Session 1974 HC.14 viii.

Davey International Ltd. and the British Rollmakers Corp. Ltd. Report by the Monopolies Commission on the proposed merger
Session 1974 HC.67 viii.

The Boots Co. Ltd. and House of Fraser, Ltd. Report by the Monopolies Commission on the proposed merger
Session 1974 HC.174 viii.

Primary batteries. Report on supply by the Monopolies and Mergers Commission
Session 1974-75 HC.1 xvii.

1975   Contraceptive sheaths. Report on supply by the Monopolies and Mergers Commission
Session 1974-75 HC.135 xvii.

H. Weidmann A.G. and B. S. and W. Whiteley Ltd. Report on the proposed merger by the Monopolies and Mergers Commission
Session 1974-75 Cmnd. 6208 xvii.

1976   Building bricks. Report on supply by the Monopolies and Mergers Commission
Session 1975-76 HC.474 xxii.

Stockbrokers' services. Report on supply of services in relation to restrictions on advertising by the Monopolies and Mergers Commission
Session 1975-76 Cmnd. 6571 xxii.

Veterinary services. Report on supply of services in relation to restrictions on advertising by the Monopolies and Mergers Commission
Session 1975-76 Cmnd. 6572 xxii.

Accountancy services. Report on the supply of services in relation to restrictions on advertising by the Monopolies and Mergers Commission
Session 1975-76 Cmnd. 6573 xxii.

See also JOHNSTON, Alexander, Sir

ROSKILL, E. A., Sir

1969-1970 Commission on the third London airport. Papers and proceedings. Vols. 1-IX
Board of Trade

1971   Commission on the third London airport. Report and index
D. of Trade and Industry

ROSS, C. R.

1973   Population panel report
Session 1972-73 Cmnd. 5258 xxviii.

ROSS, D. M.

1972   Report on the local inquiry in relation to the implementation by Lanark County Council of parts II and IV of the Housing (Financial Provisions) (Scotland) Act
Scottish Development D.

ROSS, J.

1956   Child migration to Australia. Report of a fact-finding mission
Session 1955-56 Cmd. 9832 xxiii.

ROSS, N. S.

1978   Review of the experience of the fire service—Summer 1976. Report of the joint working party
Home Office

ROSS, William David, Sir

1949   Royal Commission on the Press. Report
Session 1948-49 Cmd. 7700 xx.

ROSSE, L. M. H., Earl of

1967   Area museum services. Report
Standing Commission on Museums and Galleries

1968   Universities and museums. Report on the universities in relation to their own and other museums
Standing Commission on Museums and Galleries

1971   Preservation of technological materials. Report and recommendations
Standing Commission on Museums and Galleries

1977   University museums. Report
Standing Commission on Museums and Galleries

ROSSER, Melvyn

1977   Operation of the European regional development fund in Wales. Steering committee report
Welsh Council

ROSSETTI, H. F.

1961   Services for the disabled. 2nd ed. Standing committee on the rehabilitation and resettlement of disabled persons
M. of Labour

ROSSITER, J. R.

1973   Tides and surges. Report of the working party. In: Research in the physical marine sciences. (Publications series 'B' No. 8)
Natural Environment Research Council

ROTHSCHILD, N. M. V., Lord

1952   Foot and mouth disease research. Interim report
Agricultural Research Council

1971   The organisation and management of government R. and D. *In:* A framework for government research and development
Session 1971-72 Cmnd. 4814 xxxv.

See also DAINTON, F. S., Sir

1976   Royal Commission on Gambling
Interim report
Session 1975-76 Cmnd. 6643 viii.

1978   Final report. 2 vols.
Session 1977-78 Cmnd. 7200 vii.

ROWE, M. E., Sir

1958   Hatfield new town. Report of local inquiry into causes of damage to houses at Hatfield new town
M. of Housing and Local Government

ROWLANDS, Ted

See POSNETT, Richard

ROWNTREE, Norman, Sir

1976   Research in hydrology. Report of the working party. (Publications series 'B' No. 19)
Natural Environment Research Council

ROXBURGH, Adam

1972   Control on medicines in hospital wards and departments. Report by a joint group of the Scottish Health Service Council
Scottish Home and Health D.

ROXBURGH, R. F., Sir

1954   Land charges. Report of the committee
Session 1955-56 Cmd. 9825 xxii.

RUFFLE, J. W. B.

1978   Examinations at 18+ : the N. and F. studies. Report of the joint examinations sub-committee of the Schools Council. (Working paper No. 60)
Schools Council

RUMSBY, P. L.

1971   Application of British Standard 1377:1967 to the testing of colliery spoil. Technical memorandum issued on soil mechanics testing by the joint working party
National Coal Board

RUNCIMAN OF DOXFORD, W. L., Viscount

1953   Taxicab service. Report of the committee
Session 1952-53 Cmd. 8804 xvii.

1956   Horticultural marketing. Report of the committee
Session 1956-57 Cmnd. 61 xiv.

RUSHCLIFFE, H. B., Lord

1943   Land transfer committee report
Session 1942-43 Cmd. 6467 v.

1943   Nurses' salaries committee
1st report: salaries and emoluments of female nurses in hospitals
Session 1942-43 Cmd. 6424 v.
Supplement to 1st report
M. of Health
2nd report: salaries and emoluments of male nurses, public health nurses, district nurses and state registered nurses in nurseries
Session 1942-43 Cmd. 6487 iv.

1944   Mental nurses. Sub-committee of the nurses' salaries committee. Report
Session 1943-44 Cmd. 6542 iv.

Midwives' salaries committee. Report on salaries and emoluments of institutional domiciliary midwives, non-medical supervisors of midwives and of pupil midwives
Session 1942-43 Cmd. 6460 v.

1945   Committee on legal aid and advice in England and Wales. Report
Session 1944-45 Cmd. 6641 v.

Nurses. Report of the committee on the training of nurses for the colonies
Session 1945-46 Cmd. 6672 xiv.

RUSSELL, A., Lord

1946   Scottish lunacy and mental deficiency laws. Report of the committee
Session 1945-46 Cmnd. 6834 xiii.

RUSSELL, C. R., Sir

1966   Law of succession in relation to illegitimate persons. Report of the committee
Session 1966-67 Cmnd. 3051 xxxvi.

RUSSELL, E. L., Sir

1961   Teachers for further education. Report of an advisory sub-committee of the National Advisory Council on the training of supply of teachers
M. of Education

RUSSELL, Lionel, Sir

1973   Adult education; a plan for development. Report by a committee of inquiry
D. of Education and Science

RUSSELL, R. C. H.

1973   Surface waves. Report of the working party. *In:* Research in the physical marine sciences. (Publications series 'B' No. 8)
Natural Environmental Research Council

RUTHVEN, B. T.

1967   Organisation of courses leading to the Scottish Certificate of Education. (Consultative committee on the curriculum, curriculum papers No. 2)
Scottish Education D.

1976   Ancillary staff in secondary schools. Report of a working party
Scottish Education D.

RYAN, J.

1951   Organisation of the Ministry of Agriculture and Fisheries. Report of the committee
M. of Agriculture and Fisheries

RYDER, Don, Sir

1975   British Leyland; the next decade; an abridged version of a report by a team of inquiry
Session 1974-75 HC. 342 xiv.

RYDZ, B.
    See McLELLAN, A. G.

SACHS, Eric, Sir

1949   Pottery. Report on public inquiry into the draft Pottery (Health and Welfare) Special Regulations
M. of Labour and National Service

STAFFORD, Archibald

1949   Medical certificates. Report of the inter-departmental committee
M. of Health

SAFFORD, J. F.

1972   Structure of the pump, valve and fabricated process plant industries; France and West Germany
N.E.D.O.
    See also TINDALE, L. V. D.

SAINSBURY, A. J., Lord

1967   Relationship of the pharmaceutical industry with the National Health Service. Report of the committee of inquiry
Session 1966-67 Cmnd. 3410 xlv.

ST. ALDWYN, M. J., Earl

1955   Myxomatosis advisory committee. 2nd report
M. of Agriculture and Fisheries
    See also CARRINGTON, P. A. R., Lord

ST. JOHN WILSON, P. H.
    See WILSON, P. H. St. J.

SALISBURY, R. A. J., Marquess of

1959   Ancient monuments of the City of Cambridge. Royal Commission on the Ancient and Historical and Constructions of England. 21st interim report
Session 1958-59 Cmnd. 743 xv.

1961   Roman monuments in the City of York (EBVRACVM). 22nd interim report of the Royal Commission on Ancient and Historical Monuments and constructions of England
Session 1961-62 Cmnd. 1642 xvii.

1963   Monuments threatened or destroyed; a select list, 1956-62. Interim report of the Royal Commission on the Ancient and Historical Monuments and Constructions of England
Session 1962-63 Cmnd. 1917 xix.

SALISBURY, R. A. J., Marquess of *(continued)*

1972   Ancient monuments of north Dorset. 26th interim report of the Royal Commission on the Ancient and Historical Monuments and Constructions of England
Session 1971-72 Cmnd. 4980 xvi.

Ancient monuments of Cambridgeshire, II. 27th interim report. Royal Commission on the Ancient and Historical Monuments and Constructions of England
Session 1971-72 Cmnd. 4981 xvi.

Ancient monuments of York, II. 28th interim report of the Royal Commission on the Ancient and Historical Monuments and Constructions of England
Session 1971-72 Cmnd. 4978 xvi.

Ancient monuments of York, III. 29th interim report of the Royal Commission on Ancient and Historical Monuments and Constructions of England
Session 1971-72 Cmnd. 4979 xvi.

SALISBURY, Edward J., Sir

1950   Technical and scientific register. Present and future supply and demand for persons with professional qualifications in biology, agriculture and related sciences. Biologists' and agriculturalists' sub-committee report
M. of Labour and National Service

SALMON, C. B., Lord

1966   Royal commission on tribunals of inquiry
Report
Session 1966-67 Cmnd. 3121 li.
Documentary evidence
Minutes of oral evidence
Royal Commission on Tribunals of Inquiry

1969   Law of contempt as it affects tribunals of inquiry. Report of the interdepartmental committee
Session 1968-69 Cmnd. 4078 xlvii.

1976   Royal Commission on standards of conduct in public life. Report
Session 1975-76 Cmnd. 6524 xiv.

SALMON, B.

1966   Senior nursing staff structure. Report of the committee
M. of Health

SALMON, B. L.

1978   Supply board working group report
D. of Health and Social Security

SAMUELS, A., Sir

1951   London traffic congestion. Report by the London and home counties traffic advisory committee
M. of Transport

1953   Car parking in the inner area of London. Report of the working party
M. of Transport

1956   London traffic area. 30 m.p.h. speed limit. Report of the London and home counties traffic advisory committee
M. of Transport and Civil Aviation

Parking survey of inner London. Reports of the committee
1956   Interim report
1957   Final report
M. of Transport and Civil Aviation

1959   Victoria line. Report by the London travel committee
M. of Transport

SAMWELL, Stanley David

1978   Kuehne and Nagel Ltd. Report of investigation under the Companies Act
D. of Trade

SANDERS, H. G., Sir

1961   Toxic chemicals in agriculture and food storage. Report of the research study group
M. of Agriculture, Fisheries and Food

SANDFORD, C. J. E., Lord

1974   National park policies review committee. Report
D. of the Environment

SANDILANDS, F. E. P.

1975   Inflation accounting. Report of the inflation accounting committee
Session 1974-75 Cmnd. 6225 vii.

Inflation accounting; a brief guide to the report of the committee
D. of Trade

SANDLES, Arthur

1973   Prospects for the small hotelier. Hotel and Catering Economic Development Committee
N.E.D.O.

SANDYS, Duncan E.

1961   Southern Rhodesia constitutional conference. Report of the conference held at Salisbury, 7 February, 1961
Session 1960-61 Cmnd. 1291 xiii.

1962   British Guiana independence conference, 1962
Session 1962-63 Cmnd. 1870 x.

1963   Zanzibar independence conference, 1963
Session 1962-63 Cmnd. 2157 x.

Malta independence conference, 1963
Session 1962-63 Cmnd. 2121 x.

Kenya independence conference, 1963
Session 1962-63 Cmnd. 2156 x.

British Guiana conference, 1963
Session 1963-64 Cmnd. 2203 x.

1964   Northern Rhodesia. Report of the Northern Rhodesia independence conference, 1964
Session 1963-64 Cmnd. 2365 x.

Gambia independence conference, 1964
Session 1963-64 Cmnd. 2435 x.

SAUNDERS, A. M. Carr-, Sir
See CARR-SAUNDERS, A. M., Sir

SAVAGE, William G., Sir

1950   Hygiene in catering establishments. Report of the catering trade working party
M. of Food

SAWYER, J. S.

1976   World climatology. Report of the working party. *In* Research in applied and world climatology (publication series ' B ' No. 17)
Natural Environment Research Council

SCADDING, John G.

1968   The future of the chest services. A report by a sub-committee of the standing medical advisory committee. Central Health Services Council
M. of Health

SCAMP, A. Jack, Sir

1965   Report of a court of inquiry into the issues arising in negotiations between the British Railways Board, the Associated Society of Locomotive Engineers and Firemen, and the National Union of Railwaymen
Session 1964-65 Cmnd. 2779 xvii.

SCAMP, A. Jack, Sir (continued)

1966   Report of a court of inquiry into the causes and circumstances of the dispute between employers in membership of the Longbridge Group of Delivery Agents and their employees
Session 1965-66 Cmnd. 2905 v.

Report of a court of inquiry into the causes and circumstances of the dispute between Motor Vehicle Collections Ltd. and Avon Car Transporters Ltd., both of Solihull, on the one hand, and their respective employees on the other hand
Session 1965-66 Cmnd. 2935 v.

Motor industry joint labour council. Report on activities
M. of Labour

1967   Report of a court of inquiry into the causes and circumstances of the dispute at Birmingham Aluminium Castings Ltd., involving members of the Transport and General Workers' Union and the National Society of Metal Mechanics
Session 1966-67 Cmnd. 3201 xxxvi.

Report of a court of inquiry into the dispute between the British Air Line Pilots Association and the National Joint Council for Civil Air Transport
Session 1966-67 Cmnd. 3428 xxxvii.

Report of an inquiry into the employment of coal trimmers in the ports of Blyth, Dunston, North Shields, South Shields, Seaham Harbour and Sunderland
M. of Labour

Report of inquiry into the locally determined aspects of the system of payment and earnings opportunities of registered dock workers in the Port of Liverpool (including Birkenhead)
M. of Labour

1968   Report of a court of inquiry into a dispute concerning sewing machinists employed by the Ford Motor Co.
Session 1967-68 Cmnd. 3749 xxiii.

Report of a court of inquiry into a dispute concerning wage structure proposals for time workers employed at Pressed Steel Fisher Ltd., Cowley
Session 1967-68 Cmnd. 3688 xxiii.

Motor Industry Joint Labour Council. Report on the activities of the council
M. of Labour

1969   Report of the court of inquiry into a dispute at Vickers Ltd., Barrow-in-Furness
Session 1968-69 Cmnd. 3984 xxxiii.

1970   Report of an inquiry into employment on the loading of coal at Immingham and South Killingholme
D. of Employment and Productivity

SCARBOROUGH, L. R., Earl of

1947   Oriental, Slavonic, East European and African studies. Report of the interdepartmental commission of inquiry
Foreign Office

SCARMAN, Leslie G., Sir

1965   1st programme of the Law Commission
Lord Chancellor's D.

1966   Law Commission proposals to abolish certain ancient criminal offences
Lord Chancellor's D.

Reform of the grounds of divorce; the field of choice. Report of the Law Commission
Session 1966-67 Cmnd. 3123 xxxix.

Powers of the appeals courts to sit in private and the restrictions upon publicity in domestic proceedings
Report of the Law Commission
Session 1966-67 Cmnd. 3149 xxxix.

Proposals for reform of the law relating to maintenance and champerty. Report of the Law Commission
Lord Chancellor's Office

1st annual report of the Law Commission, 1965-66
Lord Chancellor's Office

1967   Civil liability for animals. (Law. Com. No. 13)
Lord Chancellor's Office

Imputed criminal intent. (Director of Public Prosecutions v. Smith). Law Commission
Lord Chancellor's Office

Sea Fisheries (Shellfish) Bill. Report on the consolidation of certain enactments by the Law Commission and the Scottish Law Commission
Session 1966-67 Cmnd. 3267 xxxix.

Transfer of land. Interim report on the right of title to freehold land by the Law Commission
Lord Chancellor's Office

Transfer of land. Report on restrictive covenants. (Law Com. No. 11)
Lord Chancellor's Office

Blood tests and the proof of paternity in civil proceedings. (Law Com. No. 16)
Session 1968-69 HC. 2 xxxvi.

2nd programme of law reform. (Law Com. No. 14)
Lord Chancellor's D.

1969   Landlord and tenant. Report on the Landlord and Tenant Act 1954, part II. (Law. Com. No. 17)
Session 1968-69 HC. 38 xxxvi.

Transfer of land. Report on land charges affecting unregistered land. (Law Com. No. 18)
Session 1968-69 HC. 125 xxxvi.

Proceedings against estates. (Law Com. No. 19)
Session 1968-69 Cmnd. 4010 xxxvi.

Administrative law. (Law Com. No. 20)
Session 1968-69 Cmnd. 4059 xxxvi.

The interpretation of statutes. (Law Com. No. 21) (Scot. Law Com. No. 11)
Session 1968-69 HC. 256 xxxvi.

Statute Law Revision, 1st report. Draft Statute Law (Repeals) Bill. (Law Com. No. 22)
Session 1968-69 Cmnd. 4052 xxxvi.

Proposal for the abolition of the matrimonial remedy of restitution of conjugal rights. (Law Com. No. 23)
Session 1968-69 HC. 369 xxxvii.

Exemption clauses in contracts. 1st report: amendments to the Sale of Goods Act, 1893. (Law Com. No. 24) (Scot. Law Com. No. 12)
Session 1968-69 HC. 403 xxxvii.

Family Law. Report on financial provision in matrimonial proceedings. (Law Com. No. 25)
Session 1968-69 HC. 448 xxxvii.

Breach of promise of marriage. (Law Com. No. 26)
Session 1968-69 HC. 453 xxxvii.

Trustee Savings Banks Bill. Report of the Law Commission and the Scottish Law Commission
Session 1968-69 Cmnd. 4004 xxxvii.

1970   Statute law revision, 2nd report: draft Wild Creatures and Forest Laws Bill. (Law Com. No. 28)
Session 1970-71 Cmnd. 4433 xxxi.

Criminal law report on offences of damages to property. (Law Com. No. 29)
Session 1970-71 HC. 91 xxxi.

Powers of attorney. (Law Com. No. 30)
Session 1970-71 Cmnd. 4473 xxxi.

Administration Bonds, personal representatives' rights of retainer and preference and related matters. (Law Com. No. 31)
Session 1970-71 Cmnd. 4497 xxxi.

Civil liability for dangerous things and activities. (Law Com. No. 32)
Session 1970-71 HC. 142 xxxi.

SCARMAN, Leslie G., Sir *(continued)*

Family law. Report on nullity of marriage. (Law Com. No. 33)
Session 1970-71 HC. 164 xxxi.

Hague convention on recognition of divorces and legal separations. (Law Com. No. 34) (Scot. Law Com. No. 16)
Session 1970-71 Cmnd. 4542 xxxi.

Limitation Act, 1963. (Law Com. No. 35)
Session 1970-71 Cmnd. 4532 xxxi.

Statute law revision, 3rd report. Draft Statute Law (Repeals) Bill
Session 1970-71 Cmnd. 4546 xxxi.

Coinage Bill. Report on the consolidation of certain enactments relating to coinage. (Law Com. No. 38) (Scot. Law Com. No. 18)
Session 1970-71 Cmnd. 4544 xxxi.

Vehicles (Excise) Bill. Report on the consolidation of certain enactments relating to excise duties on mechanically propelled vehicles, and to the licensing and registration of such vehicles. (Law Com. No. 39 Scot. Law Com. No. 19)
Session 1970-71 Cmnd. 4547 xxxi.

Civil liability of vendors and lessors for defective premises. (Law Com. No. 40)
Session 1970-71 HC. 184 xxxi.

1971 National Savings Bank Bill. Report on the consolidation of enactments relating to the National Savings Bank. (Law Com. No. 41) (Scot. Law Com. No. 20)
Session 1970-71 Cmnd. 4574 xxxi.

Family law. Report on polygamous marriages. (Law Com. No. 42)
Session 1970-71 HC. 227 xxxi.

Taxation of income and gains derived from land. (Law Com. No. 43) (Scot. Law Com. No. 21)
Session 1970-71 Cmnd. 4654 xxxi.

The Law Commission's second programme on consolidation and statute law revision. (Law Com. No. 44)
Session 1970-71 HC. 338 xxxi.

Town and Country Planning Bill. Report on the consolidation of certain enactments relating to town and country planning. (Law Com. No. 45)
Session 1970-71 Cmnd. 4684 xxxi.

Road Traffic Bill. Report on the consolidation of certain enactments relating to road traffic. (Law Com. No. 46) (Scot. Law Com. No. 22)
Session 1970-71 Cmnd. 4731 xxxi.

Family law. Solemnisation of marriage in England and Wales. (Working paper No. 35)
Law Commission

1972 Family law. Report on jurisdiction in matrimonial causes. (Law Com. No. 48)
Session 1971-72 HC. 464 xxi.

Draft Statute Law (Repeals) Bill. Statute law revision, 4th report. (Law Com. No. 49) (Scot Law Com. No. 26)
Session 1971-72 Cmnd. 5108 xxi.

Law Commission. 7th annual report. (Law Com. No. 50)
Session 1972-73 HC. 35 xiv.

Matrimonial Causes Bill. Report on the consolidation of certain enactments relating to matrimonial proceedings. (Law Com. No. 51)
Session 1972-73 Cmnd. 5167 xiv.

Violence and civil disturbances in Northern Ireland in 1969. Report of the tribunal of inquiry. 2 vols.
Northern Ireland Office

1973 Family law. Matrimonial proceedings in magistrates' courts. Report of a working party. (Working paper No. 53)
Law Commission

1975 Red Lion Square disorders of 15 June 1974. Report of the inquiry
Session 1974-75 Cmnd. 5919 xxx.

1976 Custody of children; jurisdiction and enforcement within the U.K. Report of a joint working party. (Working Paper No. 68; Scot. Law Com. Memo No. 23)
Law Commission *and* Scottish Law Commission

1977 Statute Law revision, 8th report. Draft Statute Law (Repeals) Bill. (Law Com. No. 80) (Scot. Law Com. No. 44)
Session 1976-77 Cmnd. 6719 xviii.

Liability for defective products. (Law Com. No. 82) (Scot. Law Com. No. 45)
Session 1976-77 Cmnd. 6831 xix.

SCHOLEFIELD, Charles E.

1965 Police areas of the county of Bedfordshire and the county borough of Luton. Report of inquiry in respect of the objections to the proposed compulsory amalgamation
Session 1964-65 Cmnd. 2676 xxi.

SCHOLFIELD, Michael

1967 Society and the young school leaver. A humanities programme for the raising of the school leaving age. (Working paper, No. 11)
Schools Council

SCHUSTER, George E., Sir

1950 Maltese Islands. Interim report on the financial and economic structure of the Maltese islands. (Colonial No. 260)
Colonial Office

Qualifications of planners. Report of the committee
Session 1950 Cmd. 8059 xiv.

SCOTT, C. Hilary, Sir

1971 Neighbourhood noise. Report by the working group of the Noise Advisory Council on the Noise Abatement Act
D. of the Environment

1973 Linked life assurance. Report of the committee on property bonds and equity-linked life assurance
Session 1972-73 Cmnd. 5281 xii.

SCOTT, J. A.

1961 The training staff of training centres for the mentally subnormal. Report of the sub-committee of the standing mental health advisory committee.
Central Health Services Council
M. of Health

SCOTT, L., Lord

1942 Land utilisation in rural areas. Report of the committee
Session 1941-42 Cmd. 6378 iv.

SCOTT, R. B.
1973 Retail sale of certain veterinary medicines to farmers. Report
Medicines Commission

SCOTT, T. E.

1949 Technical and scientific register. Present and future supply and demand for persons with professional qualifications in architecture. Architects' sub-committee report
M. of Labour and National Service

SCOTT-DOW, R. C.

1952 Preventive dental services. Report of the sub-committee of the standing dental advisory committee of the Scottish Health Services Council
D. of Health for Scotland

SCOTT HENDERSON, J.
See HENDERSON, J. S.

SCOWEN, R. T.
1975   Colliery waste tipping on Durham beaches. Interim report of the working party
D. of the Environment

SEAL, E. A., Sir
1954   Retention moneys on building and civil engineering contracts. Report of the working party appointed to examine the procedure concerning retention moneys on building and civil engineering contracts
M. of Works

SEARLE, W. F.
1950   Colonial government statisticians. 1st conference report. (Colonial No. 267)
Colonial Office

SEEBOHM, Frederick, Lord
1968   Local authority and allied personal social services. Report of the committee
Session 1967-68 Cmnd. 3703 xxxii.
1974   Naval welfare committee report
M. of Defence

SEEL, George F., Sir
1952   Development and welfare in the West Indies. Report. (Colonial No. 282)
Colonial Office
1953   Development and welfare in the West Indies. Report. (Colonial No. 291)
Colonial Office

SELIGMAN, R.
1944   Non-ferrous metals. Report by a committee convened by the British Non-Ferrous Metals Research Association. (Post-war building studies No. 13)
M. of Works

SELLERS, E. S.
1970   Survey of professional engineers, 1968. (Studies in technological manpower No. 1)
M. of Technology

SELLERS, F. A., Sir
1959   Indecency with children. 1st report of the criminal law revision committee
Session 1958-59 Cmnd. 835 xvi.
1960   Suicide. 2nd report of the Criminal Law Revision Committee
Session 1959-60 Cmnd. 1187 xvii.
1963   Insanity. 3rd report of the Criminal Law Revision Committee
Session 1962-63 Cmnd. 2149 xx.

Order of closing speeches. 4th report of the Criminal Law Revision Committee
Session 1962-63 Cmnd. 2148 xx.
1964   Criminal procedure (jurors). 5th report of the Criminal Law Revision Committee
Session 1963-64 Cmnd. 2349 xv.

Perjury and attendance of witnesses. 6th report of the Criminal Law Revision Committee
Session 1963-64 Cmnd. 2465 xv.
1965   Felonies and misdemeanours. 7th report of the Criminal Law Revision Committee
Session 1964-65 Cmnd. 2659 xviii.
1966   Theft and related offences. 8th report of the Criminal Law Revision Committee
Session 1966-67 Cmnd. 2977 xxxix.

Written statements, formal admissions and notices of alibi. 9th report of the Criminal Law Revision Committee
Session 1966-67 Cmnd. 3145 xxxix.
1968   Secrecy of jury room. 10th report of the Criminal Law Revision Committee
Session 1967-68 Cmnd. 3750 xxv.

SENDALL, Bernard
1975   Portrayal of violence on television. 2nd interim report of the working party
Independent Broadcasting Authority

SENIOR, D.
See REDCLIFFE-MAUD, J. P., Lord

SENIOR, W. H.
1972   Survey of agriculture in Caithness and Shetland (special report No. 8)
Highlands and Islands Development Board

SEROTA OF HAMPSTEAD, Bee, Baroness
1977   Length of prison sentences. Interim report of the advisory council on the penal system
Home Office

Powers of the courts dependent on imprisonment. Report of the advisory council on the penal system
Home Office
1978   Sentences of imprisonment; a review of the maximum penalties. Report of the advisory council on the penal system
Home Office

SERVICE, M. J.
1970   Safety of seamen. Report of the steering committee
Board of Trade
1975   Discipline in the fishing industry. Report of the working group
D. of Trade
1978   Safety of seamen at work. Report of the steering committee
D. of Trade

SEYMOUR-URE, Colin
1977   Studies on the press (working paper No. 3)
Royal Commission on the Press

SHACKLETON, Edward Arthur Alexander, Lord
1978   Review of the operation of the Prevention of Terrorism (Temporary Provisions) Acts, 1974 and 1976
Session 1977-78 Cmnd. 7324 xxiii.

SHACKLETON, R. M.
1973   Geotechnics and crustal studies. Reort of the working party. *In* Research in the Geological Sciences. (Publications series ' B ' No. 7)
Natural Environment Research Council

SHAKESPEARE, Geoffrey H., Sir
1940   Reception of children overseas. Report of the inter-departmental committee
Session 1939-40 Cmd. 6213 v.
1941   Conditions in reception areas. Report by a committee
M. of Health

Medical personnel (priority) committee
1941   1st interim report
1942   2nd interim report
M. of Health

SHANKLAND, Grahame
1966   Expansion of Ipswich; designation proposals. Consultants' study of the town in its sub-region
M. of Housing and Local Government

SHANKLAND, Grahame *(continued)*

1968   Expansion of Ipswich; comparative cost. A supplementary report
        M. of Housing and Local Government

1969   Ipswich draft basic plan; consultants' proposals for the expanded town
        M. of Housing and Local Government

1977   Inner London, policies for dispersal and balance. Final report of the Lambeth inner area study
        D. of the Environment

SHANKS, J.

1965   Primary education in Scotland. Report of a committee
        Scottish Education D.

SHANKS, M. J.

1971   Japan; its motor industry and market. Results of a study of the Japanese motor industry and market. Motor Manufacturing Economic Development Committee
        N.E.D.O.

SHAPIRO, D.

1975   Libraries and their finance. Information for the working party on resources set up by the Library Advisory Council for England
        D. of Education and Science

SHARP, George

1974   The future organisation of river purification boards. Report of the sub-committee of the Scottish River Purification Advisory Committee
        Scottish Development D.

SHARP, J. B.

        See WILLIAMSON, T. B.

SHARP, N.

1977   Bird control units in the R.A.F. Final report to the bird impact research and development committee (report No. 5)
        M. of Defence

SHARP, P. G.

1973   Information about industrial emissions to the atmosphere. Report by a working party of the Clean Air Council
        D. of the Environment

SHARPE, E. A., Lady

1970   Transport planning; the men for the job. A report
        M. of Transport

1977   Dartmoor. A report of a public local inquiry, December 1975 and May 1976 into the continued use of Dartmoor by the Ministry of Defence for Training Purposes
        D. of the Environment

SHARPE, Reginald T., Sir

1954   British Honduras. Report of an inquiry into allegations of contacts between People's United Party and Guatemala
        Session 1953-54 Cmd. 9139 x.

1955   Minor offences. Report of the departmental committee on the summary trial of minor offences
        Session 1955-56 Cmd. 9524 xxiii.

SHARPLES, G. B.

1944   Sound insulation and acoustics. Report of the acoustics committee of the Building Research Board of the Department of Scientific and Industrial Research (post-war building studies No. 14)
        M. of Works

SHAW, C. J. D.

        See KILBRANDON, C. J. D., Lord
        CAMERON, J., Lord

SHAW, R.

1977   Leisure and the quality of life. The report of a central steering group on four local experiments
        Vol. 1: Report
        Vol. 2: Research papers
        D. of the Environment

SHAW, Robert MacDonald

1969   The fluoridation studies in the U.K. and the results achieved after eleven years. A report of the committee on research into fluoridation. (Reports on public health and medical subjects No. 122)
        D. of Health and Social Security

SHAWCROSS, W. Hartley

1945   The rehabilitation of the catering industry. Report on an inquiry by the catering wages commission
        M. of Labour

1944   Existing methods of regulating the remuneration and conditions of employment of workers employed by the Crown in catering undertakings. Report on an inquiry by the catering wages commission
        M. of Labour

        Catering wages. Report of the catering wages commission on the recommendation for the establishment of a wages board for industrial catering, and correspondence
        Session 1943-44 Cmd. 6509 iii.

1962   Royal Commission on the Press. Report
        Session 1961-62 Cmnd. 1811 xxi.

SHEARER, I. H.

        See AVONSIDE, I. H., Lord

SHEAF, Patrick

1972   Local authority/private enterprise partnership schemes. Report of the working party
        D. of the Environment

SHEIL, C. L.

1957   Supreme court of Northern Ireland. Report of the Committee
        Session 1956-57 Cmnd. 227 xix.

SHELDON, Wilfrid P. H., Sir

1967   Child welfare centres. Report by a sub-committee of the standing medical advisory committee. Central Health Services Council
        M. of Health

1971   Special care for babies. Report of the expert group. (Reports on public health and medical subjects No. 127)
        D. of Health and Social Security

SHEPHARD, C. Y.

1944   The sugar industry of Fiji. Report. (Colonial No. 188)
        Colonial Office

SHEPHEARD, Victor G., Sir

1956   Structural steel. Admiralty advisory committee report No. P. 1. Brittle fracture research in the U.K.
Admiralty

See also SIMS, A. J., Sir

SHERIFF, P.

1976   Career patterns in the higher civil service. (Civil service studies, No. 2)
Civil Service D.

SHERRARD, Michael

1977   London Capital Group, Ltd. (formerly British Bangladesh Trust, Ltd.). Report of investigations under the Companies Act
D. of Trade

1978   Normansfield Hospital. Report of the committee of inquiry
Session 1978-79 Cmnd. 7357

SHEWAN, J. M.

1975   Research in aquatic microbiology. Report of the working party (publications series 'B' No. 11)

SHIMMIN, A. N.

1946   Industrial conditions in the cutlery trade. Report by the cutlery wages council (G.B.)
M. of Labour and National Service

1959   Catering wages commission. Final report
Session 1958-59 HC. 277 ix.

SHIPP, P. J.

1972   A study of the statistics relating to safety and health at work. Committee on safety and health at work
D. of Health and Social Security

SHOTTON, F. W.

1973   Geochronology and isotope geology. Report of the working party. *In* Research in the geological sciences. (Publications series 'B' No. 7)
Natural Environment Research Council

SHUFFREY, R. F. D.

1973   Rank structure of the fire service. Report of the joint working party
Scottish Home and Health D.

Higher training in the fire service. Report of the working party
Scottish Home and Health D.

SIBERRY, J. W. M.

1975   Fourth television service in Wales. Report of the working party
Session 1975-76 Cmnd. 6290 viii.

SIDWELL, Norman

1970   The cost of private building in Scotland. A report for the Scottish housing advisory committee
Scottish Development D.

SILK, S. J.

1970   Fumes from welding and flame cutting. Report on the shipbuilding and ship-repairing industry
D. of Employment and Productivity

SILSOE, A. Malcolm Trustram, Lord

Building apprenticeship and training council
1943   1st report
1944   2nd report
1946   3rd report
M. of Works

1947   War damage commission. Report regarding the amount of value payments
Treasury

Local Government Boundary Commission. Report for 1947
Session 1947-48 HC. 86 xiii.

1951   Scales of salaries. Teachers in primary and secondary schools maintained by local education authorities, England and Wales, 1951. Report of the Burnham committee
M. of Education

Scales of Salaries. Teaching staff of farm institutes and for teachers of agricultural (including horticultural) subjects, England and Wales, 1951
M. of Education

Scales of salaries. Teaching staff of training colleges, England and Wales, 1951. Report of the committee of representative of associations of local education authorities, training college authorities and of the Association of Teachers in Colleges and Departments of Education
M. of Education

Scales of salaries. Teachers in establishments for further education including technical and commercial colleges and institutes, art colleges and schools, England and Wales, 1951. Report of the Burnham committee
M. of Education

1955   Crown lands. Report of the committee
Session 1955-56 Cmd. 9483 xiii.

1957   Future of Regent's Park Terraces. Statement by the Crown Estate Commissioners
Crown Estate Commissioners

1959   Future of the Regent's Park Terraces. 2nd statement by the Crown Estate Commissioners
Crown Estate Commissioners

1961   Future of Carlton House Terrace. Statement by the Crown Estate Commissioners
Crown Estate Commissioners

1962   Future of Regent's Park Terraces. 3rd statement by the Crown Estate Commissioners
Crown Estate Commissioners

SIMES, C. Erskine W.

1952   Rating of site values. Report of the committee of inquiry
M. of Housing and Local Government

1956   Boundary Commission for England. Report with respect to the areas comprised in the constituencies in the City of Nottingham; and the constituencies of Colchester; Maldon; Saffron Walden; Blackpool North; North Fylde; Eccles; Farnworth; Kingston-upon-Hull East; Bridlington; Bradford North; and Shipley
Session 1955-56 HC. 227 xi.

SIMMONDS, Oliver E., Sir

Committee on brick industry
1941   1st report
1942   2nd report
1942   3rd report and appendix VII: preliminary consideration of firing of common bricks
M. of Works

SIMON, J. A., Viscount

1945   Royal Commission on population. Statement
Royal Commission on Population

SIMON OF WYTHENSHAWE, E. D., Lord

1948   Distribution of building materials and components. Report of the committee of inquiry
M. of Works

SIMONDS, G. T., Viscount

1941   Charges made in connection with the construction of militia camps. Report
Session 1940-41 Cmd. 6271 v.

1960   Powers of subpœna of disciplinary tribunals. Report of the departmental committee
Session 1959-60 Cmnd. 1033 xvii.

SIMPSON, E. E.

1976   Play for children in hospital. Report of the expert group
D. of Health and Social Security

SIMPSON, Harry

1976   Housing in multi-racial areas. Report of a working party of housing directors
Community Relations Commission

SIMPSON, W. J.

1977   Selected written evidence submitted to the advisory committee on asbestos, 1976-77
Health and Safety Commission

1978   Asbestos. Work on thermal and acoustic insulation and sprayed coatings. First report of the advisory committee
Health and Safety Commission

    Asbestos. Measurement and monitoring of asbestos in air. 2nd report of the advisory committee
Health and Safety Commission

SIMS, Alfred J., Sir

    Admiralty advisory committee on structural steel

1960   2nd report: a comparison of transition temperatures determined by small- and large-scale tests on five steels (report No. P.2)

1962   3rd report: brittle fracture in steel. Proceedings of a conference held in the engineering department, Cambridge, 28-30 September 1959 (report No. P.3)
4th report: a comparison of transition temperatures determined by small-scale and wide-plate tests on as rolled and normalized plates from the same cast of steel (report No. P.4)
Admiralty

1954   Second review of current research work in the U.K. on brittle fracture of mild steel. Navy Department Advisory Committee on Structural Steel (report No. P.5)
M. of Defence
See also SHEPHEARD, V. G., Sir

SIMS, G. D.

1971   Qualified manpower in the electronics industry; a preliminary report of the working group on scientific and technological manpower. Electronics Economic Development Committee
N.E.D.O.

SINCLAIR OF CLEEVE, R. J., Lord

1958   Financial structure of the Colonial Development Corporation. Report of the committee of inquiry
Session 1958-59 Cmnd. 786 x.

SINCLAIR, Leonard, Sir

1958   Inland telegraph service. Report of the advisory committee
Post Office

SINCLAIR, Susan

1963   The child care service at work. Report prepared for the Scottish Advisory Council on Child Care
Scottish Education D.

SINGH, Ghanshyam

1959   Cambodia. 7th interim report of the international commission for supervision and control in Cambodia for 1958. 31 August, 1959, Phnom Penh
Session 1959-60 Cmnd. 887 xxxvi.

SINGLETON, A. K. J.

1978   Communication system of physics. Final report of the physics information review committee (R&D report No. 5386)
British Library

SINGLETON, J. E.

1946   European Jewry and Palestine. Report of the Anglo-American committee of inquiry regarding the problems of European Jewry and Palestine, 20 April, 1946, Lausanne
Session 1945-46 Cmd. 6808 xxvi.

SINGLETON, Norman

1966   Appointed factory doctor service. Report by a sub-committee of the Industrial Health Advisory Committee
M. of Labour

1967   Dismissal procedures. Report of a committee of the National Joint Advisory Council
M. of Labour

SISSON, C. H.

1972   Code of practice for reducing the exposure of employed persons to noise. Prepared by the Industrial Health Advisory Committee's sub-committee
D. of the Environment

SIZER, John

1977   Life-cycle costing in the management of assets, a practical guide. Working party report
D. of Industry

SKEFFINGTON, Arthur M.

1969   People and planning. Report of the committee on public participation in planning
M. of Housing and Local Government

SKELHORN, Norman J., Sir

1959   Hide & Co. Ltd. Report. Interim and final reports of investigation under the Companies Act
Board of Trade

1964   Report of inquiry into the action of the Metropolitan Police in relation to the case of Mr. Herman Woolf
Session 1963-64 Cmnd. 2319 xviii

SKIMMINGS, W.

1976   Lonrho Ltd. Report of investigations under the Companies Act
D. of Trade

SKINNER, James B.

1972   Physical education in secondary schools. Report of the working party. (Curriculum paper No. 12)
Scottish Education D.

SKYRME, W. T. C.

1960   Expenses of legal proceedings against justices and clerks. Report of the working party
Home Office

SLADE, Gerald

1948   Medical partnerships. Report of the legal committee
Session 1948-49 Cmd. 7565 xvii.

SLIMMINGS, W. K. M.

1972   Treatment of marketing and selling expenses. Interim report on the review including the supplementary report. Review Board for Government Contracts
Treasury

1974   Profit formula for non-competitive government contracts. Report on the general review. Review Board for Government Contracts
Treasury

1977   Profit formula for non-competitive government contracts. Report on the second general review Review Board for Government Contracts
Treasury

SMART, R.

1973   Transition from school to university. Report of a working party
Scottish Education D.

SMEED, R. J.

1964   Road pricing. Economic and technical possibilities. Report of a panel
M. of Transport

SMIETON, Mary, Dame

1955   Industrial accident prevention. Industrial safety sub-committee of the national joint advisory committee. Report
M. of Labour and National Service

1958   Disabled persons. 3rd report of the standing committee on the rehabilitation and resettlement of disabled persons
M. of Labour and National Service

SMITH, A. N. EXTON-
See EXTON-SMITH, A. N.

SMITH, A. R.

1976   Manpower planning in the civil service. (Civil service studies No. 3)
Civil Service D.

SMITH, Allan Chalmers, Sir

1955   Plan for a British Caribbean Federation. Report of the judicial commission
Session 1955-56 Cmd. 9620 xii.

SMITH, Anthony D.

1972   Measurement and interpretation of service output charges
N.E.D.O.

SMITH, Cyril

1978   Public disorder and sporting events. Report by a joint panel Sports Council *and* Social Science Research Council

SMITH, F. NEWSON-, Sir
See NEWSON-SMITH, F., Sir

SMITH, G.

1975   Educational priority, vol. 4: EPA; the West Riding project
D. of Education and Science

SMITH, George

1977   Government against poverty? Liverpool community development project. Home Office, published by the Social Evaluation Unit, Oxford

SMITH, H. WILSON-, Sir
See WILSON-SMITH, H., Sir

SMITH, J. A. B.

1961   Model dairy byelaws. Report of the committee
D. of Health for Scotland

SMITH, J. C. C.

1975   Allocations to regions, 1976-77. First interim report of the resource allocation working party
D. of Health and Social Security

1976   Sharing resources for health in England. Report of the resource allocation working party
D. of Health and Social Security

SMITH, J. E.

1975   Estuaries research. Report of the working party. (Publications series 'B' No. 9)
Natural Environment Research Council

SMITH, P.

1974   Worker participation and collective bargaining in Europe. Commission on Industrial Relations. (Study No. 4)
D. of Employment

SMITH, Robin A.

1977   Scottish health authorities revenue equalisation. Report of the working party
Scottish Home and Health D.

SMITH, Sidney A., Sir

1953   Ageing population. Standing medical advisory committee. Scottish Health Services Council
D. of Health for Scotland

1955   Hospital endowments. Report of the hospital endowments commission
Session 1955-56 Cmd. 9516 xxi.

SMITH, T. D.

1966   Challenge of the changing north; a preliminary study. Northern Economic Planning Council
D. of Economic Affairs

SMITH, W. R. Verdon-, Sir
See VERDON-SMITH, W. R., Sir

SMOUT, D. A. L.

1975   Bernard Russell, Ltd. Report of investigations under the Companies Act
D. of Trade

Blanes, Ltd. (now named Black Arrow Group Ltd.). Report of investigations under the Companies Act
D. of Trade

SNELL, H., Lord

1941   Police widows' pensions. Departmental committee report
Session 1940-41 Cmd. 6312 iv.

SOLOMONIDIS, S.

1975   Modular artificial limbs. 1st report: below-knee systems
Scottish Home and Health D.

SOMERVELL OF HARROW, D. B., Lord

1952 Diplomatic immunity. Report on diplomatic immunity by an interdepartmental committee on state immunities. (Miscellaneous No. 1, 1952)
Session 1951-52 Cmd. 8460 xxx.

SORN, J. G., Lord

1944 The valuation and rating of hydro-electric under-takings in Scotland. 1st report of the committee appointed to inquire into certain aspects of the Scottish rating and valuation system
Session 1943-44 Cmd. 6526 iv.

Scottish rating system. Report of the committee appointed to inquire into (1) the effect of the rating system on the provision of houses and (2) liability for rates in respect of empty or unused premises
Session 1944-45 Cmd. 6595 v.

1954 Scottish valuation and rating committee report
Session 1953-54 Cmd. 9244 xviii.

1958 Local contributions to the Scottish universities. Report of the special committee
Session 1958-59 Cmnd. 640 xix.

1959 Proceedings of the tribunal appointed to inquiry into the allegations of assault on John Waters. Verbatim record of evidence heard by the tribunal
Scottish Home D.

Report of the tribunal appointed to inquire into the allegation of assault on John Waters
Session 1958-59 Cmnd. 718 xvi.

SORSBY, Arnold

1953 Causes of blindness in England, 1948-50. Report
M. of Health

1956 Blindness in England, 1951-54. Report
M. of Health

SOULBURY, H., Lord

1945 Ceylon. Commission on constitutional reform. Report
Session 1945-46 Cmd. 6677 x.

Teachers' salaries. Scales of salaries for teachers in primary and secondary schools, England and Wales. Report of the Burnham committee
M. of Education

Scales of salaries for teachers in technical colleges and institutes, art colleges and schools, England and Wales. Report of the Burnham committee
M. of Education

1946 Scales of salaries for teaching staff of farm institutes and for teachers of agricultural (including horticultural) subjects, England and Wales. Report of the committee
M. of Education

SOWTON, C. W.

1973 Television advisory committee, 1972. Papers of the technical sub-committee
M. of Posts and Telecommunications

SPAIN, Stephen W.

1971 Nuclear ship study. Report
D. of Trade and Industry

SPALTON, L. M.

See RIGBY, N. L.

SPENCE, James, Sir

1952 Treatment of acute dehydration in infants. Report by a working team appointed and advised by the committee on acute infections in infancy (memoranda No. 26)
Medical Research Council

SPENCER, John Carrington

1976 Army welfare inquiry committee. Report
M. of Defence

SPENS, Will P., Lord

1946 Remuneration of general practitioners. Report of the interdepartmental committee
Session 1945-46 Cmd. 6810 xii.

1948 Remuneration of general dental practitioners. Report of the interdepartmental committee
Session 1947-48 Cmd. 7402 xi.

1951 Maternity benefit. Report of the national insurance advisory committee
Session 1951-52 Cmd. 8446 xv.

1948 Remuneration of consultants and specialists. Report of the interdepartmental committee
Session 1947-48 Cmd. 7420 xi.

1952 Entertainment industry. Report of the National Insurance Advisory Committee on the classification of actors, variety artists and other persons in the entertainment industry
Session 1951-52 Cmd. 8549 xv.

Seasonal workers. Report of the National Insurance Advisory Committee on the review of the National Insurance (Seasonal Workers) Regulations
Session 1951-52 Cmd. 8558 xv.

Hospital in-patients. Report of the National Insurance Advisory Committee on the review of certain amounts payable to hospital in-patients
Session 1951-52 Cmd. 8600 xv.

National Insurance (Married Women) Amendment Regulations, draft. Report of the National Insurance Advisory Committee
Session 1953-54 HC. 49 xvi.

1953 Credits for training courses. Report of the National Insurance Advisory Committee on credits for courses of full-time training
Session 1952-53 Cmd. 8860 xiv.

Availability question. Report of the National Insurance Advisory Committee
Session 1952-53 Cmd. 8894 xiv.

National Insurance (Contributions) Amendment (No. 2) Regulations, 1953. Report of the National Insurance Advisory Committee
Session 1952-53 HC. 298 xiv.

National Insurance (Local Advisory Committees) Amendment Regulations, 1953. Report of the National Insurance Advisory Committee
Session 1952-53 HC. 294 xiv.

1954 National Insurance (Maternity Benefit and Miscellaneous Provisions) Regulations, 1954. Report of the National Insurance Advisory Committee
Session 1953-54 HC. 97 xvi.

National Insurance (Classification) Amendment Regulations, 1954. Report of the National Insurance Advisory Committee
Session 1953-54 HC. 166 xvi.

National Insurance (Unemployment and Sickness Benefit) Amendment Regulations, 1955. National Insurance Advisory Committee
Session 1954-55 HC. 40 vi.

National Insurance (Unemployment and Sickness Benefit) Amendment Regulations, 1954. Report of the National Insurance Advisory Committee
Session 1953-54 HC. 68 xvi.

1955 Liability for contributions of persons with small incomes. Report of the National Insurance Advisory Committee
Session 1954-55 Cmd. 9432 vi.

National Insurance (Maternity Benefit and Miscellaneous Provisions) Amendment Regulations, 1955. Report of the National Insurance Advisory Committee
Session 1954-55 HC. 103 vi.

SPENS, Will P., Lord (*continued*)

National Insurance (Increase of Benefit and Miscellaneous Provisions) Regulations, 1955. Report of the National Insurance Advisory Committee
Session 1954-55 HC. 102 vi.

National Insurance (Residence and Persons Abroad) Amendment Regulations, 1955. Report of the National Insurance Advisory Committee
Session 1955-56 HC. 28 xxii.

National Insurance (Contributions) Amendment Regulations, 1955. Report of the National Insurance Advisory Committee
Session 1955-56 HC. 96 xxii.

Benefit for very short spells of unemployment or sickness. Report of the National Insurance Advisory Committee
Session 1955-56 Cmnd. 9609 xxii.

National Insurance (Determination of Claims and Questions) Amendment Regulations, 1955. Report of the National Insurance Advisory Committee
Session 1955-56 HC. 131 xxii.

1956   Widows' Benefits. Report of the National Insurance Advisory Committee
Session 1955-56 Cmd. 9684 xxii.

National Insurance (Unemployment and Sickness Benefit) Amendment Regulations, 1956. Report of the National Insurance Advisory Committee
Session 1955-56 HC. 202 xxii.

Question of earnings limits for benefits. Report of the National Insurance Advisory Committee
Session 1955-56 Cmd. 9752 xxii.

Contribution conditions and credit provisions. Report of the National Insurance Advisory Committee
Session 1955-56 Cmd. 9854 xxii.

Dependency provisions. Report of the National Insurance Advisory Committee
Session 1955-56 Cmd. 9855 xxii.

Death Grants. Report of the National Insurance Advisory Committee
Session 1956-57 Cmnd. 33 xv.

National Insurance (Contributions) Amendment Regulations, 1956; National Insurance (Residence and Persons Abroad) Amendment Regulations, 1956. Report of the National Insurance Advisory Committee
Session 1956-57 HC. 29 xv.

National Insurance (New Entrants Transitional) Amendment Regulations, 1957. Report of the National Insurance Advisory Committee
Session 1956-57 HC. 91 xv.

SQUIRE, J. R.
1971   Hypogammaglobulinaemia in the U.K. MRC working party report. (Special report series No. 910)
Medical Research Council

STABLE, R. O. C.
1972   Pergamon Press, Ltd. Further interim report of investigations under the Companies Act
D. of Trade and Industry

1973   Maxwell Scientific International (Distribution Services) Ltd., Robert Maxwell & Co. Ltd., and final report of investigations under the Companies Act on Pergamon Press Ltd.
D. of Trade and Industry

STAINTON, John, Sir
1951   Local land charges. Report of the committee
Session 1951-52 Cmd. 8440 xvi.

STAMP, A. Maxwell
1970   London taxicab trade. Report of the interdepartmental committee
Session 1970-71 Cmnd. 4483 li.

STANDEN, E. J. S.
1976   Kielder water, a report on possible land-based facilities for water recreation. Standing conference of the northern sport and recreation joint working party
Northern Sports Council

STANDEN, L. F.
1975   Discipline in the merchant navy. Report of the working group
D. of Trade

STANFORD, W. P.
1963   Basutoland constitutional commission. October 3, 1963, Maseru, Basutoland. Report
Basutoland Council

STANHOPE, J. R., Earl
1948   The war years and after. 3rd report of the Standing Commission on Museums and Galleries
Standing Commission on Museums and Galleries

STANIER, William A., Sir
1949   Technical and scientific register. Present and future supply and demand for persons with professional qualifications in mechanical engineering. Mechanical engineers' panel of the engineering sub-committee. Report
M. of Labour and National Service

STANLEY, Ronald Arthur Terence
1978   Rajawella Produce Holdings, Ltd. Report of investigations under the Companies Act
D. of Trade

STANLEY-PRICE, P.
1965   Report of inquiry in respect of the objections to the proposed compulsory amalgamation of the police areas of the County of Northamptonshire and the County Borough of Northampton
Session 1964-65 Cmnd. 2593 xxi.

STARITT, J.
1974   Report of the actions of police officers concerned with the case of Kenneth Joseph Lennou
Session 1974 HC. 351 xiv.

STARK, Thomas
1977   The distribution of income in eight countries background paper No. 4)
Royal Commission on the Distribution of Income and Wealth

START, D.
1977   International price competitiveness, man-price factors and export performance
N.E.D.O.

STEAD, G.
1956   Anaesthetic explosions, including safety code for equipment and installation. Report of a working party
M. of Health

STEDMAN, Phyllis, Baroness
1978   Pop festivals and their problems. 2nd report of the working group
D. of the Environment
See also STEVENSON, D.

STEEL, J.
1951   Reception and welfare of in-patients at hospitals. Report by a sub-committee of the standing advisory committee on hospital and specialist services
D. of Health for Scotland

STEEL, J. L. S., Sir

1953   Industrial development in Jamaica, Trinidad, Barbados and British Guiana. Report of the mission of U.K. industrialists. (Colonial No. 294)
Colonial Office

STEELE, A. J.

1975   Modern language courses for non-certificate pupils. A document for discussion. Scottish central committee for modern languages
Scottish Education D.

STEERS, James Alfred

1967   Coastal preservation and development; a study of the coastline of England and Wales. The coasts of Hampshire and the Isle of Wight. Report of the regional coastal conference held in Southampton on 30 June 1966
National Parks Commission

Coastal preservation and development; the coasts of Kent and Sussex. Report of the regional coastal conference held in London on 27 May 1967
National Parks Commission

Coastal preservation and development; a study of the coastline of England and Wales. The coasts of south-west England. Report of the regional coastal conference held in Exeter on 22 July 1966
National Parks Commission

1968   Coastal preservation and development; studies of the coastline of England and Wales. Coasts of East Anglia. Report of the regional coastal conference held at Ipswich on 16 March 1967
Countryside Commission

Coastal preservation and development; studies of the coastline of England and Wales. Coasts of North-East England. Report of the regional coastal conference held at Newcastle upon Tyne on 12 January 1967
Countryside Commission

Coastal preservation and development; studies of the coastline of England and Wales. Coasts of North Wales. Report of the regional coastal conference held at Dolgellau on 15 November 1966
Countryside Commission

Coastal preservation and development; studies of the coastline of England and Wales. Coasts of north-west England. Report of the coastal conference held in Preston on 15 December 1966
Countryside Commission

The coasts of South Wales and the Severn Estuary. Reports of the regional coastal conference held in Cardiff on 18 October 1966
Countryside Commission

Coastal preservation and development; studies of the coastline of England and Wales. Coasts of Yorkshire and Lincolnshire. Report of the regional coastal conference held at York on 14 February 1967
Countryside Commission

STEINBERG, J.

1972   The eleven billion Mark market, a study of the market for ladies' outerwear in West Germany. Clothing Economic Development Committee
N.E.D.O.

STEVENS, Roger, Sir

1970   Yorkshire and Humberside regional strategy. Yorkshire and Humberside Economic Planning Council
M. of Housing and Local Government

STEVENS, R.

1976   Planning control over mineral working. Report of the committee
D. of the Environment

STEVENSON, Dennistoun

1972   Fifty million volunteers. A report on the role of voluntary organisation and youth in the environment
D. of the Environment

1973   Pop festivals. Report and code of practice by the advisory committee
D. of the Environment

1976   Free festivals. 1st report of the working group on pop festivals
D. of the Environment
See also STEDMAN, P.

STEVENSON, Matthew, Sir

1972   Crown Agents. Report of the advisory committee
Session 1977-78 HC. 50 viii.

STEWART, F.

1962   Relations between education authorities and teachers. Report of the working party on appointments to teaching posts, conditions of tenure of these posts, and arrangements for consultation between education authorities and teachers
Scottish Education D.

STEWART, F. O.

1951   Police representative organisations and negotiating machinery. Report of the Scottish Police Council
Scottish Home D.

STEWART, Frederick, Sir

1974   Advisory board for the research councils. 1st report
Session 1974 Cmnd. 5633 iv.

STEWART, J. D.

1973   Aspects of public library management. Report of a working party of the Library Advisory Council for England. (Library information series No. 3)
D. of Education and Science

STEWART, J. F.

1962   Relations between education authorities and teachers. Report of the working party on appointments to teaching posts, conditions of tenure of these posts, and arrangements for consultation between education authorities and teachers
Scottish Education D.

STEWART, J. G.

1962   Workshops for the blind. Report of the working party
M. of Labour

STEWART, John, Sir

1956   Report of a court of inquiry into the causes and circumstances of a dispute between the Iron and Steel Trades Employers' Association and the National Joint Trade Unions' Craftsmen's Iron and Steel Committee
Session 1955-56 Cmd. 9843 xxix.

STEWART, Muriel

1972   Careers education in the 1970s. Report of the working party on the transition from school to work. (Working paper No. 40)
Schools Council

STEWART, T. GRAINGER-
See GRAINGER-STEWART, T.

STEWART, William A. C.

1971   Care and treatment in a planned environment, a report on the community homes project. Advisory council on child care
Home Office

STIMPSON, D. E.

1976   Non-teaching staff in secondary schools. Report of a working party
Scottish Education D.

STOCKDALE, F. A.

1972   Adoption of children. Report of the departmental committee
Session 1971-72 Cmnd. 5107 xxxviii.

STOCKDALE, Frank, Sir

1944   West Indian conference held in Barbados, 21-30 March, 1944. Report. (Colonial No. 187)
Colonial Office

STOCKS, M. D., Baroness

1948   Midwives. Report of the working party
M. of Health

STOKES, F. H.

1978   How flexible is construction? A study of resources and participants in the construction process, by the Structural Analysis Committee
N.E.D.O.

STOLLERY, J. L.

1978   The aerodynamic problems of advanced ground transport. A report by the aerodynamics working group of the A.G.T. panel
Science Research Council

STONE, Leonard, Sir

1958   Hallmarking. Report of the departmental committee
Session 1958-59 Cmnd. 663 xv.

STONHAM, V. J., Lord

1969   Constitutional relationship between the Isle of Man and the U.K. Report of the joint working party
Home Office

STOUT, David

1977   International price competitiveness, non-price factors and export performance
N.E.D.O.

STOUT, H. P.

1972   Aircraft noise; selection of runway sites for Maplin Airport. Report of the research sub-committee
Noise Advisory Council

1974   Noise units. Report by a working party
Noise Advisory Council

        Aircraft engine noise research. Report of the Noise Advisory Council

STRACHAN, J. P, Lord

1959   Civil jury trial in Scotland. Report by a committee
Session 1959-60 Cmnd. 851 xvii.

STRAIGHT, Whitney W.

1947   Private flying. Preliminary report of the special advisory committee
M. of Civil Aviation

STRAUSS, G. R.

1947   Road safety. Final report of the committee
M. of Transport

        See also CALLAGHAN, J.
NOEL-BAKER, P.

STREATFIELD, G. H. B., Sir

1960   Business of the criminal courts. Report of the interdepartmental committee
Session 1960-61 Cmnd. 1289 xiii.

STRUTT, H. A., Sir

1950   Cremation committee report of the interdepartmental committee
Session 1950 Cmd. 8009 viii.

STRUTT, Nigel E., Sir

1970   Modern farming and the soil. Report of the agricultural advisory council on soil structure and soil fertility
M. of Agriculture, Fisheries and Food

1977   Agriculture into the 1980s. Resources and strategy. Report of the agricultural strategy group of the Agriculture Economic Development Committee
N.E.D.O.

        Agricultural exports; the role of the breed societies and their national associations
Advisory Council for Agriculture and Horticulture in England and Wales

1978   Agricultural exports; credit and finance
Advisory Council for Agriculture and Horticulture in England and Wales

        Agriculture and the countryside
Advisory Council for Agriculture and Horticulture in England and Wales

STUART-HARRIS, Charles

1977   Whooping cough vaccination. Review of the evidence by the joint committee on vaccination and immunisation
D. of Health and Social Security

SUAN, R. H.
        See PRICE, C.

SUDALE, E. W.

1976   Curricula for non-participant 16-19s. Report by H.M. Inspectorate working party
D. of Education and Science

SUMMERFIELD, Arthur

1968   Psychologists in education services. The report of a working party
D. of Education and Science

SUMMERS, Henry Forbes

1967   Housing role of the Greater London Council within London. 1st report of the standing working party on London housing
M. of Housing and Local Government

SUMMERSIDE, Pat

1977   Grass fleece experiment; a report of monitoring at Crystal Palace national Sports centre and Finsbury Park. (Study No. 12)
Sports Council

SUMNER, James

1971 Refuse disposal. Report of the working party
D. of the Environment

1973 Research into refuse collection, storage and disposal. 1st report of the standing committee
D. of the Environment

1974 Disposal of awkward household wastes. Report of the working group
D. of the Environment

1978 Co-operative programme of research on the behaviour of hazardous wastes in landfill sites. Final report of the policy review committee
D. of the Environment

SUSSMAN, N. F.

1970 Shirts in the seventies; a study of the strategic future of the U.K. shirt industry, prepared for the Clothing Industry Economic Development Committee
N.E.D.O.

SUTHERLAND, Gordon B. B. M., Sir

1967 Liaison between universities and government research establishments. Report of the working party of the Council for Scientific Policy
Session 1966-67 Cmnd. 3222 xlviii.

SUTHERLAND, John D., Sir

1943 National forest park committee report. Glentrool
Forestry Commission

SUTTON, A. S.

1972 A study of the statistics relating to safety and health at work. Committee on safety and health at work research paper
D. of Health and Social Security

SUTTON, Graham, Sir

1972 Research in the atmospheric sciences. Report of the working party (publication series 'B' No. 4)
Natural Environment Research Council

SUTTON, S. W. P. Foster, Sir
See FOSTER-SUTTON, S. W. P., Sir

SWALLOW, William, Sir

1967 Your manpower; a practical guide to the manpower statistics of the hotel and catering industry. Hotels and Catering Economic Development Committee
N.E.D.O.

Visitors to Britain. Hotels and Catering Economic Development Committee
N.E.D.O.

1969 Staff turnover; study by the Tavistock Institute of Human Relations for the Hotels and Catering Economic Development Committee
N.E.D.O.
See also RAVENHILL, A. P.

SWAN, Kenneth R., Sir

Patents and Designs Acts
1945   1st interim report of the departmental committee
Session 1944-45 Cmd. 6618 v.
1946   2nd interim report
Session 1945-46 Cmd. 6789 xiv.
1947   Final report
Session 1946-47 Cmd. 7206 xiii.

SWANN, Michael Meredith

1966 Manpower parameters for scientific growth. Interim report of the working group of the committee on manpower resources for science and technology
Session 1966-67 Cmnd. 3102 xxxix.

1968 The flow into employment of scientists, engineers and technologists. Report of the working group on manpower for scientific growth of the committee on manpower resources for science and technology
Session 1967-68 Cmnd. 3760 xxv.

1969 Use of antibiotics in animal husbandry and veterinary medicine. Report of the joint committee
Session 1969-70 Cmnd. 4190 v.

1975 Veterinary profession. Report of the committee of inquiry, and appendices. 2 vols.
Session 1974-75 Cmnd. 6143 vi.

SWANN, W. B.

1972 Survey of agriculture in Caithness and Shetland. (Special report No. 8)
Highlands and Islands Development Board

SWANWICK, G. R., Sir

1963 Sheffield police appeal inquiry report
Session 1963-64 Cmnd. 2176 xviii.

SWEETT, C. and Partners
See BUCHANAN, C. D.

SWIFT, A.

1975 Squash in the Eastern region, a re-appraisal by the liaison group
Sports Council, Eastern Region

SWIFT, S.
See GENTLEMAN, H.

SWINGLER, Stephen

1968 London Transport joint review directing group. Report. *In:* annex to Transport in London
Session 1967-68 Cmnd. 3686 xxxix.

SWISS, R. G.

1967 Dental anæsthesia. Report of a joint sub-committee of the standing dental and medical advisory committees. Central Health Services Council
M. of Health

1968 Dental technicians. Report of a sub-committee of the standing dental advisory committee. Central Health Services Council
M. of Health

TAMARI, M.

1972 A postal questionaire survey of small firms; an analysis of financial data. (Committee of inquiry on small firms research report, No. 16)
D. of Trade and Industry

TANNER, M F.

1977 Potential of towpaths as waterside footpaths. (Research report No. 1)
Water Space Amenity Commission

Water recreation in country parks. (Research report No. 2)
Water Space Amenity Commission

The recreational use of water supply reservoirs in England and Wales. (Research report No. 3)
Water Space Amenity Commission

Permit sailing on enclosed waters. (Research report No. 4)
Water Space Amenity Commission

TATCHELL, Sydney

1944   The use of standards in building. 1st progress report of the standards committee
M. of Works

Plumbing. Report of the plumbing committee of the Building Research Board of the Department of Scientific and Industrial Research. (Post-war building studies No. 4)
M. of Works

1947   Domestic drainage. The plumbing committee of the Building Research Board. 2nd report. (Post-war building studies No. 26)
M. of Works

TAVERNE, Dick

1967   Police manpower, equipment and efficiency. Reports of three working parties
Home Office

Recruitment of people with higher educational qualifications into the police service. Report of a working party
Home Office

TAYLOR, C. W. G.

1945   Police warnings. Report by the Scottish advisory council on the treatment and rehabilitation of offenders
Scottish Office

1946   Probation with a condition of residence (as it affects children and young persons). Report by the Scottish advisory council on the treatment and rehabilitation of offenders
Scottish Office

Remand homes. Report by the Scottish advisory council on the treatment and rehabilitation of offenders
Scottish Home D.

Approved schools. Report by the Scottish advisory council on the treatment and rehabilitation of offenders
Scottish Education D.

1947   The Scottish borstal system. Report by the Scottish advisory council on the treatment and rehabilitation of offenders
Scottish Home D.

1948   Psycho-therapeutic treatment of certain offenders with special reference to the case of persons convicted of sexual and unnatural offences. Report of the Scottish advisory council on the treatment and rehabilitation of offenders
Scottish Home D.

1949   The Scottish prison system. Report by the Scottish Advisory Council on the treatment and rehabilitation of offenders
Scottish Home D.

TAYLOR, Carol

1975   World invisible trade
Committee on Invisible Trade

TAYLOR, J.

1975   Water-ski-ing in the eastern region. Report by the study group
Sports Council, Eastern Region

TAYLOR, J., & SONS
    See BUCHANAN, C. D.

TAYLOR, R. R.

1973   Local inquiry in relation to the implementation by Dunfirmline Town Council of parts II and IV of the Housing (Financial Provisions) (Scotland) Act, 1972. Report
Scottish Development D.

TAYLOR, Tom

1977   New partnership for our schools. Report of the committee of inquiry
D. of Education and Science

TAYLOR, Thomas M., Sir

    Scottish Nurses' salaries committee
1943   Interim report
        Session 1942-43 Cmd. 6425 v.
        2nd report
        Session 1942-43 Cmd. 6439 iv.
        3rd report (supplement to 2nd report)
        Session 1943-44 Cmd. 6505 iv.
1943   Mental nurses. Sub-committee of the Scottish Nurses' salaries committee report
        Session 1943-44 Cmd. 6488 xiv.
        Notes on the Taylor report
        D. of Health for Scotland
1945   4th report
        Session 1945-46 Cmd. 6684 xiv.

1947   Tenure of shop premises in Scotland. Committee of inquiry report
Session 1947-48 Cmnd. 7285 xvi.

1950   Educational endowments in Scotland. Report of the committee
Scottish Education D.

1954   Crofting conditions. Report of the commission of inquiry
Session 1953-54 Cmnd. 9091 viii.

TAYLOR, W.

1950   Employment of blind persons. Report of the working party
M. of Labour and National Service

TAYLOR, W. R.

1972   Local government reform; the water service in Scotland. Report of the Scottish water advisory committee
Scottish Development D.

TAYLOR, William Ling, Sir

    Advisory committee on forestry
1955   2nd report
1956   3rd report
1960   4th report: trees in Kensington Gardens
        M. of Works
1962   5th report: Trees in Richmond Park
1963   6th report: Trees in Hampton Court and Bushy Parks
1964   7th report: Trees in Greenwich Park
        M. of Public Building and Works

TEAGLE, W. G.

1978   The endless village; wildlife of Birmingham, Dudley, Sandwell, Walsall and Wolverhampton
Nature Conservancy Council

TEMPLE, William, Archbishop of Canterbury, 1942-1945

1942   Loans (Postponement of Repayment) Measure. 86th report of the Ecclesiastical Committee
Session 1941-42 HC. 38 iv; HL. 101

New Parishes Measure. 87th report of the Ecclesiastical Committee
Session 1942-43 HC. 13 iv; HL. 6

Episcopal Endowments and Stipends Measure. 88th report of the Ecclesiastical Committee
Session 1942-43 HC. 15 iv; HL. 7

TEMPLE, William, Archbishop of Canterbury *(continued)*

1943   Diocesan Education Committee Measure. 89th report by the Ecclesiastical Committee
Session 1942-43 HC. 107 iv; HL. 50

TENBY, G., Viscount

1962   Report of the council on tribunals on the position of " third parties " at planning appeal inquiries
Session 1961-62 Cmnd. 1787 xxiv.

1964   Report of the council on tribunals on the award of costs at statutory inquiries (Scottish Committee)
Session 1963-64 Cmnd. 2471 x.

TENCH, Henry

1978   The disposal of sewage sludge by incineration. Report of the sub-committee. (Standing technical committee reports No. 14)
National Water Council

TENNANT, Mark, Sir

1965   Organisation of the scientific civil service. Report of a committee of review
Treasury

TENNENT, R. A.

1973   Maternity services. Report of the committee on integration of maternity work
Scottish Home and Health D.

TERRINGTON, H. M., Lord

1947   Report by a court of inquiry into the differences which have arisen between the two sides of the National Joint Industrial Council for the Road Haulage Industry on the trade union claims
Session 1946-47 Cmd. 7025 xiv.

1951   Air Transport Advisory Council. Report for 1951
Session 1951-52 HC. 164 viii.

1952   Post Office. Report of the Post Office (Departmental Classes) Recognition Committee
Session 1951-52 Cmd. 8470 xviii.

1960   Proposed experimental importation of Charollais cattle. Report of the committee
Session 1959-60 Cmnd. 1140 viii.

TERRY, J.

1976   The future of the British film industry. Report of the working party
Session 1975-76 Cmnd. 6372 xiii.

TETLEY, R. J.

1977   Training for health and safety at work; safety representatives and safety committees. Report of the working party
Food, Drink and Tobacco Industry Training Board

TEVIOT, C. J., Lord

Interdepartmental committee on dentistry
1944   Interim report
Session 1943-44 Cmd. 6565 iii.
1945   Final report
Session 1945-46 Cmd. 6727 xi.

THATCHER, A. R.

1975   Housing costs, weighting and other matters affecting the retail prices index. Report of the retail prices index advisory committee
Session 1974-75 Cmnd. 5905 xxxii.

THESIGER, Gerald A., Sir

1953   Road passenger services. Report of the committee on the licensing of road passenger services
M. of Transport and Civil Aviation

1971   Boundary Commission for England. Report with respect to the areas comprised in the constituencies of Abingdon; Newbury; Hertford and Stevenage; Hitchin; Bosworth; Loughborough; Leicester South; Harborough; Blyth; Hexham; Bromsgrove and Redditch; Stratford-on-Avon; Swindon; Devizes; Richmond upon Thames; Twickenham; Esher; Stockport North; Stockport South; Southwark, Bermondsey; Southwark, Dulwich; Southwark, Peckham; Bromley, Beckenham; Bromley, Chislehurst; Bromley, Orpington; and Bromley, Ravensbourne
Session 1971-72 HC. 1 vii.

1973   Boundary Commission for England. Report, January 1973
Session 1972-73 HC. 65 vi.

THOMAS, Albert Howard

1969   Cutlery Wages Council (Great Britain). Report of a commission of inquiry on a draft order to abolish the council
D. of Employment and Productivity

THOMAS, Bruce, Sir

1950   Transport tribunal. Proceedings of the permanent members of the consultative committee. Authorisation of increases in railway rates and charges for merchandise by goods and passenger train services, and in dock and canal charges
M. of Transport

Transport tribunal. Report of the permanent members sitting as a consultative committee. Applications of British Transport Commission for authorisation of additional charges in respect of railways, harbours, docks and piers, canals and inland waterways
M. of Transport

THOMAS, Charles John Howell, Sir

1943   Tithe redemption commission report
Session 1942-43 HC. 121 vi.

THOMAS, G. B.

1974   Career development in retail distribution. Labour turnover working party of the Distributive Trades Economic Development Committee
N.E.D.O.

THOMAS, George

1978   Boundary Commission for England. European Assembly constituencies
Session 1978-79 Cmnd. 7348

Boundary Commission for Wales. European Assembly constituencies
Session 1978-79 Cmnd. 7362

THOMAS, J.

1976   Guide to fostering practice. Working party report
D. of Health and Social Security

THOMAS, J. L.

1975   Retirement to the South West. Report by the South West Economic Planning Council
D. of the Environment

1976   Economic Survey of the tourist industry in the South West
South West Economic Planning Council

THOMAS, R. Lloyd

1969   Manual of principles of financial and management control for local authorities carrying out new construction by direct labour. Report by a working party
M. of Housing and Local Government

THOMAS, W. Rees
See REES-THOMAS, W.

THOMASON, George F.

1974 Report of the committee of inquiry into the dispute at Odhams (Watford) Ltd., involving the International Publishing Corporation, the Society of Lithographic Artists, Designers, Engravers and Process Workers and the National Graphical Association over the handling of photo-composed material
D. of Employment

1977 Industrial relations in the London fire service. Report of a committee of inquiry. (Report No. 8)
Advisory, Conciliation and Arbitration Service
See also MORTIMER, J. E.

THOMPSON, F. Longstreth
See also LONGSTRETH THOMPSON, F.

THOMPSON, Harold, Sir

1972 Scientific interchange. Report of the working group of the Council for Scientific Policy
Session 1971-72 Cmnd. 4843 xxxv.

THOMPSON, L. H.

1978 Control systems for the water industry. 1st interim report of the working party. (Standing technical committee reports No. 9)
National Water Council

THOMPSON, Robert H. S.

1970 Transport of nerve agents from Nancekuke to Porton and the disposal of effluent from nerve agent production. Report of a working party
M. of Defence, Army D.

THOMSON, Alexander, Lord

1968 Crime recording; the Scottish criminal statistics. Report of the departmental committee
Session 1967-68 Cmnd. 3705 xix.

1972 Criminal appeals in Scotland. 1st report by the committee
Session 1971-72 Cmnd. 5038 xx.

1975 Criminal appeals in Scotland. 2nd report by the committee
Session 1974-75 Cmnd. 6218 xv.

1977 Criminal appeals in Scotland. 3rd report by the committee
Session 1977-78 Cmnd. 7005 xix.

THOMSON, A. M. M.

1972 Data transmission: the future. The development of data transmission to meet future users' needs
N.E.D.O.

THOMSON, E. M. W.

1968 Physical education in the primary school. Report by a working party
Scottish Education D.

THOMSON, G. F.

1974 Odhams (Watford) Ltd. Report of the committee of inquiry into the dispute
D. of Employment

THORNEYCROFT OF DUNSTON, G. E. P., Baron

1970 SITPRO report 1970. Report of the U.K. committee for the simplification of international trade procedures
N.E.D.O.

THORNLEY, S. K.

1944 The painting of buildings. Report by a committee convened by the Paint Research Association. (Post-war building studies No. 5)
M. of Works

THORNTON, F. O.

1972 Medical engineering. Report of the bio-engineering study group, Scotland
Scottish Home and Health D.

THORNTON, H. G., Sir

1947 British Commonwealth scientific official conference, 1946. Specialist conference on culture collections of micro-organisms. Report of proceedings, London, August 1947
D. of Scientific and Industrial Research

THOROLD, Guy F., Sir

1961 Remuneration of milk distributors in the U.K. Report of the committee
Session 1961-62 Cmnd. 1597 xviii.

THORPE, H.

1969 Allotments. Report of the departmental committee of inquiry
Session 1968-69 Cmnd. 4166 xxxiii.

THRAVES, R. J.

1967 Teachers' experience of school based examining (English and physics). Report of the steering committee. (Examinations bulletin No. 15)
Schools Council

THRELFALL, P. M.

1972 Engineering drawing at GCE 'A' level. Report by the working group (Examinations bulletin No. 26)
Schools Council

THRELKELD, T. P.

1946 Ventilation, temperature, use of steam in humidification and lighting. Interim report of the joint advisory committee of the cotton industry
M. of Labour and National Service

1947 Cotton weaving. 1st report on spacing of machinery by the joint advisory committee of the cotton industry
M. of Labour and National Service

1948 Cotton weaving factories. Agreement concerning fencing of machinery, first aid and other safeguards, with appendices
M. of Labour and National Service

1951 Dust in card rooms. 2nd interim report of the joint advisory committee of the cotton industry
M. of Labour and National Service

Mule spinners' cancer. Joint advisory committee of the cotton industry. 2nd interim report
M. of Labour and National Service

1955 Cotton weaving factories. Agreement concerning fencing of machinery, first aid and other safeguards with appendices
M. of Labour and National Service

THURLOW, G. G.

1974 Grit and dust emissions. Report of the second working party
D. of the Environment

TINDALE, L. V. D.

1971 Market research in action. Guide for company management. Report by the Mechanical Engineering Economic Development Committee
N.E.D.O.

TIZARD, Henry, Sir

1949   Industrial productivity. 1st report of the committee
Session 1948-49 Cmd. 7665 xvii.

TIZARD, J.

1972   Children with specific reading difficulties. Report of the advisory committee on handicapped children
D. of Education and Science

TODD, A. R., Lord

1968   Royal Commission on Medical Education. Report
Session 1967-68 Cmnd. 3569 xxv.

TODD, Douglas

1972   The relative efficiency of small and large firms. (Committee of inquiry on small firms research report No. 18)
D. of Trade and Industry

TOMBS, Frank, Sir

1978   Pattern of domestic energy consumption and the growth of prices in relation to consumers' income and expenditure, 1966-77. (Energy commission paper No. 21)
Energy Commission

TOMLINSON, G.

1942   Rehabilitation and resettlement of disabled persons. Report of the interdepartmental committee
Session 1942-43 Cmd. 6415 vi.

TOOKEY, Douglas

1970   The impact of knitwear imports, a survey of buyers' attitudes. Hosiery and Knitwear Economic Development Committee
N.E.D.O.

TOOTHILL, J.

1970   Demand for garage services and labour to 1980. Motor Vehicle Distribution and Repair Economic Development Committee
N.E.D.O.

How efficient is your workshop? Motor Vehicle Distribution and Repair Economic Development Committee
N.E.D.O.

TOWNSEND, J. L.

1972   Investment in the chemical industry; a report by the investment working party. Chemicals Economic Development Committee
N.E.D.O.

TREMAYNE, Derek

1978   Sponsorship . . . who needs it? Report of the working party
West Midlands Council for Sport and Recreation

TREND, Burke St. J., Sir

1963   Organisation of civil science. Report of the committee of inquiry
Session 1963-64 Cmnd. 2171 ix.

TRESS, Ronald C.

1967   A region with a future. A draft strategy for the South West, by the South West Economic Council
D. of Economic Affairs

TRETHOWAN, W. H.

1977   The role of psychologists in the health services. Report of the sub-committee
D. of Health and Social Security

TREVELYAN, D. J.

1978   Welsh television fourth channel project. Report of the working party
Home Office

See also LITTLERS, S.

TREVELYAN, G. M.

1944   National forest park committee report. Hardknott
Forestry Commission

TREVETHIN AND OAKSEY, G., Lord

1949   Police conditions of service. Report of the committee
Part 1
Session 1948-49 Cmd. 7674 xix.
Part 2
Session 1948-49 Cmd. 7831 xix.

TRICKER, R. I.

1977   Inquiry into the prescription pricing authority. Report
D. of Health and Social Security

TROWBRIDGE, G. W.

1970   A handbook for marketing machinery. Machine Tool Economic Development Committee
N.E.D.O.

TRUEMAN, Arthur E., Sir

1949   Technology in universities, a note
University Grants Committee

TRUSTED, Harry H., Sir

1948   Disturbances in Aden in December 1947. Report of the commission of inquiry. (Colonial No. 233)
Colonial Office

TUCKER, D. G.

1971   Underwater acoustics. Report by the working group. (Publications series 'C' No. 6)

TUCKER, F. J., Lord

1949   Limitation of actions. Report of the committee
Session 1948-49 Cmd. 7740 xvii.

1954   New trials in criminal cases. Report of the departmental committee
Session 1953-54 Cmd. 9150 xi.

1958   Proceedings before examining justices. Report of the departmental committee
Session 1957-58 Cmnd. 479 xv.

TUCKER, James Millard

1951   Taxation of trading profits. Report of the committee
Session 1950-51 Cmd. 8199 xx.

1953   Taxation treatment of provisions for retirement. Report of the committee
Session 1953-54 Cmd. 9063 xix.

TUCKER, T. F.

1970   A guide to adoption practice. Advisory councils on child care for England and Wales, and for Scotland
Home Office

TULLY, J.

1977   English for slower learning children in the Scottish secondary school. Report of a sub-committee

TULLY, J. (*continued*)

of the Scottish central committee on English
Scottish Education D.

TUNBRIDGE, Ronald E., Sir

1965   The standardisation of hospital medical records.
Report of the sub-committee of the standing
medical advisory committee. Central Health
Services Council
M. of Health

1968   The care of the health of hospital staff. Report
of the joint committee of the Central and Scottish health services councils
M. of Health

1972   Rehabilitation. Report of a sub-committee of the
standing medical advisory committee of the
Central Health Services Council
D. of Health and Social Security

TUNSTALL, Jeremy

1977   Studies on the press (working paper No. 3)
Royal Commission on the Press

TURIN, D. A.

See COCKBURN, C.

TURNER, George W., Sir

1947   Motor manufacturing industry. Report on proceedings of the National Advisory Council for
the Motor Manufacturing Industry
M. of Supply

TURNER, J. Stanleigh

1944   Solid fuel installations. Report by a committee
convened by the British coal utilisation research
association. (Post-war building studies No. 10)
M. of Works

TURNER, Steve

1978   In and out of work; a study of unemployment,
low pay and income maintenance services
North Tyneside Community Development Project

TURNER, T. F.

1949   Mining subsidence. Report of the committee
Session 1948-49 Cmd. 7637 xiii.

TWEEDSMUIR, J. N. S., Lord

1954   Imperial Institute. Report of the committee of
inquiry
M. of Education

TYLER, Leslie, Sir

1962   Hospital engineers. Report of the study group on
the work, grading, training and qualifications of
hospital engineers
M. of Health

TYNDALL, A. M.

1950   Technical and scientific register. Present and
future supply and demand for persons with professional qualifications in chemical engineering.
Chemical engineers' sub-committee report
M. of Labour and National Service

TYRRELL, Chris

1976   Rates of decline; an unacceptable base of public
finance; submission to the Layfield committee
Home Office Community Development Project

ULRICH, W. O.

See THOMAS, R. L.

UNDERWOOD, J. E. A.

1955   Maladjusted children. Report of the committee
M. of Education

1959   Standards of normal weight in infancy. Report of
the committee (reports on public health and medical subjects No. 99)
M. of Health

UPJOHN, G. R., Lord

1951   Hundred of Salford. Report of the departmental
committee on the Court of Record for the Hundred of Salford
Session 1950-51 Cmd. 8364 xi.

1952   Gambia egg scheme. Colonial Development Corporation report
Session 1951-52 Cmd. 8560 ix.

URWICK, L.

1947   Education for management. Management subjects in technical and commercial colleges. Report
of a special committee
M. of Education

UTHWATT, A. Andrews

1940   War damage to property; government compensation scheme. Final report of the committees on
the principles of assessment of damage
Session 1939-40 Cmd. 6197 v.

Expert committee on compensation and better-
ment

1941   Interim report
Session 1940-41 Cmd. 6291 iv.

1942   Final report
Session 1941-42 Cmd. 6386 iv.

1949   Tenure and rents of business premises. Report of
the leasehold committee. Interim report
Session 1948-49 Cmd. 7706 xii.

UTTING, W. B.

1978   Certain aspects of the arrangement of the cast of
Stephen Menheniott. Report of the Social Work
Service
D. of Health and Social Security

VANDEPEER, Donald

1950   Agricultural Improvement Council for England
and Wales. 2nd report
M. of Agriculture and Fisheries

VARLEY, Eric

1974   Coal industry examination
        Interim report
        Final report
D. of Energy

VASSAL case

See RADCLIFFE, C. J., Viscount

VAUGHAN-LEE, A. G.

1945   Severn Barrage scheme. Report
M. of Fuel and Power

VEALE, D., Sir

1960   Training in radiological health and safety. Report
of a committee
United Kingdom Atomic Energy Authority

VEALE, J. C.

1974   Education and training. Committee for terotechnology on education and training
        1st report
        2nd report
D. of Industry

VENABLES, Peter F. R., Sir

1969   The Open University. Report of the planning committee
D. of Education and Science

VENN, J. A.

1949   Sugar industry of British Guiana. Report of a commission of inquiry
Colonial Office

VERDON-SMITH, W. Reginald, Sir

1954   Censuses of production and distribution. Report of the committee
Session 1953-54 Cmd. 9276 x.

1964   Fatstock and carcase meat marketing and distribution. Report of the committee of inquiry
Session 1963-64 Cmnd. 2282 xvi.

VERNEY, R. B.

1972   Sinews for survival. A report of the working party on the management of natural resources
D. of the Environment

1976   Aggregates; the way ahead. Report of the advisory committee
D. of the Environment

VERNON, James W.

1969   Humberside; a feasibility study. A report by the central unit on environmental planning
D. of Economic Affairs

1971   Severnside; a feasibility study. A report by the central unit for environmental planning
D. of the Environment

VERNON, M. D.

1972   Education of the visually handicapped. Report of the committee of inquiry
D. of Education and Science

VERSTAGE, M.

See COCKBURN, C.

VIAL, V. E.

See WRIGHT, A. C. S.

VICK, Arnold O. R.

1976   Hops Marketing Scheme, 1932 (as amended). Report of the public inquiry on proposed amendments, 11 to 22 October, 1976
M. of Agriculture, Fisheries and Food

VICK, Godfrey Russell, Sir

1945   Remand homes. Report of the committee of inquiry on London County Council remand homes
Session 1944-45 Cmd. 6594 v.

1948   Evasions of petrol rationing control. Report of the committee of inquiry
Session 1947-48 Cmd. 7372 xiv.

1958   Allegations of ill-treatment of prisoners in Her Majesty's Prison, Liverpool. Report of inquiry and subsequent proceedings
Session 1957-58 Cmnd. 503 xvii.

VILE, M. J. C.

1973   Federalism in the United States, Canada and Australia. (Research papers No. 2)
Commission on the Constitution

VINEY, A.

1974   Rights of consumers. Report by the consumer protection advisory committee
Session 1974-75 HC. 6 vii.

1975   Prepayment for goods. Report on practices relating to prepayment in mail order transactions and in shops by the consumer protection advisory committee
Session 1975-76 HC. 285 ix.

1976   Disguised business sales. Report on the practice of seeking to sell goods without revealing that they are being sold in the course of a business, by the consumer protection advisory committee
Session 1975-76 HC. 355 ix.

1977   VAT-exclusive prices. Report by the consumer protection advisory committee on practices relating to advertising, displaying or otherwise quoting VAT-exclusive prices or charges
Session 1976-77 HC. 146 vii.

VIVIAN, Sylvanus Percival, Sir

1942   Electoral machinery. Report of the committee
Session 1942-43 Cmd. 6408 iv.

VOWDEN, D. H. W.

1972   The fire at Coldharbour Hospital, Sherborne on 5 July, 1972. Report of the committee of inquiry
Session 1972-73 Cmnd. 5170 x.

WADDELL, James, Sir

1978   School examinations. Report of the steering committee to consider proposals for replacing the GCE 'O'-level and CSE examinations
      Part 1: report of the steering committee
      Part 2: report of the sub-groups
Session 1977-78 Cmnd. 7281-I, 7281-II x.

WADDILOVE, Lewis

1977   Co-operatives and housing policy; report in response to the consultative document on housing policy by the advisory committee on co-operatives
Co-operative Housing Agency

WADDINGTON, E. J., Sir

1951   Brtish Guiana. Report of the constitutional commission and despatch from the Secretary of State for the Colonies to the Governor of British Guiana
Colonial Office

WAIN, D. B.

1977   Comments on "The Water Industry in England and Wales, the Next Steps"
Inland Waterways Amenity Advisory Council

WALDEGRAVE, G. N., Earl of

1961   Some problems of horticultural co-operative marketing in England and Wales. Report of a departmental working party. (Economic series No. 52)
M. of Agriculture, Fisheries and Food

WALERAN OF UFFCULME, W. G. H., Lord

1949   Petrol stations. Report of the technical committee
M. of Transport

WALEY, David, Sir

1947   European economic co-operation. Report of the committee (Marshall Plan)
Foreign Office

Payments agreements. Report of the committee
Foreign Office

WALKDEN, A. C., Lord

1949   Water softening sub-committee of the central advisory water committee. Report
M. of Health

See ADAMS, J. R.

WALKER, Arthur

1978   Doctor manpower, 1975-2000; alternative forecasts and their resource implications. (Research paper No. 4)
Royal Commission on the National Health Service

WALKER, G. F. F., Sir

See LLEWELYN-DAVIES, R., Lord

WALKER, J., Lord

1956   Law relating to (a) the liability of an occupier of land or other property to persons suffering injury while on the property, and (b) the obligations of a lessor towards third parties invited or allowed by the lessor to be on the subjects let. 1st report of the Law Reform Committee for Scotland
Session 1956-57 Cmnd. 88 xv.

1957   Procedural law relating to actions of removing and actions of ejection. 2nd report of the Law Reform Committee for Scotland
Session 1956-57 Cmnd. 114 xv.

Rules governing the date from which interest on an award of damages is, or may be, ordered by the court to run. 3rd report of the Law Reform Committee for Scotland
Session 1956-57 Cmnd. 141 xv.

Effect on the liability of insurance companies of special conditions and exceptions in insurance policies and of non-disclosure of facts by persons effecting such policies. 4th report of the Law Reform Committee for Scotland
Session 1957-58 Cmnd. 330 xv.

Need for provision allowing the enforcement in Scotland of orders for maintenance made by the courts of other Commonwealth countries (except England and Wales) and, reciprocally, the enforcements in those other countries of orders for aliment made by Scottish courts. 5th report of the Law Reform Committee for Scotland
Session 1957-58 Cmnd. 449 xv.

The relevance, in a question of the assessment of damages, of any liability to tax of the person entitled to the damages, with particular reference to the decision in British Transport Commission v. Gourley (1956 A.C. 185). 6th report of the Law Reform Committee for Scotland
Session 1958-59 Cmnd. 635 xvi.

1959   Procedure in actions in the Sheriff Courts between spouses for payment of aliment. 7th report of the Law Reform Committee for Scotland
Session 1959-60 Cmnd. 907 xvii.

1960   Constitution of security over movable property; and floating charges. 8th report of the Law Reform Committee for Scotland
Session 1959-60 Cmnd. 1017 xvii.

Power of trustees to sell, purchase or otherwise deal with heritable property; and the variation of trust purposes. 9th report of the Law Reform Committee of Scotland
Session 1959-60 Cmnd. 1102 xxii.

The title of a person' relatives to sue in respect of the death of that person, with particular reference to Laidlaw v. National Coal Board (1957 S.C. 49); and the right to solatium for the death of a relative or spouse. 10th report of the Law Reform Committee for Scotland
Session 1960-61 Cmnd. 1103 xviii.

1963   The desirability of enabling an employer to recover damages for loss suffered by him in consequence of a wrong to his employee by a third person. 11th report of the Law Reform Committee for Scotland
Session 1962-63 Cmnd. 1997 xx.

The law relating to civil liability for loss, injury and damage caused by animals. 12th report of the Law Reform Committee for Scotland
Session 1963-64 Cmnd. 2185 xv.

1964   The law relating to civil liability for loss, injury and damage caused by dangerous agencies escaping from land. 13th report of the Law Reform Committee for Scotland
Session 1963-64 Cmnd. 2348 xv.

The position in relation to diligence of creditors of goods in the possession of but not belonging to a debtor. 14th report of the Law Reform Committee for Scotland
Session 1963-64 Cmnd. 2343 xv.

WALKER, J.

1967   Hospital medical records in Scotland, development and standardisation. Report of a sub-committee of the Standing Medical Advisory Committee. Scottish Health Services Council
Scottish Home and Health D.

1973   Standardisation of hospital medical records. Report of the working group
Scottish Home and Health D.

WALKER, N. D.

1961   Degrees of mental handicap. Report of the working party on standards of ascertainment for Scottish school children
Scottish Education D.

WALKER, Robert Bryce, Sir

1945   Water rates and charges. Report of the committee on water rating in Scotland
Session 1945-46 Cmd. 6765 xiv.

WALL, J. I.

1950   Celluloid storage. Report of the committee
Session 1950 Cmd. 7929 vii.

WALSH, D. P., Sir

1969   Field monuments. Report of the committee of inquiry into the arrangements for the protection of field monuments
Session 1968-69 Cmnd. 3904 xxxii.

WALTON, Raymond

1975   Boundary Commission for England. Report, December 1975
Session 1975-76 HC. 25 viii.

WARBOYS, Walter, Sir

1963   Traffic signs, 1963. Report of the committee on traffic signs for all-purpose roads
M. of Transport

WARD, A., Frank

1950   Inspection of Bristol Rovers Football Club Ltd., and in the matter of the Companies Act, 1948. Report
Board of Trade

WARD, Alan G.

1965   Fish and meat pastes. Report of the food standards committee
M. of Agriculture, Fisheries and Food

1966   Claims and misleading descriptions. Report of the food standards committee
M. of Agriculture, Fisheries and Food

WARD, Alan G. *(continued)*

1967   Cream. Report of the food standards committee
M. of Agriculture, Fisheries and Food

1968   Soups. Report of the food standards committee
M. of Agriculture, Fisheries and Food

1969   Jams and other preserves. Report of the food
standards committee
M. of Agriculture, Fisheries and Food

        Condensed milk. Report of the food standards
committee
M. of Agriculture, Fisheries and Food

1970   Pre-1955 compositional orders concerning baking
powder and golden raising powder, edible gelatine,
mustard, curry powder, tomato ketchup, fish cakes
and suet. Report of the food standards committee
M. of Agriculture, Fisheries and Food

1972   Offals in meat products. Report of the food standards committee
M. of Agriculture, Fisheries and Food

        Date marking of food. Report of the food stan-
dards committee
M. of Agriculture, Fisheries and Food

1973   Vinegars. Report of the food standards committee
M. of Agriculture, Fisheries and Food

1974   Novel protein foods. Report of the food standards
committee
M. of Agriculture, Fisheries and Food

1977   Review of food labelling, part 1: the use of
fructose in foods specially prepared for diabetics.
Report of the food standards committee
M. of Agriculture, Fisheries and Food

WARD, F. J.

1964   Costing of management and maintenance of local
authority housing. Report of the working party
M. of Housing and Local Government

WARD, J. A.

        Misuse of drugs in Scotland. Sub-committee of the
consultative committee of the medical officers of
health

1972   2nd report
1975   3rd report
Scottish Home and Health D.

1973   Routine medical examination of school children.
Report of a sub-committee of the consultative
committee of medical officers of health
Scottish Home and Health D.

WARD, W. E. F.

1948   Education for citizenship in Africa. Report of a
sub-committee of the advisory committee on education in the colonies
Colonial Office

WARD-JACKSON, A. M.

1972   Consumers' committee for G.B. Report on the
effect of the potato marketing scheme on consumers
M. of Agriculture, Fisheries and Food

1974   Consumers' committee for England and Wales.
Report on the effect of the milk marketing scheme
on consumers
M. of Agriculture, Fisheries and Food

WARDLE, P. A.

1971   Operational research and managerial economics
of forestry. Proceedings of a meeting of a working
group of the International Union of Forest Research Organisations held at the Forestry Commission Research Station, Alice Holt Lodge,
September 1970
Forestry Commission

WARE, Inquiry
    See JOLLY, J. C.

WARE, R. R.

        Agricultural valuation. Report of the committee
1948   1st report
1950   2nd report
M. of Agriculture and Fisheries

    See also HOOPER, L. J.
    DOBB, E. E.

WARFORD, J. J.

1969   The South Atcham scheme; an economic appraisal
M. of Housing and Local Government

WARING, A. B., Sir

1954   Human relations in industry, 1953-54. 1st report
of the joint committee
D. of Scientific and Industrial Research *and* Medical Research Council

WARK, I. L., Lord

1943   Report by a court of inquiry concerning a dispute
at an engineering undertaking in Scotland
Session 1942-43 Cmd. 6474 v.

WARNER, Frederick, Sir

1971   A survey of manufacturing capacity. Report on a
survey of manufacturing capacity in certain sectors of the process plant manufacturing industry
N.E.D.O.

1975   Necessary partnership. Reconciling conflicting
objectives in the supply of process plant. Process
plant Working Party
N.E.D.O.

1977   Standards and specifications in the engineering
industries. A report
N.E.D.O.

WARNOCK, H. Mary

1978   Special educational needs. Report of the committee of inquiry into the education of handicapped children and young people
Session 1977-78 Cmnd. 7212 x.

WARR, H. E. D. B. De La, Earl
    See DE LA WARR, H. E. D. B., Earl

WATERHOUSE, Ronald

        Rabies. Committee of inquiry
1970   Interim report
Session 1970-71 Cmnd. 4457 v.
1971   Final report
Session 1970-71 Cmnd. 4696 v.

1975   Dwyfor. Special community review draft propo-
sals
Local Government Boundary Commission for
Wales

        Isle of Anglesey. Special community review draft
proposals
Local Government Boundary Commission for
Wales

        Ogwr. Special community review draft proposals
Local Government Boundary Commission for
Wales

        Swansea. Special community review draft propo-
sal
Local Government Boundary Commission for
Wales

WATERHOUSE, Ronald (*continued*)

1976 Vale of Glamorgan. Special community review draft proposals
Local Government Boundary Commission for Wales

Borough of Afan. Special community review report and proposals
Local Government Boundary Commission for Wales

Cardiff. Special community review draft proposals
Local Government Boundary Commission for Wales

Colwyn. Special community review draft proposals
Local Government Boundary Commission for Wales

Cynon Valley. Special community review draft proposals
Local Government Boundary Commission for Wales

Dinefwr/Lliw Valley. Boundary review draft proposals
Local Government Boundary Commission for Wales

District of Ceredigion and district of Preseli. Boundary review report and proposals
Local Government Boundary Commission for Wales

Glyndwr. Special community review draft proposals
Local Government Boundary Commission for Wales

Llanelli. Special community review draft proposals
Local Government Boundary Commission for Wales

Merionnydd. Special community review draft proposals
Local Government Boundary Commission for Wales

Merthyr Tydfil. Special community review draft proposals
Local Government Boundary Commission for Wales

Newport. Special community review draft proposals
Local Government Boundary Commission for Wales

Preseli/Ceredigion. Boundary review draft proposals
Local Government Boundary Commission for Wales

Preseli/South Pembrokeshire. Boundary review draft proposals
Local Government Boundary Commission for Wales

Radnor. Special community review draft proposals
Local Government Boundary Commission for Wales

Rhondda. Special community review draft proposals
Local Government Boundary Commission for Wales

Rhuddlan. Special community review draft proposals
Local Government Boundary Commission for Wales

Rhymney Valley/Iswyn. Boundary review draft prosopals
Local Government Boundary Commission for Wales

Taff-Ely. Special community review draft proposals
Local Government Boundary Commission for Wales

Vale of Glamorgan. Special community review

draft proposals
Local Government Boundary Commission for Wales

Wrexham Maelor. Special community review draft proposals
Local Government Boundary Commission for Wales

1977 Alyn and Deeside. Special community review draft proposals
Local Government Boundary Commission for Wales

Arfon. Special community review draft proposals
Local Government Boundary Commission for Wales

Blaenau Gwent. Special community review draft proposals
Local Government Boundary Commission for Wales

Borough of Cynon Valley. Special community review report and proposals
Local Government Boundary Commission for Wales

Delyn. Special community review draft proposals
Local Government Boundary Commission for Wales

District of Rhymney Valley and Borough of Islwyn boundary review report
Local Government Boundary Commission for Wales

Maldwyn. Special community review draft prosopals
Local Government Boundary Commission for Wales

Monmouth. Special community review draft proposals
Local Government Boundary Commission for Wales

Montgomery. Special community review draft prosopals
Local Government Boundary Commission for Wales

Neath. Special community review draft proposals
Local Government Boundary Commission for Wales

1978 Brecknock. Special community review draft proposals
Local Government Boundary Commission for Wales

Ceredigion. Special community review draft proposals
Local Government Boundary Commission for Wales

WATERS, A. H. S., Sir

 Sand and gravel. Report of the advisory committee
1948-52 Parts 1-18
 M. of Town and Country Planning
1953 Parts 1-6 repr.
 M. of Town and Country Planning
 Parts 7-8 repr.
 M. of Housing and Local Government

WATERS, John
 See SORN, J. G., Lord

WATKINS, I. Lloyd
1978 Problems of physically handicapped children in Wales. Report of the health and social services panel
 Welsh Council

WATKINS, Tasker
1970   Farleigh Hospital committee of inquiry report
       Session 1970-71 Cmnd. 4557 xx.

WATKINSON, H. A., Viscount
1953   Employment of older men and women. 1st report
       of the national advisory committee
       Session 1952-53 Cmd. 8963 xi.

1955   Employment of older men and women. 2nd report
       of the national advisory committee
       Session 1955-56 Cmd. 9628 xvii.

WATSON, A. H.
1976   Reporting of road accident statistics. 1st and 2nd
       reports of the steering group
       D. of Transport

1977   Road accident statistics; a revised reporting
       system. Report by the steering group
       D. of Transport

WATSON, Aiken
1948   Disturbances in the Gold Coast. Report of the
       commission of inquiry
       Colonial Office

WATSON, C. E.
1975   Guarding of foundry machinery. 3rd report of
       the sub-committee on machinery safety of the
       joint standing committee on health, safety and
       welfare in foundries
       D. of Employment

       Guarding of foundry machinery. 4th report of
       the sub-committee on machinery safety of the
       joint standing committee on health, safety and
       welfare in foundries
       D. of Employment

1977   The guarding of automatic foundries. 5th report
       of the sub-committee on the guarding of foundry
       machinery of the joint standing committee on
       health, safety and welfare in foundries
       Health and Safety Executive

       The philosophy of guarding. 6th report of the
       sub-committee on the guarding of foundry
       machinery of the joint standing committee on
       health, safety and welfare in foundries
       Health and Safety Executive

       See also HARVEY, B. H.

WATSON, C. J.
1977   Assessing housing needs; a manual of guidance.
       Working party on assessment of housing need.
       (Scottish housing handbook No. 1)
       Scottish Development D.

       See also CULLINGWORTH, J. B.

WATSON, H.
1956   Marketing of woodland produce. Report of the
       committee
       Forestry Commission

WATSON, J. Wreford
1968   The central borders; a plan for expansion
              Vol. 1: Plan and physical study
              Vol. 2: Economic and geographical report
       Scottish Development D.

WATSON, L. Hill, Lord
       See HILL WATSON, L., Lord

WATSON, R.
       See LACEY, G.

WATSON, Stewart M.
1977   Local government staff commission for Wales.
       Report
       Welsh Office

WATT, James
1952   Standardisation of radiological terminology in
       pulmonary disease and standardisation of tech-
       nique in chest radiography. Report of the joint
       committee of the joint tuberculosis council
       M. of Health

WATTS, Hugh E., Sir
1950   Ammonium nitrate working party report
       Home Office

1954   Carriage of dangerous goods and explosives in
       ships. Report of the departmental committee
       M. of Transport

1956   Carriage of dangerous goods and explosives in
       ships. Minister's Standing Advisory Committee
       report
       M. of Transport and Civil Aviation

1961   Carriage of dangerous goods and explosives in
       ships. Report of the Minister's Standing Advisory
       Committee. Consolidated edition
       M. of Transport

WAVERLEY, J., Viscount
1952   Export of works of art, etc. Report of a com-
       mittee
       Treasury

       Coastal flooding
1953   Interim report of the departmental committee
           Session 1952-53 Cmd. 8923 xi.
1954   Report of the departmental committee
           Session 1953-54 Cmd. 9165 xiii.

       Forces medical and dental services. Report of
       the committee
1955   Report
1956   2nd report
       M. of Defence

WAY, Richard
1975   Dispute between the National Union of Blast-
       furnacemen and the British Steel Corporation.
       Report of the court of inquiry (Report No. 3)
       Advisory, Conciliation and Arbitration Service

WAY, Richard G. K., Sir
1971   Machine tool industry. Report of the machine
       tool expert committee
       D. of Trade and Industry

WAYNE, Edward J., Sir
1969   Cannabis. Report by the advisory committee on
       drug dependence
       Home Office

       The rehabilitation of drug addicts. Report of the
       advisory committee on drug dependence
       Home Office

1970   The amphetamines and lysergic acid diethyla-
       mide (LSD). Report by the advisory committee
       on drug dependence
       Home Office

       Powers of arrest and search in relation to drug
       offences. Report of the advisory committee on
       drug dependence
       Home Office

WEAVER, Tobias R.
1957   Educational maintenance allowances. Report of
       the working party
       M. of Education

WEAVER, Tobias R. *(continued)*

1966   Government of colleges of education. Report of the study group
D. of Education and Science

1970   Teaching council for England and Wales. Report of the working party
D. of Education and Science

WEBB, W.

1976   Coastguard; an official history of H.M. Coastguard
D. of Trade

WEDGWOOD, Ralph, Sir

1943   Matrimonial Causes (trial in the provinces) committee report
Session 1942-43 Cmd. 6480 v.

WEEDON, Basil C. L.

1970   Emulsifiers and Stabilisers in Food Regulations, 1962. Report on the review by the food additives and contaminants committee
M. of Agriculture, Fisheries and Food

1972   Preservatives in Food Regulations, 1962. Report on the review by the food additives and contaminants committee
M. of Agriculture, Fisheries and Food

1974   Antioxidant in Food Regulations, 1966 and 1972. Report by the food additives and contaminants committee. (FAC-REP 18)
M. of Agriculture, Fisheries and Food

1975   Lead in Food Regulations, 1961. Report on the review by the food additives and contaminants committee
M. of Agriculture, Fisheries and Food

1977   Sulphur dioxide. Report of a representation for the use of sulphur dioxide as an alternative to permitted colouring in canned garden peas by the food additives and contaminants committee
M. of Agriculture, Fisheries and Food

1978   The review of additives and processing aids used in the production of beer. Report of the food additives and contaminants committee. (FAC/REP/26)
M. of Agriculture, Fisheries and Food

Review of solvents in food. Report of the food additives and contaminants committee. (FAC/REP/25)
M. of Agriculture, Fisheries and Food

**See also MORTON, R. A.
LLEWELYN-DAVIES, R., Lord**

WEEKS, Hugh, Sir

1970   A look at wholesaling. Report to the wholesale sub-committee on wholesale warehousing and use of labour. Distributive Trades Economic Development Committee
N.E.D.O.

WEEKS, Ronald M., Sir

1950   Future development of higher technical education. Report of the National Advisory Council on Education for Industry and Commerce
M. of Education

WEILER, Terence G.

1971   Habitual drunken offenders. Report of the working party
Home Office

1975   Adjudication procedures in prisons. Report of the working party
Home Office

WEIR, Cecil, Sir

1942   Small retailers of pottery. Scheme for ensuring fair shares of supplies
Board of Trade

1959   Electricity and gas boards. Report of the committee on co-operation between area and Scottish electricity and gas boards
Session 1958-59 Cmnd. 695 xiii.

WELLS, G. S.

1950   District heating working party. Interim report
M. of Local Government and Planning

See also ELLIOTT, R. A.

WELSH, James

1946   Modernising our homes. A report by the Scottish housing advisory committee
D. of Health for Scotland

WEMYSS, Lord
    See WEMYSS AND MARCH, F. D. C., Earl of

WEMYSS AND MARCH, F. D. C., Earl of

1950   Monuments and constructions in the City of Edinburgh. 13th report of the Royal Commission on Ancient and Historical Monuments and Constructions of Scotland
Session 1950 Cmd. 7967 xii.

1955   Ancient monuments of Roxburghshire. 14th report of the Royal Commission on the Ancient and Historical Monuments and Constructions of Scotland
Session 1955-56 Cmd. 9735 xxi.

1956   Ancient monuments of Selkirkshire. 15th report of the Royal Commission on the Ancient and Historical Monuments and Constructions of Scotland
Session 1956-57 Cmnd. 276 xiv.

1963   Ancient and Historical monuments of Stirlingshire. 16th report of the Royal Commission on the Ancient and Historical Monuments and Constructions of Scotland
Session 1962-63 Cmnd. 1860 xix.

1972   Ancient and Historical monuments of Argyll. Vol. 1: Kintyre. 18th report of the Royal Commission on Ancient and Historical Monuments of Scotland
Session 1971-72 Cmnd. 4808 xvi.

1975   Ancient and historical monuments of Argyll. Vol. 2: Lorn. 19th report of the Royal Commission on the Ancient and Historical Monuments of Scotland
Session 1974-75 Cmnd. 6010 xi.

1978   The prehistoric and Roman monuments of Lanarkshire. 20th report of the Royal Commission on Ancient and Historical Monuments of Scotland
Session 1977-78 Cmnd. 7201 xvi.

WESTON, W. G.

1944   United Maritime authority planning committee report
M. of War Transport

1948   Turn-round of shipping in the U.K. ports. Reports of the working party
M. of Transport

WESTWICK, C.

1971   Study of profitability in the hosiery and knitwear industry. Hosiery and Knitwear Economic Development Committee
N.E.D.O.

WESTWOOD, W., Lord

1949   Mineral development. Report of the committee
        Session 1948-49 Cmd. 7732 xviii.

WETHERED, E. H. C.

1952   Bristol Rovers Football Club Ltd. Investigation
        under the Companies Act
        Board of Trade

WHEARE, K. C., Sir

1950   Children and the cinema. Report of the depart-
        mental committee
        Session 1950 Cmd. 7945 vii.

WHEATCROFT, S. F.

1973   The freight forwarder. Follow-up report by a
        working party of the Movement of Exports
        Economic Development Committee
        N.E.D.O.

WHEATLEY, John, Lord

1947   Scottish nurses' salaries committee. 5th and
        supplementary reports
        Session 1947-48 Cmd. 7238 xvi.

        Mental nurses. Sub-committee of the Scottish
        nurses' salaries committee. 6th and supplementary
        reports
        Session 1947-48 Cmd. 7239 xvi.

1963   The teaching profession in Scotland. Arrange-
        ments for the award and withdrawal of cer-
        tificates of competency to teach. Report of the
        committee
        Session 1962-63 Cmnd. 2066 xv.

1969   Royal Commission on Local Government in
        Scotland. Report and appendices
        Session 1968-69 Cmnd. 4150 xxxix.

        Scotland; local government reform. Short ver-
        sion of the report of the Royal Commission on
        Local Government in Scotland
        Session 1968-69 Cmnd. 4150-I xxxix.

1972   Crowd safety at sports grounds. Report of the
        inquiry
        Session 1971-72 Cmnd. 4952 ix.

WHEATLEY, J. D.

1973   Coastal recreation in south west England. Report
        of a working party
        South Western Sports Council

WHELAN, C. B.
        See GODDARD, R., Lord

WHITE, A. M. W.

1971   The state enrolled nurse. A report by the sub-
        committee of the standing nursing advisory com-
        mittee. Central Health Services Council
        D. of Health and Social Security

WHITE, C. L.

1977   The women's periodical press in Britain, 1946-76.
        (Working paper No. 4)
        Royal Commission on the Press

WHITE, G. H. Graham-
        See GRAHAM-WHITE, G. H.

WHITE, R. G.

1952   Hill farm research. Scottish Hill farm research
        committee. 2nd report
        D. of Agriculture for Scotland

WHITE, S. F.

1974   Backsiphonage in water installations. Report of
        the committee
        D. of the Environment

1976   Domestic unvented hot water systems. Report of
        the standing technical committee on water regu-
        lations. (Standing technical committee reports
        No. 3)
        National Water Council

WHITE, Thomas

1977   New Brighton Association Football and Athletic
        Club Co. Ltd. Report of investigations under the
        Companies Act
        D. of Trade

WHITE, Tom

1978   Multi-racial Britain; the social services response.
        A working party report
        Commission for Racial Equality

WHITFIELD, Sylvia

1977   People in paper chains. (Birmingham community
        development project final report No. 3)
        Home Office, published by the Social Evaluation
        Unit, Oxford

WHITFORD, John

1977   Copyright and designs law. Report of the
        committee
        Session 1976-77 Cmnd. 6732 vii.

WHITLEY, H. C.

1950   Child care after-care committee of the Scottish
        advisory council. Report
        Scottish Home D.

WHITLEY, R. L.

1977   Materials handling; pallet usage and wastage.
        Report of the pallets survey steering panel
        D of Industry

WHITTINGTON, G.

1976   Financing of quoted companies in the U.K.
        (Background paper No. 1)
        Royal Commission on Distribution of Income
        and Wealth

WIDGERY, John Passmore, Lord

1966   Legal aid in criminal proceedings. Report of the
        departmental committee
        Session 1965-66 Cmnd. 2934 vi.

1970   Reparation by the offender. Report of the sub-
        committee of the advisory council on the penal
        system
        Home Office

1972   Report of the tribunal to inquiry into the events
        on Sunday 30 January 1972 (Bloody Sunday)
        which led to loss of life in connection with the
        procession in Londonderry
        Session 1971-72 HC. 220 xxxii; HL. 101

WIGODER, Basil Thomas, Lord

1978   Transfer of pay beds from the Royal Salop
        Infirmary to Shrewsbury Hospital, Copthorne.
        Proposal made by the Health Services Board
        Session 1977-78 HC. 139 xvi.

        Withdrawal of authorisations for the use of
        N.H.S. hospital accommodation and services by
        private patients. Health Services Board's second
        proposals
        Session 1977-78 HC. 358 xvi.

WIGODER, Basil Thomas, Lord

Relocation of pay bed authorisations at hospitals of the Newcastle Area Health Authority (Teaching). Proposal by the Health Services Board
Session 1977-78 HC. 505 xv.

Withdrawal of authorisations for the use of N.H.S. hospital accommodation and services by private patients. Health Service Boards third set of proposals
Session 1978-79 HC. 4

Relocation of private practice facilities at national health service hospitals. Proposals made by the Health Service Board
Session 1978-79 HC. 5

WILBERFORCE, R. O., Lord

1965   Positive covenants affecting land. Report of the committee
Session 1964-65 Cmnd. 2719 xviii.

1971   Court of inquiry into a dispute between the parties represented on the National Joint Industrial Council for the Electricity Supply Industry. Report
Session 1970-71 Cmnd. 4594 xxv.

1972   Dispute between the National Coal Board and the National Union of Mineworkers. Report of a court of inquiry
Session 1971-72 Cmnd. 4903 xviii.

WILCOCK, C. A. B.

1948   Civil aviation. Report by the committee on recruitment, training and licensing of personnel for civil aviation
Session 1948-49 Cmd. 7746 xi.

WILDING, R. W. L.

1978   Longer term review of administrative computing in central government. Report by the steering committee
Civil Service D.

WILES, Harold H.

1946   The rehabilitation and resettlement of disabled persons. Report of the standing committee
M. of Labour and National Service

1948   The rehabilitation and resettlement of disabled persons. 2nd report of the standing committee
M. of Labour and National Service

1955   Services for the disabled. Standing committee on the rehabilitation and resettlement of disabled persons
M. of Labour and National Service

WILKINSON, S. F.

Requisitioned properties in use for housing
1952   Interim report
1953   2nd interim report
1953   3rd and final report
M. of Housing and Local Government

WILLETT, H. L.

Coal dust explosions. Reports of the working party
1960   Report
1967   Final report
National Coal Board

1961   Stone dust barriers on coal conveyor roads. Report
National Coal Board

1965   Outbursts of firedamp from the floor of coal seams. Report of the working party
National Coal Board

WILLIAMS, A. J.

1977   Aggregates. South Wales working party interim report
D. of the Environment

WILLIAMS, C. E.

1970   The costing of handling and storage in warehouses, 1: Coventional warehouses
D. of Trade and Industry

WILLIAMS, Charles C. P.

1978   Fuel cost adjustment for the supply of electricity. Price Commission report
Session 1977-78 HC. 133 xlvii.

Barclays Bank Ltd. Charges for money transmission services to the Post Office, the British Gas Corporation and the Electricity Council. Report by the Price Commission
Session 1977-78 HC. 134 xlvii.

Metal Box Ltd. Open-top food and beverage and aerosol cans. Report of the Price Commission
Session 1977-78 HC. 135 xlvii.

Fisons Ltd., Agrochemical Division. Agrochemical and horticultural products. Report by the Price Commission
Session 1977-78 HC. 151 xlvii.

U.K. Glass Containers Ltd. Prices of glass containers. Report by the Price Commission
Session 1977-78 HC. 170 xlviii.

Margins of coal merchants in West Wales. Report by the Price Commission
Session 1977-78 HC. 214 xlvii.

Tate & Lyle Refineries Ltd. Sugar and sugar products. Report by the Price Commission
Session 1977-78 HC. 224 xlviii.

British Railways Board. Increases in passenger fares. Report by the Price Commission
Session 1977-78 HC. 225 xlvii.

Prices, costs and margins in the importation and distribution of bacon. Report by the Price Commission
Session 1977-78 HC. 229 xlvii.

Ever Ready Co. (G.B.) Ltd. Dry (primary) batteries. Report by the Price Commission
Session 1977-78 HC. 284 xlvii.

Cadbury Schweppes Foods Ltd. Grocery products. Report by the Price Commission
Session 1977-78 HC. 293 xlvii.

Imperial Chemical Industries Ltd. Sodium carbonate. Report by the Price Commission
Session 1977-78 HC. 332 xlvii.

Weetabix Ltd. Cereal and muesli products. Price Commission report
Session 1977-78 HC. 336 xlviii.

Banks; charges for money transmission services. Price Commission report
Session 1977-78 HC. 337 xlvii.

Prices, costs and margins in the production and distribution of compound feedingstuff for cattle, pigs and poultry. Price Commission report
Session 1977-78 HC. 338 xlvii.

Allied Breweries (U.K.) Ltd. Brewing and wholesaling of beer and sales in managed houses. Price Commission report
Session 1977-78 HC. 415 xvlii.

Southalls (Birmingham) Ltd. Sanitary protection and other hygiene products. Price Commission report
Session 1977-78 HC. 436 xlviii.

Prices, costs and margins in the production and distribution of proprietary non-ethical medicines. Price Commission report
Session 1977-78 HC. 469 xlviii.

WILLIAMS, Charles C. P. *(continued)*

IPC Magazines Ltd. Increases in cover prices. Price Commission report
Session 1977-78 HC. 481 xlvii.

Associated Portland Cement Manufacturers Ltd. Increases in cement price. Price Commission report
Session 1977-78 HC. 495 xlvii.

Thames Water Authority. Water, sewage and environmental services. Price Commission report
Session 1977-78 HC. 496 xlviii.

Prices, costs and margins in the distribution of footwear in the U.K. Price Commission report
Session 1977-78 HC. 498 xlvii.

Prices, costs and margins in the publishing, printing and binding, and distribution of books. Price Commission report
Session 1977-78 HC. 527 xlviii.

South of Scotland Electricity Board. Price increases in the supply of electricity. Price Commission report
Session 1977-78 HC. 535 xlviii.

Pricing of beds. Price Commission report
Session 1977-78 HC. 650 xlviii.

Trust Houses Forte Hotels Ltd. Charges for hotel services in the U.K. Price Commission report
Session 1977-78 HC. 651 xlviii.

Prices, costs and margins in the provision of taxicab and private hire car services. Price Commission report
Session 1977-78 HC. 655 xlviii.

Charges, costs and margins in the hiring of television sets for domestic use. Price Commission report
Session 1977-78 HC. 656 xlvii.

British Gypsum Ltd. Increases in the prices of gypsum-related products. Price Commission report
Session 1977-78 HC. 663 xlvii.

London Transport Executive. Increases in passenger fares. Report of the Price Commission
Session 1977-78 HC. 594 xlvii.

Lever Brothers Ltd. Soaps, detergents and related products. Price Commission report
Session 1977-78 HC. 657 xlvii.

Royal Doulton Tableware Ltd. China and earthenware tableware and ornamental items. Price Commission report
Session 1977-78 HC. 658 xlviii.

The road haulage industry. Price Commission report
Session 1977-78 HC. 698 xlviii.

Procter and Gamble, Ltd. Soaps and detergents. Price Commission report
Session 1978-79 HC. 1

Imperial Tobacco Ltd. Cigarettes and cigarillos. Price Commission report
Session 1978-79 HC. 28

General Paper and Box Manufacturing Co. Ltd. and Rizla Ltd. Cigarette paper booklets, filter tips and accessories. Price Commission report
Session 1978-79 HC. 50

Prices, costs and margins in the distribution of jeans. Price Commission report
Session 1978-79 HC. 67

Air Products Ltd. Merchant industrial gases. Prices Commission report
Session 1978-79 HC. 124

Prices, costs and margins in the production and distribution of toothpaste. Price Commission report
Session 1978-79 HC. 125

Tea prices (report No. 32)
Price Commission

Decorative paint (report No. 33)
Price Commission

WILLIAMS, D. R. REES-
See REES-WILLIAMS, D. R.

WILLIAMS, E. C.

1974　Report on the incident in building B204 at the Windscale works of British Nuclear Fuels, Ltd. on 26 September 1973
Session 1974 Cmnd. 5703 iii.

WILLIAMS, G. G., Sir

1948　University awards. Working party report
M. of Education

WILLIAMS, H. Lloyd-
See LLOYD-WILLIAMS, H.

WILLIAMS, I. C.

1972　The predictive value of C.S.E. grades for further education. (Examinations bulletin, No. 24)
Schools Council

WILLIAMS, J. C. Hanbury-
See HANBURY-WILLIAMS, J. C.

WILLIAMS, R.

1978　Berwick-upon-Tweed. Report of the working party on environmental and traffic problems
D. of the Environment

WILLIAMS, R. Morton
See MORTON-WILLIAMS, R.

WILLIAMS, Robert, Sir

1976　Genetic manipulation. Report of the working party on the practice
Session 1975-76 Cmnd. 6600 xliii.

WILLIAMS, T.

1976　Professions in the construction industries. Building and Civil Engineering Economic Development Committees
N.E.D.O.

WILLIAMS, W. D. A.

1948　Milk distribution. Report of the committee
Session 1947-48 Cmd. 7414 xiii.

WILLIAMS, William Emrys, Sir

1970　The theatre today in England and Wales. Report of the Arts Council theatre enquiry
Arts Council

WILLIAMSON, T. B.

1977　Nutrition education. Report of a working party
D. of Health and Social Security

WILLINK, Henry U., Sir

1949-
1950　Betting, Lotteries and Gaming, Royal Commission

Minutes of evidence taken before the Royal Commission. 25 days

1951　Report
Session 1950-51 Cmd. 8190 viii.

1957　Medical practitioners. Report of the committee to consider the future numbers of medical practitioners and the appropriate intake of medical students
M. of Health

WILLINK, Henry V., Sir *(continued)*

1958   Nigeria. Report of the commission appointed to inquire into the fears of minorities and the means of allaying them
Session 1957-58 Cmnd. 505 ix.

     Royal Commission on the Police
1960   Interim report
           Session 1960-61 Cmnd. 1222 xx.
1960-   Minutes of evidence. 10 days. With appen-
1961   dix to minutes of evidence (1-10). Selection of witnesses supplementary evidence, 11th to 27th days
1962   Final report
           Session 1961-62 Cmnd. 1728 xx.

WILLIS, H.

1972   Redevelopment proposals for the Richmond Terrace - New Scotland Yard site. Report of a public inquiry
D. of the Environment

WILLIS, J. Ramsey, Sir

1958   Lymm. Report of inquiry into the proposed development of land at Lymm for Manchester overspill
M. of Housing and Local Government

1965   Licensing planning. Report of the departmental committee
Session 1964-65 Cmnd. 2709 xviii.

WILLIS, W. J. A.

1958   Police uniform. Report of the committee of the Police Council for England and Wales
Home Office

WILSON, Alan Hemes, Sir

1960   Report of the committee on coal derivatives
Session 1959-60 Cmnd. 1120 ix.

1962   Noise from motor vehicles. Interim report of the committee of the problem of noise
Session 1961-62 Cmnd. 1780 xix.

1963   Noise. Final report of the committee on the problem of noise
Session 1962-63 Cmnd. 2056 xxii.

1969   Delays in commissioning C.E.G.B. power stations. Report of the committee of enquiry
Session 1968-69 Cmnd. 3960 xxix.

1971   Future management of water in England and Wales. Report by the central advisory water committee
D. of the Environment

WILSON, Andrew

1969   Collection of residue data; a report by the advisory committee on pesticides and other toxic chemicals covering a report by its working party
D. of Education and Science

     Further review of certain persistent organo-chlorine pesticides used in G.B. Report by the advisory committee on pesticides and other toxic chemicals
D. of Education and Science

1973   General sale list of medical products for human use. Report
Medicines Commission

     Prescription only medicines and related matters. Report
Medicines Commission

WILSON, Alfred Harold

1946   London airport. Report of the layout panel (M.C.A.P. 4)
M. of Civil Aviation

WILSON, Arton, Sir

1956   Agriculture, Fisheries and Food. Report of the committee appointed to review the provincial and local organisations and procedures of the Ministry of Agriculture, Fisheries and Food
Session 1955-56 Cmd. 9732 x.

1959   Caravans as homes. Report
Session 1959-60 Cmnd. 872 ix.

WILSON, Charles H., Sir

1973   The future of the Dundee Institute of Art and Technology. Report of a committee
Scottish Education D.

WILSON, Duncan R.

1940   Lighting in factories. 5th report of the departmental committee
M. of Labour

WILSON, G.

1974   Solvents in food. Supplementary report of the toxicity sub-committee of the food additives and contaminants committee
M. of Agriculture, Fisheries and Food

WILSON, H.

1976   Construction into the early 1980s. Building and Civil Engineering Economic Development Committees
N.E.D.O.

1977   Change or decay; final report of the Liverpool inner area study
D. of the Environment

WILSON, Harold, Sir

     Committee to review the functioning of financial institutions

1977   Progress report on the financing of industry and trade
Treasury
     Evidence on financing of industry and trade
         Vol. 1: Treasury, Department of Industry
         Vol. 2: CBI, TUC, Association on Independent Businesses
1978   Vol. 3: Export Credits Guarantee Department, Insurance Company Associations; National Association of Pension Funds, Stock Exchange
         Vol. 4: National Enterprise Board, Finance for Industry Ltd., Equity Capital for Industry
         Vol. 5: Accepting Houses Committee, Committee of London Clearing Banks, Bank of England
         Vol. 6: Committee of Scottish Clearing Bankers, Scottish Development Agency
         Vol. 7: Association of Investment Trust Companies, Unit Trust Association, Association of British Chambers of Commerce
     Treasury

     Proposals for setting up of a British film authority. Report of the interim action committee on the film industry
Session 1977-78 Cmnd. 7071 xiv.

WILSON, Hugh

1967   Irvine new town. Final report on planning proposals
Scottish Development D.

1971   Teesside survey and plan. Final report to the steering committee. Vol. 2: Analysis. 2 parts
D. of the Environment
See also ALLISON, C. W., Sir

WILSON, Hugh (*continued*)

1978 New industrial development. Report of a working party
Environmental Board

WILSON, I. M.
See KIDD, J.

WILSON, J. Callan

1956 Housing subsidies in Scotland. Report of the working party
D. of Health for Scotland

WILSON, P. H. St. John

1954 Training of supervisors. Report of the committee of inquiry
M. of Housing and Local Government

1959 Lister v. the Romford Ice and Cold Storage Co. Ltd. Report of the inter-departmental committee
M. of Labour and National Service

1962 Index of retail prices. Report of revision by the cost of living advisory committee
Session 1961-62 Cmnd. 1657 xii.

WILSON, Reginald H., Sir

1968 Bristol Siddeley Engines Ltd. Report of the committee of inquiry into certain contracts.
Session 1967-68 HC. 129 xvii.

1970 National Freight Corporation. Report on organisation
Session 1969-70 HC. 72 xxviii.

WILSON, Roy M., Sir

1958 Smithfield market. Report of the committee of inquiry to inquire whether there are any causes of industrial unrest arising from the present arrangements for the delivery, handling and distribution of meat in Smithfield Market
M. of Labour and National Service

1964 Report of the committee of investigation to inquire into the difference existing in the Yorkshire area of the coalmining industry involving members of the National Union of Mineworkers employed by the National Coal Board and the National Coal Board
M. of Labour

1965 Report of the committee of inquiry into the causes and circumstances of the difference existing between the two sides of the National Council for the Omnibus Industry
M. of Labour

1966 Report of a court of inquiry into the causes and circumstances of a strike by members of the National Amalgamated Stevedores and Dockers in the Port of London and into practices relevant thereto
Session 1966-67 Cmnd. 3146 xxxvi.

1967 Immigration appeals. Report of the committee
Session 1966-67 Cmnd. 3387 xxxvi.

WILSON-DICKSON, P.

1978 Fire risks of new materials. Report of the technical sub-committee
Home Office

WILSON-SMITH, Henry, Sir

1946 Pensionability of unestablished civil service. Report of a committee of the Civil Service National Whitley Council
Session 1945-46 Cmd. 6942 x.

1954 Duty free entry of machinery into the U.K. Report of a committee
Board of Trade

WINDEYER, Brian W., Sir

1968 Code of practice for the protection of persons exposed to ionising radiations in research teaching. 2nd ed.
D. of Employment

1970 Organisation of radioactive isotope services. Report for the working party. (Reports on public health and medical subjects, No. 128)
D. of Health and Social Security

1972 Lead poisoning at the RTZ smelter at Avonmouth. Report of the committee
Session 1971-72 Cmnd. 5042 xvi.

WINDLE, H. R.

1971 Marketing education in the U.K. Report of the marketing sub-committee of the Management Education, Training and Development Committee
N.E.D.O.

WINN, C. R. N., Sir

1965 Report of the standing security commission
Session 1964-65 Cmnd. 2722 xxii.

1968 Personal injuries litigation. Report of the committee
Session 1967-68 Cmnd. 3691 xxx.

Report of the Security Commission. Douglas Ronald Britten
Session 1968-69 Cmnd. 3856 xiv.

1969 Report of the Security Commission. Clive Edwin Bland
Session 1968-69 Cmnd. 3892 xlv.

WINNER, Albertine, Dame

1978 Collaboration in community care, a discussion document prepared by the working party
D. of Health and Social Security

WINNIFRITH, A. J. D., Sir

1960 Agricultural improvement council for England and Wales. 4th report
M. of Agriculture, Fisheries and Food

WINSBURY, R.

1975 New technology and the press; study of experience in the U.S. (Working paper No. 1)
Royal Commission on the Press

WINSTEN, C. B.

1977 Structural model of British retail trade. Preliminary report; methodology and historical analysis.
Distributive Trades Economic Development Committee
N.E.D.O.

WINTERBOTTOM, I., Lord

1969 Building maintenance; an interim report. R & D bulletin
M. of Public Building and Works

WINTON, R. C.

1972 The electronics industry and the schools. Report of the sub-committee of the Electronics Economic Development Committee
N.E.D.O.

WISE, M. J.

1966 Statutory smallholdings provided by local

WISE, M. J. *(continued)*
authorities in England and Wales. 1st report of the departmental committee
Session 1965-66 Cmnd. 2936 vii.

Statutory smallholdings. Final report of the departmental committee. Statutory smallholdings provided by the Minister of Agriculture, Fisheries and Food
Session 1966-67 Cmnd. 3303 xix.

WITNEY, K. P.

1973   Lotteries. Report of the interdepartmental working party
Session 1973-74 Cmnd. 5506 iii.

WOLF, N.
See WATSON, J. W.

WOLFENDEN, John F., Sir

1952   Examinations in secondary schools. 2nd report of the secondary schools examination council
M. of Education

1956   National service men. Report of the committee of the employment of national service men in the U.K.
Session 1956-57 Cmnd. 35 xvii.

1957   Homosexual offences and prostitution. Report of the committee
Session 1956-57 Cmnd. 247 xiv.

1968   Non-recurrent grants; notes on procedure. 3rd ed.
University Grants Committee

1978   The future of voluntary organisations
Croom Helm for the Rowntree Memorial Trust and the Carnegie U.K. Trust (not a government publication)

WOLRIGE-GORDON, J.

1964   The staffing of the midwifery services in Scotland. Report by a committee of the Scottish Health Services Council

WOLSTENCROFT, A.

1960   Mobile radio committee. 4th report
Post Office

WOLSTENHOLME, Gordon, Sir

1978   Genetic manipulation advisory group. 1st report
Session 1977-78 Cmnd. 7215 li.

WOLVERSON, W. A.

1956   Mobile radio committee. 2nd report
Post Office

1959   Mobile radio committee. 3rd report
Post Office

WOMERSLEY, L.
See WILSON, H.

WOOD, A.

1976   Older areas. Interim report of the sub-group
Environmental Board

WOOD, John

1975   Dispute between British Leyland, Cowley and AUEW and TGWU concerning mechanical rectifiers. Report of the panel of investigation. (Report No. 1)
Advisory, Conciliation and Arbitration Service

WOOD, John C.

1969   Report of a court of inquiry into a dispute at the Woodend Avenue, Liverpool plant of Standard-Triumph (Liverpool) Ltd.
Session 1969-70 Cmnd. 4220 xvi.

1970   Report of a court of inquiry into a dispute between Pilkington Brothers Ltd. and certain of their employees
D. of Employment and Productivity

Report of a commission of inquiry on a draft order varying the field of operation of the Road Haulage Wages Council
D. of Employment and Productivity

1971   Salaries for teachers in establishments for further education. Report of the arbitral body
D. of Education and Science

1973   Disputes involving teachers in the area of the Teesside local education authority. Report of the committee of inquiry
D. of Education and Science

WOOD, J. I.

1971   Workwear; the changing scene. A study of the strategic picture of the U.K. overall industry. Overall industry study group of the Clothing Economic Development Committee
N.E.D.O.

WOOD, K.

1975   Public client and the construction industries. Building and Civil Engineering Economic Development Committees
N.E.D.O.

WOOD, Robert S., Sir

1943   Standard construction for schools. Report by a committee (Post-war building studies No. 2)
M. of Works

1947   The recruitment and training of nurses. Report of the working party
M. of Health

1954   Agricultural education, British Caribbean territories. Report on the provision of agricultural education of university degree standard in the British Caribbean Territories. (Colonial No. 313)
Colonial Office

WOOD, S. D.

1971   A common system of examining at 16+. Report of the working party (Examinations bulletin No. 23)
Schools Council

WOODCOCK, George

1969   The Associated Octel Co. Ltd. (Commission on Industrial Relations report No. 1)
Session 1969-70 Cmnd. 4246 xvi.

General Accident, Fire and Life Assurance Corporation Ltd. (Commission on Industrial Relations report No. 2)
Session 1969-70 Cmnd. 4247 xvi.

W. Stevenson & Sons; Suttons Cornwall Ltd. (Commission on Industrial Relations report No. 3)
Session 1969-70 Cmnd. 4248 xvi.

Birmingham Aluminium Casting (1903) Co. Ltd.; Dartmouth Auto Castings Ltd.; Midland Motor Cylinder Co. Ltd. (Commission in Industrial Relations report No. 4)
Session 1969-70 Cmnd. 4264 xvi.

B.S.R. Ltd. (Commission on Industrial Relations report No. 5)
Session 1969-70 Cmnd. 4274 xvi.

Elliotts of Newbury Ltd. (Commission on Industrial Relations report No. 6)
Session 1969-70 Cmnd. 4311 xvi.

Brock's Fireworks Ltd. (Commission on Industrial Relations report No. 7)
Session 1969-70 Cmnd. 4325 xvi.

WOODCOCK, George (*continued*)

Frederick Parker Ltd. (Commission on Industrial Relations report No. 8)
Session 1969-70 Cmnd. 4374 xvi.

1970   Commission on Industrial Relations. 1st general report (report No. 9)
Session 1970-71 Cmnd. 4417 xxv.

International Harvester Co. of G.B. Ltd. (Commission on Industrial Relations report No. 10)
Session 1970-71 Cmnd. 4469 xxv.

Hover Ltd. (Commission on Industrial Relations report No. 11)
Session 1970-71 Cmnd. 4537 xxv.

Medical Research Council. (Commission on Industrial Relations report No. 12)
Session 1970-71 Cmnd. 5431 xxv.

Armstrong Patents Co. Ltd. (Commission on Industrial Relations report No. 13)
Session 1970-71 Cmnd. 4541 xxv.

1971   Standard Telephone and Cables Ltd. (Commission on Industrial Relations report No. 14)
Session 1970-71 Cmnd. 4598 xxv.

Clayton Dewandre Co. Ltd. (Commission on Industrial Relations report No. 15)
Session 1970-71 Cmnd. 4640 xxv.

Commercial Union Assurance Co. Ltd. (Commission on Industrial Relations report No. 16)
Session 1970-71 Cmnd. 4642 xxv.

Facilities afforded to shop stewards. (Commission on Industrial Relations report No. 17)
Session 1970-71 Cmnd. 4668 xxv.

Electrolux Ltd. (Commission on Industrial Relations report No. 18)
Session 1970-71 Cmnd. 4697 xxv.

Scottish Stamping and Engineering Co. Ltd. (Commission on Industrial Relations report No. 19)
Session 1970-71 Cmnd. 4702 xxv.

Joseph Lucas Ltd. (Commission on Industrial Relations report No. 20)
Session 1970-71 Cmnd 4718 xxv.

Electric Windings (London) Ltd. (Commission on Industrial Relations report No. 21)
Session 1970-71 Cmnd. 4730 xxv.

Shipbuilding and ship repairing. (Commission on Industrial Relations report No. 22)
Session 1970-71 Cmnd. 4756 xxv.

See also HERON, Conrad F.

WOODHAM, J. B.

1974   Water services; estimates and accounts. Report of the working party
D. of the Environment

WOODHAMS, A. S.

1976   U.K. Chemicals, 1975-85; strategies and opportunities for the industry. Industrial review working party of the Chemicals Economic Development Committee
N.E.D.O.

WOODHEAD, Michael

1975   A study of two local labour markets; short summary of a report on research carried out in Manchester and Liverpool
N.E.D.O.

WOODING, Hugh Olliviere Beresford

1970   Anguilla problem. Report of the commission of inquiry. (Miscellaneous No. 23, 1970)
Session 1970-71 Cmnd. 4510 viii.

WOODLAND, A. W.

1973   Data processing in geology and geophysics. Report of the working party. *In* Research in the geological sciences. (Publication series 'B' No. 7)
Natural Environment Research Council

WOODROOFE, Ernest, Sir

1975   Review Body on Doctors' and Dentists' Remuneration
5th report
Session 1974-75 Cmnd. 6032 xxxii.
Supplement to the 5th report
Session 1974-75 Cmnd. 6243 xxxii.
2nd supplement. **See HALSBURY, Lord**

1976   3rd supplement to the 5th report
Session 1975-76 Cmnd. 6406 xli.
6th report
Session 1975-76 Cmnd. 6473 xli.

1977   7th report
Session 1976-77 Cmnd. 6800 xlii.

1978   8th report
Session 1977-78 Cmnd. 7176 xlviii.

WOODS, C. Roland

1946   Fire grading of buildings, part 1: General principles and structural precautions. Report by a joint committee. (Post-war building studies No. 20)
M. of Works

1948   Precautions against fire and explosion in underground car parks. Report by a joint committee. (Post-war building studies No. 28)
M. of Works

1949   Fire grading of buildings, part 2: Fire fighting equipment, part 3: Personal safety. Part 4: Chimneys and flues. Report by a joint committee. (Post-war building studies No. 29)
M. of Works

WOODS, H.

1952   The prevention of accidents in paper mills. 2nd report of the committee
M. of Labour (repr. with amendments, 1962)

1961   Conditions in steel foundries. 1st report of the joint standing committee
M. of Labour

1963   Foundry goggles. Report of the joint advisory committee
M. of Labour

1964   Safety in paper mills. Joint standing committee for paper mills. 1st report
M. of Labour

1965   Power press safety code. 5th report of proceedings of the joint standing committee on safety in the use of power presses
M. of Labour

WOODS, Wilfred, Sir

1945   Malta. Report on the finances of the government of Malta. (Colonial No. 196)
Colonial Office

WOOLF, Herman
  See SKELHORN, N. J., Sir

WOOLFE, J. N.

1972   Methods of payment of wages. A report by a sub-committee of the national joint advisory council
D. of Employment

WOOSTER, C. E. D.

1967   Network analysis in construction design. Research and development. (R. & D. Building management handbook No. 3)
M. of Public Building and Works

WORDIE, John S.

1967   Report of the committee on scales of salaries for the teaching staff of colleges of education, England and Wales
D. of Education and Science

Scales of salaries for teachers in primary and secondary schools, England and Wales
D. of Education and Science

1968   Scales of salaries for teachers in establishments for further education, England and Wales
D. of Education and Science

Scales of salaries for the teaching staff of farm institutes and for teachers of agricultural (including horticultural) subjects, England and Wales
D. of Education and Science

Compulsory retirement age of dock workers. Report of a committee
M. of Labour

1969   Report of the committee on scales of salaries for the teaching staff of colleges of education, England and Wales
D. of Education and Science

Scales of salaries for teachers in establishments for further education, England and Wales
D. of Education and Science

Scales of salaries for teachers in primary and secondary schools, England and Wales
D. of Education and Science

Scales of salaries for the teaching staff of farm institutes and teachers of agricultural (including horticultural) subjects, England and Wales
D. of Education and Science

1971   Scales of salaries for teachers in primary and secondary schools, England and Wales
D. of Education and Science

WORTINGTON, E. B.

1963   Grey seals and fisheries. Report of the consultative committee on grey seals and fisheries
Nature Conservancy

WRAGG, Richard

1977   Study of the passenger transport needs of urban Wales
Welsh Council

WRAY, K. O. Roberts-, Sir

See ROBERTS-WRAY, K. O., Sir

WRENCH, K. J.

1977   Accidents are colour-blind. Industrial accidents and the immigrant worker, a pilot study
Community Relations Commission

WRIGHT, A. C. S.

1954   Land in British Honduras. Report of the British Honduras land use survey team. (Colonial research publication No. 24)
Colonial Office

WRIGHT, C. W.

1973   Provincial museums and galleries. Report of a committee
D. of Education and Science

WRIGHT, J. H.

1964   Medical staffing structure in Scottish hospitals. Report of a committee
Scottish Home and Health D.

WRIGHT, M. O.

1969   Standard system of hotel accounting. An aid to achieving profits by the application of a uniform system of management accounting to hotel operations. Advisory Committee on Uniform Hotel Accounts. Hotel and Catering Economic Development Committee
N.E.D.O.

WRIGHT, Norman C., Sir

1951   Urban working-class household diet. 1st report of the national food survey committee
M. of Food

1954   Report on lead; revised recommendations for limits for lead content of foods. Food Standards Committee
M. of Food

Antioxidants. Revised recommendations relating to the use of antioxidants in foods. Report of the Food Standards Committee
M. of Food

Colouring matters. Recommendations relating to the use of colouring matters in foods. Report of the Food Standards Committee
M. of Food

1955   Colouring matters. Supplementary report by the Food Standards Committee
M. of Agriculture, Fisheries and Food

Arsenic. Revised recommendations for limits for arsenic in foods. Report of the Food Standards Committee
M. of Food

1956   Sausages. Report of the Food Standards Committee
M. of Agriculture, Fisheries and Food

Diets. Studies in urban household diets, 1944-49. 2nd report of the National Food Survey Committee
M. of Agriculture, Fisheries and Food

Emulsifying and stabilising agents in foods. Recommendations relating to the use of emulsifying and stabilising agents in foods. Report of the Food Standards Committee
M. of Agriculture, Fisheries and Food

Processed cheese and cheese spread, report. 2nd report of the Food Standards Committee
M. of Agriculture, Fisheries and Food

1957   Fluorine. Revised recommendations for limits for fluorine content of foods. Report of the Food Standards Committee
M. of Agriculture, Fisheries and Food

Ice cream standard. Report of the Food Standards Committee
M. of Agriculture, Fisheries and Food

1958   Soft drinks. Report of the Food Standards Committee
M. of Agriculture, Fisheries and Food

WRIGHT, R.

1968   Eggs. Report of the reorganisation commission
Session 1967-68 Cmnd. 3669 xix.

WRIGHT, Ray W.

1969   Report of the process plant expert committee
M. of Technology

WRIGHT, Ray W. *(continued)*

1973 Industrial review to 1977: Electronics. Electronics Economic Development Committee
N.E.D.O.

WYNN, Arthur H. A.

1968 Change to the metric system in the U.K. Report by the standing joint committee on metrication
M. of Technology

WYNN PARRY, Henry, Sir

1954 Private international law committee. 1st report
Session 1953-54 Cmd. 9068 xvi.

1958 Private international law committee. 4th report: formal validity of wills
Session 1957-58 Cmnd. 491 xv.

Prison services. Report of the committee on remuneration and conditions of service of certain grades in the prison services
Session 1957-58 Cmnd. 544 xvii.

1962 British Guiana. Report of a commission of inquiry into the disturbances in British Guiana in February 1962. (Colonial No. 354)
Colonial Office

WYNNE-EDWARDS, R. M., Sir

1964 Building regulations advisory committee. 1st report
Session 1963-64 Cmnd. 2279 ix.

1966 Reports on shortages of gas supplies in the West Midlands during the winter of 1965-66
M. of Power

WYNNE-FINCH, J. C.

1954 Monmouthshire Moors investigation. Report of the Welsh agricultural land sub-commission report
M. of Agriculture, Fisheries and Food

1955 Mid-Wales investigation. Report of the Welsh agricultural land sub-commission
Session 1955-56 Cmd. 9631 x.

YAPP, W. B.

1969 The weekend motorist in the Lake District. The report of a survey
Countryside Commission

YATES, Anne

1978 Recreation management training committee. Interim report
D. of the Environment

YATES, R.

1942 Murton colliery, Durham. Report on the causes of and circumstances attending the explosion which occurred on June 26, 1942
Session 1942-43 Cmd. 6413 vi.

1957 Clearances on transport roads in coal mines. Report of the committee
M. of Power

YATES, R. C.

1959 Growing demand for water. 1st report of the sub-committee of the Central Advisory Water Committee
M. of Housing and Local Government

YONGE, C. M., Sir

Freshwater and salmon fisheries research. Report by the supervisory committee for brown trout research

1950 Report for 1948-49, No. 1
1952 Report for 1951-52, No. 4
Scottish Home D.

YOUNG, E.

1977 Drama in Scottish schools, a discussion document. Report of the working party
Scottish Education D.

YOUNG, Frank G., Sir

1964 Irradiation of food. Report of the working party of the committee on medical and nutritional aspects of food policy
M. of Health

YOUNG, L. E. C.

1973 Training for data processing management. Report by a joint committee of industrial training boards
D. of Employment

YOUNG, R. S.

See JONES, S. L.

YOUNGER, J. P., Sir

1950 Tuberculosis. Report of the Scottish Health Services Council's committee on tuberculosis
D. of Health for Scotland

See also STEEL, J.

YOUNGER, Kenneth G.

1968 Detention of girls in a detention centre. Interim report of the advisory council on the penal system
Home Office

The regime for long-term prisoners in conditions of maximum security. Report of the advisory council on the penal system
Home Office

1970 Detention centres. Report of the advisory council on the penal system
Home Office

Non-custodial and semi-custodial penalties. Report of the advisory council on the penal system
Home Office

1972 Privacy. Report of the committee
Session 1971-72 Cmnd. 5012 xxii.

1974 Young adult offenders. Report of the advisory council on the penal system
Home Office

1977 Powers of the courts dependent on imprisonment. Report of the advisory council on the penal system
Home Office

See also SEROTA OF HAMPSTEAD, Bee, Baroness

YOUNGER, W. McEwan, Sir

1964 Organisation and practices for building and civil engineering. Report of the working party on building and civil engineering procedure in Scotland
M. of Public Building and Works

YOUNGHUSBAND, E. L., Dame

1959 Social workers in the local authority health and welfare services. Report of the working party
M. of Health

YOUNGMAN, P.

See BUCHANAN, C. D.

ZIMAN, J. M.

1978 Communications system of physics. Final report of the physics information review committee. (R. & D. report No. 5386)
British Library

ZUCKERMAN, Solly, Sir

1951 Toxic chemicals in agriculture. Report of the working party on precautionary measures
M. of Agriculture and Fisheries

1953 Toxic chemicals in agriculture. Residues in food. Report of the working party on precautionary measures
M. of Agriculture and Fisheries

1954 The use of towns' wastes in agriculture. A study by the natural resources (technical) committee
D. of Scientific and Industrial Research

1955 Toxic chemicals in agriculture. Risks to wild life. Report of the working party on precautionary measures
M. of Agriculture, Fisheries and Food

   Recruitment of scientists and engineers by the engineering industry. Report of the scientific manpower committee of the scientific policy advisory council
Lord Presidents' Office

1956 Scientific engineering manpower in G.B. Report on the number of scientists and engineers employed in G.B. and a study of the likely trend in future demand. Advisory council on scientific policy
M. of Labour and National Service

1957 Forestry, agriculture and marginal land. Report by the natural resources (technical) committee
D. of Scientific and Industrial Research

1958 Sheep industry in Britain. Report by the natural resources (technical) committee
D. of Scientific and Industrial Research

1959 Scientific and engineering manpower in G.B., 1959. Report of the committee on scientific manpower of the advisory council on scientific policy
Session 1959-60 Cmnd. 902 xx.

1960 Scale of enterprise in farming. Report by the natural resources (technical) committee sub-committee on agriculture
Office of the Minister for Science

1961 Management and control of research and development. Report of the committee on management and
Office of the Minister for Science

   Long-term demand for scientific manpower. Committee on scientific manpower, statistics sub-committee of the advisory council on scientific policy. Report
Session 1960-61 Cmnd. 1490 xx.

1963 Scientific and technological manpower in G.B., 1962. Report of the committee on scientific manpower in G.B.
Session 1962-63 Cmnd. 2146 xxiv.

1968 Hospital scientific and technical services. Report of the committee
D. of Health and Social Security

   Technical innovation in Britain. Report of the central advisory council for science and technology
Cabinet Office

   The Torrey Canyon. Report of the committee of scientists on the scientific and technological aspects of the Torrey Canyon disaster
Cabinet Office

1972 Cancer research
Cabinet Office